D0512995

EYEWITNESS TRAVEL

SYDNEY

EYEWITNESS TRAVEL
SYDNEY

MAIN CONTRIBUTORS: KEN BRASS & KIRSTY MCKENZIE

LONDON, NEW YORK,
MELBOURNE, MUNICH AND DELHI
www.dk.com

PRODUCED BY The Watermark Press,
Sydney, Australia
PROJECT EDITOR Siobhán O'Connor
ART EDITOR Claire Edwards
EDITORS Robert Coupe, Leith Hillard, Jane Sheard
DESIGNERS Katie Peacock, Claire Ricketts, Noel Wendtman

Dorling Kindersley Limited
SENIOR EDITOR Fay Franklin
SENIOR ART EDITOR Jane Ewart
SENIOR REVISIONS EDITOR Esther Labi

CONTRIBUTORS
Anna Bruechert, John Dengate, Carrie Hutchinson, Graham Jahn,
Kim Saville, Susan Skelly

PHOTOGRAPHERS
Max Alexander, Simon Blackall, Michael Nicholson, Rob Reichenfeld,
Alan Williams

ILLUSTRATORS
Richard Draper, Stephen Gyapay, Alex Lavroff Associates, The Overall
Picture, Robbie Polley

Printed and bound by South China Printing Company Ltd., China

First published in Great Britain in 1996
by Dorling Kindersley Limited
80 Strand, London, WC2R 0RL
12 13 14 15 10 9 8 7 6 5 4 3 2 1

Reprinted with revisions 1997, 1999, 2000, 2001,
2002 (twice), 2003, 2005, 2006, 2008, 2010, 2012

Copyright 1997, 2012 © Dorling Kindersley Limited, London
A Penguin Company

A CIP CATALOGUE RECORD IS AVAILABLE FROM THE BRITISH LIBRARY

ISBN 978-1-4053-7082-0
Front cover main image: Sydney Opera House

MIX
Paper from
responsible sources
FSC™ C018179

**The information in this
DK Eyewitness Travel Guide is checked regularly.**

Every effort has been made to ensure that this book is as up-to-
date as possible at the time of going to press. Some details,
however, such as telephone numbers, opening hours, prices,
gallery hanging arrangements and travel information, are liable to
change. The publishers cannot accept responsibility for any
consequences arising from the use of this book, nor for any
material on third party websites, and cannot guarantee that any
website address in this book will be a suitable source of travel
information. We value the views and suggestions of our readers
highly. Please write to: The Publisher, DK Eyewitness Travel
Guides, 80 Strand, London, WC2R 0RL, or email: travelguides@dk.com.

CONTENTS

HOW TO USE THIS GUIDE 6

INTRODUCING SYDNEY

**A view of the Royal Botanic Garden
and city skyline**

Tamarama beach and surf club

Façade of Sydney Town Hall

Wattleseed, pepperberry and
lemon myrtle

Stained-glass window,
Queen Victoria Building

Opera House

HOW TO USE THIS GUIDE

This guide helps you to get the most from your visit to Sydney. It provides both expert recommendations and detailed practical information. *Introducing Sydney* locates the city geographically, sets modern Sydney in its historical and cultural context and describes events through the entire year. *Sydney at a Glance* is an overview of the city's main attractions, including a feature on the city shoreline and Sydney's best beaches. *Sydney Area*

Strolling at the Royal Easter Show

by Area is the main sightseeing section, covering all the sights, with photographs, maps and drawings. *Further Afield* looks at sights just outside the city centre while *Beyond Sydney* explores other places close to Sydney. Carefully researched tips on hotels, restaurants, pubs and entertainment venues are found in *Travellers' Needs*. The *Survival Guide* contains useful practical advice on everything from the Australian telephone system to public transport.

FINDING YOUR WAY AROUND THE SIGHTSEEING SECTION

The centre of Sydney has been divided into six sightseeing areas. Each area has its own chapter and is colour-coded for easy reference. Every chapter opens with a list of the sights described. All sights are numbered and plotted on an *Area Map*. Detailed information for each sight is presented in numerical order, making it easy to locate within the chapter.

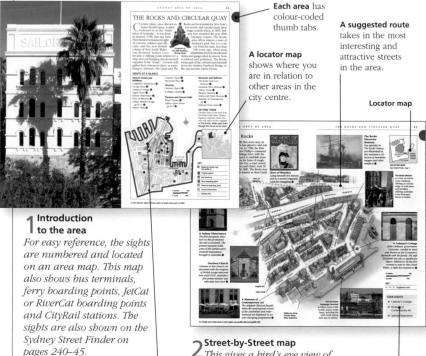

Each area has colour-coded thumb tabs.

A suggested route takes in the most interesting and attractive streets in the area.

A locator map shows where you are in relation to other areas in the city centre.

Locator map

1 Introduction to the area
For easy reference, the sights are numbered and located on an area map. This map also shows bus terminals, ferry boarding points, JetCat or RiverCat boarding points and CityRail stations. The sights are also shown on the Sydney Street Finder on pages 240–45.

The area shaded pink is shown in greater detail on the Street-by-Street map on the following pages.

2 Street-by-Street map
This gives a bird's eye view of the most important parts of each sightseeing area. The numbering of the sights ties in with the area map and the fuller descriptions on the pages that follow.

The list of star sights recommends the places that no visitor should miss.

SYDNEY AREA MAP

The coloured areas shown on this map *(see pp16-17)* are the six main sightseeing areas - each covered by a full chapter in *Sydney Area by Area (pp60-149)*. The six areas are highlighted on other maps throughout the book. In *Sydney at a Glance (pp32-47)*, for example, they help locate the top sights, including art galleries and museums and parks and reserves. They are also used to show some of the best hotels *(pp172-7)*, the top restaurants, cafés and pubs *(pp184-97)* and great shopping areas *(pp200-1)*.

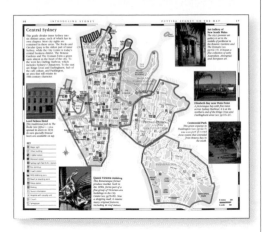

Façades of important buildings are often shown to help you recognize them quickly.

Practical information lists all the information you need to visit every sight, including a map reference to the Street Finder *(pp240-5)*.

Numbers refer to each sight's position on the area map and its place in the chapter.

The visitors' checklist provides all the practical information needed to plan your visit.

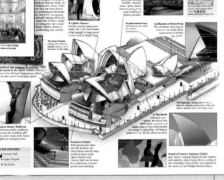

3 Detailed information on each sight
All the important sights in Sydney are described individually. They are listed in order, following the numbering on the area map. Addresses and practical information are provided. The key to the symbols used in the information block is on the back flap.

Stars indicate the features no visitor should miss.

4 Sydney's top sights
Museums and galleries have colour-coded floorplans to help you locate the most interesting exhibits; historic buildings are dissected to reveal their interiors.

INTRODUCING
SYDNEY

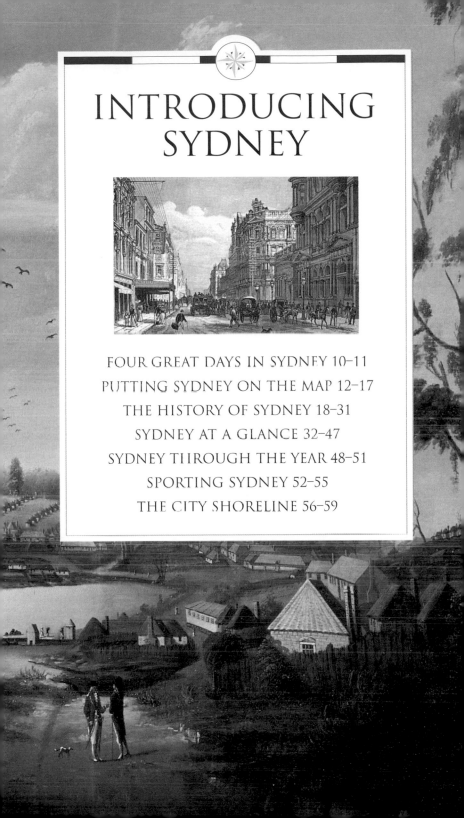

FOUR GREAT DAYS IN SYDNEY

Planning a one-day itinerary to take in the best that Sydney has to offer need not be a challenge. The magnificent harbour or beaches, as well as cultural and architectural highlights, would ideally be included. These four itineraries offer a mix of activities in different parts of

Koala at Taronga Zoo

Sydney, all accessible by public transport. They are designed to be flexible – you might choose to leave out some stops or include other attractions that are nearby. Prices show the cost for two adults or for a family of two adults and two children, including food and drinks.

Sydney Opera House and Harbour Bridge by night

AROUND THE HARBOUR

- **The view from Sydney Harbour Bridge**
- **A tour of The Rocks**
- **Ferry ride to Manly**
- **Sunset over the harbour**

TWO ADULTS allow at least A$110

Morning
Start early at an Australian icon, the **Sydney Harbour Bridge** (see pp70–71), built in 1932. Cross on the pedestrian walkway or, from $198 per person, let BridgeClimb guide you to the top of the steel arch bridge (bookings are essential). Climbs depart every ten minutes, and take 3.5 hours including orientation. The view at the top is well worth it. Recharge with a pit stop at the Gumnut Café (see p195), where you can choose from fresh fruit juices, cakes and scones. Explore the historic Rocks area where you'll find the convict-carved Argyle Cut and the military **Garrison Church**

(see pp68–9). Cobblestoned alleys lead to the original docks of Old Sydney Town at **Campbell's Storehouses** (see p66) and **Cadman's Cottage** (see p68), Sydney's oldest surviving dwelling.

Afternoon
Enjoy a classic ferry trip to **Manly** (see p133). Once there, stroll down the Corso to the ocean beach or walk around the headland (pp146–7). Buy

Henry Moore sculpture outside the Art Gallery of New South Wales

fish and chips and eat them on the beach, or try some parasailing, boating or kayaking on offer at the jetty. Treat yourself to a beer at the Manly Wharf Hotel (see p191) where you can find a window seat and watch the sunset over the harbour. End the day with the fast ferry back to Circular Quay.

ART AND OPERA

- **Colonial buildings on Macquarie Street**
- **Aboriginal art at the Yiribana Gallery**
- **The Royal Botanic Garden**
- **Sydney Opera House**

TWO ADULTS allow at least A$140

Morning
Stroll down **Macquarie Street** (see pp112–15), named after Governor Lachlan Macquarie. You can still see several of the buildings he commissioned here. Other architectural gems include the **Hyde Park Barracks** (see pp114–15) and **St James' Church** (see p115) both designed by convict James Greenway. The old Rum Hospital now houses the **Sydney Mint** (see p114) and **Parliament House** (see pp112–13) where free tours run every half hour. At the **State Library of NSW** (see p112), you can tread on a mosaic replica of the Tasman Map, illustrating 17th-century voyages to Australia.

Afternoon
Across **The Domain** (see p107), the **Art Gallery of New South Wales** (see pp108–11) houses both traditional and

modern Aboriginal art in the Yiribana Gallery, the largest space in the world devoted to the art of Indigenous Australians. Rest weary legs with lunch in the gallery's café *(see p195)*, then stroll along to the scenic **Mrs Macquaries Chair** *(see p106)* for a fine view across the harbour before taking the Fleet Steps down the hill into the **Royal Botanic Garden** *(see pp104–5)*. On the other side of Farm Cove is **Sydney Opera House** *(see pp74–7)*. Stop in at the Opera Bar *(see p197)*, then take a tour of the world-famous building (booking is recommended). If you want to make an evening of it, for an extra cost you can book tickets for an opera, play or concert. Last-minute tickets are sometimes available.

Giraffe at Taronga Zoo, on the foreshore of Sydney Harbour

BEACHES AND BROWSING

- **Breakfast at Bondi**
- **A cliff-top constitutional**
- **Fashion, terraces and galleries in Paddington**
- **Cocktails on the Finger Wharf**

TWO ADULTS allow at least A$114

Morning
Have breakfast at **Bondi Beach**'s Icebergs Bistro *(see p195)* at the legendary Bondi Icebergs (on weekends) or at the Crabbe Hole *(see p191)*. Admire the view and watch the die-hard swimmers do laps. Then stretch your legs with the Bondi-to-Bronte section of the famous cliff

walk *(see pp144–5)*. When you reach Bronte, order a juice at Swell *(see p195)* then head to Oxford Street, Paddington, to begin browsing the glamorous boutiques. The renowned **Paddington Markets** *(see p126)* are open every Saturday.

Afternoon
Take lunch in the courtyard at Sloane's *(see p195)* then, if you wish, spend all your cash at Collette Dinnigan's store *(see p205)*. Stop by the London Tavern *(see p124)*, the area's oldest pub, before exploring the streets of ter raced houses near Five Ways. Admire the art at Tim Olsen Gallery (No. 63 Jersey Road), Australian Galleries Works On Paper (No. 24 Glenmore Road) and Hogarth Galleries (No. 7 Walker Lane). Later, have a drink at the Tilbury Hotel *(see p197)* in Woolloomooloo and cap off the day with a pie from Harry's Café de Wheels *(see p195)* on the Finger Wharf.

FAMILY FUN

- **A spin on the Monorail**
- **Ferry and Sky Safari**
- **Koalas, kangaroos and platypuses at Taronga Zoo**
- **Up high in Sydney Tower**

FAMILY OF 4 allow at least A$196

Morning
Start with a 12-minute loop on the Monorail *(see pp232–3)*, which offers good views of Darling Harbour, Chinatown and odd peeks into office windows. Buy a ZooPass from Circular Quay then take a ferry to **Taronga Zoo** *(see pp134–5)*. Once there, your ZooPass includes the Sky Safari cable car ride to the main entrance. Here you'll find information on koala viewing and the daily seal and bird shows. Spend the morning exploring the zoo, making sure you stop by all of the native Australian animals, including monotremes, platypuses and echidnas. Buy ice creams to eat as you walk.

Afternoon
Have lunch at one of the many kiosks in the zoo, before heading back to the wharf for the return ferry. Finish off the day at **Sydney Tower** *(see p83)*. Ride the lift to the Sydney Tower Eye Observation Deck and take in a tour of Sydney in the 4-D cinema. Use a telescope to spot the zoo and other land-marks, or enjoy the sunset.

Bathers enjoying the golden sand and surf at Bronte Beach

Putting Sydney on the Map

Situated on Australia's eastern coastline within the state of New South Wales, Sydney spreads with the rare luxury of space – 3,700 sq km (1,430 sq miles) in all – around what is often described as one of the finest harbours in the world. Greater Sydney is home to over 4 million people and, while it is not the nation's capital, it is Australia's oldest and largest city, as well as its media and financial centre. Sydney is also the main gateway to Australia and it enjoys good air, road and rail links to other major centres.

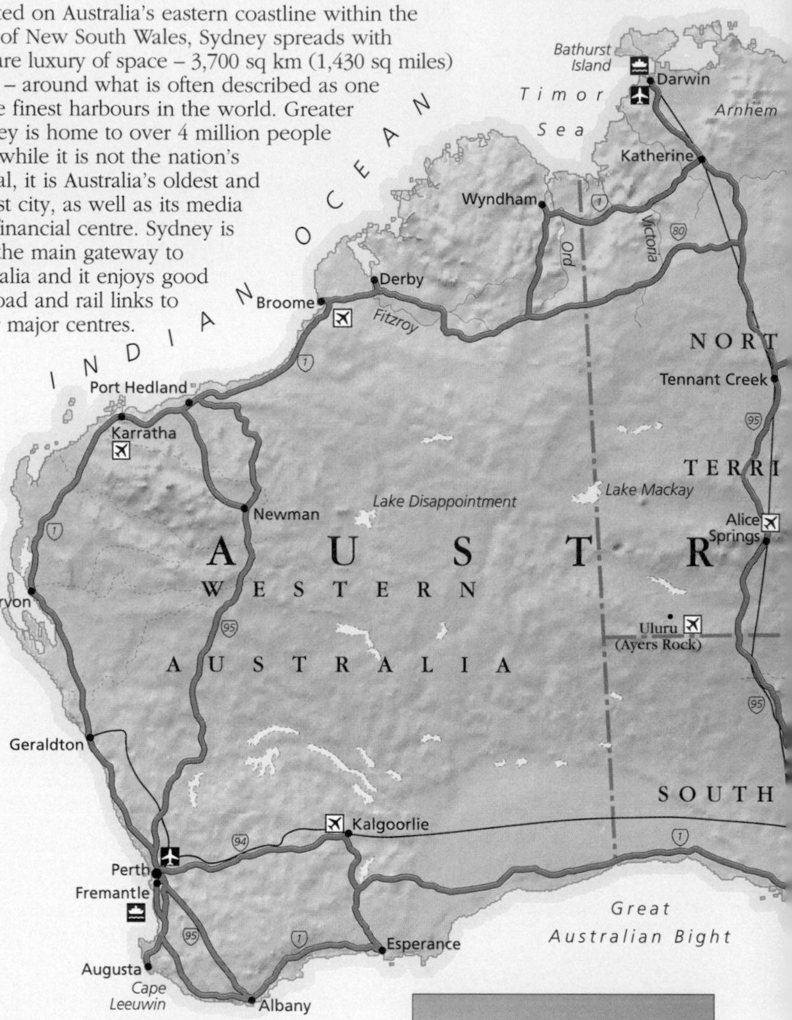

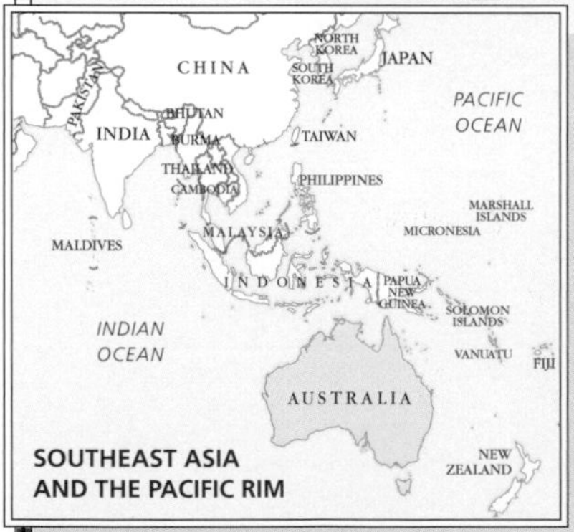

INDIAN OCEAN

Timor Sea

Bathurst Island
Darwin
Arnhem
Katherine
Wyndham
Ord
Victoria
Derby
Broome
Fitzroy
Port Hedland
Karratha
Newman
Lake Disappointment
Lake Mackay
Carnarvon

A U S T R A
W E S T E R N
A U S T R A L I A

N O R T
Tennant Creek
T E R R I
Alice Springs
Uluru (Ayers Rock)

Geraldton

Kalgoorlie
Perth
Fremantle
Augusta
Cape Leeuwin
Albany
Esperance

Great Australian Bight

S O U T H

SOUTHEAST ASIA
AND THE PACIFIC RIM

CHINA
NORTH KOREA
SOUTH KOREA
JAPAN
INDIA
BHUTAN
BURMA
TAIWAN
PACIFIC OCEAN
THAILAND
CAMBODIA
PHILIPPINES
MALDIVES
MALAYSIA
MARSHALL ISLANDS
MICRONESIA
INDONESIA
PAPUA NEW GUINEA
SOLOMON ISLANDS
INDIAN OCEAN
VANUATU
FIJI
AUSTRALIA
NEW ZEALAND

Aerial view of Sydney, looking from the mouth of Port Jackson towards the city

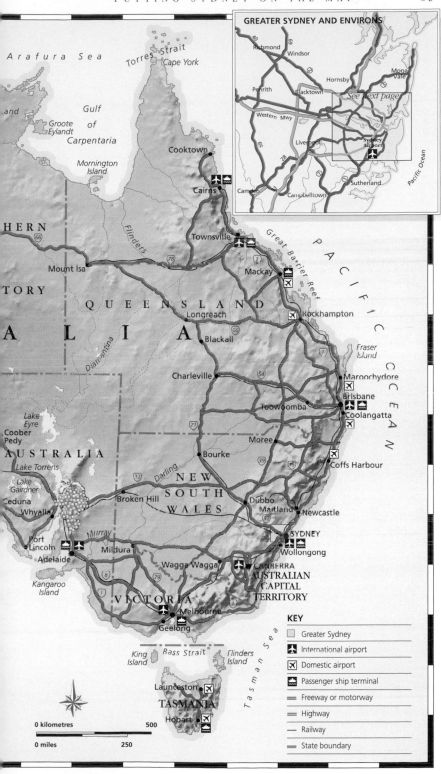

GREATER SYDNEY AND ENVIRONS

Richmond
Windsor
Hornsby
Mona Vale
Penrith
Blacktown
Western Mwy
See next page
Liverpool
Sydney Airport
Camden
Campbelltown
Sutherland
Pacific Ocean

Arafura Sea
Torres Strait
Cape York
...and
Gulf of Carpentaria
Groote Eylandt
Mornington Island
Cooktown
Cairns
HERN
Flinders
Townsville
Great Barrier Reef
TORY
Mount Isa
Mackay
ALIA
QUEENSLAND
Longreach
Rockhampton
Blackall
Diamantina
Fraser Island
Charleville
Maroochydore
Brisbane
Toowoomba
Coolangatta
Lake Eyre
Coober Pedy
AUSTRALIA
Moree
Lake Torrens
Bourke
Coffs Harbour
Lake Gairdner
Darling
NEW
Ceduna
Broken Hill
SOUTH
Whyalla
WALES
Dubbo
Port Lincoln
Murray
Maitland
Newcastle
Adelaide
Mildura
SYDNEY
Kangaroo Island
Wagga Wagga
Wollongong
CANBERRA
AUSTRALIAN
CAPITAL
TERRITORY
VICTORIA
Melbourne
Geelong

PACIFIC OCEAN

KEY

Greater Sydney

✈ International airport

✈ Domestic airport

⚓ Passenger ship terminal

Freeway or motorway

Highway

Railway

State boundary

King Island
Bass Strait
Flinders Island
Tasman Sea
Launceston
TASMANIA
Hobart

0 kilometres   500

0 miles   250

Central Sydney and Suburbs

Sydney has gradually expanded to fill both sides
of the harbour. Parramatta to the west was once a
separate settlement, but is now very much a part
of the city. To the east are the beaches and seaside
suburbs that have come to typify Sydney living.
The area as a whole is served by CityRail lines
and roads.

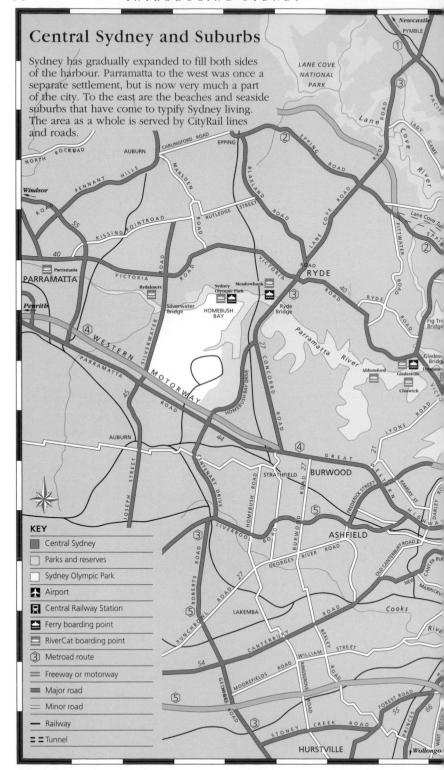

KEY

- Central Sydney
- Parks and reserves
- Sydney Olympic Park
- Airport
- Central Railway Station
- Ferry boarding point
- RiverCat boarding point
- ③ Metroad route
- Freeway or motorway
- Major road
- Minor road
- Railway
- Tunnel

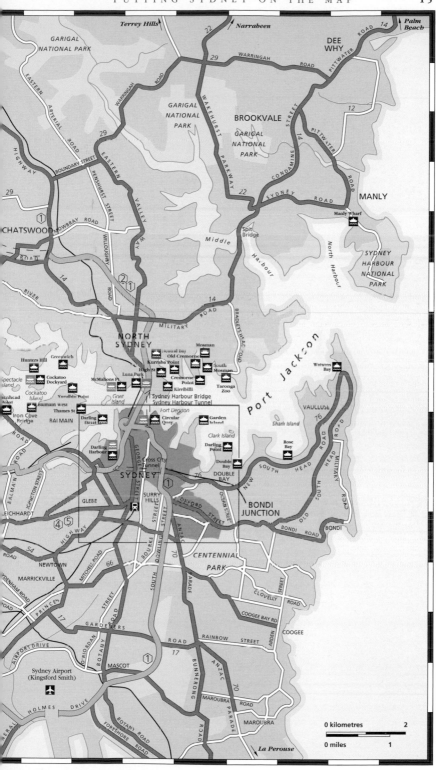

Central Sydney

This guide divides inner Sydney into six distinct areas, each of which has its own chapter. Most city sights are contained in these areas. The Rocks and Circular Quay is the oldest part of inner Sydney, while the City Centre is today's central business district. The Botanic Gardens and The Domain form a green oasis almost in the heart of the city. To the west lies Darling Harbour, which includes Sydney's Chinatown. To the east are Kings Cross and Darlinghurst, hub of the café culture, and Paddington, an area that still retains its 19th-century character.

Lord Nelson Hotel
This traditional pub in The Rocks (see pp62–77) first opened its doors in 1834. Its own specially brewed beers are available on tap.

KEY

▮	Major sight
▮	Other building
⬘	CityRail station
⬘	Monorail station
⬘	Metro Light Rail station
⬘	Bus terminus
⬘	Coach station
⬘	Ferry boarding point
⬘	RiverCat boarding point
⬘	Police station
P	Parking
i	Tourist information
✚	Hospital with casualty unit
✝	Church
✡	Synagogue

Queen Victoria Building
This Romanesque former produce market, built in the 1890s, forms part of a fine group of Victorian-era buildings in the City Centre (see pp78–89). Now a shopping mall, it retains many original features, including its roof statues.

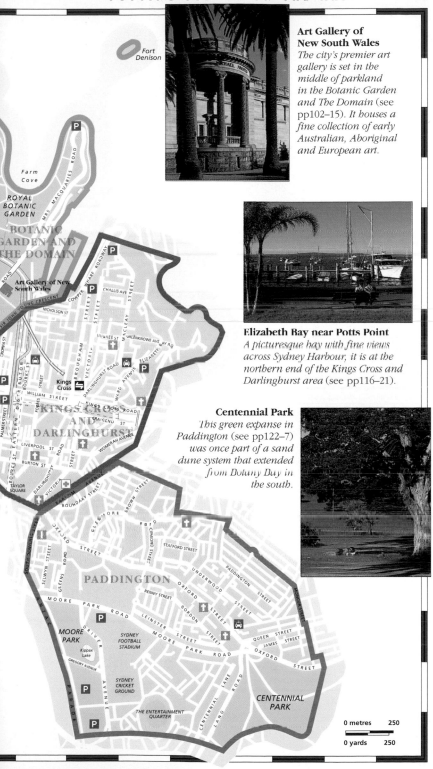

Art Gallery of New South Wales

The city's premier art gallery is set in the middle of parkland in the Botanic Garden and The Domain (see pp102–15). *It houses a fine collection of early Australian, Aboriginal and European art.*

Elizabeth Bay near Potts Point

A picturesque bay with fine views across Sydney Harbour, it is at the northern end of the Kings Cross and Darlinghurst area (see pp116–21).

Centennial Park

This green expanse in Paddington (see pp122–7) *was once part of a sand dune system that extended from Botany Bay in the south.*

0 metres 250

0 yards 250

THE HISTORY OF SYDNEY

The first inhabitants of Australia were the Aboriginal peoples. Their history began in a time called the Dreaming when the Ancestor Spirits emerged from the earth and gave form to the landscape. Anthropologists believe the Aboriginal peoples arrived from Asia more than 50,000 years ago. Clans lived in the area now known as Sydney, until the Europeans caused violent disruption to this world.

Sydney's coat of arms, Sydney Town Hall

In 1768, Captain James Cook began a search for the fabled "great south land". Travelling in the wake of other European explorers, he was the first to set foot on the east coast of the land the Dutch had named New Holland, and claimed it for King and country. He landed at Botany Bay in 1770, naming the coast New South Wales.

At the suggestion of Sir Joseph Banks, Cook's botanist on the *Endeavour*, a penal colony was established here to relieve Britain's overflowing prisons. The First Fleet of 11 ships reached Botany Bay in 1788, commanded by Captain Arthur Phillip. He felt the land there was swampy and the bay windswept. Just to the north, however, he found "one of the finest harbours in the world," naming it Sydney Cove,

after the Home Department's Secretary of State. Here, 1,485 convicts, guards, officers, officials, wives and children landed. This marked the beginning of the rapid devastation of the Aboriginal peoples, as they fell to introduced diseases and battled an undeclared war against the settlers. Full citizenship rights were finally granted to the Aboriginal peoples in 1973, and their traditions are now accorded respect.

The city of Sydney soon flourished, with the construction of impressive public buildings befitting an emerging maritime power. In 1901, amid a burgeoning nationalism, the federation drew the country's six colonies together and New South Wales became a state of Australia.

In its two centuries of European settlement, Sydney has experienced alternating periods of growth and decline. It has weathered the effects of gold rush and trade booms, depressions and world wars, to establish a distinctive city marked by a vibrant eclecticism. The underlying British culture, married with Aboriginal influences and successive waves of Asian and European migration, has produced today's modern cosmopolitan city.

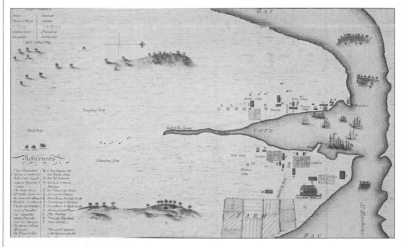

Sketch & Description of the Settlement at Sydney Cove (1788) by transported convict Francis Fowkes

◁ *Desmond, a New South Wales Chief* (about 1825) by Augustus Earle

Sydney's Original Inhabitants

Hafted
stone axe

Anthropologists believe that Aboriginal peoples reached Sydney Harbour at least 50,000 years ago. One of the clans of coastal Sydney was the Eora. Their campsites were usually close to the shore, particularly in the summer when fish were plentiful. Plant and animal foods supplemented their seafood diet. Artistic expression was a way of life, with their shields decorated with ochre, designs carved on their implements, and their bodies adorned with scars, animal teeth and feathers. Sacred and social ceremonies are still vital today. Oral traditions recount stories of the Dreaming (see p19) and describe the Eora's strong attachment to the land.

Aborigines Fishing *(1819)*
Sixty-seven Eora canoes were counted in the harbour on a single day. Spears were used as tools and weapons.

Berowra
Waters

This Berowra Waters carving is hard to interpret; experts believe that it may represent a koala.

Glenbrook Crossing
The Red Hand Caves near Glenbrook in the lower Blue Mountains contain stencils where ochre was blown over outstretched hands.

Glenbrook

The name Parramatta means place where eels lie down or sleep, or the head of the river.

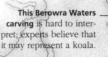

Parramatta •

Glenbrook Caves ochre hand stencils

Cabramatta •

Cabramatta means land where the *cobra* grub is found.

Red Ochre and Shell Paint Holder
Ochre was a commonly used material in rock painting. Finely ground, then mixed with water and a binding agent, it would be applied by brush or hand.

ABORIGINAL ROCK ART

There are appxroximately 5,500 known rock art sites in the Sydney basin alone. Early colonists such as Watkin Tench said that paintings and engravings were on every kind of surface. The history of colonization was also recorded in rock engravings, with depictions of the arrival of ships and fighting.

TIMELINE

43,000–38,000BC Tools found in a gravel pit beside Nepean River are among the oldest firmly dated signs of human occupation in Australia

Diprotodon

20,000 Humans lived in the Blue Mountains despite extreme conditions. Remains found of the largest mammal, *Diprotodon,* date back to this period

11,000 Burial site excavated in Victoria of more than 40 individuals of this period

50,000 BC	20,000 BC

28,000 Funerary rites at Lake Mungo, NSW. Complete skeleton has been found of man buried at this time

18,000 People now inhabit the entire continent, from the deserts to the mountains

23,000 One of the world's earliest known cremations carried out in Western NSW

13,000 Final stages of Ice Age, with small glaciers in the Snowy Mountains

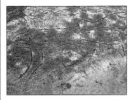

Ku-ring-gai is named after clans who lived in this coastal district. It is rich in rock engravings.

Hunting and Fishing Implements

Multi-pronged Eora spears were used for fishing, while canoes were shaped from a single piece of bark. Boomerangs are still used today for hunting and music making.

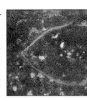

Fish Carving at West Head

This area in Ku-ring-gai Chase has 51 figures and is acknowledged as one of the richest sites in the greater Sydney region.

Gumbooya Reserve *in suburban Allambie Heights has a collection of 68 rock carvings. This human figure appears to be inside or on top of a whale.*

Allambie Heights

Bondi is from *boondi*, the sound of water crashing. This carving is of a shark and fish.

Bondi

Shell Fish-Hooks

Introduced from the Torres Strait, these hooks were ground-down mollusc shells.

Coogee

Coogee means bad smell of rotten seaweed washed ashore.

Maroubra

This python skeleton *is on view at the Australian Museum (see pp88–9), along with a large collection of Aboriginal artifacts.*

Maroubra comes either from the *merooberah* tribe, or means place where shells are found.

Water Carrier

These bags were usually made of kangaroo skin. The skin was removed in one piece and either turned inside out or tanned with the sap from a gum tree.

This carving of a leaping kangaroo is found in the Royal National Park.

Bundeena

8,000 BC The oldest returning boomerangs are in use in South Australia

5,000 BC Dingo reaches Australia, thought to have been brought by seafarers

Captain James Cook

AD 1606 Dutch ship, *Duyfken*, records first European sighting of the continent. Lands on the eastern coast of Gulf of Carpentaria

10,000–8,500 BC Tasmania is separated from mainland Australia by rising seas

Copperplate print of a dingo

AD 1700 Macassans search for trepang or sea slugs off Australia's north coast

AD 1770 James Cook lands at Botany Bay

The Early Colony

Hat made from cabbage palm

The colony's beginnings were rugged and hungry, imbued with a spirit that would give Sydney its unique character. Convicts were put to work establishing roads and constructing buildings out of mud, reeds, unseasoned wood and mortar made from a crushed shell mixture. From these simple beginnings, a town grew. Officers of the New South Wales Corps became farmers, encouraged to work their land alongside convict labour. Because the soldiers paid for work and goods in rum, they soon became known as the Rum Corps, in 1808 overthrowing Governor Bligh (of *Bounty* fame) when he threatened their privileges. By the early 1800s farms were producing crops, with supplies arriving more regularly – as were convicts and settlers with more appropriate skills and trades.

GROWTH OF THE CITY

☐ Today   ■ 1810

First Fleet Ship *(c.1787)*
This painting by Francis Holman shows three angles of the Borrowdale, *one of the fleet's three commercial storeships.*

Scrimshaw
Engraving bone or shell was a skilful way to pass time during long months spent at sea.

Boat building at the Government dockyard

Pitts Row

Government House

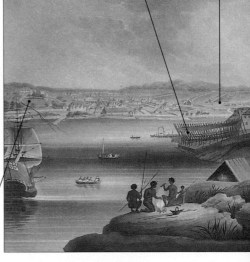

A VIEW OF SYDNEY COVE

This idyllic image, drawn by Edward Dayes and engraved by F Jukes in 1804, shows the Aboriginal peoples living peacefully within the infant colony alongside the flourishing maritime and agricultural industries. In fact, they had been entirely ostracized from the life and prosperity of the town by this time.

TIMELINE

1787 The First Fleet leaves Portsmouth, bound for Botany Bay

1788 First white child born in the colony – and the first man hanged

Barrington, the convict and thespian star of The Revenge

1796 *The Revenge* opens Sydney's first, but short-lived, playhouse, simply named The Theatre

1785	1790	1795

Bennelong pictured in European finery

1789 The Aboriginal Bennelong is held captive and ordered to act as an intermediary between the whites and blacks

1790 First detachment of the New South Wales Corps arrives in the colony. Fears of starvation are lessened with the arrival of the supply ship *Lady Juliana*

1793 Arrival of the first free settlers

1797 Merino sheep arrive from Cape of Good Hope

The Arrest of Bligh
This shameful, and invented, scene shows the hated Governor William Bligh, in full regalia, hiding under a servant's bed to avoid arrest by the NSW Rum Corps in 1808.

The buildings may look impressive, but most were poorly built with inferior materials.

Male and female convicts housed separately

Waratah *(1803)*
John Lewin, naturalist and engraver, drew delicate and faithful representations of the local flora and fauna.

Barracks housing NSW Rum Corps

Kangaroo *(1813)*
Naturalists were amazed at Sydney's vast array of strange plant and animal species. The first pictures sent back to England caused a sensation.

WHERE TO SEE EARLY COLONIAL SYDNEY
The Rocks was the hub of early Sydney. Wharves, warehouses, hotels, rough houses and even rougher characters gave it its colour. Dramatic cuts were made in the rocky point to provide building materials and filling for the construction of Circular Quay, and allow for streets. The houses are gone, except for Cadman's Cottage (*see p68*), but the irregular, labyrinthine lanes are still give the flavour of convict history.

Elizabeth Farm (pp138–9) *at Parramatta is the oldest surviving building in Australia. It was built by convicts using lime mortar from the penal colony of Norfolk Island.*

Experiment Farm Cottage, *an early dwelling (see p139), displays marked convict-made bricks. Masons also marked each brick, as they were paid according to the number laid.*

1799 Explorers Bass and Flinders complete their circumnavigation of Van Diemen's Land (now Tasmania), before returning to Port Jackson

1803 The first issue of the weekly Sydney Gazette, Australia's first newspaper, is published

1808 Rum Rebellion brings social upheaval. Estimated population of New South Wales stands at 9,100

1800   **1805**   **1810**

1801 Ticket-of-leave system introduced, enabling the convicts to work for wages and to choose their own master

1804 Irish convict uprising at Castle Hill

1802 Aboriginal leader Pemulwy is shot and killed following the killing of four white men by Aboriginal men

Love token

1810 New convict arrivals craft such items as love tokens

The Georgian Era

Merino sheep for export wool

Sydney's early decades were times of turbulence and growth. Lachlan Macquarie, governor from 1810 to 1821, was one of the most significant figures. He took over a town-cum-jail and left behind a fully fledged city with a sense of civic pride. Noted for his sympathetic attitude to convicts and freed women and men, he commissioned many fine buildings, including work by convict Francis Greenway *(see p114)*. When Macquarie left in 1822, Sydney boasted main roads, regular streets and an organized police system. By the 1830s, trade had expanded, and labour and land were plentiful. In 1840, transportation of convicts was abolished. A decade of lively debate followed: on immigration, religion and education.

GROWTH OF THE CITY

☐ *Today* ■ *1825*

The domed saloon is elliptical, and has a cantilevered staircase.

Bedroom

The breakfast room was used for informal dining.

View from the Summit
Blaxland, Lawson and Wentworth were the first Europeans to cross the Blue Mountains in 1813. Augustus Earle's painting shows convicts working on a road into this fertile area.

The kitchen was originally in a separate block to avoid the danger of fire.

The Macquaries
Governor Macquarie and his wife Elizabeth arrived in the city with a brief to "improve the morals of the Colonists".

ELIZABETH BAY HOUSE
This extravagant Regency villa was built from 1835–9 for Colonial Secretary Alexander Macleay *(see p120)*. After only six years' occupancy, lavish building and household expenses forced him into bankruptcy.

TIMELINE

1814 Holey dollar eases coin shortage

Holey dollar and dump, made from Spanish coins

1820 Macquarie Chair crafted of she-oak and wallaby skin

Macquarie Chair

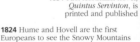

1830 Sir Thomas Mitchell discovers megafauna fossils in New South Wales

1810	1815	1820	1825	1830

1816 Convict architect Francis Greenway designs his first building, Macquarie Lighthouse

1817 The Bank of NSW opens. Macquarie recommends adoption of the name Australia for the continent, as suggested by explorer Matthew Flinders

1831 First Australian novel, *Quintus Servinton*, is printed and published

1824 Hume and Hovell are the first Europeans to see the Snowy Mountains

Lyrebird (1813)
As the colony continued to expand, more exotic birds and animals were found. The male of this species has an impressive tail that spreads into the shape of a lyre.

WHERE TO SEE GEORGIAN SYDNEY

Governor Macquarie designated the street now bearing his name *(see pp112–15)* as the ceremonial centre of the city. It has an elegant collection of buildings: the Hyde Park Barracks, St James' Church, the Sydney Mint, Parliament House and Sydney Hospital. Other fine examples are the Victoria Barracks *(p127)*, Vaucluse House *(p136)* and Macquarie Lighthouse *(p137)*.

Servants' quarters

Aboriginal Explorer
Bungaree took part in the first circumnavigation of the continent, sailing with Matthew Flinders.

Old Government House, *the oldest surviving public building in Australia (see p139), was erected in 1799. Additions ordered by Governor Macquarie were completed in 1816.*

Drawing room

The Classical design was to be complemented by a colonnade, but money ran out.

High Fashion, 1838
Stylish ladies would promenade through Hyde Park (see pp86–7) in the very latest London fashions, which were available from the David Jones department store.

The dining room was furnished in a florid style out of keeping with the Neo-Classical architecture.

Naturalist and author, Charles Darwin

1842 Sydney town becomes a city

1837 Victoria is crowned Queen of England

1844 Edward Geoghegan's Australian musical comedy, *The Currency Lass*, first performed

1848 Parramatta's Female Factory, a notorious women's prison, closes down

1835	1840	1845	1850

1836 Charles Darwin visits Sydney on HMS *Beagle*

1841 Female Immigrants' Home established in Sydney by Caroline Chisholm. Gas lights illuminate Sydney

1850 Work begins on NSW's first railway line, from Sydney to Parramatta

1838 Myall Creek massacre of Aboriginal peoples

1840 Transportation of convicts to NSW is abolished

Caroline Chisholm, philanthropist

Victorian Sydney

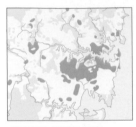

Gold rush memorabilia

In the 1850s, gold was discovered in New South Wales and Sydney came alive with gold seekers, big spenders and a new wave of settlers. It was the start of a peaceful period of solid growth. Education became compulsory, an art gallery was opened and the Australian Academy of Arts held its first exhibition. The city skyline became more complex, with spires and "tall" buildings. Terrace houses proliferated. Victorian decorum and social behaviour borrowed from the mother country flourished, with much social visiting and sporting enthusiasm. It was an age of pleasure gardens and regattas, but also a time of unruliness and political agitation. In the 1890s, as the country moved towards Federation, fervent nationalism and an Australian identity began to take shape.

GROWTH OF THE CITY

☐ *Today*   ■ *1881*

The structure was built of hollow pine.

The dome was 30 m (98 ft) in diameter.

Mrs Macquaries Chair *(1855)*
This prime harbour viewing spot (see p106), with the seat carved from rock for the governor's wife, was "the daily resort of all the fashionable people in Sydney".

Boer War
The 1st Australian Horse division was praised for its bushcraft, horsemanship and accurate shooting.

THE GARDEN PALACE

Built in the Botanic Garden especially for the occasion, in 1879–80, the Garden Palace hosted the first international exhibition held in the southern hemisphere. Twenty nations took part. Sadly, the building and most of its contents were destroyed by fire in 1882.

TIMELINE

1851 The discovery of gold near Bathurst, west of the Blue Mountains, sparks a gold rush

1868 The Duke of Edinburgh visits and survives an assassination attempt. The Prince Alfred Hospital is later named in his honour

Henry Parkes

1872 Henry Parkes elected NSW Premier

1850	1860	1870

1867 Henry Lawson born

1857 *Dunbar* wrecked at The Gap with the loss of 121 lives and only one survivor

Henry Lawson, notable poet and author of short stories

1869 Trend in the colony towards the segregation of Aboriginal peoples on reserves and settlements

1870 The last British troops withdraw from the colony

The Waverly
This clipper brig, with its extra sails and tall masts, enabled the fast transport of wool exports and fortune seekers hastening to newly discovered colonial gold fields.

The "Strasburg" Clock
In 1887, Sydney clockmaker Richard Smith began work on this astronomical model now in the Powerhouse Museum (see pp100–101).

Some of the exhibits held in the Powerhouse Museum *(see pp100–101)* were rescued from this burning building.

The exhibition attracted over one million people.

Arthur Streeton
In 1891, Streeton and Tom Roberts, both Australian Impressionist painters, set up an artists' camp overlooking Sydney Harbour in Mosman.

WHERE TO SEE VICTORIAN SYDNEY

Sydney's buildings reflect the spirit of the age. The Queen Victoria Building *(see p82)*, Sydney Town Hall *(p87)* and Martin Place *(p84)* mark grand civic spaces. In stark contrast, the Argyle Terraces and Susannah Place *(p67)* in The Rocks give some idea of the cramped living conditions endured by the working class.

St Mary's Cathedral (see p86), *built in Gothic Revival style, is thought to be the largest Christian church in the former "Empire", outside Britain.*

Victorian terrace houses, *decorated with iron lace, began to fill the streets of Paddington (see pp122–7) and Glebe (p131) from the 1870s onwards.*

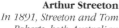

1880 The *Bulletin* is launched, and becomes a literary icon. Captain Moonlight, a notorious bushranger, is hanged

1890 First electric trams run between Bondi Junction and Waverley

Tivoli Theatre programme

1896 Moving pictures come to the Tivoli Theatre

1880

1890

1879 Steam tramway travels from the city to Redfern

Steam tram

1891 Labor Party enters the political arena

1877 Caroline Chisholm, a philanthropist who helped immigrant women, dies

1888 Louisa Lawson's journal *Dawn* published

1900 Queen Victoria consents to the formation of the Commonwealth of Australia. Bubonic plague breaks out

Sydney Between the Wars

Federation took place on 1 January 1901 and New South Wales became a state of the Australian nation. In Sydney, new wharves were built, roads widened and slums cleared. The 1920s were colourful and optimistic in "the city of pleasure". The skyline bristled

Vegemite spread created in 1923

with cranes as modern structures replaced their ornate predecessors. The country was hit hard by the Great Depression in 1931, but economic salvation came in the form of rising wool prices and growth in manufacturing. The opening of the Sydney Harbour Bridge in 1932 was a consolidation of all the changes brought by Federation and urbanization.

GROWTH OF THE CITY

☐ *Today*   ■ *1945*

The poster depicts the youthful vigour of the nation.

Home in the Suburbs
The Federation bungalow became a unique architectural style (see p39). Verandas, gables and chimneys featured amid much red brick.

Surf lifesaver

Bronzed Lifesavers
No surf beach was complete without these icons, forever looking to sea.

"Making Do"
This chair, made in 1910, used packing case timber, cotton reels, fencing wire and the mouldings of picture frames.

SYDNEY CELEBR
MARCH 19th 1932

SYDNEY HARBOUR BRIDGE
After nine years of construction, the largest crowd ever seen in Sydney greeted the bridge's opening. Considered a wonder of engineering at the time, it linked the harbour's north and south shores.

TIMELINE

1901 Miles Franklin's *My Brilliant Career* is published

Miles Franklin

1912 High-rise era begins in Sydney with the erection of the 14-storey Culwulla Chambers in Macquarie Street. First surfboard arrives in Sydney from Hawaii

1920 Prince Edward, the Prince of Wales, visits

1918 Sydneysiders greet the Armistice riotously

1900   **1910**   **1920**

1902 Women win the right to vote in New South Wales

1901 Proclamation of the Commonwealth of Australia. Edmund Barton elected as first prime minister

1907 Trunk line between Melbourne and Sydney opens

Poster for telephone trunk line

the TRUNK LINE SERVICE

1919 The Archibald Prize for portraiture is first awarded. Influenza epidemic hits Sydney

1915 Anzacs land at Gallipoli

Luna Park

This harbourside amusement park opened in 1935 (see p132). A maniacally grinning face looms at the entranceway. Millions of Australians recall the terrifying thrill of running the gauntlet through the gaping mouth as children.

One million people crossed the bridge on its opening day.

Donald Bradman

The 1932 English team used "dirty" tactics to outsmart this brilliant cricketer, almost causing a diplomatic rift with Great Britain.

Australian Women's weekly

This magazine, first published in 1933, becomes a family institution full of homespun wisdom, recipes, stories and handy hints.

WHERE TO SEE EARLY 20TH-CENTURY SYDNEY

The years after Federation yielded stylish and sensible buildings like Central Railway Station, the Commonwealth Bank in Martin Place *(see pp40–41)* and the State Library of New South Wales. The suburbs of Haberfield and Strathfield best exemplify the Federation style of gentrified residential housing.

The Anzac Memorial *(1934) is in Hyde Park (see pp86–7). The Art Deco memorial, with its reflecting pool, commemorates all Australians killed in wars.*

The wireless *became almost a fixture in sitting rooms in the 1930s. This 1935 AWA Radiolette is held at the Powerhouse Museum (see pp100–1).*

1924 Sydney swimmer Andrew "Boy" Charlton wins a gold medal at the Paris Olympics

Painted glass pub sign

1937 Heyday of painted glass pub art depicting local heroes

1938 Sydney celebrates her 150th anniversary

1939 Australia declares war on Germany

1930

1940

1928 Kingsford Smith and Ulm make first flight across Pacific in the *Southern Cross*

Kingsford Smith, Ulm

1932 Sydney Harbour Bridge opens

1935 Luna Park opens

1941 Australia declares war on Japan

1942 Japanese midget submarines enter Sydney Harbour

1945 Street celebrations mark the end of World War II

Postwar Sydney

1950s Holden sedan

The postwar baby boom was accompanied by mass immigration and the suburban sprawl. The hippie movement gave youth an extrovert voice that imbued the 1960s with an air of flamboyance. Australian involvement in the Vietnam War led to political unrest in the early 1970s, relieved for one seminal moment by the 1973 opening of the Sydney Opera House *(see pp74–7)*. In the 1980s, vast sums were spent on skyscrapers and glossy redevelopments like Darling Harbour, and on bicentennial celebrations. The city's potential was recognized in 1993 with the announcement that Sydney would host the year 2000 Olympics.

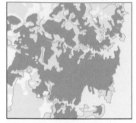

GROWTH OF THE CITY

☐ *Today*   ■ *1966*

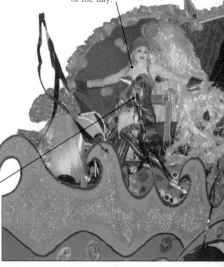

Drag queens pose in their Hollywood-style sequined finery or lampoon public figures of the day.

Sydney to Hobart Yacht Race
Australia's most prestigious and treacherous yacht race runs over 1,167 km (725 miles). Each Boxing Day since 1945, spectators have watched yachts jostle at the starting line.

Elaborate floats and costumes can take a year to make, with prizes given to the best.

Bicentenary
The re-enactment of the First Fleet's journey ended in Sydney Harbour on Australia Day, 1988. A chaotic flotilla greeted the "tall ships".

NEW MARDI GRAS FESTIVAL

What began as a protest march involving 1,000 people in 1978 is now a multi-million dollar boost for Australian tourism. While the parade lasts for one rude and riotous night only *(see p49)*, the surrounding international festival offers a month of art, sporting and community events.

TIMELINE

Johnny O'Keefe

Patrick White

1950	1960	1970	1980
1950 Petrol, butter and tea rationing ends	**1958** Qantas Airlines embarks on its first round-the-world flights	**1965** Conscription re-introduced; first regular army battalion sent to Vietnam	**1973** Official opening of the Sydney Opera House	**1979** Sydney's Eastern Suburbs Railway opens
1954 Elizabeth II is the first reigning monarch to visit Australia	**1959** Population of Australia reaches 10 million	**1964** Rocker Johnny O'Keefe, "The Wild One", continues to top the music charts	**1973** Patrick White wins the Nobel Prize for Literature	**1978** Brett Whiteley wins Archibald Prize, Wynne Prize and Sulman Prize for three works of art

Green Bans

In the 1970s, the militant building union placed work bans on developments in the inner city considered destructive to the environment or cultural heritage.

The parade of ornate floats and showy dance troupes stretches for over 2 km (1¼ miles).

MR ETERNITY

Arthur Stace (1885–1967), a reformed alcoholic, was inspired by an evangelist who said that he wanted to "shout eternity through the streets of Sydney". "I felt a powerful call from the Lord to write 'Eternity'." At least 50 times a day, for over 30 years, he chalked this word in perfect copperplate on the footpaths and walls of the city. A plaque in Sydney Square pays tribute to Mr Eternity's endeavours.

Arthur Stace and "Eternity", 1963

Ned Kelly

This 1946 portrait of legendary hero Ned Kelly is by Sir Sidney Nolan (1917–92), an important postwar painter.

Floats are marshalled in Elizabeth Street, before travelling along Oxford and Flinders Streets.

Oz Magazine, 1963–73

This satirical magazine, which had a major international influence, was the mouthpiece of an irreverent generation. It was declared obscene in 1964.

Aboriginal Land Rights

In 1975, the first handover of land was made to Vincent Lingiari, representative of the Gurindji people, by Prime Minister Gough Whitlam.

1990		2000		2010		2020

1990 Population of Australia reaches 17 million

1997 INXS singer Michael Hutchence commits suicide in a Sydney hotel

2003 Memorial unveiled to the 202 people killed in Bali bombing (2002)

2006 Sydney stages first Live Earth concert replicated simultaneously worldwide

2010 Population of Australia reaches 22 million

1992 Sydney Harbour Tunnel opens

1989 Earthquake strikes Newcastle causing extensive damage

2008 Sydney hosts World Youth Day

2000 Sydney plays host to the first Olympic Games of the new millennium

2010 Julia Gillard becomes the country's first female Prime Minister

SYDNEY AT A GLANCE

There are more than 100 places of interest described in the *Area by Area* section of this book. A broad range of sights is covered: from the colonial simplicity of Hyde Park Barracks *(see p114)* to the ornate Victorian terraces of Paddington; from the tranquillity of Centennial Park *(see p127)* to the bustle of the cafés and shops of Oxford Street. To help you make the most of your stay, the following 14 pages are a time-saving guide to the best Sydney has to offer. Museums and galleries, architecture and parks and reserves all have sections of their own. There is also a guide to the diverse cultures that have helped to shape the city into what it is today. Below is a selection of attractions that no visitor should miss.

SYDNEY'S TOP TEN ATTRACTIONS

The Rocks
See pp62–77

Sydney Opera House
See pp74–7

Royal Botanic Garden
See pp104–5

Art Gallery of New South Wales
See pp108–11

Sydney Tower
See p83

Oxford Street and Paddington
See pp116–27

Darling Harbour and Chinatown
See pp90–101

Taronga Zoo
See pp134–5

Harbour ferries
See pp234–5

Sydney's beaches
See pp54–5

◁ Sydney Harbour Bridge, opened in 1932 *(see pp70–71)*

Sydney's Best: Museums and Galleries

Sydney is well endowed with museums and galleries, and, following the current appreciation of social history, much emphasis is placed on the lifestyles of past and present Sydneysiders. Small museums are also a feature of the Sydney scene, with a number of historic houses recalling the colonial days. These are covered in greater depth on pages 36–7. Most of the major collections are housed in architecturally significant buildings – the Classical façade of the Art Gallery of NSW makes it a city landmark, while the Museum of Contemporary Art has given new life to a 1950s Art Deco-style building at Circular Quay.

Bima figure, Powerhouse Museum

Museum of Sydney
The Edge of the Trees is an interactive installation by the entrance.

THE ROCKS AND CIRCULAR QUAY

Museum of Contemporary Art
This waterfront space is Australia's only museum dedicated to exhibiting national and international contemporary art.

CITY CENTRE

The National Maritime Museum
The museum is the home port for HMS Endeavour, a replica of the vessel that charted Australia's east coast in 1770, with Captain Cook in command.

DARLING HARBOUR

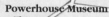

Powerhouse Museum
This museum, set in a former power station, uses both traditional and interactive displays to explore Australian innovations in science and technology.

0 metres   500
0 yards   500

Art Gallery of New South Wales
The Australian collection includes colonial watercolours which, to avoid deterioration, are only shown for a few weeks each year. Charles Meere's Australian Beach Pattern *(1940) is among more recent works.*

Elizabeth Bay House
The dining room is elegantly furnished to the 1840s period, when the Colonial Secretary Alexander Macleay briefly lived in the house that ultimately caused his bankruptcy.

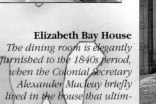

BOTANIC GARDEN AND THE DOMAIN

KINGS CROSS AND DARLINGHURST

Hyde Park Barracks Museum
Originally built by convicts for their own incarceration, these barracks were later home to poor female immigrants. Exhibits recall the daily life of these occupants.

Australian Museum
Discover the Earth's age, find out about meteorites, volcanic activity and dinosaurs at Australia's largest natural history museum.

PADDINGTON

Sydney Jewish Museum
The history of the city's Jewish community is documented here. Included is a reconstruction of George Street in 1848, a major location for Jewish businesses.

Exploring Sydney's Museums and Galleries

Sydney boasts a rich variety of museums and galleries that reflects the cultural, artistic and historical heritage of this, the country's oldest city – and of Australia as a whole. The growth of such

Nautilus scrimshaw, National Maritime Museum

institutions parallels a corresponding growth in public interest in all things cultural, a phenomenon that seems at odds with Sydney's predominantly hedonistic image. In fact, Sydney has a long-standing cultural tradition, one that has not always been widely recognized. It may even surprise some people that museums and galleries attract more people than do high-profile football matches.

Detail from *Window of Dreams* at the National Maritime Museum

Collage on one of the internal doors of the Brett Whiteley Studio

VISUAL ARTS

The **Art Gallery of NSW** has one of the finest existing collections of modern Australian and Aboriginal art. It also boasts an outstanding collection of late 19th- and early 20th-century English and Australian works as

well as a gallery devoted to Asian art and a collection of contemporary and photo-graphic works. Thematic temporary exhibitions are also a regular feature here.

The far newer **Museum of Contemporary Art** (MCA) is best known for its impressive blockbuster exhibitions. Many of these take advantage of its prime harbour site to create a fine sense of spectacle. It also has a considerable permanent collection, and hosts literary readings and talks.

The **Brett Whiteley Studio**, housed in the studio of the late artist, commemorates the life and works of perhaps the most celebrated and contro-versial Sydney painter of the late 20th century.

The substantial collection of Australian painting and sculpture held by the **S.H. Ervin Gallery** is supplemented by frequent thematic and other specialized exhibitions.

TECHNOLOGY AND NATURAL HISTORY

The undisputed leader in this area is the **Powerhouse**, with traditional and interactive displays covering fields as diverse as space travel, silent films and solar energy. The **Australian National Maritime Museum** has the world's fastest boat, *Spirit of Australia*, as part of its indoor/outdoor display. Also part of their fleet are the destroyer HMAS *Vampire*, the *Onslow* (a sub-marine), and the *James Craig* (1874), a three-masted barque.

The **Australian Museum**, in contrast, emphasizes natural history with its displays of the exotic and extinct: from birds, insects and rock samples to giant Australian megafauna.

ABORIGINAL CULTURE

With more than 200 works, both traditional and contem-porary, on display, the **Art Gallery of NSW**'s Yiribana Gallery has the best and most

Jabarrgwa Wurrabadalumba's *Dugong Hunt* (1948), Art Gallery of NSW

comprehensive collection of Aboriginal art in the country. The **Australian Museum** has displays ranging from rocks and minerals, birds and insects to the permanent indigenous exhibition. In its community access space, it also presents performances that celebrate Aboriginal culture.

The First Australians exhibit at the **Australian National Maritime Museum** includes audio and video material, with traditional tools made by Aboriginal communities.

The **Museum of Sydney** uses images, artifacts and oral histories to evoke the life of the Eora, the indigenous people of the Sydney region, up to the years of first contact with the European colonists.

COLONIAL HISTORY

Elizabeth Bay House's superb interior is furnished to show early colonial life at its most elegant, but while at first the house may appear to celebrate a success story, the enormous cost of its construction brought bankruptcy to its owner. Also built in grand style, **Vaucluse House** celebrates the life and times of WC Wentworth, explorer and politician.

Experiment Farm Cottage, Hambledon Cottage and **Elizabeth Farm** in and around Parramatta are testament to the crucial role of agriculture in the survival of a colony that was brought to the brink of starvation. The former has been restored as a gentleman's cottage of the mid-19th century, while the latter two have been furnished to the period of 1820–50. Parramatta's **Old Government House** was once the vice-regal "inland" residence when Parramatta had more people than Sydney. The colonial furniture on display predates 1855.

The **Museum of Sydney** is built on the site of the first Government House, close to Sydney Cove. On display are unearthed relics from that

The Georgian-style front bedroom in the cottage at Elizabeth Farm

building, some of which are visible under windows at the entrance to the museum.

Susannah Place Museum looks at working-class life in the 19th century. **Cadman's Cottage**, also in The Rocks, is a simple stone dwelling dating from 1816 and the city's oldest extant building. Adjacent is the **Sailors' Home**, built in 1864 as lodgings for visiting sailors. It now houses the Billich Art Gallery, as well as a restaurant and the Sailors Thai Canteen noodle bar (see p184). The important role of gold in the history of Australia and how it determined patterns of migration and expansion are shown at the **Powerhouse Museum. Hyde Park Barracks Museum** evokes the often brutal lives and times of the convicts who were housed there in the early 19th century, while not neglecting its other place in history as an immigration depot.

Water dip at Experiment Farm Cottage

SPECIALIST MUSEUMS

Author May Gibbs' home on the harbour, **Nutcote**, has been refurbished in the style of the 1930s. The **Justice and Police Museum** examines a far less comfortable history, investigating Australian crime and punishment, while the **Westpac Museum** traces local financial transactions from first coins through to credit cards. Experiences of Jewish migrants to Australia and the story of the Holocaust are examined at the **Sydney Jewish Museum**.

Side view of the veranda at Elizabeth Farm, near Parramatta

Sydney's Best: Architecture

For such a young city, Sydney possesses a remarkable diversity of architectural styles. They range from the simplicity of Francis Greenway's Georgian buildings *(see p114)* to Jørn Utzon's Expressionist Sydney Opera House *(see pp74–7)*. Practical Colonial structures gave way to elaborate Victorian edifices such as Sydney Town Hall, and the same passion for detail is seen on a smaller scale in Paddington's terraces. Later, Federation warehouses and bungalows brought in a particularly Australian style.

Colonial Convict
The first structures were very simple yet formal English-style cottages with shingled roofs and no verandas. Cadman's Cottage is a fine repre-sentative of this style.

Contemporary
Governor Phillip Tower is a modern commercial building incorporating a historical site (see p85).

THE ROCKS AND CIRCULAR QUAY

Colonial Georgian
Francis Greenway's courthouse design was ordered to be adapted to suit the purposes of a church. St James' Church is the result.

American Revivalism
Shopping arcades connecting streets, such as the Queen Victoria Building, were 1890s vogue.

CITY CENTRE

Victorian
The Town Hall interior includes Australia's first pressed metal ceiling, installed for fear that the organ would vib-rate a plaster one loose.

DARLING HARBOUR

Contemporary Expressionism
Innovations in sports stadiums and museum architecture, such as the National Maritime Museum, empha-size roof design and the silhouette.

Interwar Architecture
Bruce Dellit's Anzac Memorial in Hyde Park, with sculptures by Rayner Hoff, encapsulates the spirit, form and detail of Art Deco.

| 0 metres | 500 |
| 0 yards | 500 |

Modern Expressionism

One of the world's greatest examples of 20th-century architecture, Jørn Utzon's Sydney Opera House beat 234 entries in a design competition. Work commenced in 1959 and, despite the architect's resignation in 1966, it was opened in 1973.

Early Colonial

The first buildings of character and quality, such as Hyde Park Barracks, were for the government.

BOTANIC
GARDEN AND
THE DOMAIN

Australian Regency

During the 1830s, the best designed villas were the work of John Verge. Elizabeth Bay House was his masterpiece.

KINGS CROSS AND
DARLINGHURST

Colonial Military

Victoria Barracks, designed by engineers, is an impressive example of a well-preserved Georgian military compound.

PADDINGTON

Colonial Grecian

Greek Revival was the major style for public buildings, such as the Darlinghurst Court House, designed by the Colonial Architect in the 1820–50 period.

Victorian Iron Lace

Festooned with a filigree of cast-iron lace in a wide range of prefabricated patterns, Paddington verandas demonstrate 1880s workmanship.

Exploring Sydney's Architecture

Federation-era stained glass

While European settlement in Sydney has a relatively short history, architectural styles have rapidly evolved from provincial British buildings and the simplicity of convict structures. From the mid-19th century until the present day, architectural innovations have borrowed from a range of international trends to create vernacular styles more suited to local materials and conditions. The signs of affluence and austerity, from gold rush to depression, are also manifested in bricks and mortar.

Façade of the Colonial Susannah Place, with corner shop window

COLONIAL ARCHITECTURE

Little remains of the Colonial buildings from 1790–1830. The few structures still standing have a simple robustness and unassuming dignity. They rely more on form, proportion and mass than on detail.

The Rocks area has one of the best collections of early Colonial buildings: **Cadman's Cottage** (1816), the **Argyle Stores** (1826) and **Susannah Place Museum** (1844). The Georgian **Hyde Park Barracks** (1819) and **St James' Church** (1820), by Francis Greenway *(see p114)*, as well as the Greek Revival **Darlinghurst Court House** (1835) and **Victoria Barracks**(1841–8) are excellent examples of this period.

AUSTRALIAN REGENCY

Just as the Colonial style was reaching its zenith, the city's increasingly moneyed society abandoned it as undignified and unfashionable. London's residential architecture, exemplified by John Soane under the Prince Regent's patronage, was in favour from the 1830s to the 1850s. Fine examples of this shift towards Regency are John Verge's stylish town houses at **39–41 Lower Fort Street** (1834–6), The Rocks, and the adjoining **Bligh House** built for a wealthy merchant in 1833 in High Colonial style complete with Greek Classical Doric veranda columns.

Regency-style homes often had Grecian, French and Italian details. **Elizabeth Bay House** (1835–8), internally the finest of all John Verge's works, is particularly noted for its cantilevered staircase rising to the arcaded gallery. The cast-iron Ionic-columned **Tusculum Villa** (1831) by the same architect at Potts Point *(see p118)* is unusual in that it is encircled by a double-storeyed veranda, now partially enclosed.

Entrance detail from the Victorian St Patrick's Seminary in Manly

VICTORIAN

This prosperous era featured confident business people and merchants who designed their own premises. Tracts of the city west of York Street and south of Bathurst Street are testimony to these self-assured projects. The cast-iron and glass **Strand Arcade** (1891) by JB Spencer originally included a gas and electricity system, and hydraulic lifts.

Government architect James Barnet's best work includes the "Venetian Renaissance" style **General Post Office**, Martin Place (1864–87), and the extravagant **Lands Department Building** (1877–90) with its four iron staircases and, originally, patent lifts operated by water power. The **Great Synagogue** (1878), **St Mary's Cathedral** (1882), **St Patrick's Seminary** (1885), **Sydney Town Hall** and **Paddington Street** are also of this period.

AMERICAN REVIVALISM

After federation in 1901, architects looked to styles such as Edwardian, American Romanesque and Beaux Arts from overseas for commercial buildings. The former **National Mutual Building** (1892) by Edward Raht set the change of direction, followed by warehouse buildings in Sussex and Kent Streets. The Romanesque **Queen Victoria Building**

The Australian Regency-style Bligh House in Dawes Point

(1893–98) was a grand council project by George McRae. The Beaux Arts **Commonwealth Savings Bank** (1928) features an elaborate chamber in Neo-Classical style.

INTERWAR ARCHITECTURE

Architecture between World Wars I and II produced skyscrapers such as the **City Mutual Life Assurance Building** (1936), by Emil Sodersten. This building exhibits German Expressionist influences such as pleated or zigzag windows.

Two important structures are the **ANZAC Memorial** (1929–34) in Hyde Park and **Delfin House** (1938–40), by the Art Deco architect Bruce Dellit. The latter, a skyscraper, features a vaulted ceiling and a granite arch decorated with an allegory of modern life.

MODERN ARCHITECTURE

Modern MLC Centre, Martin Place

From the mid-1950s, modern architecture was introduced to the city through glass-clad curtain-walled office blocks, proportioned like matchboxes on their ends. The contrasting expressed frame approach of **Australia Square** (1961–7) gives structural stability to one of the world's tallest lightweight concrete office towers. This city block was formed by amalgamating 30 properties. Harry Seidler's **MLC Centre** (1975–8) is a 65-storey office

FEDERATION ARCHITECTURE

This distinctly urban style of architecture developed to meet the demands of the prosperous, newly emerging middle classes at the time of Federation in 1901. Particular features are high-pitched roofs, which form a picturesque composition or architectural tableau, incorporating intricate gables, wide verandas and chimneys. The decorative timber fretwork the verandas and archways and the leadlight windows reveal the influence of the Art Nouveau period, as do the vibrant red roof tiles. Patriotic references are seen throughout, and Australian flora and fauna are recurring decorative motifs.

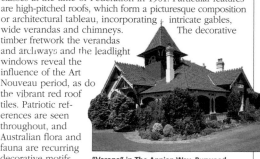

"Verona" in The Appian Way, Burwood

tower comprising a reinforced concrete tube structure with column-free floors.

Jørn Utzon's **Sydney Opera House** (1959–73) is widely regarded as one of the architectural wonders of the world.

CONTEMPORARY ARCHITECTURE

The elliptical **Sydney Football Stadium** (1985–8) and the **Australian National Maritime Museum** (1986–9), both by Philip Cox, make use of advanced steel engineering systems. Detailed masonry has made a return to commercial buildings such as the highly regarded **Governor Phillip Tower** (1989–94). The dictates of office design do not detract from the historical Museum of Sydney, ingeniously sited on the lower floors.

The **ABN-AMRO Tower** at Aurora Place (2000) was designed by Renzo Piano and was awarded the Sulman Prize for Architecture in 2004.

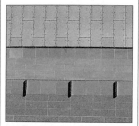

Masonry detail from the contemporary Governor Phillip Tower

WHERE TO FIND THE BUILDINGS

Sydney's Many Cultures

Sydney has one of the world's most cosmopolitan societies, reflected in the extraordinary variety of restaurants, religions, community centres and cultural activities to be found throughout the city and its environs. Over 235 birthplaces outside Australia were named in the last census. Indeed, the Sydney telephone directory lists interpreting services for 22 languages, including Greek, Italian, Spanish, Chinese, Vietnamese, Turkish, Korean and Arabic, and many of these groups have their own newspapers. While immigrants have settled all over the city, there are still pockets of Sydney that retain a distinctive ethnic flavour.

Thai Community
Thai culinary traditions have caused a revolution in Sydney eating houses. The Loy Krathong Festival in Parramatta celebrates the transplanted Thai culture.

Auburn Mosque
This lavish mosque rises above the thriving Turkish businesses nearby. Halal meat markets and sweet shops are proof of their influence.

Thailand

Turkey

Cambodian
Cabramatta is the hub of the Cambodian community. Songkran, the three-day new year celebration is held at Bonnyrigg.

Cambodia

Vietnam

Filipinos
Over 60 per cent of this rapidly expanding migrant group arrive as the brides of Australian men.

Philippines

Lebanon

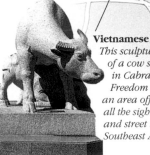

Vietnamese
This sculpture of a cow stands in Cabramatta's Freedom Plaza, an area offering all the sights, smells and street life of Southeast Asia.

Lakemba
A living monument to Islam, the fastest growing religion in Australia, this centre is a meeting place for local Lebanese people.

0 kilometres 4

0 miles 2

Irish Parade
Sydney's first settlers, many of them Irish, made their home in The Rocks. With its proliferation of pubs, it is the focal point for jubilant St Patrick's Day celebrations on 17 March each year.

Little Italy
Long home to the Italian community, Leichhardt evokes the flavour of Europe with its bars, cafés, restaurants and a sprawling annual street fair.

Jewish Delicatessen
The sizeable Jewish community in the city's eastern suburbs, about half of whom were born in Australia, is well served by kosher supermarkets and butchers' shops.

Ireland

Italy   China

Israel

Greece

Indigenous
Australia

Aboriginal Peoples
Redfern Park hosts a Survival concert every 26 January, the culmination of a week of cultural exchange.

Chinese New Year
Each year, revellers pack Dixon Street, at the heart of Chinatown, to celebrate with fireworks and Chinese dragons.

St Nicholas Church
Marrickville's Greek Orthodox church is the home of worship for the community, mostly based in the southern suburbs.

Sydney's Best: Parks and Reserves

Flannel
flower

Sydney is almost completely surrounded by national parks and intact bushland. There are also a number of national parks and reserves within Greater Sydney itself. Here, the visitor can gain some idea of how the landscape looked before the arrival of European settlers. The city parks, too, are filled with plant and animal life. The more formal plantings of both native and exotic species are countered by the indigenous birds and animals that have adapted and made the urban environment their home. One of the highlights of a trip to Sydney is the huge variety of birds to be seen, from large birds of prey such as sea eagles and kites, to the shyer species such as wrens and tiny finches.

Garigal National Park
Rainforest and moist gullies provide shelter for superb lyrebirds and sugar gliders.

North Arm Walk
In spring, grevilleas and flannel flowers bloom profusely on this foreshore walk.

Lane Cove National Park
The open eucalypt forest is dotted with grass trees, as well as fine stands of red and blue gums. The rosella, a type of parrot, is common.

Bicentennial Park
Situated at Homebush Bay on the Parramatta River, the park features a mangrove habitat. It attracts many water birds, including pelicans.

Hyde Park
Situated on the edge of the city centre, the park provides a peaceful respite from the hectic streets. The native iris is just one of the plants found in the lush gardens. The sacred ibis, a water bird, is often seen.

Middle Head and Obelisk Bay

Gun emplacements, tunnels and bunkers built in the 1870s to protect Sydney from invasion by sea dot the area. The superb fairy wren lives here and water dragons can at times be seen basking on rocks.

North Head

Coastal heathland, with banksias, tea trees and casuarinas, dominates the cliff tops. On the leeward side, moist forest surrounds tiny harbour beaches.

Grotto Point

Bottlebrushes, grevilleas and flannel flowers line paths winding through the bush to the lighthouse.

Bradleys Head

The headland is a nesting place for the ringtail possum. Noisy flocks of rainbow lorikeets are also often in residence.

South Head

Unique plant species such as the sundew cover this heathland.

Nielsen Park

The kookaburra is easily identified by its call, which sounds like laughter.

The Domain

Palms and Moreton Bay figs are a feature of this former common. The Australian magpie, with its black and white plumage, is a frequent visitor.

Moore Park

Huge Moreton Bay figs provide an urban habitat for the flying fox.

Centennial Park

Open expanses and groves of paperbark and eucalypt trees bring sulphur-crested cockatoos en masse. The brushtail possum is a shy creature that comes out at night.

0 kilometres   4

0 miles   2

Exploring the Parks and Reserves

Despite 200 years of European settlement, Sydney's parks and reserves contain a surprising variety of native wildlife. Approximately 2,000 species of native plants, 1,000 cultivated and weed species and 300 bird species have managed to adapt favourably to the changes.

Several quite distinct vegetation types are protected in the bushland around Sydney, and these in turn provide shelter for a wide range of birds and animals. Even the more formal parks such as Hyde Park and the Royal Botanic Garden are home to many indigenous species, allowing the visitor a glimpse of the city's diverse wildlife.

Colourful and noisy rainbow lorikeets at Manly's Collins Beach

COASTAL HINTERLAND

One reason Sydney has so many heathland parks, such as those found at South Head and North Head, is that the soil along the city's coastline is deficient in almost every known nutrient. What these areas lack in fertility, they make up for in species diversity.

Heathland contains literally hundreds of species of plants, including some unique flora that have adapted to the poor soil. The most surprising ones are the carnivorous plants, which rely on passing insects for their food. The tiny sundew *(Drosera spatulata)*, so called because of its sparkling foliage, is the commonest of the carnivorous species. This low-growing plant snares insects on its sticky, reddish leaves, which lie flat on the ground. You will often stumble across them where walking tracks pass through swampy ground, waiting patiently for a victim.

Red bottlebrush
(Callistemon sp.)

Two other distinctive plants are casuarinas *(Allocasuarina* species) and banksias *(Banksia* species), both of which attract smaller birds such as honey-eaters and blue wrens.

RAINFOREST AND MOIST FOREST

Rainforest remnants do exist in a few parts of Sydney, especially in the Royal National Park to the south of the city *(see pp164–5)*. Small pockets can also be found in Garigal National Park, Ku-ring-gai Chase *(see pp154–5)* and some gullies running down to Middle Harbour. The superb lyrebird *(Menura novaehollandiae)* is a feature of these forest areas. The sugar glider *(Petaurus breviceps)*, a small species of possum, can sometimes be heard calling to its mate during the night.

The deadliest spider in the world, the Sydney funnel-web *(Atrax robustus, see p89)*, also lives here, but you are unlikely to see one unless you poke under rocks and logs. A common plant in this habitat is the cabbage tree palm *(Livistona australis)*. Its heart was used as a vegetable by the early European settlers.

The soft tree fern *(Dicksonia antartctica)* decorates the gullies and creeks of moist forest. You may see a ringtail possum *(Pseudocheirus peregrinus)* nest at the top of one of these ferns at Bradleys Head. The nest looks rather like a hairy football and is found in hollow trees or ferns and shrubs.

Rainbow lorikeets *(Trichoglossus haematodus)* also inhabit Bradleys Head, as well as Clifton Gardens and Collins Beach. Early in the morning, they shoot through the forest canopy like iridescent bullets.

OPEN EUCALYPT FOREST

Some of Sydney's finest smooth-barked apple gums *(Angophora costata)* are in the Lane Cove National Park. These ancient trees, with their gnarled pinkish trunks, lend an almost "lost world" feeling.

Tall and straight blue gums *(Eucalyptus saligna)* stand in the lower reaches of the park, where the soil is better, while the smaller grey-white scribbly gum *(Eucalyptus rossii)*, with its distinctive gum veins, lives on higher slopes. If you examine the markings on a scribbly gum closely, you will see they start out thin, gradually become thicker, then take a U-turn and stop. This is the track made by an *ogmograptis* caterpillar the previous year. The grubs that made the track

Coastal heathland lining the cliff tops at Manly's North Head

become small, brownish-grey moths and are commonly seen in eucalypt or gum forests.

Grass trees (*Xanthorrhoea* species), also common in open eucalypt forest, are an ancient plant species with a tall spike that bears white flowers in spring. Lyrebirds, echidnas, currawongs and black snakes are predominant wildlife. The snakes, although beautiful, should be treated with caution.

A smooth-barked apple gum in Lane Cove National Park

WETLANDS

More than 60 per cent of New South Wales' coastal wetlands have been lost. This makes the remaining areas of wetland especially important. Most of Sydney's wetlands are mangrove swamps, with some of the best preserved examples at Bicentennial Park and the North Arm Walking Track.

Mangrove swamps are one of the most hostile places for a plant or animal to live. There

A grey mangrove swamp near the Lane Cove National Park

is no fresh water and, unlike soil, the mud has no oxygen whatsoever below the very surface level. Mangroves have developed some fascinating ways around these problems.

First, excess salt is excreted from their leaves. Secondly, they get oxygen to the roots by pushing special peg-like roots, called pneumatophores, into the air. At low tide, these can be clearly seen around the base of most mangroves. They allow air to diffuse down into the roots so that they can survive the stifling conditions under the mud. The Sydney rock oyster (*Saccostrea commercialis*), a popular local delicacy, is found in mangrove areas, particularly around the Hawkesbury and Botany Bay.

CITY PARKS

An amazing number of birds and animals make the city parks their home. Silver gulls (*Larus novaehollandiae*) and sulphur-crested cockatoos (*Cacatua galerita*) are frequent daytime visitors to Hyde Park, Centennial Park, The Domain and the Botanic Garden.

After dark, brush-tailed possums (*Trichosurus vulpecula*) go in search of food and may be seen scavenging in rubbish bins. Also a night creature, the fruit-eating grey-headed flying fox (*Pteropus poliocephalus*) can be seen swooping through the trees. There is sometimes

The nocturnal grey-headed flying fox, at rest during the daytime

a temporary colony of these mammals in the Botanic Garden, where they hang upside down from trees in the park. Most of Sydney's flying foxes come from a large colony in Gordon, in the city's north.

Moore Park and The Domain are good places to spot flying foxes and they also have wonderful specimens of Moreton Bay and other fig species.

While paperbarks (*Melaleuca* species) are a feature of Centennial Park, a range of palms can be seen in the Botanic Garden. The exquisite superb fairy-wren (*Malurus cyaneus*) can also be seen here, flitting between shrubs, while overhead honeyeaters dart after each other in the tree canopy.

STRANGLER FIGS

The majestic figs in the city parks hide a dark secret. While most of the Moreton Bay figs (*Ficus macrophylla*) you see have been grown by gardeners long past, in the wild these trees have a different approach. They start as a tiny seedling, sprouted from a seed dropped by a bird in the fork of a tree. Over decades, the pencil-thin roots grow downwards. Once they reach the ground, new roots are sent down, forming a lacy network around the trunk of the host tree. They eventually become an iron-hard cage around the host tree's trunk so that it dies and rots away, leaving the fig with a hollow trunk.

The Moreton Bay fig, with its massive spreading canopy

SYDNEY THROUGH THE YEAR

Sydney's temperate climate allows for the enjoyment of outdoor activities throughout the year. Seasons in Sydney are the opposite of those in the northern hemisphere. September ushers in the three months of spring; summer stretches from December to February; March, April and May are the autumn months; while the shorter days and falling temperatures of June announce the onset of winter. In reality, however, Sydney seasons often merge into one another with little to mark their changeover. Balmy nights, the sweet, pervasive scent of jasmine blossom and the colourful blooming of shrubs and flowers are typical of spring. Summer caters for sun- and surf-lovers as well as being Sydney's festival season. Autumn, with warm days and cooler nights, is often perfect for bushwalks and picnics. And the crisp days of winter are ideal for historic walks and exploring art galleries and museums.

Reveller at the Mardi Gras

SPRING

With the warmer weather, the profusion of spring flowers brings the city's parks and gardens excitingly to life. Food, art and music festivals abound. Footballers finish their seasons with action-packed grand finals, professional and backyard cricketers warm up for their summer competitions and the horse-racing fraternity gets ready to place its bets.

Spring display of tulip beds at the Leura Garden Festival

SEPTEMBER

David Jones Spring Flower Show (*first two weeks*), Elizabeth Street department store. Breathtaking floral artwork fills the ground floor.
Primavera (*Sep–mid-Nov*). Highly regarded talent-spotting show at the Museum of Contemporary Art (*see p73*).
Tulip Time Bowral (*late Sep–early Oct*), Bowral (*see p162*). A two-week festival of open gardens, talks, specialist shows and 100,000 tulips in bloom.
Spring Racing Carnival (*Sep–Oct*). The horse-racing action is shared between Rosehill racecourse and the Royal Randwick racecourse.
Festival of the Winds (*dates vary*), Bondi Beach (*see p137*). Multicultural kite-flying festival; music, dance.
New South Wales Rugby Union Grand Final, Sydney Football Stadium (*see p52*).

OCTOBER

Australian Rugby League Grand Final (*first Sun*), Stadium Australia, Homebush.
Manly International Jazz Festival (*Labour Day weekend*). World-class jazz at a variety of venues (*see p133*).
Fiesta (*Labour Day weekend*), Darling Harbour (*see pp92–3*). Fiestas, parades and festivals from all nations, including music, arts, dance, puppets and fireworks.
Leura Garden Festival (*early Oct*), Blue Mountains (*see pp160–61*). A village fair launches the festival, when magnificent private gardens featuring flower displays of a particularly high standard may be viewed.
Australian International Motor Show (*mid-Oct*), Sydney Convention and Exhibition Centre, Darling Harbour (*see p92*).

NOVEMBER

Melbourne Cup Day (*first Tue*). The city almost grinds to a halt mid-afternoon to tune in to Australia's most popular horse race. Restaurants and hotels offer special luncheons on the day.
Sydney to the Gong Bicycle Ride (*first Sun*). From Moore Park to Wollongong. Over 10,000 cyclists of all standards do this 92-km (57-mile) ride.
Sculpture by the Sea (*early Nov*), Bondi Beach. Hugely popular outdoor exhibition of fantastic sculptures on the path between Bondi and Tamarama beaches.

Sacred ibis stilt-dancer at the Sydney in Bloom festival

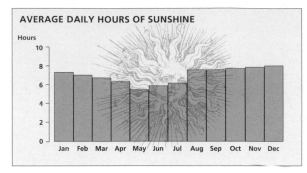

AVERAGE DAILY HOURS OF SUNSHINE

Hours

Jan Feb Mar Apr May Jun Jul Aug Sep Oct Nov Dec

Sunshine Hours
A sunny climate is one of Sydney's main attractions. There are very few days with no sunshine at all, even in the middle of winter. An up-to-date weather forecast is available by telephoning 1196. Coastal weather conditions can be obtained by dialling 11541.

SUMMER

Sydney turns festive in the summer months. Christmas pageants and open-air carol singing in The Domain mark the start of the season. Then there is the Sydney Festival, three weeks of cultural events and other popular entertainment, culminating in Australia Day celebrations on 26 January. Summer, too, brings a feast for sport lovers, with surfing and lifesaving events, yacht races and both local and international cricket matches.

"Santa Claus" at the surf: Christmas Day celebrations on Bondi Beach

DECEMBER

Carols in The Domain *(second Sat before Christmas)*. Carols by candlelight in the parkland of the city's favourite outdoor gathering spot *(see p107)*.
Christmas at Bondi Beach *(25 Dec)*. Holidaymakers hold their own unofficial party on this famous beach *(see p137)*.
Sydney to Hobart Yacht Race *(26 Dec)*. The harbour teems with small craft as they escort racing yachts out to sea for the start of their journey.
New Year's Eve *(31 Dec)*. Street parties in The Rocks and Circular Quay and fireworks displays in Sydney Harbour.

JANUARY

Opera in the Domain *(one Sat)*, The Domain *(see p107)*. A free performance of highlights from productions by Opera Australia.
Symphony under the Stars *(one Sat)*, The Domain *(see p107)*. Free concert by the Sydney Symphony Orchestra.
Cricket Test matches and one-day internationals at Sydney Cricket Ground *(see p52)*.
Flickerfest *(early–mid-Jan)*, Bondi Pavilion *(see pp144–5)*. Festival of Australian and international short films and animation.
Festival of Sydney *(second weekend)*. Fantastic music, theatre, sport and art events.
Big Day Out *(around 26 Jan)*, Olympic Park, Homebush. Outdoor concert attracting huge crowds and hip acts.
Ferrython *(26 Jan)*, Sydney Harbour. Ferries compete for line honours, as do rigged

competitors in the Tall Ships Race held on the same day.
Australia Day Concert *(26 Jan)*. Concerts take place all over the city.
Chinese New Year *(late Jan or early Feb)*. Lion dancing, firecrackers and other New Year festivities take place in Chinatown *(see p99)*, Darling Harbour and Cabramatta *(p42)*.

FEBRUARY

New Mardi Gras Festival, various inner-city venues *(see pp30–31)*. A month of events culminating in a street parade, mainly on Oxford Street, usually held early March.
North Bondi Classic Ocean Swim *(one Sun in early Feb)*, North Bondi *(see p137)*. A 2-km (1½-mile) race. Any swimmer can enter.
Coogee Surf Carnival *(first weekend)*, Coogee *(see p55)*.
Tropfest *(third Sun)*, Darlinghurst and The Domain. Hugely popular short-film festival.

Chinese New Year lion

Australia Day Tall Ships race in Sydney Harbour

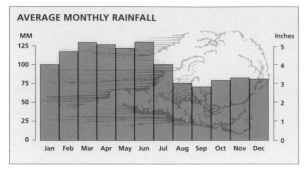

AVERAGE MONTHLY RAINFALL

Rainfall
Autumn is Sydney's rainiest season, with March being the wettest month, while spring is the driest time of year. Rainfall, however, can often be unpredictable. Long stretches of sunny weather are common, but so, too, are periods of unrelenting rain.

AUTUMN

After the humidity of the summer, autumn brings fresh mornings and cooler days that are tailor-made for outdoor pursuits. There are many sporting and cultural events – some of them colourful and eccentric – to tempt the visitor. For many, the Royal Easter Show is the highlight of the season. Anzac Day (25 April) is a national holiday on which Australians commemorate their war dead.

MARCH

Dragon Boat Races Festival *(late Feb–early Mar)*, Darling Harbour *(see pp92–3)*. Brilliantly decorated Chinese dragon boats race across Cockle Bay.
St Patrick's Day Parade *(17 Mar, or closest Sun)*. Hyde Park *(see pp86–7)* to The Domain. Pubs serve green beer on the day.
Sydney Harbour Week *(early*

St Patrick's Day beer

Mar). A programme of more than 40 events, many free, including swimming, sailing, snorkelling, heritage tours and the Sydney Harbour Regatta.
Archibald, Wynne and Sulman exhibitions *(Mar)*, Art Gallery of NSW *(pp108–11)*. Annual exhibition of that year's entries in the portraiture, landscape, genre works and drawing competitions.
Autumn Racing Carnival *(six weeks during Mar and Apr)*. Top-class races and big prize money, at Rosehill and Royal Randwick racecourses.

EASTER

Sydney Royal Easter Show *(opens for two weeks over Easter period)*, Olympic Park. Homebush. Country meets city for around 14 days of ring events, livestock and produce judging, woodchopping competitions, sheepdog trials, arts and crafts displays and sideshow alley attractions.

Woodchopping at the Easter Show

Darling Harbour Hoopla *(Easter long weekend)*, Darling Harbour *(see pp92–3)*. Circus acts and street theatre by magicians, acrobats, mime and other artists.

APRIL

National Trust Heritage Festival *(dates vary)*. Celebration of the natural and cultural heritage of Sydney. www.nsw.nationaltrust.org.au
Anzac Day *(25 Apr)*. Dawn remembrance service held at the Cenotaph, Martin Place *(see p84)*, with a parade by war veterans along George Street.

MAY

Sydney Writers' Festival *(dates vary)*, Pier 4/5 Hickson Road, Walsh Bay.
Bridge to Bridge Power Boat Classic *(first Sun)*. Race from Brooklyn Bridge to Upper Hawkesbury Power Boat Club, Windsor *(see pp156–7)*.
Sydney Half Marathon *(Sun in May)*, from Pier One, The Rocks. A 21-km (13-mile) run open to all standards.

Traditional decorative dragon boats on Darling Harbour's Cockle Bay

AVERAGE MONTHLY TEMPERATURE

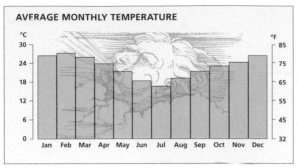

°C / °F chart with bars for Jan Feb Mar Apr May Jun Jul Aug Sep Oct Nov Dec

°C scale: 30, 24, 18, 12, 6, 0
°F scale: 85, 75, 65, 55, 45, 32

Temperature
This chart gives the average minimum and maximum temperatures for Sydney. Spring and autumn are generally free of extremes, but be prepared for sudden cold snaps in winter and occasional bursts of oppressive humid heat in summer.

WINTER

Winter in Sydney can be cold enough to require warm jackets; temperatures at night may drop dramatically away from the coast. The days are often clear and sometimes surprisingly mild. Arts are a major feature of winter. There are lots of exhibitions and the Sydney Film Festival, which no film buff will want to miss.

JUNE

Manly Food and Wine Festival *(first weekend)*, Manly Beach *(see p133)*. Annual food and wine festival plus train rides, bouncy castles and more for children.
Darling Harbour Jazz and Blues Festival *(Queen's Birthday weekend)*, Darling Harbour *(see pp92–3)*. Constantly changing line up of jazz, blues, country, gospel and world music performers.
Sydney Film Festival *(two weeks mid-Jun)*, State Theatre *(see p82)*. The latest short and feature films, as well as retrospectives and showcases.
Winter Magic Festival *(weekend closest to the winter solstice)*, Katoomba. Celebrate the winter solstice with elves and fairies in an enchanting street parade.

JULY

Biennale of Sydney *(two months, mid-year)*, various venues. International festival, held in even-numbered years,

Australian soldiers or "Diggers" at an Anzac Day ceremony

The familiar logo of the Film Festival

encompassing many forms of visual art, from painting and installations to photography and performance art.
Yulefest *(throughout winter)*, Blue Mountains *(see pp160–61)*. Hotels, guesthouses and some restaurants celebrate a midwinter "Christmas" with log fires and all the Yuletide trimmings.
NAIDOC (National Aboriginal and Torres Strait Islander) Week *(dates vary)*. Week-long celebrations to build awareness and understanding of Aboriginal culture and history.
The Rocks Aroma Festival *(late Jul)*, The Rocks *(see pp64–5)*. A festival celebrating ground coffee, spices and teas.

AUGUST

Sydney International Boat Show *(early Aug)*, Convention and Exhibition Centre and Cockle Bay Marina, Darling Harbour *(see p98)*.

PUBLIC HOLIDAYS

New Year's Day (1 Jan)
Australia Day (26 Jan)
Good Friday (variable)
Easter Monday (variable)
Anzac Day (25 Apr)
Queen's Birthday (second Mon in Jun)
Bank Holiday (first Mon in Aug: only banks and some financial institutions are closed)
Labour Day (first Mon in Oct)
Christmas Day (25 Dec)
Boxing Day (26 Dec)

City to Surf Race *(second Sun)*. From the city to Bondi Beach *(see p137)*. A 14-km (9-mile) community event that attracts all types, from amateurs to leading marathon runners.
Japan Festival *(dates vary)*, various venues. Ikebana, tea ceremonies, sports and music, with visiting acts of all kinds.

Runners in the City to Surf Race, surging down William Street

SPORTING SYDNEY

Throughout Australia sport is a way of life and Sydney is no exception. On any day you'll see locals on golf courses at dawn, running around the streets keeping fit, or having a quick set of tennis after work. At weekends, during summer and winter, there is no end to the variety of sports you can watch. Thousands gather at Sydney Football Stadium and Sydney Cricket Ground every weekend while, for those who cannot make it, sport reigns supreme on weekend television.

CRICKET

During the summer months Test cricket and one-day internationals are played at the Sydney Cricket Ground (SCG). Tickets for weekday sessions of the Tests can often be bought at the gate, although it is advisable to book well in advance (through **Ticketek**) for weekend sessions of Test matches and for all the one-day international matches.

RUGBY LEAGUE AND RUGBY UNION

The popularity of rugby league knows no bounds here. This is what people are referring to when they talk about "the footie". There are three major competition levels: national, State of Origin – which matches Queensland against New South Wales – and Tests. The National Rugby League (NRL) competition fields teams from all over Sydney as well as Newcastle, Canberra, Melbourne, Brisbane, the Gold Coast, Far North Queensland and Auckland, New Zealand.

Many of these matches are held in different areas of Sydney, although the Telstra

Australia versus the All Blacks, SFS

Stadium at Sydney Olympic Park is by far the biggest venue. Tickets for State of Origin and Test matches often sell out instantly.

Rugby union is the second most popular football code. Again, matches at Test level sell out very quickly. For some premium trans-Tasman rivalry, catch a Test match between Australia's "Wallabies" and the New Zealand "All Blacks".

GOLF AND TENNIS

Golf enthusiasts need not do without their round of golf. There are many courses throughout Sydney where visitors are welcome at all times. These include **Moore Park**,

St Michael's and Warringah golf courses. It is sensible to phone beforehand for a booking, especially at weekends.

Tennis is another favoured sport. Courts available for hire can be found all over Sydney. Many centres also have flood-lit courts available for night time. Try **Cooper Park** or **Parkland Sports** Centre.

Playing golf at Moore Park, one of Sydney's public courses

AUSTRALIAN RULES FOOTBALL

Although not as popular as in Melbourne, "Aussie Rules" has a strong following in Sydney. The original local team, the Sydney Swans, plays its home games at the Sydney Cricket Ground. A second Sydney-based team, the Greater Western Sydney Giants, plays at Homebush. Check a local paper for details.

Rivalry between the Sydney supporters and their Melbourne counterparts is always strong. Tickets can usually be bought at the ground on match day.

BASKETBALL

Basketball is a popular spectator and recreational sport in the city. Sydney has male and female teams competing in the National Basketball League. The men's games, held at the Sydney Entertainment Centre,

One-day cricket match between Australia and the West Indies, SCG

Aerial view of the Sydney Football Stadium at Moore Park

Haymarket, have much of the pizzazz, colour and excitement of American basketball. Tickets can be purchased from Ticketek, on the phone or on the Internet.

CYCLING AND INLINE SKATING

Sydney boasts excellent, safe locations for the whole family to go cycling. One of the most frequented is Centennial Park (see p127). You can hire bicycles and safety helmets from **Centennial Park Cycles**.

Another increasingly popular pastime in summer is in-line skating, and skaters can often be seen on the paths of the city's parks as well as on the streets.

Rollerblading.com.au runs tours starting at Milsons Point to all parts of Sydney. If you're unsteady, they also do group and private lessons.

For those who like to keep both feet firmly on the ground, you can watch skateboarders and inline skaters practising their moves at the ramps at Bondi Beach (see p137).

Inline skaters enjoying a summer evening on the city's streets

HORSE RIDING

For a leisurely ride, head to Centennial Park or contact the **Centennial Parklands Equestrian Centre**. They will give details of the four riding schools that operate in the park. **Samarai Park Riding School** conducts trail rides through Ku-ring-gai Chase National Park (see pp154–5).

Further afield, you can enjoy the scenery of the Blue Mountains (see pp160–61) on horseback. The **Megalong Australian Heritage Centre** has rides lasting from one hour to overnight. All levels of experience are catered for.

Horse riding in one of the parks surrounding the city centre

ADVENTURE SPORTS

You can participate in guided bushwalking, mountain biking, canyoning, rock climbing and abseiling expeditions in the nearby Blue Mountains National Park. The **Blue Mountains Adventure Company** runs one-day or multi-day courses and trips for all standards of adventurer.

In the city, **BridgeClimb** offers 2½- and 3½-hour guided climbs to the summit of Sydney Harbour Bridge.

DIRECTORY

Blue Mountains Adventure Company
84a Bathurst Rd, Katoomba.
Tel 4782 1271.
www.bmac.com.au

BridgeClimb
3 Cumberland St,
The Rocks, Sydney.
Tel 8274 7777.
www.bridgeclimb.com.

Centennial Park Cycles
50 Clovelly Rd, Randwick.
Tel 9398 5027.
www.cyclehire.com.au

Centennial Parklands Equestrian Centre
Cnr Lang & Cook Rds,
Moore Park. **Map** 5 D5.
Tel 9332 2809.
www.cpequestrian.com.au

Cooper Park Tennis Courts
Off Suttie Rd, Double Bay.
Tel 9389 3100.
www.cptennis.com.au

Megalong Australian Heritage Centre
Megalong Valley Rd, Megalong Valley. *Tel 4787 8188.*
www.megalongcc.com.au

Moore Park Golf Club
Cnr Cleveland St & Anzac Parade,
Moore Park. **Map** 5 B5.
Tel 9663 1064.
www.mooreparkgolf.com.au

Parkland Sports
Cnr Anzac Parade & Lang Rd,
Moore Park.
Tel 9662 7033.

Rollerblading.com.au
Tel 0411 872 022.

St Michael's Golf Club
Jennifer St, Little Bay.
Tel 9311 0688.
www.stmichaelsgolf.com.au

Samarai Park Riding School
90 Booralie Rd, Terrey Hills.
Tel 9450 1745.
www.samaraipark.com

Ticketek
Tel 132849.
www.ticketek.com.au

Warringah Golf Club
397 Condamine St, North Manly.
Tel 9905 4028.

Sydney's Beaches

Being a city built around the water, it is no wonder that many of Sydney's recreational activities involve the sand, sea and sun. There are many harbour and surf beaches throughout Sydney, most of them accessible by bus *(see p231)*. Even if you're not a swimmer, the beaches offer a chance to get away from it all for a day or weekend and enjoy the fresh air and relaxed way of life.

Scuba diving at Gordons Bay

SWIMMING

Harbour beaches such as Camp Cove, Shark Bay and Balmoral Beach are generally smaller and more sheltered than the ocean beaches. The latter have surf lifesavers in distinctive red and yellow caps. Surf lifesaving carnivals are held throughout summer. Call **Surf Life Saving NSW** for a calendar of events. District councils also provide their own lifeguards, who wear blue uniforms. Rules about swimming are rigorously enforced, so try to familiarize yourself with beach signage.

The beaches can sometimes become polluted. The **Beach Watch and Harbour Watch Info Line** gives information about pollution levels.

SURFING

Surfing is more a way of life than a leisure activity for some Sydneysiders. If you're a beginner, try Bondi, Bronte, Palm Beach or Collaroy.

Two of the best surf beaches are Maroubra and Narrabeen. Bear in mind that local surfers know one another well and do not take kindly to "intruders" who drop in on their waves

or leave litter on their beaches. To hire a surfboard, try Bondi Surf Co on Campbell Parade, Bondi Beach, or Aloha Surf on Pittwater Road, Manly. If you would like to learn, there are two surf schools: **Manly Surf School** and **Lets Go Surfing** at Bondi Beach. They also hire out boards and wetsuits.

WINDSURFING AND SAILING

There are locations around Sydney suitable for every level of windsurfer. Boards can be hired from **Balmoral Sailing School** at Balmoral Beach. Good spots include Palm Beach, Narrabeen Lakes, La Perouse, Brighton-Le-Sands and Kurnell Point (for beginner and intermediate boarders) and Long Reef Beach, Palm Beach and Collaroy (for the more experienced windsurfer).

One of the best ways to see the harbour is while sailing. A sailing boat, including a skipper, can be hired for the afternoon from the **East Sail** sailing club. If you'd like to learn how to sail, the sailing club has two-day courses and also hires out sailing boats and motor cruisers to experienced sailors.

SCUBA DIVING

There are some excellent dive spots around Sydney, especially in winter when the water is clear, if a little cold. More favoured spots are Gordons Bay, Shelly Beach, and Camp Cove.

Pro Dive Coogee offers a complete range of courses, escorted dives, introductory dives for beginners, and hire equipment. **Dive Centre Manly** also runs courses and introductory dives, hires equipment and conducts boat dives seven days a week.

DIRECTORY

Balmoral Sailing School
Balmoral Sailing Club, Balmoral Beach. *Tel* 9960 5344.
www.sailboard.net.au

Beach Watch and Harbour Watch Info Line
Tel 1800 036 677.

Dive Centre Manly
10 Belgrave St, Manly. *Tel* 9977 4355. www.divesydney.com.au

East Sail
d'Albora Marinas, New Beach Rd, Rushcutters Bay. *Tel* 9326 2355.
www.eastsail.com.au

Lets Go Surfing
128 Ramsgate Ave North Bondi.
Tel 9365 1800.
www.letsgosurfing.com.au

Manly Surf School
North Steyne Rd, Manly.
Tel 9977 6977.
www.manlysurfschool.com

Pro Dive Coogee
27 Alfreda St, Coogee.
Tel 1800 820 820.

Surf Life Saving NSW
Tel 9984 7188.
www.surflifesaving.com.au

Rock baths and surf lifesaving club at Coogee Beach

TOP 30 BEACHES

The beaches shown here have been selected for their safe swimming, water sports, facilities available or their picturesque setting.

	SWIMMING POOL	SURFING	WINDSURFING	FISHING	SCUBA DIVING	PICNIC/BARBECUE	RESTAURANT/CAFE
Avalon	●	■	●	■		■	
Balmoral	●		●	■	■	■	●
The Basin	●					■	
Bilgola							
Bondi Beach	●	■		■	●	■	●
Bronte	●	■		■	●	■	●
Camp Cove					●		
Clifton Gardens	●		●	■	●	■	
Clovelly	●			■	●	■	●
Coogee	●		●	■	●	■	●
Curl Curl	●	■		■			
Dee Why	●	■		■	●	■	●
Fairy Bower					●		
Fishermans Beach		■	●	■	●		
Freshwater	●	■		■	●	■	
Gordons Bay				■	●		
Long Reef		■	●	■	●		
Manly Beach	●	■			●	■	●
Maroubra		■	●	■	●	■	●
Narrabeen	●	■		■		■	
Newport Beach	●	■	●	■		■	
Obelisk Bay (naturist)							
Palm Beach	●	■	●	■		■	●
Parsley Bay	●					■	
Seven Shillings Beach	●					■	
Shark Bay	●					■	●
Shelly Beach					●	■	●
Tamarama		■			●	■	●
Watsons Bay	●		●	■			●
Whale Beach	●	■	●	■		■	●

THE TYPES OF WAVES

Cresting waves *can be identified by the foam that is created as they break from the top. These waves are ideal for board riding and body surfing.*

Plunging waves *curl into a tube before breaking close to the shore. Fondly known as "dumpers", these waves should only be tackled by experienced surfers.*

Surging waves *are those that don't appear to break. They often travel all the way into the beach before breaking and can easily sweep a toddler or child off its feet.*

Garden Island to Farm Cove

Waterlily in the Royal
Botanic Garden

Sydney's vast harbour, also named
Port Jackson after a Secretary in the
British Admiralty who promptly
changed his name, is a drowned
river valley which was transformed
over millions of years. Its intricate
coastal geography of headlands and
secluded bays can sometimes confound even life-
long residents. This waterway was the lifeblood of
the early colony, with the maritime industry a vital
source of wealth and supply. The legacies of alter-
nate recessions and booms can be viewed along the
shoreline: a representative story in a nation where an
estimated 70 per cent of the population cling to the
coastal cities, especially along the eastern seaboard.

The city skyline *is a result of random
development. The 1960s indiscrimin-
ate destruction of architectural history
was halted, and towers now stand
amid Victorian buildings.*

Two harbour beacons,
*known as "wedding cakes"
because of their three
tiers, are solar powered
and equipped with a
fail-safe back-up. There
are around 350 buoys
and beacons now
in operation.*

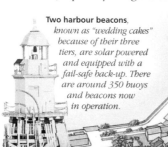

The barracks for
the naval garrison
date from 1888.

Garden Island
marks a 1940s con-
struction project
with 12 ha (30
acres) reclaimed
from the harbour.

Sailing on the harbour *is a pastime not
exclusively reserved for the rich and elite. Of
the several hundred thousand pleasure boats
registered, some are available for hire while
others take out groups of inexperienced sailors.*

Mrs Macquaries Chair *is a carved rock seat by
Mrs Macquaries Road (see p106). In the early
days of the colony, this was the site of a fruit and
vegetable garden which was farmed until 1805.*

| 0 metres | 250 |
| 0 yards | 250 |

The Andrew (Boy) Charlton Pool *is a favourite bathing spot for inner-city residents, and is named after the Sydneysider who, at the age of 16, won an Olympic gold medal in 1924. It was erected in 1963 on the Domain Baths' site, which had a grandstand for 1,700.*

Woolloomooloo Finger Wharf has been developed as a dynamic entertainment and residential complex.

LOCATOR MAP
See Street Finder, *map 2*

Harry's Café de Wheels, *a snack van, is a Sydney culinary institution, and has been operating continuously since 1945. Photographs of celebrity customers are pinned to the van.*

The Royal Botanic Garden *displays a profusion of both flowering and non-flowering plants. The first trees were planted by the newly arrived European colonists. Some of these plants survive today.*

Farm Cove *has long been a mooring place for visiting naval vessels. The land opposite, now the Botanic Garden, has been continuously cultivated for over 200 years.*

Sydney Cove to Walsh Bay

Conservatorium of Music

It is estimated that over 70 km (43 miles) of harbour foreshore have been lost as a result of the massive land reclamation projects carried out since the 1840s. That the 13 islands existing when the First Fleet arrived in 1788 have now been reduced to just eight is a startling indication of rapid and profound geographical transformation.

Detail from railing at Circular Quay

Redevelopments around the Circular Quay and Walsh Bay area from the 1980s have opened up the waterfront for public use and enjoyment, acknowledging it as the city's greatest natural asset. Sydney's environmental and architectural aspirations recognize the need to integrate city and harbour.

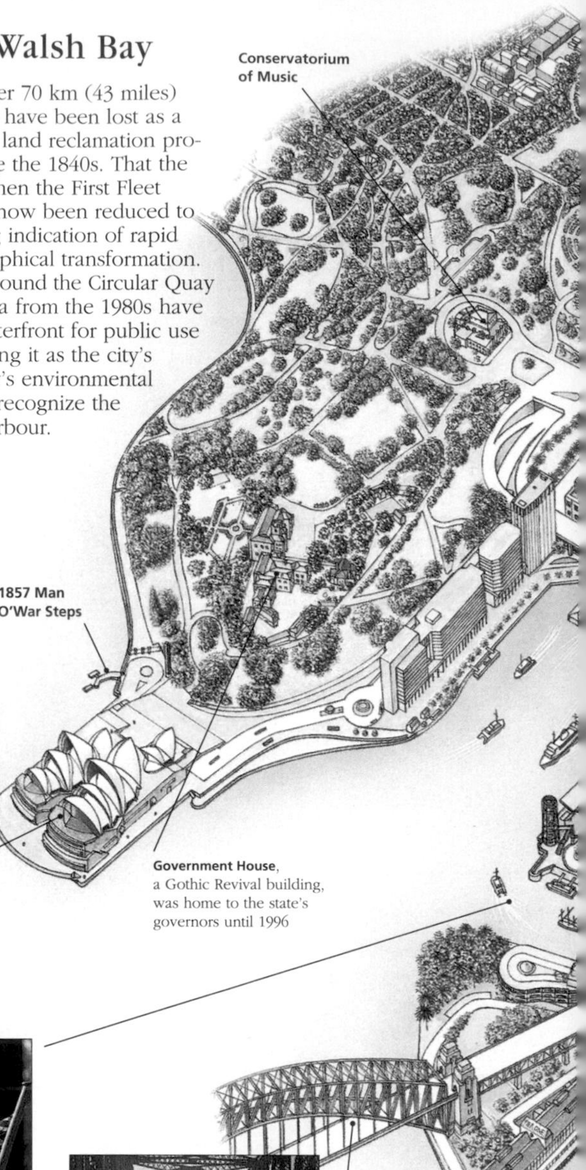

1857 Man O'War Steps

The Sydney Opera House *was designed to take advantage of its spectacular setting. The roofs shine during the day and seem to glow at night. The building can appear as a visionary land-scape to the pedestrian onlooker.*

Government House, a Gothic Revival building, was home to the state's governors until 1996

Harbour cruises *regularly depart from Circular Quay, taking visitors out and about both during the day and in the evening. They are an incomparable way to see the city and its waterways.*

The Sydney Harbour Bridge *was also known as the "Iron Lung" at the time of its construction. During the Great Depression it provided on-site work for approximately 1,400, while many more were employed in the specialist workshops.*

| 0 metres | 250 |
| 0 yards | 250 |

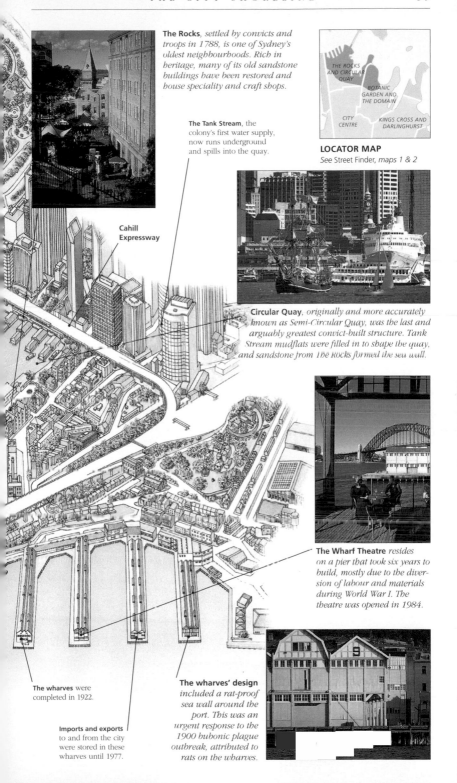

The Rocks, *settled by convicts and troops in 1788, is one of Sydney's oldest neighbourhoods. Rich in heritage, many of its old sandstone buildings have been restored and house speciality and craft shops.*

The Tank Stream, the colony's first water supply, now runs underground and spills into the quay.

LOCATOR MAP
See Street Finder, *maps 1 & 2*

THE ROCKS AND CIRCULAR QUAY

BOTANIC GARDEN AND THE DOMAIN

CITY CENTRE

KINGS CROSS AND DARLINGHURST

Cahill Expressway

Circular Quay, *originally and more accurately known as Semi-Circular Quay, was the last and arguably greatest convict-built structure. Tank Stream mudflats were filled in to shape the quay, and sandstone from The Rocks formed the sea wall.*

The Wharf Theatre *resides on a pier that took six years to build, mostly due to the diversion of labour and materials during World War I. The theatre was opened in 1984.*

The wharves were completed in 1922.

Imports and exports to and from the city were stored in these wharves until 1977.

The wharves' design *included a rat-proof sea wall around the port. This was an urgent response to the 1900 bubonic plague outbreak, attributed to rats on the wharves.*

SYDNEY AREA BY AREA

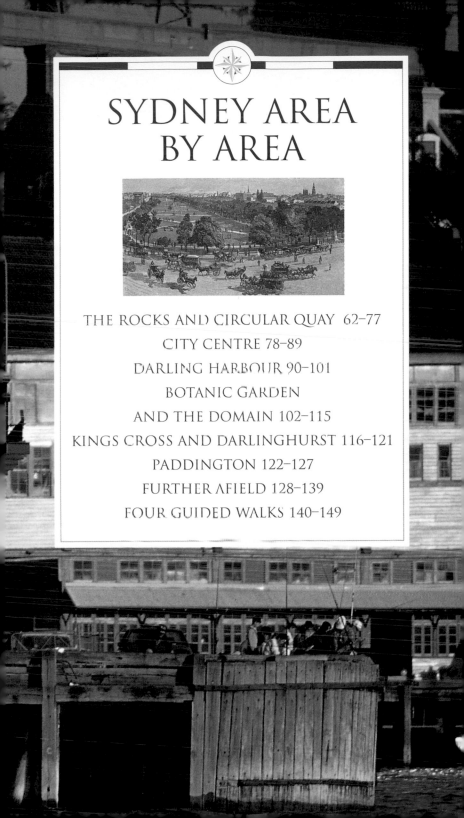

THE ROCKS AND CIRCULAR QUAY

Circular Quay, once known as Semi-Circular Quay, is often referred to as the "birthplace of Australia". It was here, in January 1788, that the First Fleet landed its human freight of convicts, soldiers and officials, and the new British colony of New South Wales was declared. Sydney Cove became a rallying point whenever a ship arrived bringing much-needed supplies from "home". Crowds still gather here whenever there is something to celebrate. The Quay and The Rocks are focal points for New Year's Eve revels, and Circular Quay drew huge crowds when, in 1993, Sydney was awarded the year 2000 Olympic Games. The Rocks area offers visitors a taste of Sydney's past, but it is a far cry from the time, less than 100 years ago, when most inhabitants lived in rat-infested slums and gangs ruled its streets. Now scrubbed and polished, The Rocks forms part of the colourful promenade from the Sydney Harbour Bridge to the spectacular Opera House.

Sculpture on the AMP Building, Circular Quay

SIGHTS AT A GLANCE

Historic Streets and Buildings
Campbell's Storehouses ❶
George Street ❷
Cadman's Cottage ❻
Argyle Stores ❽
Sydney Observatory ❿
Hero of Waterloo ⓫
Sydney Harbour Bridge pp70–71 ⓭
Writers' Walk ⓯

Customs House ⓱
Macquarie Place ⓲

Churches
Garrison Church ❾
St Philip's Church ㉑

Theatres and Concert Halls
Wharf Theatre ⓬
Sydney Opera House pp74–7 ⓮

Museums and Galleries
The Rocks Discovery Museum ❸
Susannah Place Museum ❹
Sailors' Home ❺
Westpac Museum ❼
Justice and Police Museum ⓰
Museum of Contemporary Art ⓳
National Trust Centre ⓴

GETTING THERE
Circular Quay is the best stop for ferries and trains. Sydney Explorer and bus routes 431, 432, 433 and 434 run regularly to The Rocks, while most buses through the city go to the Quay.

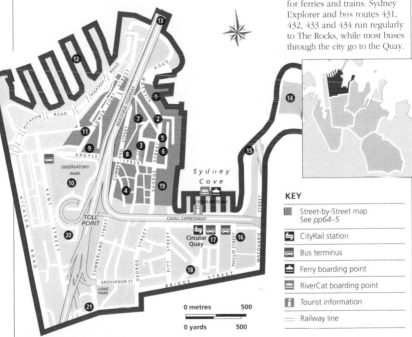

KEY

- Street-by-Street map See *pp64–5*
- CityRail station
- Bus terminus
- Ferry boarding point
- RiverCat boarding point
- Tourist information
- Railway line

0 metres 500
0 yards 500

◁ **The historic Sailors' Home, parts of which date back to 1864**

Street-by-Street: The Rocks

Governor Arthur Phillip

Named for the rugged cliffs that were once its dominant feature, this area has played a vital role in Sydney's development. In 1788, the First Fleeters under Governor Phillip's command erected makeshift buildings here, with the convicts' hard labour used to establish more permanent structures in the form of rough-hewn streets. The Argyle Cut, a road carved through solid rock using just hammer and chisel, took 18 years to build, beginning in 1843. By 1900, The Rocks was overrun with disease; the street now known as Suez Canal was once Sewer's Canal. Today, the area is still rich in colonial history and colour.

Hero of Waterloo
Lying beneath this historic pub is a tunnel originally used for smuggling ⑪

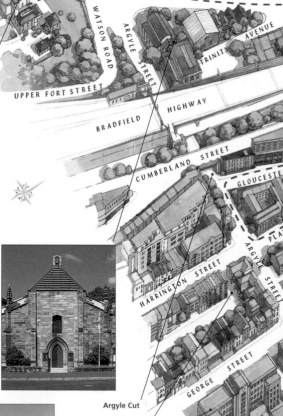

Hero of Waterloo ↑

LOWER

WATSON ROAD

ARGYLE STREET

TRINITY AVENUE

UPPER FORT STREET

HIGHWAY

BRADFIELD

CUMBERLAND STREET

GLOUCESTER

PLAYFAIR

ARGYLE STREET

HARRINGTON STREET

GEORGE STREET

★ Sydney Observatory
The first European structure on this prominent site was a windmill. The present museum holds some of the earliest astronomical instruments brought to Australia ⑩

Garrison Church
Columns in this church are decorated with the insignia of British troops stationed here until 1870. Australia's first prime minister was educated next door ⑨

Argyle Cut

Suez Canal

★ Museum of Contemporary Art
The Classical façade belies the contemporary nature of the Australian and international art displayed in an ever-changing programme ⑲

Walkway along
Circular Quay
West foreshore

The Rocks Discovery Museum

Key episodes in The Rocks' history are illustrated by this museum's collection of maritime images and other artifacts ❸

LOCATOR MAP
See Street Finder, map 1

The Rocks Market

is a hive of activity every weekend, offering an eclectic range of craft items and jewellery utilizing Australian icons from gum leaves to koalas.

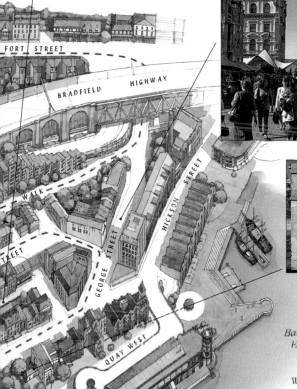

FORT STREET

BRADFIELD HIGHWAY

WALK

HICKSON STREET

GEORGE STREET

QUAY WEST

CIRCULAR

★ **Cadman's Cottage**
John Cadman, government coxswain, resided in what was known as the Coxswain's Barracks with his family. His wife Elizabeth was also a significant figure, believed to be the first woman to vote in New South Wales, a right she insisted on ❺

0 metres	100
0 yards	100

KEY

– – – Suggested route

The Overseas Passenger Terminal is where some of the world's luxury cruise liners berth during their stay in Sydney.

STAR SIGHTS

★ Cadman's Cottage

★ Museum of Contemporary Art

★ Sydney Observatory

Campbell's Storehouses ❶

7–27 Circular Quay West; The Rocks. **Map** 1 B2. ▦ *Sydney Explorer, 431, 432, 433, 434.* 📷 ♿

In 1798, the Scottish merchant Robert Campbell sailed into Sydney Cove and soon established himself as a founding father of commerce for the new colony. With trade links already established in Calcutta, his business blossomed. In 1839, Campbell began constructing a private wharf and stores to house the tea, sugar, spirits and cloth he imported from India. Twelve sandstone bays had been built by 1861 and a brick upper storey was added in about 1890. Part of the old sea wall and 11 of the original stores still remain. The area soon took on the name of Campbell's Cove, which it retains to this day.

Today the bond stores contain several harbourside restaurants catering for a range of tastes, from contemporary to Chinese and Italian. It is a delightful area in which to relax with a meal and watch the bustling boats in the harbour go by. The pulleys that were used to raise cargo from the wharf can still be seen on the outside, near the top of the building.

George Street ❷

Map 1 B2. ▦ *Sydney Explorer, 431, 432, 433, 434.*

Formerly the preserve of wealthy merchants, sailors and the city's working class, George Street today is a popular attraction with visitors to Sydney, who are drawn to its restaurants, art galleries, museums, jewellery stores and craft souvenir shops. For one-stop memento and gift shopping it is ideal, with little of the mass-produced and tacky, but a great deal in the way of modern Australian craft of a very high calibre, with many unique pieces.

One of Sydney's original thoroughfares – some say Australia's first street – it ran from the main water supply, the Tank Stream, to the tiny community in the Rocks, and was known as Spring Street. In 1810 it was renamed in honour of George III. George Street today runs all the way from the Harbour Bridge to the Central Railway Station north of Chinatown.

Many 19th-century buildings remain, such as the 1844 Counting House at No. 43, the Old Police station at No. 127 (1882), and the Russell Hotel at No. 143 (1887).

But it is The Rocks end that most reflects what the early colony must have looked like, characterized by cobbled pavements, narrow side streets, warehouses, bond stores, pubs and shop fronts that reflect the area's maritime history. Even the Museum of Contemporary Art *(see p73)*, constructed during the 1950s, began its life as the Maritime Services Board's administration offices.

In the early 1970s union workers placed "green bans" on the demolition of The Rocks *(see p31)*. These streets had been considered slum areas by the government of the day. However many of the buildings in George Street were restored and are now listed by the National Trust. The Rocks remains a vibrant part of the city, with George Street at its hub. A market is held here every weekend, when part of the street is closed off to traffic *(see p203)*.

The Rocks Discovery Museum ❸

2–6 Kendall Lane, The Rocks. **Map** 1 B2. **Tel** 9240 8680. 🚋 *Circular Quay.* ▦ *Sydney Explorer, 431, 432, 433, 434.* ◯ *10am–5:30pm daily.*

This museum is in a restored 1850s sandstone coach house, and has exhibitions on the

Umbrellas shade the terrace restaurants overlooking the waterfront at Campbell's Storehouses

Old-style Australian products at the corner shop, Susannah Place

history of the The Rocks, including displays on its first Aboriginal inhabitants, the Cadigal people, and Sydney's maritime history and traditions in the 18th and 19th centuries.

A unique collection of archaeological artifacts, such as an illegal alcohol still, and historical images dating from the early establishment of the European colony to the postwar era, helps visitors explore the eventful and colourful history of this neighbourhood. The displays are enhanced by interactive high-tech touch screens and audiovisual exhibits, bringing the history of the area alive.

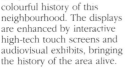

Billy Tea on sale at the Susannah Place shop

Susannah Place Museum ❹

58–64 Gloucester St, The Rocks. **Map** 1 B2. **Tel** 9241 1893. 🚋 Circular Quay, Wynyard. 🚌 Sydney Explorer, 431, 432, 433, 434. ◯ 10am–5pm Sat & Sun, daily in Jan & NSW school hols. ◯ Good Fri, 25 Dec. 🅿️ 🔊 🎫

This 1844 terrace of four brick and sandstone houses has a rare history of continuous domestic occupancy from the 1840s right through to 1990.

The museum now housed here examines this working class domestic history, evoking the living conditions of its inhabitants. Rather than re-creating a single period, the museum retains the many renovations made by successive tenants.

Built for Edward and Mary Riley, who arrived from Ireland with their niece Susannah in 1838, these solid houses have basement kitchens and backyard outhouses. Connections to piped water and sewerage had probably arrived by the mid-1850s. The museum surveys the houses' development over the years, from wood and coal to gas and electricity, which enables the visitor to gauge the gradual lightening of the burden of domestic labour.

The terrace, including a corner grocer's shop, escaped the wholesale demolitions that occurred after the outbreak of bubonic plague in 1900, as well as later clearings of land to make way for the Sydney Harbour Bridge and the Cahill Expressway. In the 1970s, it was saved once again when the Builders Labourers' Federation, under the leadership of activist Jack

Mundey, imposed a conservation "green ban" on The Rocks (see p31), temporarily halting all demolition and redevelopment work.

Sailors' Home ❺

106 George St, The Rocks. **Map** 1 B2. **Tel** 9255 1788. 🚌 Sydney Explorer, 339, 340, 431, 432, 433, 434. ◯ to the public.

Built in 1864 to provide cheap lodgings for visiting seamen, the Sailors' Home is now used as an art gallery. The building's original north wing is Romanesque Revival in design. The L-shaped wing that fronts onto George Street was added in 1926.

At the time it was built, the Sailors' Home was a welcome alternative to the many seedy inns and brothels in the area, saving sailors from the perils of "crimping". "Crimps" would tempt newly arrived men into lodgings and bars providing much-sought-after entertainment. While drunk, the sailors would be sold on to departing ships, waking miles out at sea and returning home in debt.

Sailors used the home until 1980, when it was adapted for use as a puppet theatre. The house is now home to the Billich Gallery, a privately owned art gallery that is open to the public. In the basement is the Sailor's Thai restaurant (see p189), one of Sydney's top dining spots.

Interior of the Sailors' Home, viewed from an upper level

Façade of Cadman's Cottage, the oldest extant building in the city

Cadman's Cottage **6**

110 George St, The Rocks. **Map** 1 B2. **Tel** 9247 5033. 🚌 431, 432, 433 434. ◻ 9:30am–4:30pm Mon–Fri, 10am–4:30pm Sat & Sun. 🌑 Good Fri, 25 Dec. 📷

Dwarfed by the adjacent Sailors' Home, of which it was once part, the upper level of this sandstone cottage serves as the information centre for the Sydney Harbour National Park and has information about guided harbour tours. Built in 1816 to house the crews of the governor's boats, it is Sydney's oldest surviving dwelling.

The cottage is named after John Cadman, a convict who was transported in 1798 for stealing horses. By 1813, he was coxswain of a timber boat and the following year received an unconditional pardon. In 1821, he was granted a full pardon. Six years later, he was made boat superintendent of govern-ment craft and took up resi-dence in the four-room cottage that now bears his name.

Cadman married Elizabeth Mortimer in 1830. She had also arrived in Sydney as a convict, sentenced to seven years trans-portation for the theft of one hairbrush. The couple, along with Elizabeth's two daughters, lived in the cottage until 1846.

When Cadman's Cottage was built it stood on the foreshore of Sydney Harbour. At high tide, the water used to lap just 2.5 m (8 ft) from the door.

Now, as a result of successive land reclamations such as the filling in of Circular Quay in the 1870s, it is set well back from the waterfront.

Westpac Museum **7**

6–8 Playfair St, The Rocks. **Map** 1 B2. **Tel** 9763 5670. 🚌 Sydney Explorer, 431, 432, 433, 434. ◻ 9am–noon, 1–4pm Mon–Fri. 🌑 public hols.

From 1817, when the "holey" dollar was in circulation and Sydney's first bank opened, to present-day plastic credit cards, this museum, located on the first floor, traces the history of banking in Australia. It also covers the Olympic history in 1956 and 2000 as Westpac was a sponsor of both of these games. There is a self-guided tour with interactive and holographic displays but this small museum can be seen in less than an hour.

Argyle Stores **8**

18–24 Argyle St, The Rocks. **Map** 1 B2. 🚌 Sydney Explorer, 431, 432, 433, 434. ◻ 10am–6pm daily. 🌑 Good Fri, 25 Dec. 📷 ♿

The Argyle Stores consists of a number of warehouses around a cobbled courtyard. They have been converted into a retail complex of mostly accessories and fashion shops that retains its period character.

Built between 1826 and the early 1880s, the stores held imported goods such as spirits. All goods forfeited for the non-payment of duties were auctioned in the courtyard. The oldest store was built for Captain John Piper, but it was confiscated and sold after his arrest for embezzlement.

Argyle Centre from the courtyard

Garrison Church **9**

Cnr Argyle and Lower Fort Sts, Millers Point. **Map** 1 A2. **Tel** 9247 1268. 🚌 431, 433. ◻ 9am–6pm daily. 📷 ♿

Officially named the Holy Trinity Church, this was dubbed the Garrison Church because it was the colony's first military church. Officers and men from various British

Bank of New South Wales one pound note from around 1830

regiments, stationed at Dawes Point fort, attended morning prayers here until 1870.

Henry Ginn designed the church and, in 1840, the foundation stone was laid. In 1855, the architect Edmund Blacket was engaged to enlarge the church to accommodate up to 600 people. These extensions, minus the spire that Blacket proposed, were completed in 1878. Regimental plaques hung along interior walls recall the church's military associations.

Other features to look out for are the brilliantly coloured east window and the carved red cedar pulpit. The window was donated by a devout parishioner, Dr James Mitchell, scion of a leading Sydney family. The church also houses a museum displaying early Australian military and historical items.

East window, Garrison Church

Sydney Observatory ⑩

Watson Rd, Observatory Hill, The Rocks. **Map** 1 A2. **Tel** 9921 3485. ▦ *Sydney Explorer, 343, 431, 432* ⏰ *10am–5pm daily.* **Night viewings** *phone to book.* ⬤ *25 Dec.* ▦ ◉ ⬤ ▦ **www.**sydneyobservatory.com.au

In 1982, this domed building, which had been a centre for astronomical observation and research for almost 125 years, became the city's astronomy museum. It has interactive equipment and games, along with night sky viewings; it is essential to book for these.

The building began life in the 1850s as a time-ball tower. At 1pm daily, the ball on top of the tower dropped to signal the correct time. A cannon was fired simultaneously at Fort Denison. This custom continues today *(see p107).*

In the 1880s, some of the first astronomical photographs of the southern sky were taken here. From 1890–1962, the observatory mapped 750,000 stars as part of an international project that produced an atlas of the entire night sky.

Hero of Waterloo ⑪

81 Lower Fort St, The Rocks. **Map** 1 A2. **Tel** 9252 4553. ▦ *431, 432, 433, 434.* ⏰ *10am–11pm Mon & Tue, 10am–11:30pm Wed–Sat, 10am–10pm Sun.* ⬤ *Good Fri, 25 Dec.* ◉ ⬤ *ground floor only.*

This picturesque old inn is welcoming in the winter, when its log fires and cosy ambience offer respite from the chill outside. Built in 1844 from sandstone excavated from the Argyle Cut, this was a favourite drinking place for the nearby garrison's soldiers. Unscrupulous sea captains were said to use the hotel to recruit. Patrons who drank themselves into a stupor were pushed into the cellars through a trapdoor. From here they were carried along underground tunnels to the wharves nearby and onto waiting ships.

Wharf Theatre ⑫

Pier 4, Hickson Rd, Walsh Bay. **Map** 1 A1. **Tel** 9250 1700. ▦ *430, 431, 432, 433, 434.* **Box office Tel** 9250 1777. ⏰ *9am–7pm Mon, 9am–8:30pm Tue–Fri, 11am–8:30pm Sat.* ◉ ⬤ *phone in advance.* **www.**sydneytheatre.com.au *See* **Entertainment** *p210.*

The then recently formed Sydney Theatre Company took possession of this early

The corner façade of the Hero of Waterloo hotel in Millers Point

20th-century finger wharf at Walsh Bay in 1984. Pier 4/5 is one of four finger wharves at Walsh Bay, reminders of the time when this was a busy part of the city's maritime industry.

The site fulfilled the Sydney Theatre Company's need for a base large enough to hold theatres, rehearsal rooms and administration offices. The ingenious conversion of the once-derelict heritage building into a modern theatre complex is recognized as an outstanding architectural achievement.

Since then, the main theatre has been a venue for many of the company's productions. It has seen premieres of plays from leading Australian playwrights such as Michael Gow and David Williamson, as well as performances of new works from overseas.

At the tip of the wharf, the bar area and Wharf Restaurant *(see p185)* command superb harbour views across to the Harbour Bridge *(see pp70–71).*

The Wharf Theatre, a former finger wharf, jutting on to Walsh Bay

Sydney Harbour Bridge

Completed in 1932, the construction of the
Sydney Harbour Bridge was an economic feat,
given the depressed times, as well as an engineering triumph. Prior to this, the only links
between the city centre on the south side of the
harbour and the residential north side were by ferry
or a circuitous 20-km (12½-mile) road route with
five bridge crossings. Known as the "Coathanger",

**Ceremonial
scissors**

the single-span arch bridge was manufactured in
sections and took eight years to build, including
the railway line. Loans for the total cost of
approximately 6.25 million Australian pounds were paid
off in 1988. Intrepid visitors can make the vertiginous
climb to its summit, with spectacular views as reward.

The 1932 Opening
*The ceremony was disrupted
when zealous royalist Francis
de Groot rode forward and
cut the ribbon in honour, he
claimed, of King and Empire.*

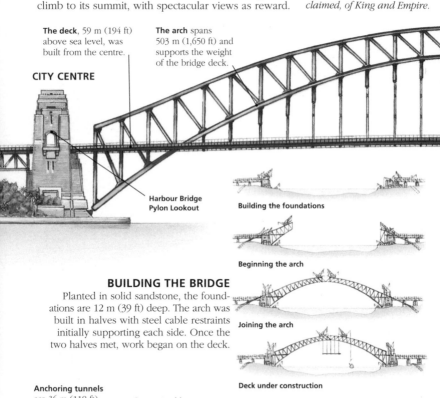

The deck, 59 m (194 ft)
above sea level, was
built from the centre.

The arch spans
503 m (1,650 ft) and
supports the weight
of the bridge deck.

CITY CENTRE

Harbour Bridge
Pylon Lookout

Building the foundations

Beginning the arch

BUILDING THE BRIDGE
Planted in solid sandstone, the foundations are 12 m (39 ft) deep. The arch was
built in halves with steel cable restraints
initially supporting each side. Once the
two halves met, work began on the deck.

Joining the arch

Deck under construction

Anchoring tunnels
are 36 m (118 ft)
long and dug into
rock at each end.

Support cables were
slackened over a
12-day period, enabling
both halves to join.

Temporary
attachment plate

The Bridge Design
*The steel arch of the bridge
supports the deck, with hinges
at either end bearing the bridge's
full weight and spreading the load
to the foundations. The hinges allow the
structure to move as the steel expands
and contracts in response to wind
and extreme temperatures.*

BridgeClimb
Thousands of people have enjoyed the spectacular bridge-top views after a 2.5- or 3.5-hour guided tour up ladders, catwalks and finally the upper arch of the bridge (see p53).

(see p53).

VISITORS' CHECKLIST

Map 1 B1. 🚌 all routes to The Rocks. 🚉 Circular Quay. 🚢 Circular Quay, Milsons Point. **Bridge Climb** *Tel* 8274 7777. 📷 **Pylon Lookout & Mus** *Tel* 9240 1100. ◯ 10am–5pm daily. ● 25 Dec. 🖥 www.bridgeclimb.com www.pylonlookout.com.au

Over 150,000 vehicles cross the bridge each day, about 15 times as many as in 1932.

Bridge Workers
The bridge was built by 1,400 workers, 16 of whom were killed in accidents during construction.

NORTH SHORE

Maintenance
Painting the bridge has become a metaphor for an endless task. Approximately 30,000 litres (6,593 gal) of paint are required for each coat, enough to cover an area equivalent to 60 soccer pitches.

The vertical hangers support the slanting crossbeams which, in turn, carry the deck.

FATHER OF THE BRIDGE
Chief engineer Dr John Bradfield shakes the hand of the driver of the first train to cross the bridge. Over a 20-year period, Bradfield supervised all aspects of the bridge's design and construction. At the opening ceremony, the highway linking the harbour's south side and northern suburbs was named in his honour.

Paying the Toll
The initial toll of sixpence helped pay off the construction loan. The toll is now used for maintenance and to pay for the 1992 Sydney Harbour Tunnel.

Strolling along a section of the Writers' Walk at Circular Quay

Sydney Opera House ⑭

See pp74–7.

Writers' Walk ⑮

Circular Quay. **Map** 1 C2.
Circular Quay routes.

This series of plaques is set in the pavement at regular intervals between East and West Circular Quay. It gives the visitor the chance to ponder the observations of famous Australian writers, both past and present, on their home country, as well as the musings of some noted literary visitors.

Each plaque is dedicated to a particular writer, with a quotation and a brief biographical note. Australian writers include novelists Miles Franklin and Peter Carey, poets Oodgeroo Noonuccal and Judith Wright, humorists Barry Humphries and Clive James, and the influential feminist writer Germaine Greer. Among visiting writers are Charles Darwin, Joseph Conrad and Mark Twain.

Justice and Police Museum ⑯

Cnr Albert & Phillip sts. **Map** 1 C3.
***Tel** 9252 1144.* Circular Quay routes. 10am–5pm Sat & Sun (daily Jan & NSW school hols). Good Fri, 25 Dec. restricted.

The museum's buildings were originally the Water Police Court, designed by Edmund Blacket in 1856; Water Police

Station, designed by Alexander Dawson in 1858; and Police Court designed by James Barnet in 1885. Here the rough-and-tumble underworld of quayside crime, from the petty to the violent, was dealt swift and, at times, harsh justice. The museum exhibits bear vivid testimony to that turbulent period, as they document and re-create legal and criminal history. Late Victorian legal proceedings can be easily imagined in the fully restored courtroom.

Menacing implements from knuckledusters to bludgeons are displayed as the macabre relics of violent and notorious crimes. Other aspects of policing and justice are highlighted in regularly changing exhibitions. The bushranger exhibit, prison artifacts, and forensic display powerfully evoke the realities of the justice system in Australia.

Detail from Customs House

Montage of criminal "mug shots", Justice and Police Museum

Customs House ⑰

31 Alfred St, Circular Quay. **Map** 1 B3.
***Tel** 9242 8595.* Circular Quay routes. 8am–7pm Mon–Fri, 10am–4pm Sat, noon–4pm Sun. Good Fri, 25 Dec.

Colonial architect James Barnet designed this 1885 sandstone Classical Revival building on the site of an earlier Customs House. It recalls the days when trading ships loaded and unloaded their goods at the quay. Features include columns in polished granite, a sculpted coat of arms and a clock face, added in 1897, bearing a pair of tridents and dolphins.

Customs House reopened in 2005 after major refurbishment. Facilities include a City Library with a reading room and exhibition space, and an open lounge area with an international newspaper and magazine salon, Internet access and bar. On the roof, Café Sydney offers great views.

Macquarie Place ⑱

Map 1 B3. Circular Quay routes.

In 1810, governor Lachlan Macquarie created this park on what was once part of the vegetable garden of the first Government House. The sandstone obelisk, designed by convict architect Francis Greenway *(see p114)*, was erected in 1818 to mark the starting point for all roads in the colony. The gas lamps recall the fact that this was also the site of Sydney's first street lamp, installed in 1826.

Also in this little triangle of history are the remains of the bow anchor and cannon from HMS *Sirius*, flagship of the First Fleet. There is also a statue of Thomas Mort, a 19th-century industrialist whose vast business interests embraced gold, coal and copper mining, dairy and cotton farming, wool auctioning and ship repair. These days his statue is a marshalling place for the city's somewhat kamikaze bicycle couriers.

Façade of the Museum of Contemporary Art

Museum of Contemporary Art ⑲

Circular Quay West, The Rocks.
Map 1 B2. **Tel** 9245 2400. 🚌 *Sydney Explorer, 431, 432, 433, 434.* 🕐 *10am–5pm daily.* 🟢 *25 Dec.* 📷 🕊 ✚
www.mca.com.au

Sydney's substantial collection of contemporary art has grown steadily, but largely out of public view, since 1943. This was the year John Power died, leaving his art collection and a financial bequest to the University of Sydney.

In 1991 the permanent collection, including works by Hockney, Warhol, Lichtenstein and Christo, was transferred to this 1950s Art Deco-style former Maritime Services Board Building. The museum also hosts temporary exhibitions of works by both Australian and international artists.

The grassed area at the front of the building is an ideal location for a harbour-front picnic. The MCA Store sells distinctive gifts by Australian designers, as well as books on contemporary art and design.

National Trust Centre ⑳

Observatory Hill, Watson Rd, The Rocks. **Map** 1 A3. **Tel** 9258 0123 🚌 *Sydney Explorer, 343, 431, 432, 433, 434.* 🕐 *9am–5pm Mon–Fri.* **Gallery** 🕐 *11am–5pm Tue–Sun.* 🟢 *public hols.* 🕊 🏛 📷

The buildings that form the headquarters of the conservation organization, the National Trust of Australia (NSW), date from 1815, when Macquarie chose the site on Observatory Hill for a military hospital.

Today they house a café and the S.H. Ervin Gallery, with changing exhibitions throughout the year, designed to explore the richness and diversity of Australian Art.

St Philip's Church ㉑

3 York St (enter from Jamison St)
Map 1 A3. **Tel** 9247 1071. 🚌 *George St routes.* 🕐 *9am–5pm Mon–Fri.* 🟢 *26 Jan.* 📷 🕊 ✚ *8:30am, 10:15am, 6pm Sun.*
www.yorkstreetanglican.com

Despite its elevated site, this Victorian Gothic church seems overshadowed in its modern setting. Yet, when it was first built, the tall square tower with its decorative pinnacles was a local landmark.

Begun in 1848, St Philip's is by Edmund Blacket, dubbed "the Christopher Wren of Australia" for the 58 churches he designed. In 1851, work was disrupted when its stonemasons left for the gold fields, but was completed by 1856.

A peal of bells was donated in 1858, with another added in 1888 to mark Sydney's centenary. These bells are still in use.

The interior and pipe organ of St Philip's Anglican church

A FLAGPOLE ON THE MUDFLATS

The Founding of Australia by Algernon Talmage, which hangs in Parliament House (see pp112–13)

It is easy to miss the modest flagpole in Loftus Street near Customs House. It flies a flag, the Union Jack, on the spot where Australia's first ceremonial flag-raising took place. On 26 January 1788, Captain Arthur Phillip came ashore to hoist the flag and declare the foundation of the colony. A toast to the King was drunk and a musket volley fired. On the same day, the rest of the First Fleet arrived from Botany Bay to join Phillip and his men. (On this date each year, the country marks Australia Day with a national holiday.) In 1788, the flagpole was on the edge of mudflats on Sydney Cove. Today, because of the large amount of land reclaimed to build Circular Quay, it is some distance from the water's edge.

Sydney Opera House ⑭

No building on earth looks like the Sydney Opera House. Popularly known as the "Opera House" long before the building was complete, it is, in fact, a complex of theatres and halls linked beneath its famous shells. Its birth was long and complicated. Many of the construction problems had not been faced before, resulting in an architectural adventure which lasted 14 years *(see p77)*. An appeal fund was set up, eventually raising $900,000, while the Opera House Lottery raised the balance of the $102 million final cost. As well as being the city's most popular tourist attraction, the Sydney Opera House is also one of the world's busiest performing arts centres.

★ **Opera Theatre**
Mainly used for opera and ballet, this 1,507-seat theatre is big enough to stage grand operas such as Verdi's Aida.

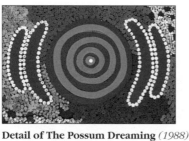

Detail of The Possum Dreaming *(1988)*
The mural in the Opera Theatre's northern foyer is by Michael Tjakamarra Nelson from the central Australian desert.

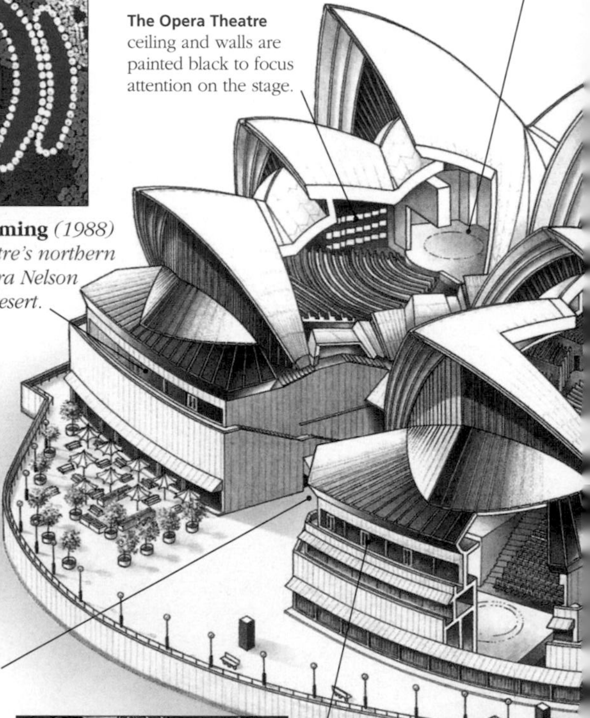

The Opera Theatre ceiling and walls are painted black to focus attention on the stage.

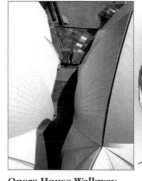

Opera House Walkway
Extensive public walkways around the building offer the visitor views from many different vantage points.

Northern Foyers
With spectacular views over the harbour, the Utzon Room and the large northern foyers of the Opera Theatre and Concert Hall can be hired for conferences, lunches, parties and weddings.

STAR FEATURES

★ Concert Hall

★ Opera Theatre

★ The Roofs

★ **Concert Hall**
This is the largest hall, with seating for 2,679. It is used for symphony, choral, jazz, folk and pop concerts, chamber music, opera, dance and everything from body building to fashion parades.

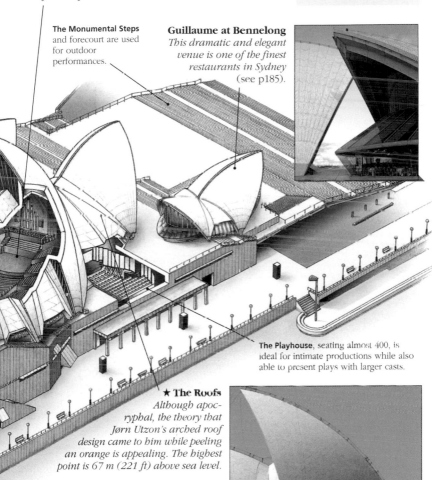

The Monumental Steps and forecourt are used for outdoor performances.

Guillaume at Bennelong
This dramatic and elegant venue is one of the finest restaurants in Sydney (see p185).

The Playhouse, seating almost 400, is ideal for intimate productions while also able to present plays with larger casts.

★ **The Roofs**
Although apocryphal, the theory that Jørn Utzon's arched roof design came to him while peeling an orange is appealing. The highest point is 67 m (221 ft) above sea level.

Detail of Utzon's Tapestry (2004)
Jørn Utzon's original design for this Gobelin-style tapestry, which hangs floor to ceiling in the remodelled Utzon Room, was inspired by the music of Carl Philipp Emanuel Bach.

Exploring Sydney Opera House

The Sydney Opera House covers almost 2 ha (4.5 acres), and is the fourth building to stand on this prominent site. Underneath the ten spectacular roofs of varying planes and textures lies a complex maze of more than 1,000 rooms of all shapes and sizes. One of the world's busiest performing arts centres, the Opera House hosts more than 3,000 events every year.

Coppelia in the Opera Theatre

OPERA THEATRE

The relatively compact size of this venue is a bonus for patrons who savour intimacy. Stage designers continue to demonstrate the opera theatre's great versatility for both opera and dance. The proscenium opening is 12 m (39 ft) wide, and the stage extends back

25 m (82 ft), while the orchestra pit accommodates up to 70–80 musicians. It is rumoured that Box C plays host to a resident ghost.

CONCERT HALL

The rich concert acoustics under the vaulted ceiling of this venue are much admired. Sumptuous Australian wood panelling and the 18 acoustic rings above the stage clearly reflect back the sound. The 10,500 pipe Grand Organ was designed and built by Ronald Sharp from 1969–79.

DRAMA THEATRE, STUDIO AND PLAYHOUSE

The Drama Theatre was not in the original building plan, so jackhammers were brought in to hack it out of the concrete. Refrigerated aluminium

Sydney Dance Company poster

panels in the ceiling control the temperature.

The Playhouse is used for small-cast plays and is also a fully-equipped cinema. The Sydney Theatre Company *(see p69)* puts on at least one performance here every year.

The Studio hosts innovative, contemporary music and performances in an intimate space that seats just 350 people.

BACKSTAGE

Artists performing at the Opera House have the use of five rehearsal studios, 60 dressing rooms and suites and a green room complete with restaurant, bar and lounge.

The scene-changing machinery works on very well-oiled wheels; most crucial in the Opera Theatre where there is regularly a nightly change of performance, with an average of 14 operas being performed in repertoire each year.

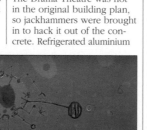

John Olsen's *Salute to Five Bells* (1973) in the Concert Hall foyer

TIMELINE

	1955 International design competition announced		**1957** Utzon's design wins and a lottery is established to finance the building		*Roof in mid-construction*	
	1948 Sir Eugene Goossens lobbies government and Bennelong Point is chosen as opera house site			**1963** Building of roof shells begins		**1973** Opera House officially opened by Queen Elizabeth II
1945	**1950**	**1955**		**1960**	**1965**	**1970**
		1959 Construction begins	**1963** Utzon opens Sydney office		**1967** Concrete roof shells completed	
		Old tram shed at Bennelong Point	**1966** Utzon resigns. Australian architects appointed to complete interior design		**1973** Prokofiev's opera *War and Peace* is the first public performance in Opera House	

The Design of the Opera House

In 1957, Jørn Utzon won the international competition to design the Sydney Opera House. He envisaged a living sculpture that could be viewed from any angle – land, air or sea – with the roofs as a "fifth façade". It was boldly conceived, posing architectural and engineering problems that Utzon's initial compendium of sketches did not begin to solve. When construction began in 1959, the intricate design proved impossible to execute and had to be greatly modified. The project remained so controversial that Utzon resigned in 1966 and an Australian design team completed the building's interior. In 1999 Utzon agreed to be involved in guiding future changes to the building. Since Utzon's death in 2008, his son Jan has taken on this role.

Jørn Utzon

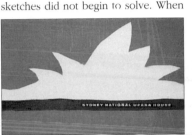

The Red Book, *as submitted for the 1957 design competition, contains Utzon's original concept sketches for the Sydney Opera House.*

Segmented globe

Segments separated

Roof comes into view

Several pieces *cut out of a globe were used in an ingenious manner by architect Jørn Utzon to make up the now familiar shell roof structure.*

UTZON'S OPERA HOUSE MODEL

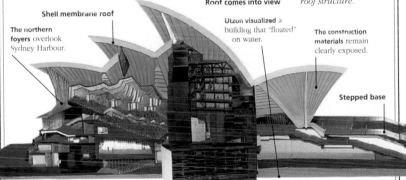

Shell membrane roof

The northern foyers overlook Sydney Harbour.

Utzon visualized a building that "floated" on water.

The construction materials remain clearly exposed.

Stepped base

Utzon's original interiors *and many of his design features now exist only in model form. The architect donated his models and plans to the State Library of NSW (see p112).*

The pre-cast roof *has its inspiration in nature. The basic idea for the formwork of the roof was taken from the fanlike ribs of a palm. Realizing this deceptively simple idea took Utzon six years of design work.*

The roof tiles *were not fixed in place individually, but installed in panels to create the smooth and continuous roof surface.*

CITY CENTRE

Mosaic floor detail, St Mary's Cathedral

Australia's first thorough-fare, George Street, was originally lined with clusters of mud and wattle huts. The gold rushes brought bustling prosperity, and by the 1880s shops and the archi-tecturally majestic edifices of banks dominated the area. The city's first skyscraper - Culwulla Chambers in Castlereagh Street – was completed in 1913, but the city council then imposed a 46-m (150-ft) height restriction which remained in place until 1956. Hyde Park, on the edge of the city centre, was first used as a race course, attracting illegal betting and gambling taverns to Eliza-beth Street. The park later hosted other amusements: wrestling matches, circuses, public hangings and, from 1804 onwards, cricket matches between the army and the town. Today it provides a peaceful oasis, while the city's com-mercial centre is an area of glamorous boutiques, department stores, arcades and malls. Various exercise needs are also catered for: the Cook & Phillip Park Centre in College Street is a great pool and gym complex.

SIGHTS AT A GLANCE

Historic Streets and Buildings
Marble Bar ❶
Queen Victoria Building ❷
Strand Arcade ❺
Martin Place ❻
Lands Department Building ❼
Sydney Town Hall ⓬

Museums and Galleries
Museum of Sydney ❽
Australian Museum pp88–9 ⓮

Landmarks
Sydney Tower p83 ❹

Cathedrals and Synagogues
St Mary's Cathedral ❾
Great Synagogue ⓫
St Andrew's Cathedral ⓭

Parks and Gardens
Hyde Park ❿

Theatres
State Theatre ❸

GETTING THERE
Town Hall, Wynyard, Martin Place, St James and Museum railway stations serve the area. There are frequent buses, par-ticularly along Elizabeth and George Streets. Monorail stops are at City Centre, Galeries Victoria and World Square.

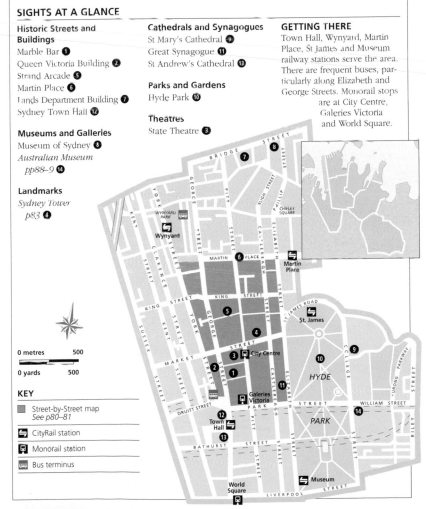

KEY

◼	Street-by-Street map See p80–81
🚇	CityRail station
🚊	Monorail station
🚌	Bus terminus

0 metres 500
0 yards 500

◁ **Mythological figures in the Archibald Fountain, Hyde Park**

Street-by-Street: City Centre

Sculpture outside the MLC Centre

Although closely rivalled by Melbourne, this is the business and commercial capital of Australia. Vibrant by day, at night the streets are far less busy when office workers and shoppers have gone home. The comparatively small city centre of this sprawling metropolis seems to be almost jammed into a few city blocks. Because Sydney grew in such a haphazard fashion, with many of today's streets following tracks from the harbour originally made by bullocks, there was no allowance for the expansion of the burgeoning city into what has become a major international centre. A colourful night scene of cafés, restaurants and theatres is emerging, however, as more people return to the city centre to live.

★ **Queen Victoria Building**
Taking up an entire city block, this 1898 former produce market has been lovingly restored and is now a shopping mall ②

State Theatre
A gem from the era when the movies reigned, this glittering and richly decorated 1929 cinema was once hailed as "the Empire's greatest theatre" ③

YORK STREET

STREET

GEORGE

To Sydney Town Hall

STREET

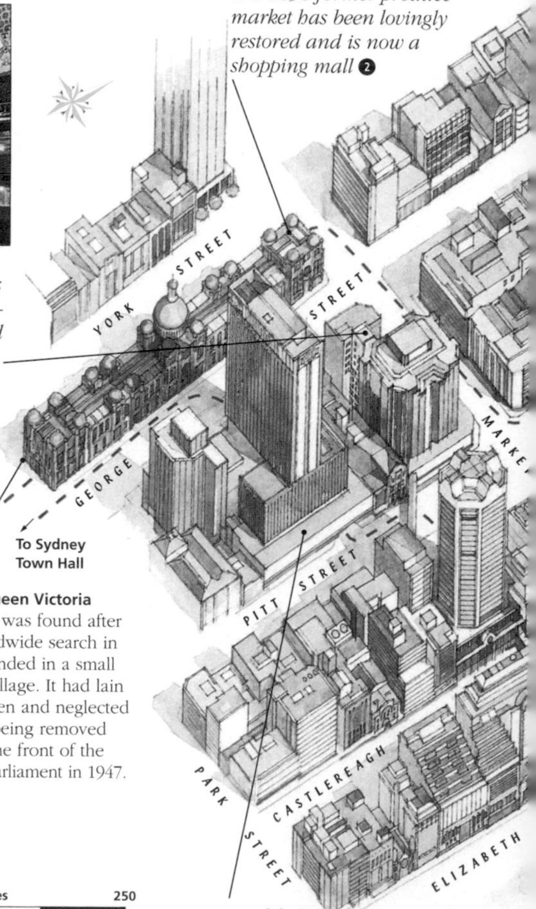

The Queen Victoria Statue was found after a worldwide search in 1983 ended in a small Irish village. It had lain forgotten and neglected since being removed from the front of the Irish Parliament in 1947.

PITT STREET

PARK STREET

CASTLEREAGH

ELIZABETH

MARKET

STAR SIGHTS

★ Queen Victoria Building

★ Sydney Tower

★ Martin Place

| 0 metres | 250 |
| 0 yards | 250 |

KEY

– – – Suggested route

Marble Bar
Once a landmark bar in the 1893 Tattersalls hotel, it was dismantled and re-erected in the Sydney Hilton in 1973 ①

Strand Arcade

A reminder of the late 19th century Victorian era when Sydney was famed as a city of elegant shopping arcades, this faithfully restored example is said to have been the finest of them all ❺

LOCATOR MAP
See Street Finder, maps 1 & 4

MLC Centre
(see p41)

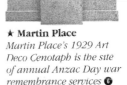

★ **Martin Place**
Martin Place's 1929 Art Deco Cenotaph is the site of annual Anzac Day war remembrance services ❻

Theatre
Royal

Westfield Sydney is an upscale shopping mall housing a wide range of both local and international designer labels.

Hyde Park's
northern end

★ **Sydney Tower**
The tower tops the city skyline, giving a bird's eye view of the whole of Sydney. It rises 305 m (1,000 ft) above the ground and can be seen from as far away as the Blue Mountains ❹

Entrance to the Marble Bar

The Marble Bar ❶

488 George St. **Map** 1 B5. **Tel** 9266 2000. George St routes. 3–11pm Mon–Wed, 3pm–midnight Thu, 3pm–2am Fri, 5pm–2am Sat. public hols. See **Restaurants, Cafés and Pubs** p197.

The Marble Bar, originally part of George Adams' Tattersalls Hotel built in 1893, is an inspired link with the Sydney of an earlier era. The bar, whose rich and decadent Italian Renaissance style had made it a local institution, was dismantled before the demolition of the hotel in 1969. Its colonnade entrance, fireplaces and counters were re-erected in the Sydney Hilton basement and reopened in 1973.

During the week, the bar attracts a broad range of city workers for after-work drinks. On Fridays and at weekends if a band is playing, the bar bustles with a younger crowd who come to hear the mostly jazz and rhythm and blues music.

Queen Victoria Building ❷

455 George St. **Map** 1 B5. **Tel** 9264 9209. George St routes. 9am–6pm Mon–Wed, 9am–9pm Thu, 9am–6pm Fri & Sat, 11am–5pm Sun & public hols. see **Shops and Markets** pp198 and 200.

French Designer Pierre Cardin called the Queen Victoria Building "the most beautiful shopping centre in the world". Yet this spacious, ornate Romanesque building, better known as the QVB, began life as the Sydney produce market. The dust, flies, grime and shouts as horses struggled with heavy loads on the slippery ramps are now difficult to imagine. Completed to the design of City Architect George McRae in 1898, the dominant features are the central dome, sheathed in copper, as are the 20 smaller domes, and the glass barrel vault roof which lets in a flood of natural light.

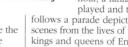

Roof detail, Queen Victoria Building

The market closed at the end of World War I and the building fell into disrepair. It had various roles during this time, including that of City Library. By the 1950s, after extensive remodelling and neglect, it was threatened with demolition.

Refurbished at a cost of over A$75 million, the QVB reopened in 1986 as a grand shopping gallery, with over 190 shops and boutiques on four levels. At the Town Hall end a wishing well incorporates a stone from Blarney Castle,

Ireland and a sculpture of Islay, beloved dog of Queen Victoria. In 1983, a worldwide search began for a statue of the queen herself. One was finally found in the village of Daingean, Republic of Ireland, where it had lain forgotten since its removal from the front of the Irish Parliament in 1947.

Fully restored, the Queen Victoria Statue stands near the wishing well. Inside the QVB, suspended from the ceiling, is the Royal Clock. Weighing more than 1 tonne and over 5 m (17 ft) tall, the clock was designed by Neil Glasser in 1982. The upper structure features part of Balmoral Castle above a copy of the four dials of Big Ben. At one minute to every hour, a fanfare is played and there follows a parade depicting six scenes from the lives of various kings and queens of England.

State Theatre ❸

49 Market St. **Map** 1 B5. **Tel** 9373 6655. George St routes. **Box office** 9am–5:30pm Mon–Fri. Good Fri, 25 Dec. bookings essential. **www**.statetheatre.com.au.

When it opened in 1929, this picture palace was hailed as the finest that local craftsmanship could achieve. The State Theatre is one of the best examples in Australia of the architectural fantasies used to entice people to the movies.

Its Cinema Baroque style is evident right from the Gothic foyer, with its vaulted ceiling, mosaic floor, richly decorated marble columns and statues. Inside the brass and bronze doors, the auditorium, which seats over 2,000 people, is lit by a 20,000-piece chandelier. The Wurlitzer organ (currently under repair) rises from below stage just before performances. Now one of Sydney's premier concert and theatre venues, it is also the main base for the Sydney Film Festival, held in June of each year (see p51).

The ornately decorated Gothic foyer of the State Theatre

Sydney Tower ❹

The highest observation deck in the southern hemisphere, the Sydney Tower was conceived as part of a 1970s shopping centre, but was not completed until 1981. About one million visitors a year admire the stunning views, often stretching for over 85 km (53 miles). A landmark in itself, it can be seen from almost anywhere in the city, and far beyond. Visitors can also take a 45-minute Skywalk tour over the roof of the tower.

VISITORS' CHECKLIST

100 Market St. **Map** 1 B5.
Tel 9333 9222. 🚌 *Sydney Explorer, all city routes.* 🚌 *Darling Harbour.* 🚉 *St James, Town Hall.* 🚍 *City Centre.* **Sydney Tower** ◯ *9am–10:30pm daily.* **Skywalk** ◯ *9:30am–8:45pm daily.* ● 25 Dec. 📷 ♿ 🚻 🎁 🍴 ♿
www.sydneytowereye.com.au

Sydney Tower Eye Observation Deck
Views stretch to Pittwater in the north, Botany Bay to the south, westwards to the Blue Mountains, and out to the sea.

The 30-m (98-ft) spire completes the total 305 m (1,000 ft) of the tower's height.

The water tank holds 162,000 litres (35,500 gallons) and acts as an enormous stabilizer on very windy days.

Skywalk

Level 4: Observation

Level 3: Coffee shop

Level 2: Buffet restaurant

Level 1: A la carte restaurant

The turret's nine levels include two restaurants, a café and the Observation Level.

The windows comprise three layers. The outer has a gold dust coating. The frame design prevents panes falling outwards.

The 56 cables weigh seven tonnes each. If laid end to end, they would reach from New Zealand to Sydney.

The shaft is designed to withstand wind speeds expected only once in 500 years.

The stairs are two separate, fireproofed emergency escape routes.

Double-decker lifts can carry up to 2,000 people per hour. At full speed, a lift takes only 40 seconds to ascend the 76 floors to the Observation Level.

Construction of Turret
The nine turret levels were erected on the roof of the base building, then hoisted up the shaft using hydraulic jacks.

The 4-D cinema experience takes you on a journey around Sydney.

New Year's Eve
Every year, visitors flock to Sydney's highest observation deck to watch the fireworks over the city and Harbour Bridge.

Strand Arcade ❺

412–414 George St. **Map** 1 B5.
Tel 9232 4199. 🚌 George St
routes. ⬜ 9am–5:30pm Mon–Wed
& Fri, 9am–9pm Thu, 9am–4pm Sat,
11am–4pm Sun. ⬤ some public
hols, 25 & 26 Dec. ♿ 📷 See **Shops
and Markets** pp198–201.

Victorian Sydney was a city of
grand shopping arcades. The
Strand, joining George and
Pitt Streets and designed by
English architect John Spencer,
was the finest jewel in the city's
crown. The blaze of publicity
surrounding its opening in
April 1892 was equalled only
by the natural light pouring
through the glass roof and the
artificial glare from the chan-
deliers, each carrying 50 jets
of gas as well as 50 lamps.

The boutiques and shops
in the galleries make window
shopping a delight in this airy
building which, after a fire in
1976, was restored to its original splendour. Be sure to stop,
as shoppers have done since
opening day, for refreshments
at one of the beautiful coffee
shops in the arcade.

Interior of National Australia Bank, George Street end of Martin Place

**The Pitt Street entrance to the
majestic Strand Arcade**

Martin Place ❻

Map 1 B4. 🚌 George St & Elizabeth
St routes. 🚇 Martin Place.

Running from George Street
across Pitt, Castlereagh and
Elizabeth Streets to Macquarie
Street, this plaza was opened
in 1891 and made a traffic-free
precinct in 1971. It is busiest at
lunchtime when city workers
enjoy their sandwiches while
watching free entertainment,

sponsored by the Sydney City
Council, in a performance
space near Castlereagh Street.

Every Anzac Day, a national
day of war remembrance on
25 April, the focus moves to
the Cenotaph at the George
Street end. Thousands of past
and present servicemen and
women attend a dawn service
and wreath-laying ceremony,
followed by a march-past. The
shrine, with bronze statues of a
soldier and a sailor on a granite
base, by Bertram MacKennal,
was unveiled in 1929.

On the southern side of the
Cenotaph is the symmetrical
façade of the Renaissance-
style General Post Office,
considered to be the finest
building by James Barnet,
Colonial Architect. Con-
struction of the GPO, as
Sydneysiders call it, took
place between 1866 and
1874, with additions in
Pitt Street between 1881
and 1885. Most contro-
versial were the relief
figures executed by
Tomaso Sani. Although
Barnet declared that
the figures represented
Australians in realistic form,
they were labelled "grotesque".

A stainless steel sculpture
of upended cubes, the Dobell
Memorial Sculpture stands
above a waterfall which was

**Statue of explorer
Gregory Blaxland**

funded by public subscription
following a donation by artist
Lloyd Rees. The sculpture, a
tribute to the artist William
Dobell (see p31), was created
by Bert Flugelman in 1979.

Lands Department
Building ❼

23 Bridge St. **Map** 1 B3. 🚌 325,
George St routes. ⬜ only 2 weeks,
dates vary. ♿

Designed by the Colonial
Architect James Barnet, the
three-storey Classical Revival
sandstone edifice was built
between 1877 and 1890.

As for the GPO building,
Pyrmont sandstone was
used for the exterior.
Decisions about the sub-
division of much of rural
eastern Australia were
made in offices within.
Statues of explorers and
legislators who "pro-
moted settlement" fill
23 of the façade's 48
niches; the remainder
are still empty. The
luminaries include the
explorers Hovell and Hume,
Sir Thomas Mitchell, Blaxland,
Lawson and Wentworth (see
p136), Ludwig Leichhardt, Bass
and Matthew Flinders and the
botanist Sir Joseph Banks.

Museum of Sydney ❽

Cnr Bridge & Phillip Sts. **Map** 1 B3.
Tel *9251 5988.* 🚌 *Circular Quay routes.* 🔵 *9:30am–5pm daily.*
⚫ *Good Fri, 25 Dec.* 🎫 🖻 🍴 🛒
📷 ♿ *www.*hht.net.au/museums

Situated at the base of Governor Phillip Tower, the Museum of Sydney is on the site of the first Government House, the home, office and seat of authority for the first nine governors of NSW from 1788 until its demolition in 1846. The design assimilates a valuable archaeological site into a modern office block. The museum itself traces the city's turbulent history, from the 1788 arrival of the British colonists until the present day.

Indigenous Peoples

The museum sits on Cadigal land. A gallery explores the culture, history, continuity and place of Sydney's original Aboriginal inhabitants, and the "turning point" of colonization/invasion. Collectors' chests hold items of daily use such as flint and ochre, each piece painstakingly catalogued and evocatively interpreted.

There are two audio-visual exhibits which explore the history of indigenous peoples

The Viewing Cube, Level 3, overlooking the piazza to Circular Quay

from a contemporary perspective. In the square at the front of the complex, the acclaimed *Edge of the Trees* sculpture, a collection of 29 sandstone, steel and wooden pillars, symbolizes the first contact between the Aboriginal peoples and Europeans. Haunting voices in the Eora tongue fill the space. Inscribed in the wood are signatures of the First Fleeters and names of botanical species in both the indigenous language and Latin. Incisions made in the pillars are filled with organic materials such as ash, feathers, bone, shells and human hair.

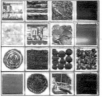

The Trade Wall display on Level 2

History of Sydney

Outside the museum, a paving pattern outlines the site of the first Government House. Original foundations, lost under street level for many years, can be seen here through a window. Inside the entrance a viewing floor reveals more foundations. A segment of wall has been reconstructed using sandstone excavated during archaeological exploration of the site.

The Colony display on Level 2 focuses on Sydney during the critical decade of the 1840s when convict transportation ended, the town officially became a city and suffered an economic depression. There is also a set of scale models of the 11 First Fleet ships. The Museum presents stories of the Fleet's journey, arrival, first contacts with Indigenous people and the survival challenges faced by those on board. On Level 3, 20th century Sydney is explored with panoramic images of the developing city providing a vivid backdrop. The Museum of Sydney has a regular changing exhibition program.

Edge of the Trees **sculptural installation by Janet Laurence and Fiona Foley (1995)**

Interior of the 19th-century Great Synagogue

St Mary's Cathedral ❾

St. Mary's Rd. **Map** 1 C5. *Tel 9220 0400.* 🚌 *Elizabeth St routes.* ⏱ *6:30am–6pm Mon–Fri, 6:30am–7pm Sat & Sun.* ♿ *with advance notice.* **www**.stmaryscathedral.org.au

Although Catholics arrived with the First Fleet, the celebration of Mass was at first prohibited in case the priests provoked civil strife among the colony's large Irish Catholic population. The first priests were appointed in 1820 and services allowed. In 1821, Governor Macquarie laid the foundation stone for St Mary's Chapel on the site

of today's cathedral, the first land granted to the Catholic Church in Australia.

The initial section of the Gothic Revival-style cathedral was opened in 1882. In 1928, the building was completed, but without the twin southern spires proposed by the architect, William Wardell. By the entrance steps are statues of Australia's first cardinal, Moran, and Archbishop Kelly who laid the stone for the final stage in 1913. They were sculpted by Bertram MacKennal, also responsible

for the Martin Place Cenotaph *(see p84)* and the Shakespeare group outside the State Library *(see p112).* The crypt houses a historical exhibition of the early Sydney church. The terrazzo mosaic floor here took 15 years to complete.

Great Synagogue ⓫

187 Elizabeth St, entrance on 166 Castlereagh St. **Map** 1 B5. *Tel 9267 2477.* 🚌 *333, 380, 394.* ⏱ *for services and tours.* 🕎 *public & Jewish hols.* ♿ *advance notice.* 📧 🌐 **www**.greatsynagogue.org.au

The longest established Jewish Orthodox congregation in Australia assembles in this synagogue, consecrated in 1878. Although Jews had arrived with the First Fleet, worship did not begin until the 1820s. With its carved entrance columns and magnificent stained-glass windows, the synagogue is perhaps the finest work of Thomas Rowe, the architect of Sydney Hospital *(see p113).* The panelled ceiling is decorated with hundreds of tiny gold leaf stars.

Candelabra from the Great Synagogue

Hyde Park ❿

Map 1 B5. 🚌 *Elizabeth St routes.*

Fenced and named after its London equivalent by Governor Macquarie in 1810, Hyde Park marked the outskirts of the township. It was a popular exercise field for garrison troops and later

Tomb of the Unknown Soldier in the Art Deco Anzac Memorial

incorporated a racecourse and a cricket pitch. Though much smaller today than the original park, it still provides a peaceful haven in the middle of the bustling city centre.

Anzac Memorial
The 30-m- (98-ft-) high Art Deco memorial, reflected in the poplar-lined Pool of Remembrance, commemorates those Australians who were killed at war in the service of their country. Opened in 1934, the Anzac Memorial now includes a photographic and military artifact exhibition downstairs.

Sandringham Garden
In spring, the pergola in this sunken garden is a cascade of mauve-flowering wisteria. The garden, a memorial to the English kings George V and George VI, was opened by Queen Elizabeth II in 1954.

Diana, goddess of purity and the chase, Archibald Fountain

Archibald Fountain
This bronze and granite fountain commemorates the French and Australian World War I alliance. It was completed by François Sicard in 1932 and donated by JF Archibald, one of the founders of the *Bulletin*, a popular literary magazine which encouraged the work of Henry Lawson and "Banjo" Paterson, among many others. It was Archibald's bequest that established the Archibald Prize for portraiture *(see p50).*

The Grand Organ in Sydney Town Hall's Centennial Hall

Sydney Town Hall ⑫

483 George St. **Map** 4 F2.
Tel 9265 9333. George St
routes. 8:30am–6pm Mon–Fri.
public hols. www.
cityofsydneyvenues.com.au

The steps of this sandstone building, central to George Street's Victorian architecture, have been a favourite Sydney meeting place since it opened in 1869. Walled burial grounds had originally covered the site.

It is a fine example of high Victorian architecture. The original architect, JH Wilson,

died during its construction, as did several of the architects who followed. The vestibule – an elegant salon with intricate plasterwork, lavish stained glass and a crystal chandelier – is the work of Albert Bond. The Bradbridge brothers completed the clock tower in 1884. From 1888–9, other architects were used for the Centennial Hall, with its coffered zinc ceiling and the imposing 19th-century Grand Organ with over 8,500 pipes.

On the façade, you will see numerous carved lion heads. Just to the north of the main entrance, facing George Street, a lion has been carved with one eye shut. This oddity appeared because of the head stonemason's habit of checking the line of the stonework by closing one eye. The sly joke was not found until work was finished. Some people have concluded that Sydney Town Hall became the city's most elaborate building by accident, as each architect strove to outdo similar buildings in Manchester and Liverpool. Today, it makes a magnificent event venue.

The Great Bible, St Andrew's Cathedral

St Andrew's Cathedral ⑬

Sydney Square, Cnr George & Bathurst Sts. **Map** 4 E3. **Tel** 9265 1661. George St routes.
contact the cathedral for opening hours and tour times.
www.cathedral.sydney.anglican.asn.au

While the foundation stone or the country's oldest cathedral was laid in 1819, almost 50 years elapsed before the building was consecrated in 1868. The Gothic Revival design is by Edmund Blacket, whose ashes are interred here. Inspired by York Minster in England, the twin towers were completed in 1874. In 1949, the main entrance was moved to the eastern end near George Street. Inside are memorials to Sydney pioneers, including Thomas Mort (see p72), as well as a collection of religious memorabilia.

The southern wall incorporates stones from London's St Paul's Cathedral, Westminster Abbey and the House of Lords.

Obelisk
This monument was dubbed "Thornton's Scent Bottle" after the mayor of Sydney who had it erected in 1857. The mock-Egyptian edifice is in fact a ventilator for a sewer.

Emden Gun
Standing at the corner of College and Liverpool Streets, this monument commemorates a World War I naval action. HMAS *Sydney* destroyed the German raider *Emden* off the Cocos Islands on 9 November 1914, and 180 crew members were taken prisoner.

City Circle Railway
The park we see today bears very little resemblance to the Hyde Park of old. In fact, the dictates of city railway tunnels have largely created its present landscape. Tunnels were excavated through an open cut that

ran through the park, and after the rail system was opened in 1926 the entire area had to be remodelled and replanted.

Busby's Bore Fountain
This is a reminder of Busby's Bore, the city's first piped water supply opened in 1837.

John Busby, a civil engineer, conceived and supervised the construction of the 4.4-km (2¾-mile) tunnel. It carried water from bores on Lachlan Swamp, now within Centennial Park (see p127), to horse-drawn water carriers on the corner of Elizabeth and Park Streets.

Game in progress on the giant chessboard, near Busby's Bore Fountain

Australian Museum ⑭

Model head of
Tyrannosaurus rex

The Australian Museum, the nation's leading natural science museum, founded in 1827, was the first museum established and remains the premier showcase of Australian natural history. The main building, an impressive sandstone structure with a marble staircase, faces Hyde Park. Architect Mortimer Lewis was forced to resign his position when building costs began to far exceed the budget. Construction was completed in the 1860s by James Barnet. The collection provides a journey across Australia and the near Pacific, covering biology and both natural and cultural history. Australian Aboriginal traditions are celebrated in a community access space also used for dance and other performances.

Museum Entrance
The façade features massive Corinthian square pillars or piers.

Planet of Minerals
This section features a walk-through re-creation of an underground mine with a display of gems and minerals.

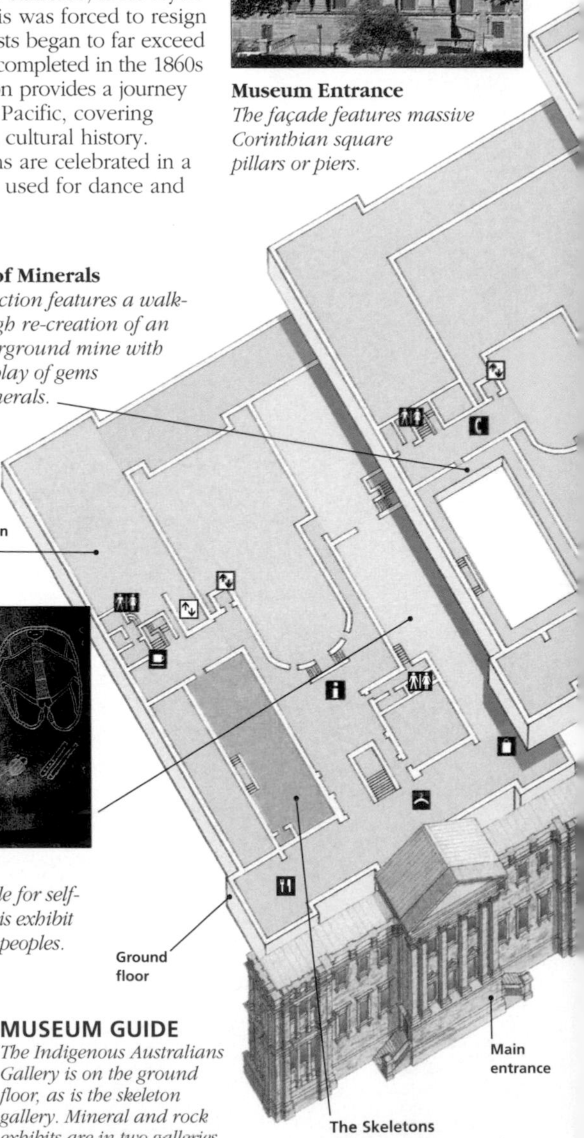

Rhodochrosite   Cuprite

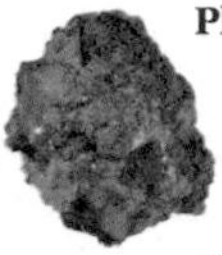

Mesolite with green apophyllite

Special exhibition space

★ **Indigenous Australians**
From the Dreaming to the struggle for self-determination and land rights, this exhibit tells the stories of Australia's first peoples.

Ground floor

Main entrance

STAR EXHIBITS

- ★ Indigenous Australians
- ★ Kidspace
- ★ Search & Discover

MUSEUM GUIDE

The Indigenous Australians Gallery is on the ground floor, as is the skeleton gallery. Mineral and rock exhibits are in two galleries on level 1. Birds and Insects are found on level 2, along with Kidspace, Surviving Australia and Dinosaurs.

The Skeletons Gallery, on the ground floor, provides a different perspective on natural history.

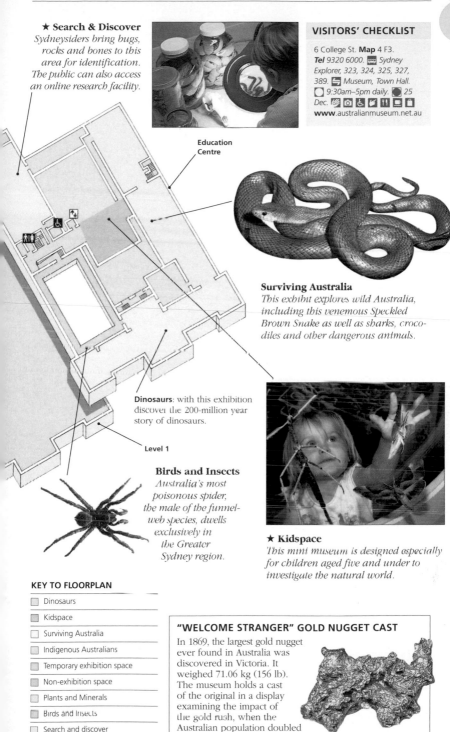

★ Search & Discover
Sydneysiders bring bugs, rocks and bones to this area for identification. The public can also access an online research facility.

VISITORS' CHECKLIST

6 College St. **Map** 4 F3.
***Tel** 9320 6000.* 🚌 *Sydney Explorer, 323, 324, 325, 327, 389.* 🚇 *Museum, Town Hall.*
🕘 *9:30am–5pm daily.* 🔴 *25 Dec.* 🎟️ 📷 ♿ ✏️ 🍴 🛍️ 📖
www.australianmuseum.net.au

Education Centre

Surviving Australia
This exhibit explores wild Australia, including this venomous Speckled Brown Snake as well as sharks, crocodiles and other dangerous animals.

Dinosaurs: with this exhibition discover the 200-million year story of dinosaurs.

Level 1

Birds and Insects
Australia's most poisonous spider, the male of the funnel-web species, dwells exclusively in the Greater Sydney region.

★ Kidspace
This mini museum is designed especially for children aged five and under to investigate the natural world.

KEY TO FLOORPLAN

- ☐ Dinosaurs
- ☐ Kidspace
- ☐ Surviving Australia
- ☐ Indigenous Australians
- ☐ Temporary exhibition space
- ☐ Non-exhibition space
- ☐ Plants and Minerals
- ☐ Birds and Insects
- ☐ Search and discover
- ☐ Skeletons Gallery

"WELCOME STRANGER" GOLD NUGGET CAST

In 1869, the largest gold nugget ever found in Australia was discovered in Victoria. It weighed 71.06 kg (156 lb). The museum holds a cast of the original in a display examining the impact of the gold rush, when the Australian population doubled in ten years.

◄——67.5 cm (26½ in) wide——►

DARLING HARBOUR

Named in honour of the seventh governor of New South Wales, Ralph Darling, this area was originally called Cockle Bay because of the molluscs early European settlers collected here. Darling Harbour was an unsavoury place in the late 19th century, known for its thieves' dens and bawdy houses. Its docks, backed by a railway yard, were an embarkation point for wool and other exports. The country's industrial age began here in 1815 with the opening of a steam mill. Darling

Horatio Nelson, National Maritime Museum

Harbour continued as, first, a grimy workplace and, later, with the industrial decline of Sydney Harbour, an obsolete and run-down backwater. In the 1980s, it was decided to make this prime city site a focal point of the 1988 Bicentenary. The project was the largest urban redevelopment ever carried out in Australia. Today Darling Harbour is an extension of the city centre with a mixture of fine museums, shopping and open space. It has become a popular and lively area of Sydney.

SIGHTS AT A GLANCE

Historic Districts and Buildings
Pyrmont Bridge **4**
King Street Wharf **5**
Chinatown **8**

Museums and Galleries
Australian National Maritime Museum pp94–5 **1**
Powerhouse Museum pp100–1 **11**

Parks and Gardens
Chinese Garden of Friendship **7**

Entertainment
Sydney Aquarium p96 **2**
Wild Life Sydney p97 **3**
Convention and Exhibition Centre **6**

Theatres
Capitol Theatre **9**

Markets
Paddy's Markets **10**

GETTING THERE
Harbourside, Convention and Paddy's Markets monorail stations are convenient. Ferries run to Darling Harbour wharf, while the most useful buses are the Sydney Explorer, 456 and 501.

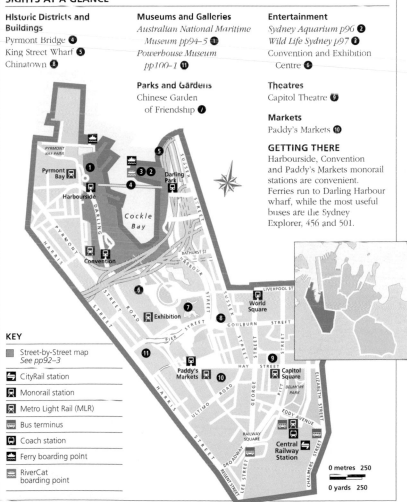

KEY

■	Street-by-Street map *See pp92–3*
🚆	CityRail station
🚈	Monorail station
🚈	Metro Light Rail (MLR)
🚌	Bus terminus
🚍	Coach station
⛴	Ferry boarding point
🚤	RiverCat boarding point

0 metres 250
0 yards 250

◁ **View from Harbourside Shopping Centre looking east towards the city**

Street-by-Street: Darling Harbour

**Carpentaria lightship,
National Maritime Museum**

Darling Harbour was New South Wales' bicentennial gift to itself. This imaginative urban redevelopment, in the heart of Sydney, covers a 54-ha (133-acre) site that was once a busy industrial centre and international shipping terminal catering for the developing local wool, grain, timber and coal trades. In 1984 the Darling Harbour Authority was formed to examine the area's commercial options. The resulting complex opened in 1988, complete with the Australian National Maritime Museum and Sydney Aquarium, two of the city's tourist highlights. Free outdoor entertainment, for children in particular, is a regular feature, and there are many shops, cafés and restaurants, as well as several major hotels overlooking the bay.

Harbourside Complex offers restaurants and cafés with superb views over the water to the city skyline. There is also a wide range of speciality shops, selling unusual gifts and other items.

Convention and Exhibition Centre
This complex presents an alternating range of trade shows displaying everything from home decorating suggestions to bridal wear ❻

DARLING DRIVE

WESTERN DISTRIBUTOR

WESTERN DISTRIBUTOR

The Tidal Cascades sunken fountain was designed by Robert Woodward, also responsible for the El Alamein Fountain *(see p120)*. The double spiral of water and paths replicates the circular shape of the Convention Centre.

IMAX large-screen cinema

Chinese Garden of Friendship

The Chinese Garden of Friendship is a haven of peace and tranquillity in the heart of Sydney. Its landscaping, with winding pathways, waterfalls, lakes and pavilions, offers an insight into the rich culture of China.

STAR SIGHTS

★ Australian National Maritime Museum

★ Sydney Aquarium

Pyrmont Bridge
The swingspan bridge opens for vessels up to 14 m (46 ft) tall. The monorail track running above the walkway also opens up to allow access for even taller boats **❹**

LOCATOR MAP
See Street Finder, maps 3 & 4

A historic fleet of 14 vessels is docked at the museum's wharves, making it one of the world's largest collections held at a museum.

Star City Casino

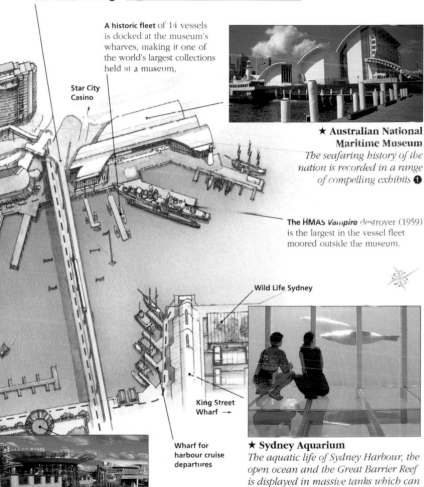

★ **Australian National Maritime Museum**
The seafaring history of the nation is recorded in a range of compelling exhibits **❶**

The HMAS *Vampire* destroyer (1959) is the largest in the vessel fleet moored outside the museum.

Wild Life Sydney

King Street Wharf →

Wharf for harbour cruise departures

★ **Sydney Aquarium**
The aquatic life of Sydney Harbour, the open ocean and the Great Barrier Reef is displayed in massive tanks which can be seen from underwater walkways **❷**

Cockle Bay Wharf
is vibrant and colourful, and an exciting food and entertainment precinct.

| 0 metres | 100 |
| 0 yards | 100 |

KEY

– – – Suggested route

Australian National Maritime Museum ❶

1602 Willem Blaeu Celestial Globe

Bounded as it is by the sea, Australia's history is inextricably linked to maritime traditions. The museum displays material in a broad range of permanent and temporary thematic exhibits, many with inter-active elements. As well as artifacts relating to the enduring Aboriginal maritime cultures, the exhibits survey the history of European exploratory voyages in the Pacific, the arrival of convict ships, successive waves of migration, water sports and recreation, and naval life. Historic vessels on show at the wharf include a flimsy Vietnamese refugee boat, sailing, fishing and pearling boats, a navy patrol boat and a World War II commando raider.

Museum Façade
The billowing steel roof design by Philip Cox suggests both the surging sea and the sails of a ship.

Passengers
The model of the Orcades *reflects the grace of 1950s liners. This display also charts harrowing sea voyages made by migrants and refugees.*

Eora – First People traces the seafaring traditions of Aboriginal peoples and Torres Strait Islanders.

The Tasman Light was used in a Tasmanian lighthouse.

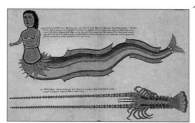

★ **Navigators**
This 1754 engraving of an East Indian sea creature is a European vision of the un-charted, exotic "great south".

The *Sirius* **anchor** is from a 1790 wreck off Norfolk Island.

Main entrance (sea level)

The Navy exhibit examines naval life in war and peace, as well as the history of colonial navies.

Linked by the Sea honours enduring links between the US and Australia. American traders stopped off in Australia on their way to China.

KEY TO FLOORPLAN

☐	Navigators and Eora – First People
☐	Passengers
☐	Commerce
☐	Watermarks
☐	Navy
■	Linked by the Sea: USA Gallery
☐	Temporary exhibitions
☐	Non-exhibition space

STAR EXHIBITS

★ HMAS Vampire

★ Navigators and Eora – First People

★ Watermarks

Commerce
This 1903 Painters' and Dockers' Union banner was carried by waterfront workers in marches. It shows the Niagara entering the dry dock at Cockatoo Island (see p106).

★ Watermarks
This 1960s poster for Bondi beach is part of the museum's Watermarks – adventure, sport and play exhibition. The displays, including fully rigged boats and profiles of world champion scullers and swimmers, celebrate Australia's love affair with the water.

Level 1

Gallery One

A replica of Captain Cook's *Endeavour* is based at the museum

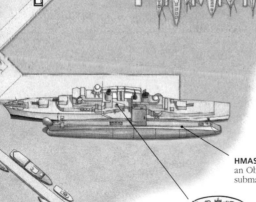

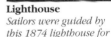

Lighthouse
Sailors were guided by this 1874 lighthouse for over a century. It was rebuilt complete with original kerosene lamp.

HMAS Onslow
an Oberon-class submarine.

★ HMAS Vampire
The museum's largest vessel is the 1959 Royal Australian Navy destroyer, whose insignia is shown. Tours of "The Bat" are accompanied by simulated battle action sounds.

MUSEUM GUIDE
The Watermarks, Navy and Linked by the Sea: USA Gallery exhibits are located on the main entrance level (sea level). The Eora – First People, Navigators, Passengers and Commerce sections are found on the first level.

Sydney Aquarium ❷

Tropical sea star

Sydney Aquarium contains the largest, most comprehensive collection of Australian aquatic wildlife, with over 12,000 animals from 650 species. Both freshwater and marine exhibits simulate the animals' natural environments. For many visitors, the highlight is a walk "on the ocean floor" through the floating oceanarium with 165 m (480 ft) of acrylic underwater tunnels. These allow close observation of sharks, stingrays and schools of fish. None of the displays is harmful to the creatures, and many of the tanks display practical information about environmental hazards.

Exploring the Tropical Touch Pool

EXPLORING SYDNEY AQUARIUM

Built on a pier in Darling Harbour, Sydney Aquarium comprises over 4,000 sq m (43,000 sq ft) of exhibition space and is one of the largest aquariums in the world. Exhibits are organised by theme and take the visitor on a journey through the different marine habitats of the Australian continent. On entering, visitors are led through the Northern Rivers and Southern Rivers sections, featuring animals such as platypuses and freshwater fish, before reaching the Southern Oceans and Northern Oceans areas where the oceanariums and touch pool can be found.

It is worth checking the website to coincide a visit with one of the feeding times. There are also "tank talks" (1:30pm daily) when a trained diver can be asked questions while they are feeding sharks in the Great Barrier Reef Oceanarium. Also, for an added cost, visitors can ride out on a glass-bottom boat to watch and feed the sharks first hand (11am daily).

ATTRACTIONS

Sydney Aquarium offers a great variety of exhibits and animal encounters.

Platypuses

Endemic to the rivers, streams, billabongs and lakes of the east coast and Tasmania, the platypus is an iconic symbol of Australia. When discovered by Europeans, the animal's strange collection of physical attributes, including a duck-like bill and otter's tail, were once thought to be some kind of elaborate hoax.

Claws

This exhibit features the world's largest crab species – the Japanese Spider Crab. It can grow to a claw-to-claw span of almost 4 m (13 ft).

Mermaid Lagoon

An exciting addition to the aquarium in 2008 were two of only six dugongs (sea cows) to be held in captivity. These

docile, herbivorous mammals can reach up to 3 m (9.8 ft) in length and live for more than 70 years. Named "Pig" and "Wuru" (an Aboriginal word meaning "young child"), the dugongs were originally rescued as orphaned calves.

Touch Pool

There is a touch pool in the aquarium, giving the visitor the rare chance to touch, with care, marine life found along the coastline. It includes sea urchins, tubeworms, crabs and sea stars.

Open Ocean Oceanarium

Through an underwater tunnel, visitors can encounter huge stingrays, shoals of fish as well as the largest sharks on display in the aquarium – the grey nurse shark.

Great Barrier Reef Oceanarium

The world's largest coral reef extends along 2,300 km (1,430 miles) of Australia's coast. Vibrant tangs, angelfish and spiny lionfish are on display as well as tropical sharks and rays. At the end of the oceanarium, the floor-to-ceiling Reef Theatre glass panel offers an unparalleled spectacle of the colourful, exotic creatures.

Sharks and hundreds of other fish on view from the Reef Theatre

Wild Life Sydney ③

King parrot

Wild Life Sydney contains over 100 Australian land-dwelling species, including insects, birds, snakes, reptiles and mammals. Together with the Sydney Aquarium the complex comprises the world's largest collection of native Australian animal species to be housed in one location. In the heart of Darling Harbour, the undulating see-through mesh roof is a sight to behold in itself. Although compact in size, the zoo contains nine different temperature- and humidity-controlled habitats, and the experience is enhanced by soundscapes, graphics and interactive models.

VISITORS' CHECKLIST

Aquarium Wharf, Darling Harbour. **Map** 4 D2. **Tel** 9333 9288. 🚌 Sydney Explorer. 🚢 Darling Harbour. 🚊 Town Hall. 🚊 Darling Park. ◷ 9am–6pm daily (last adm 4:30pm). 🎫 📷 🚻 📷 🛒 ▯
🖥 www.wildlifesydney.com.au

Visitors can get close to kangaroos at Wild Life Sydney

EXPLORING WILD LIFE SYDNEY

There are joint tickets available for Wild Life Sydney and Sydney Aquarium and both sites can be visited in one day; another pass also includes Sydney Tower Eye.

Exhibits are laid out over three floors with one kilometre (0.6 miles) of enclosed walkways. The habitats are climate controlled and visitors largely view the animals through vast viewing panels.

Throughout the day feeds and talks are given by the keepers, and visitors get the chance to get closer to and sometimes touch the animals, under supervision. Another good option is to book a group or "VIP" guided tour.

ATTRACTIONS

Wild Life Sydney groups the animals by their natural habitats, housing intriguing, often unique, species that are native to the Australian continent.

Butterfly Tropics
The butterfly tropics zone contains such spectacular species as the Zebra, Blue Triangle and Ulysses butterflies, the latter with its huge 14-cm (5.5-in) wingspan. During guided tours visitors get to gently hold the butterflies.

Frilled-Neck Lizard
Native to the dry landscape of the Kimberley in north Western Australia, this bizarre-looking lizard flares the folds of skin around its neck when feeling threatened or scared. It will also hiss and lunge to ward off predators. It used to feature on the Australian 2c coin.

Flight Canyon
This large open-air aviary is filled with colourful birds, such as the vibrant King Parrot and Rainbow Lorikeet. There are also ground-dwelling birds such as the Southern Cassowary. Around half of the bird species of Australia are found nowhere else in the world.

Invertebrates
This habitat contains all kinds of creepy crawlies such as the carnivorous praying mantis, the giant rhinoceros cockroach and the world's most dangerous spider – the Sydney funnel-web.

Koalas
A raised walkway under the open-air mesh roof winds through the koala and wallaby habitats and allows visitors to get closer to these cuddly, iconic animals and even have a photo taken with them. The koala's diet of eucalyptus leaves is so low in nutrients, it has to conserve energy by moving slowly and sleeping a lot.

Yellow-Footed Rock Wallaby
Bounding about on rocks in the Wallaby Cliff habitat, this stripy-tailed wallaby is perhaps the most attractive of the kangaroo species, so much so it used to be hunted for its beautiful fur. Its huge feet have strong muscles and a brush of stiff hairs to help it get around over rocky terrain.

Koala

Southern Cassowary
This distinctive blue-necked bird, a close relation of the emu, is considered the most dangerous bird in the world. It has powerful talons and one spear-like inner claw which can reach up to 12 cm (4.7 in) in length. This flightless bird is capable of killing dogs and even humans if provoked.

Pyrmont Bridge ❹

Darling Harbour. **Map** 1 A5.
🚉 Darling Park, Harbourside.
📷 ♿ ✔

Pyrmont Bridge opened
in 1902. The world's
oldest electrically operated
swingspan bridge, it was fully
functional before Sydney's
streets were lit by electricity.
It was the second Pyrmont
Bridge and provided access
to what, at the time, was a
busy international shipping
terminal with warehouses and
wool stores. Electricity for the
new bridge came from the
Ultimo power station, the
building that now houses the
city's Powerhouse Museum
(see pp100–101).
   Percy Allan, the bridge's
designer, achieved overseas
recognition for his two central
steel swingspans and went on
to design 583 more bridges
in the course of his career. J.J.
Bradfield, the designer of the
Sydney Harbour Bridge *(see
pp70–71),* was also involved
in construction of this bridge.
   The 369-m- (1,200-ft-) long
Pyrmont Bridge has 14 spans,
with only the two central
swingspans being made of
steel. The remaining spans
are made of ironbark, an
Australian hardwood timber.
The bridge was permanently
closed to road traffic in 1981,
but reopened to pedestrians
when the Darling Harbour
complex opened in 1988. A
portion of the monorail route

The architectural geometry of the Convention and Exhibition Centre

travels along the bridge. The
central steel swingspans are
still driven by their original
motor. The bridge is opened
regularly to allow boats access
to and from Cockle Bay.

**Night lights at King Street Wharf,
Darling Harbour**

King Street Wharf ❺

Lime St, between King and Erskine
sts. **Map** 4 D1. 🚉 Darling Park. 🚌
🍴 📷 🏛 ♿ **www**.ksw.com.au

Journalists from nearby
newspaper offices and
city workers flock to this
harbourside venue, which
combines an aggressively
modern glass and steel shrine
to café society with a working
wharf. Passengers arrive and
depart in style on ferries,
water taxis and rivercats.
   The complex is flush with
bars that vie for the best
views, and restaurants including Thai, Japanese, Italian and
Modern Australian. Midway
along the wharf is a boutique
brewery that caters for those
who revere the best kind of
cleansing ales. There are
residents here as well in low-
rise apartments set back from
the water on the city side.

Convention and Exhibition Centre ❻

Darling Drive, Darling Harbour. **Map**
3 C3. **Tel** 9282 5000. 🚉 Convention. ☐ daily (check in advance). 📷
🖥 ♿ **www**.darlingharbour.com

This purpose-built facility was
completed in 1988. Major
conventions are held in the
main auditorium. For trade
shows and exhibitions, the
Exhibition Centre's five halls
can be combined to form a
column-free area the size of
five sports fields. The roof is
supported by a system of sail-
like masts and rigging, which
reflects the maritime history
of Darling Harbour. Works of
art by such noted Australian
artists as Brett Whiteley and
John Olsen hang within.

Chinese Garden of Friendship ❼

Darling Harbour. **Map** 4 D3. **Tel** 9240
8500. 🚉 Paddy's Markets.
☐ 9:30am–5pm daily. 🌳 Good Fri,
25 Dec. 🎟 📷 🖥 ♿ limited.
www.chinesegardens.com.au

The Chinese Garden of
Friendship was built in 1984.
It is a tranquil refuge from the
city streets. The garden's design
was a gift to Sydney from its
Chinese sister city of Guangdong. The Dragon Wall is in
the lower section beside the
lake. It has glazed carvings of
two dragons, one representing
Guangdong province and the
other the state of New South
Wales. In the centre of the wall,
a carved pearl, symbolizing
prosperity, is lifted by the

**The view from Pyrmont Bridge
looking up towards the city centre**

waves. The lake is covered with lotus and water lilies for much of the year and a rock monster guards against evil. On the other side of the lake is the Twin Pavilion. Waratahs (New South Wales's floral symbol) and flowering apricots are carved into its woodwork, and also grow at its base.

A tea house, found at the top of the stairs in the Tea House Courtyard, serves traditional Chinese tea and cakes.

Chinatown ⑧

Dixon St Plaza, Sydney **Map** 4 D4. 🚇 *Paddy's Markets.*

Originally concentrated around Dixon and Hay Streets, Chinatown is expanding to fill Sydney's Haymarket area, stretching west to Harris Street, south to Broadway and east to Castlereagh Street. It is close to the Sydney Entertainment Centre, where some of the world's best-known rock and pop stars perform and indoor sporting events are held.

For years, Chinatown was a run-down district at the edge of the city's produce markets where many Chinese migrants worked. Today Dixon Street, its main thoroughfare, has been

Chinatown entrance, Dixon Street

spruced up, with street lanterns and archways, and a new wave of Asian migrants fills the now upmarket restaurants.

Chinatown is a distinctive area with greengrocers, traditional herbalists and butchers' shops with wind-dried ducks hanging in their windows. Jewellers, clothing shops and confectioners fill the arcades. There are also two Chinese-language cinema complexes.

Capitol Theatre ⑨

13 Campbell St, Haymarket. **Map** 4 E4. **Tel** 9320 5000. 🚌 *George St routes.* 🎭 *performances only.* **Box office** 🕘 *9am–5pm Mon–Fri.* ♿ **www.** capitoltheatre.com.au

In the mid-1800s a cattle and corn market was situated here. It became Paddy's Market Bazaar with sideshows and an

outdoor theatre, which were in turn replaced by a circus with a floodable ring. The present building was erected in the 1920s as a luxurious picture palace. In the mid-1990s, the cinema was restored, in keeping with the original theme of a Florentine Garden.

The Capitol reopened as a lyric theatre with productions being staged beneath its Mediterranean-blue ceiling studded with twinkling stars reflecting the southern sky.

The lavishly renovated Capitol Theatre in Chinatown

Paddy's Markets ⑩

Cnr Thomas & Hay sts, Haymarket. **Map** 4 D4. **Tel** 1300 361 589. 🚇 *Paddy's Markets.* 🕘 *9am–5pm Wed–Sun & pub. hols.* 🔒 *25 Apr, 25 Dec.* 📷 ♿ *See also Shops and Markets p203.* www.paddysmarkets.com.au

Haymarket, in Chinatown, is home to Paddy's Markets, Sydney's oldest market. It has been in this area, on a number of sites, since 1869 (with only one five-year absence). The name's origin is uncertain, but is believed to have come from either the Chinese who originally supplied much of its produce, or the Irish, their main customers.

Once the shopping centre for the inner-city poor, Paddy's Markets is now an integral part of an ambitious development including residential apartments and the Market City Shopping Centre, with fashion outlet stores, an Asian food court and a cinema complex. However, the familiar clamour and chaotic bargain-hunting atmosphere of the original marketplace remain. Every weekend the market has up to 800 stalls selling everything from fresh produce to chickens, puppies, electrical products and leather goods.

Pavilion in the grounds of the Chinese Garden of Friendship

Powerhouse Museum ⑱

This former power station, completed in 1902 to provide power for Sydney's tramway system, was redesigned to cater for the needs of an interactive, hands-on museum. Revamped, the Powerhouse opened in 1988. The early collection was held in the Garden Palace where the 1879 international exhibition of invention and industry from around the world was held. Few exhibits survived the devastating 1882 fire, and today's huge and ever-expanding collection was gathered after this disaster. The building's monumental scale provides an ideal context for the epic sweep of ideas encompassed within: everything from the realm of space and technology to the decorative and domestic arts. The museum emphasizes Australian innovations and achievements, celebrating both the extraordinary and the everyday.

Silver cricket trophy

What's It Like to Live in Space?
Find out how astronauts live and work in space, and experience weightlessness in the zero gravity space lab.

Level 2

★ **Experimentations**
Explore the principles of temperature, pressure, electricity, magnetism, light, gravity, motion and chemistry in this exciting interactive exhibit.

Level 1

Thinkspace
This is a state-of-the-art digital studio for the exploration of sound and music projects.

Cyberworlds: Computers and Connections
These toy robots are part of an interactive exploration of the past, present and future of computers.

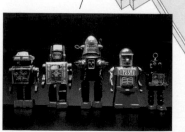

Ecologic shows the science behind global warming and what can be done to prevent it.

MUSEUM GUIDE

The museum is housed in two buildings: the former power-house and the Neville Wran building. There are over 20 exhibitions on four levels, descending from Level 4. The shop, entrance and temporary exhibits are on Level 3. Level 2 has thematic exhibits. Level 1 has experiments and displays on space, transport, computers.

VISITORS' CHECKLIST

500 Harris St, Ultimo. **Map** 4 D4.
Tel *9217 0111.* 449, 501.
Darling Harbour. Central.
Paddy's Markets. 10am–
5pm daily. 25 Dec.
www.powerhouse
museum.com

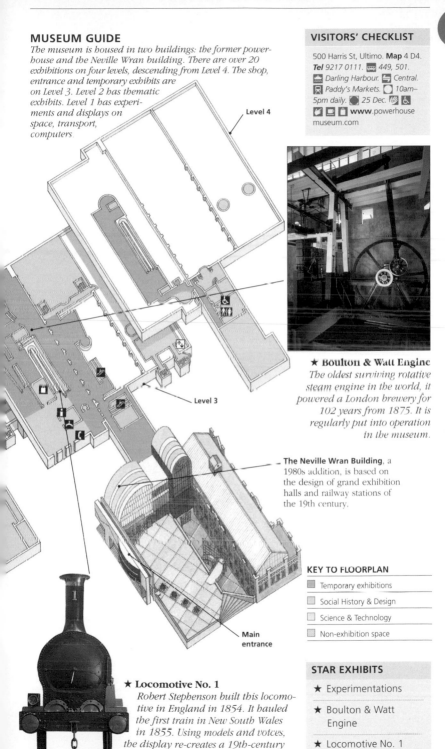

Level 4

Level 3

★ **Boulton & Watt Engine**
The oldest surviving rotative steam engine in the world, it powered a London brewery for 102 years from 1875. It is regularly put into operation in the museum.

The Neville Wran Building, a 1980s addition, is based on the design of grand exhibition halls and railway stations of the 19th century.

KEY TO FLOORPLAN

- Temporary exhibitions
- Social History & Design
- Science & Technology
- Non-exhibition space

Main entrance

★ **Locomotive No. 1**
Robert Stephenson built this locomotive in England in 1854. It hauled the first train in New South Wales in 1855. Using models and voices, the display re-creates a 19th-century day trip for a group of Sydneysiders.

STAR EXHIBITS

★ Experimentations

★ Boulton & Watt Engine

★ Locomotive No. 1

BOTANIC GARDEN AND THE DOMAIN

This tranquil part of Sydney can seem a world away from the bustle of the city centre. It is rich in the remnants of Sydney's convict and colonial past: the site of the first farm, and the boulevard-like Macquarie Street where the barracks, hospital, church and mint – bastions of civic power – are among the oldest surviving public buildings in Australia. This street continues to assert its dominance today as the home of the state government of New South Wales. The Domain, an open, grassy space, was originally set aside by the colony's first governor for his private use. Today it is a democratic place with joggers and touch footballers sidestepping picnickers. In January, during the Festival of Sydney, it hosts outdoor concerts with thousands of people enjoying fine music. The Botanic Garden, which with The Domain was the site of Australia's first park, is a haven where visitors can stroll around and enjoy the extensive collection of native and exotic flora.

Wooden angel, St James' Church

SIGHTS AT A GLANCE

Historic Streets and Buildings
Conservatorium of Music 2
Government House 3
Woolloomooloo Finger Wharf 6
State Library of NSW 9
Parliament House 10
Sydney Hospital 11
The Mint 12
Hyde Park Barracks 13

Museums and Galleries
Art Gallery of New South Wales pp108–11 7

Churches
St James' Church 14

Islands
Fort Denison 5

Monuments
Mrs Macquaries Chair 4

Parks and Gardens
Royal Botanic Garden pp104–5 1
The Domain 8

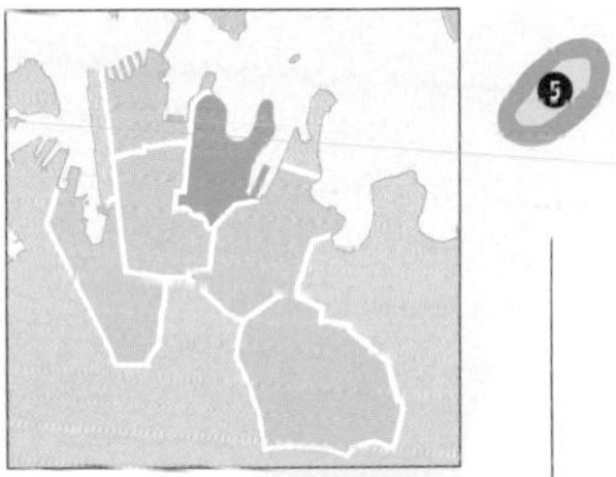

GETTING THERE
Visit on foot, if possible. St James and Martin Place train stations are near most of the sights. The 311 bus from Circular Quay runs near the Art Gallery of NSW and past the Woolloomooloo Finger Wharf. The Sydney Explorer also stops at several sights.

0 metres 500
0 yards 500

KEY
Royal Botanic Garden *See pp104–5*
CityRail station

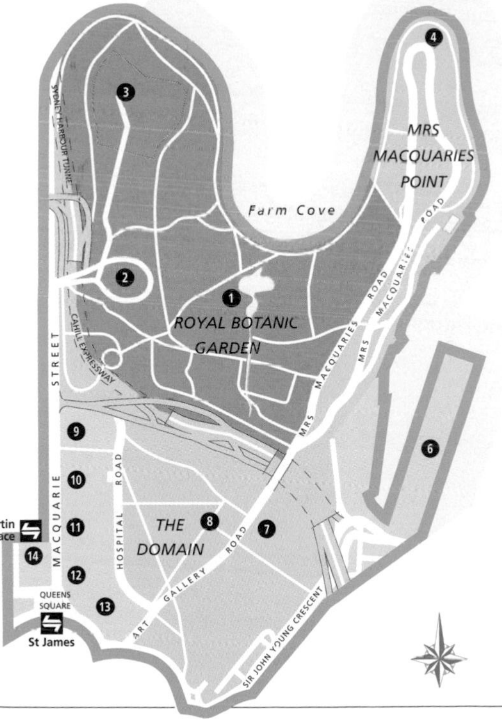

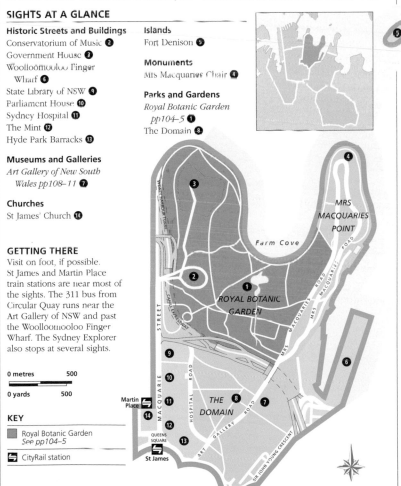

◁ Succulents and cacti from the Succulent Garden in the Royal Botanic Garden

Royal Botanic Garden ❶

Statue in the Botanic Garden

The Royal Botanic Garden, an oasis of 30 ha (74 acres) in the heart of the city, occupies a superb position, wrapped around Farm Cove at the harbour's edge. Established in 1816 as a series of pathways through shrubbery, it is the oldest scientific institution in the country and houses an outstanding collection of plants from Australia and overseas. A living museum, the garden is also the site of the first farm in the fledgling colony. Fountains, statues and monuments are today scattered throughout. Plant specimens collected by Joseph Banks on Captain James Cook's epic voyage along the east coast of Australia in 1770 are displayed in the National Herbarium of New South Wales, an important centre for research on Australian plants.

LOCATOR MAP
See Street Finder, maps 1 & 2

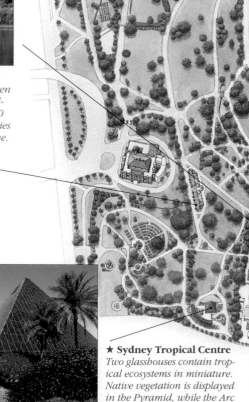

Government House (1897)

★ **Palm Grove**
Begun in 1862, this cool summer haven is one of the world's finest outdoor collections of palms. There are about 180 species. Borders planted with kaffir lilies make a colourful display in springtime.

★ **Herb Garden**
Herbs from around the world used for a wide variety of purposes – culinary, medicinal and aromatic – are on display here. A sensory fountain and a sundial modelled on the celestial sphere are also features.

★ **Sydney Tropical Centre**
Two glasshouses contain tropical ecosystems in miniature. Native vegetation is displayed in the Pyramid, while the Arc holds plants not found locally, commonly known as exotics.

Macquarie Wall
In 1810, work began on this 290-m- (950-ft-) long wall intended to separate the convict domain from the town's "respectable Class of Inhabitants". Only a small section remains standing today.

Choragic Monument *(1870)*
This replica of the marble monument of Lysicrates in Athens was sculpted in sandstone by Walter McGill.

0 metres	200
0 yards	200

Mrs Macquarie's Chair

Cadi Jam Ora, a bush tucker display, features native plants that would have grown on the site prior to colonial settlement.

★ Australia's First Farm
It is claimed that some Middle Garden oblong beds follow the direction of the first furrows ploughed in the colony

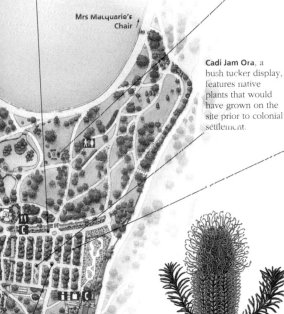

National Herbarium of New South Wales
Over one million dried plant specimens document biological diversity. The charting of new plants provides essential information for conservation decision making.

Wollemi Pine

STAR SIGHTS

- ★ Australia's First Farm
- ★ Herb Garden
- ★ Palm Grove
- ★ Sydney Tropical Centre

Conservatorium of Music ❷

Macquarie St. **Map** 1 C3. **Tel** 9351 1222. 🚌 Sydney Explorer, Circular Quay routes. ⬜ 9am–5pm Mon–Fri, 9am–4pm Sat (public areas only). ⬤ pub hols, Easter Sat, 24 Dec–2 Jan. 📷 ♿ 📷 by appt (phone 9351 1382). **Free concerts** 1:10pm Wed (donation).

When it was finished in 821, this striking castellated Colonial Gothic building was meant to be stables and servants' quarters for Government House, but construction of the latter was delayed for almost 25 years. That stables should be built in so grand a style, and at such great cost, brought forth cries of outrage and led to bitter arguments between the architect, Francis Greenway (see p114), and Governor Macquarie – and a decree that all future building plans be submitted to London.

Between 1908 and 1915, "Greenway's folly" underwent a dramatic transformation. A concert hall, roofed in grey slate, was built on the central courtyard and the building in its entirety was converted for the use of the new Sydney Conservatorium of Music.

The Conservatorium's facilities include a café which holds lunchtime concerts during the school term and an upper level with harbour views. "The Con" continues to be a training ground for future musicians as well as being a great place to visit.

The Conservatorium of Music at the edge of the Royal Botanic Garden

---

THE HISTORY OF COCKATOO ISLAND

HMS *Orlando* in dry dock at Cockatoo Island in the 1890s

Now deserted, the largest of the 12 Sydney Harbour islands was used to store grain from the 1830s. It was a penal establishment from the 1840s to 1908, with prisoners being put to work constructing dock facilities. The infamous bushranger "Captain Thunderbolt" made his escape from Cockatoo in 1863 by swimming across to the mainland. From the 1870s to the 1960s, Cockatoo Island was a thriving naval dockyard and shipyard, the hub of Australian industry.

Government House ❸

Macquarie St. **Map** 1 C2. **Tel** 9931 5222. 🚌 Sydney Explorer, Circular Quay routes. **House** ⬜ 10:30am–3pm Fri–Sun. ⬤ Good Fri, 25 Dec. **Garden** ⬜ 10am–4pm daily. 📷 ♿ 📷 every 30 mins. **www**.hht.net.au/museums

What used to be the official residence of the governor of New South Wales overlooks the harbour from within the Royal Botanic Garden, but the grandiose, somewhat sombre, turreted Gothic Revival edifice seems curiously out of place in its beautiful park setting.

It was built of local sandstone and cedar between 1837 and 1845. A fine collection of 19th- and early 20th-century furnishings is housed within.

Resting on the carved stone seat of Mrs Macquaries Chair

Mrs Macquaries Chair ❹

Mrs Macquaries Rd. **Map** 2 E2. 🚌 Sydney Explorer, 888. ♿

The scenic Mrs Macquaries Road winds alongside much of what is now the city's Royal Botanic Garden, from Farm Cove to Woolloomooloo Bay and back again. The road was built in 1816 at the instigation of Elizabeth Macquarie, wife of the Governor. In the same year, a stone bench, inscribed with details of the new road, was carved into the rock at the point where Mrs Macquarie would stop to admire the view on her daily constitutional.

Although today the outlook from this famous landmark is much changed, it is just as arresting, taking in the broad sweep of the harbour and foreshore with all its landmarks.

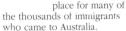

Historic Woolloomooloo Finger Wharf redevelopment, including apartments, restaurants and a hotel

Fort Denison ❺

Sydney Harbour. **Map** 2 F1. *Tel* 9247 5033. 🚢 *from Circular Quay.* 🔴 *25 Dec.* 📷 📷 📷 📷 *phone to book.* **www.**fortdenison.com.au

First named Rock Island, this prominent, rocky outcrop in Sydney Harbour was very quickly dubbed "Pinchgut". This was probably because of the meagre rations given to convicts who were confined there as punishment. It had a grim history of incarceration in the early years of the colony.

In 1796, convicted murderer Francis Morgan was hanged on the island in chains. His body was left to rot on the gallows for three years as a grisly warning to the other convicts.

Between 1855 and 1857, the Martello tower (the only one in Australia), gun battery and barracks that now occupy the island were built as part of Sydney's defences and the site was renamed after the governor of the time. The gun, still fired at 1pm each day, was an important aid for navigation, allowing mariners to set their ships' chronometers.

Today the island is a popular tourist spot, commanding spectacular views of Sydney

Harbour, the Opera House and Kirribilli. To explore Fort Denison, book a boat tour from Cadman Cottage.

Woolloomooloo Finger Wharf ❻

Cowper Wharf Roadway, Woolloomooloo. **Map** 2 E4. 🚌 *Sydney Explorer, 311.* 📷

This is the largest of several finger wharves that jut out into the harbour. The wharf, completed in 1914, was one of the points of embarkation for soldiers bound for both world wars. Following World War II, it was a landing place for many of the thousands of immigrants who came to Australia.

The wharf was the subject of public controversy in the late 1980s and early 1990s, when demolition plans were thwarted by conservation groups. Since then, this National Trust-listed maritime site has been redeveloped to include a hotel, lively restaurants and bars, and apartments.

Art Gallery of New South Wales ❼

See pp108–11.

Fort Denison in 1907

The Domain ❽

Art Gallery Rd. **Map** 1 C4. 🚌 *Sydney Explorer, 111, 411.* 📷 ♿

People who swarm to the January concerts and other Festival of Sydney events in The Domain (see p49) are part of a long-standing tradition.

This extensive public space has long been a rallying point for crowds of Sydneysiders whenever emotive issues of public importance have arisen, such as the attempt in 1916 to introduce military conscription or the dismissal of the elected federal government by the then governor-general in 1975.

From the 1890s, part of The Domain was also used as the Sydney version of "Speakers' Corner". Today, you are more likely to see joggers or office workers playing touch football in their lunch hours, or simply enjoying the shade.

A dramatic view of Sydney Opera House from Mrs Macquaries Chair

Art Gallery of New South Wales ❺

Established in 1874, the art gallery has occupied its present imposing building since 1897. Designed by the Colonial Architect WL Vernon, the gallery doubled in size following 1988 building extensions. Two equestrian bronzes – *The Offerings of Peace* and *The Offerings of War* – greet the visitor on entry. The gallery itself houses some of the finest works of art in Australia, with permanent collections of Australian, Aboriginal, European, Asian and contemporary art. The Yiribana Gallery is one of the largest in the world to exclusively exhibit Aboriginal and Torres Strait Islander art and culture. Free guided tours take place daily, covering Aboriginal art, highlights of the collection or major exhibitions.

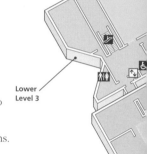

Lower
Level 3

Mars and the Vestal Virgin *(1638)*
This oil on canvas by Parisian painter Jacques Blanchard (1600–38) depicts Mars's encounter with a Vestal Virgin, who subsequently gave birth to Romulus and Remus, founders of Rome.

Sunbaker *(1937)*
Max Dupain's iconic, almost abstract, Australian photograph of hedonism and sun worship uses clean lines, strong light, and geometric form. The image's power lies in its simplicity.

Sofala *(1947)*
Russell Drysdale's visions of Australia show "ghost" towns laid waste by devastating natural forces such as drought.

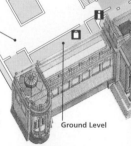

Ground Level

GALLERY GUIDE

There are five levels. The Ground Level and Lower Level 1 host temporary exhibitions. The Ground Level also showcases European and Australian works. The Contemporary Galleries on Lower Level 2 have the most comprehensive collection of contemporary art in the country. On Lower Level 3 is the Yiribana Aboriginal Gallery.

STAR EXHIBITS

★ The Golden Fleece by Tom Roberts

★ Pukumani Grave Posts

★ **Pukumani Grave Posts** *(1958)*
Carved by Tiwi artists of Melville Island (north of Australia), these magnificent funerary posts were specially commissioned for the art gallery.

Guardians, Tang Dynasty
These 7th-century Chinese figures are part of a collection highlighting different traditions, periods and cultures from the many countries of Asia.

Lower
Level 2

★ **The Golden Fleece** *(1894)*
Also known as Shearing at Newstead, *this work by Tom Roberts marks the coming of age of Australian Impressionist art.*

Lower
Level 1

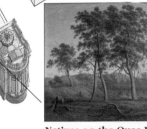

Natives on the Ouse River, Van Diemen's Land *(1838)*
English-Australian artist John Glover was dubbed the father of Australian landscape painting for his bright depictions of the Van Dieman's Land bush (now Tasmania).

The sandstone entrance was added in 1909.

KEY TO FLOORPLAN

- Australian Art
- European Art
- Asian Art
- 20th and 21st Century International Art
- Contemporary Art
- Domain Theatre
- Yiribana Aboriginal Gallery
- Temporary exhibition space
- Photography gallery
- Non-exhibition space

Exploring the Art Gallery's Collection

Although local works had been collected since 1875 the gallery did not seriously begin seeking Australian and non-British art until the 1920s, and not until the 1940s did it begin acquiring Aboriginal and Torres Strait Islander paintings. These contrasting collections are now its great strength. Major temporary exhibitions are also regularly staged, with the annual Archibald, Wynne and Sulman prizes being most controversial and highly entertaining.

Grace Cossington Smith's *The Curve of the Bridge* (1928–9)

AUSTRALIAN ART

Among the most important colonial works is John Glover's *Natives on the Ouse River, Van Diemen's Land* (1838), an image of doomed Tasmanian Aborigines.

The old wing holds paintings from the Heidelberg school of Australian Impressionism. Charles Conder's *Departure of the Orient – Circular Quay* (1888) and Tom Robert's *The Golden Fleece – Shearing at Newstead* (1894) hang alongside fine works by Frederick McCubbin and Arthur Streeton. Rupert Bunny's sensuous *Summer Time* (c.1907)

and *A Summer Morning* (c.1908), and George Lambert's heroic *Across the black soil plains* (1899), impress with their huge size and complex compositions.

Australia was slow to take up Modernism. *Implement blue* (1927) and *Western Australian Gum Blossom* (1928), both by Margaret Preston, are her most assertive of the 1920s. Sidney Nolan's works range from *Boy in Township* (1943) to *Burke* (c.1962), exploiting myths of early Australian history. There are fine holdings of William Dobell and Russell Drysdale, as well as important collections of Arthur Boyd, Fred Williams, Grace Cossington Smith and Brett Whiteley (*see p130*).

EUROPEAN ART

The scope of the scattered European collection ranges from the medieval to the modern. British art from the late 19th to the early 20th centuries forms an outstanding component.

Among the Old Masters are some significant Italian works that reflect Caravaggio's influence. There are also several notable works from the Renaissance in Sienese

Three Bathers, an Ernst Ludwig Kirchner painting from 1913

and Florentine styles. Hogarth, Turner and Joshua Reynolds are represented, as are Neo-Classical works. *The Visit of the Queen of Sheba to King Solomon* (1884–90) by Edward Poynter has been on display since 1892. Ford Madox Brown's *Chaucer at the Court of Edward III* (1845–51) is the most commanding work in the Pre-Raphaelite collection.

The Impressionists and Post-Impressionists, represented by late 1880s Pissarro and Monet, are housed in the newest gallery wing. Bonnard, Kandinsky, Braque and many other well-known European artists are also here. *Old Woman in Ermine* (1946) by Max Beckmann and *Three Bathers* (1913) by Ernst Ludwig Kirchner are strong examples of German Expressionism. The gallery's first Picasso, *Nude in a Rocking Chair* (1956), was purchased in 1981. Among distinguished sculptures is Henry Moore's *Reclining Figure: Angles* (1980), found resting by the side of the entrance.

PHOTOGRAPHY

Australian photography from 1975 to today, represented in all its various forms, is a major part of the collection. In recent years, however, the emphasis has been on building up a body of 19th-century Australian work in a range of early mediums. Nearly 3,000

Brett Whiteley's vivid *The Balcony (2)* from 1975

prints constitute this collection with pieces by Charles Kerry, Charles Bayliss and Harold Cazneaux, the latter a major figure of early 20th-century Pictorialism. Such international photographers as Muybridge, Robert Mapplethorpe and Man Ray are also represented here.

ASIAN ART

This collection is one of the finest in Australia. Chinese art is represented by a chronological presentation of works from the pre-Shang dynasty (c.1600–1027 BC) to the 20th century. The Ming porcelains, earthenware funerary pieces *(mingqi)* and the sculptures deserve close attention.

The Japanese painting collection contains fine examples by major artists of the Edo period (1615–1867). The Indian and Southeast Asian holdings consist of lacquer, ceramics and sculptures, with painting displays changing regularly.

PRINTS AND DRAWINGS

As so many of the works in this collection are fragile, the exhibitions are changed frequently. The collection represents the European tradition from the High Renaissance to the 19th and 20th centuries, with work by Rembrandt, Constable, William Blake and Edvard Munch. A strong bias towards Sydney artists from the past 100 years has resulted in a fine gathering of work by Thea Proctor, Norman and Lionel Lindsay and Lloyd Rees.

Egon Schiele's *Poster for the Vienna Secession* (1918)

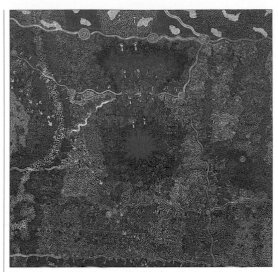

Warlugulong by Clifford Possum Tjapaltjarri and Tim Leura Tjapaltjarri

CONTEMPORARY ART

The significance of the art of our time is reflected in the collection of recent work by international and Australian artists, only a fraction of which can be displayed at any time. The collection highlights the artistic themes that have been central to art practice of the last three decades. Works by Australian artists, such as *Pataphysical Man* (Imants Tillers, 1984) and *Suspended Stone Circle II* (Ken Unsworth, 1988), are on display alongside pieces by notable international artists of the calibre of Cindy Sherman, Yves Klein, Philip Guston and Anselm Kiefer. The gallery also has a contemporary project space that features temporary experimental installations.

YIRIBANA GALLERY

Devoted to the exhibition of Aboriginal and Torres Strait Islander artworks bought since the 1940s, traditional bark paintings hang alongside innovative works from both desert and urban areas, including stone and wood carvings, ceramics and weavings. The ability of contemporary artists to apply traditional ceremonial body and sand painting styles to new media forms, and the endurance of "Aboriginality", are repeatedly demonstrated. The significant early purchases are mainly natural pigment paintings on bark and card, often containing a simple, figurative motif of everyday life. Also of interest are two sandstone carvings by Queenslanders Linda Craigie and Nora Nathan, the only women artists in the collection until 1985. Topographical, geographical and cultural mapping of the land is displayed in a number of intricate landscapes. The qualities and forms of the natural world, and the actions and tracks of Ancestral Beings, are coded within the images. These paintings are maps of Ancestral journeys and events. The bark painting *Three Mimis Dancing* (1964) by Samuel Wagbara examines the habitation of the land by Spirits and the recurrence of the Creation Cycles.

Pukumani Grave Posts Melville Island (1958) is a solemn ceremonial work dealing with death, while the eminent Emily Kame Kngwarreye honours the land from which she comes. The canvases of her intricate dot paintings, created using new tools and technology, appear to move and shimmer, telling stories of the animals and food to be found there.

Mosaic replica of the Tasman Map in the State Library of NSW

The newest section, a modern structure facing Macquarie St, houses the State Reference Library and a gourmet café.

Outside the library, also facing Macquarie Street, is a statue of explorer Matthew Flinders. Behind him on the windowsill is a statue of his co-voyager, his faithful cat, Trim.

Parliament House ⑩

Macquarie St. **Map** 4 F1. **Tel** 9230 2111. 🚌 Sydney Explorer, Elizabeth St routes. 🚆 Martin Place. 📋 book in advance 9230 3444. 🕙 9am–5pm Mon–Fri. ⬤ most public hols. ♿ www.parliament.nsw.gov.au

The central section of this building, which houses the State Parliament, is part of the original Sydney Hospital built from 1811–16. It has been a seat of government since 1829 when the newly appointed Legislative Council first held meetings here. The building was extended twice during the 19th century and again during the 1970s and 1980s. The current building contains the chambers for both houses of state parliament, as well as parliamentary offices.

State Library of NSW ⑨

Macquarie St. **Map** 4 F1. **Tel** 9273 1414. 🚌 Sydney Explorer, Elizabeth St routes. 🕙 9am–8pm Mon–Thu, 9am–5pm Fri, 10am–5pm Sat & Sun. ⬤ pub hols; Mitchell Library closed Sun. 💻 🏛 ♿ 📋 www.sl.nsw.gov.au

The State Library is housed in two separate buildings connected by a passageway and a glass bridge. The older building, the Mitchell Library wing (1910), is a majestic sandstone edifice facing the Royal Botanic Garden. Huge stone columns supporting a vaulted

ceiling frame the impressive vestibule. On the vestibule floor is a mosaic replica of an old map illustrating the two voyages made to Australia by Dutch navigator Abel Tasman in the 1640s. The original Tasman Map is held in the Mitchell Library as part of its large collection of historic Australian paintings, books, documents and pictorial records.

The Mitchell wing's vast reading room, with its huge skylight and oak panelling, is just beyond the main vestibule.

Malby's celestial globe, Parliament House

MACQUARIE STREET

Described in the 1860s as one of the gloomiest streets in Sydney, this could now claim to be the most elegant. Open on the northeastern side to the harbour breezes and the greenery of The Domain, a leisurely walk down this tree-lined street is one of the most pleasurable ways to view the architectural heritage of Sydney.

The new wing of the library was built in 1988 and connected to the old section by a glass walkway.

The Mitchell Library wing's portico (1906) has Ionic columns.

The Legislative Assembly, the lower house of state parliament, is furnished in the traditional green of the British House of Commons.

Parliament House was once the convict-built Rum Hospital's northern wing.

STATE LIBRARY OF NSW (1906–41)   **PARLIAMENT HOUSE** (1811–16)

Parliamentary memorabilia is on view in the Jubilee Room, as are displays showing Parliament House's development and the legislative history of New South Wales.

The corrugated iron building with a cast-iron façade tacked on at the southern end was a pre-fabricated kit from England. It was originally intended as a chapel for the gold fields, but was diverted from this purpose and sent to Sydney. In 1856, this dismantled kit became the chamber for the new Legislative Council. Its packing cases were used to line this chamber; the rough timber is still on view inside.

Stained glass at Sydney Hospital

the Rum Hospital because the builders were paid by being allowed to import rum for resale. Both the north and south wings of the Rum Hospital survive as Parliament House and the Sydney Mint. The central wing, which was in danger of collapsing, was demolished in 1879 and the new hospital, which still functions today, was completed in 1894. The Classical Revival building boasts a Baroque staircase and elegant floral stained-glass windows in its entrance hall.

Florence Nightingale approved the design of the 1867 nurses' wing. In the inner courtyard, there is a brightly coloured Art Deco fountain (1907).

At the front of the hospital sits *Il Porcellino*, a brass boar. It is a copy of a 17th-century fountain in Florence's Mercato Nuovo. Donated in 1968 by an Italian woman whose relatives had worked at the hospital, the statue is an enduring symbol of the close friendship between Italy and Australia.

Like his Florentine counterpart, *Il Porcellino* is supposed to bring good luck to all those who rub his snout. All coins tossed in the shallow pool at his feet for luck and fortune are collected for the hospital.

Sydney Hospital ⓫

Macquarie St. **Map** 1 C4.
Tel *9382 7111.* Sydney Explorer, Elizabeth St routes. ◯ *daily.* ◻ *for tours.* ◙ ♿ ◪ *must be booked in advance by telephone.*

This imposing collection of Victorian sandstone buildings stands on the site of what was once the central section of the original convict-built Sydney Hospital – known as

Il Porcellino, **the brass boar in front of Sydney Hospital**

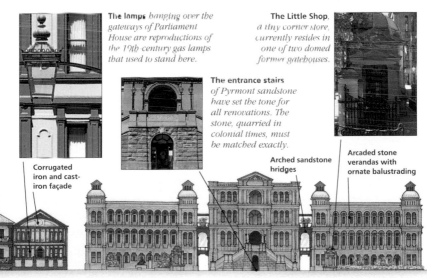

The lamps *hanging over the gateways of Parliament House are reproductions of the 19th-century gas lamps that used to stand here.*

The Little Shop, *a tiny corner store, currently resides in one of two domed former gatehouses.*

The entrance stairs *of Pyrmont sandstone have set the tone for all renovations. The stone, quarried in colonial times, must be matched exactly.*

Corrugated iron and cast-iron façade

Arched sandstone bridges

Arcaded stone verandas with ornate balustrading

SYDNEY HOSPITAL *(1868–94)*

The Mint ⑫

10 Macquarie St. **Map** 1 C5.
Tel *8239 2288.* 🚌 *Sydney Explorer,*
Elizabeth St routes. 🕙 *9am–5pm*
Mon–Fri. ⚫ *Good Fri, 25 Dec.*
📷 🅰 ⚫ *ground floor only.*
www.hht.net.au/museums

The gold rushes of the mid-19th century transformed colonial Australia. The Sydney Mint opened in the 1816 Rum Hospital's south wing in 1854 to turn recently discovered gold into bullion and currency.

It was the first branch of the Royal Mint to be established outside London. The Mint was closed in 1927 as it was no longer competitive with the Melbourne and Perth Mints. The Georgian building went into its own decline after it was converted into government offices. In the 1950s, the front courtyard was even used as a car park. In 1982, it opened as a branch of the Powerhouse Museum (*see pp100–101*), but the collection moved to the main museum in Harris Street.

This building is now the head office of the Historic Houses Trust of NSW and you can wander through the front of the building, or view the small historical display near the entrance.

Replica convict hammocks on the third floor of Hyde Park Barracks

FRANCIS GREENWAY, CONVICT ARCHITECT

Until the 1990s, Australian A$10 notes bore the portrait of the early colonial architect Francis Greenway, the only currency in the world to pay tribute to a convicted forger. Greenway was transported to Sydney in 1814 to serve 14 years for his crime. Under the patronage of Governor Macquarie, who appointed him Civil Architect in 1816, Greenway designed more than 40 buildings, of which only 11 remain today. He received a full pardon in 1819, but soon fell out of favour as he persisted in charging large fees while still on a government salary. Greenway died in poverty in 1837.

Francis Greenway (1777–1837)

Hyde Park Barracks Museum ⑬

Queens Square, Macquarie St. **Map** 1 C5. ***Tel*** *8239 2311.* 🚇 *St James, Martin Place.* 🕙 *9:30am–5pm daily.* ⚫ *Good Fri, 25 Dec.* 📷 📷 ⚫ *level one only.* 🎧 *on request.* **www.hht.net.au/museums**

Described by Governor Macquarie as "spacious" and "well-aired", the beautifully proportioned barracks are the work of Francis Greenway and are considered his masterpiece. They were completed in 1819

MACQUARIE STREET

Fine examples of Francis Greenway's Georgian style are within an easy walk of one another at the Hyde Park end of Macquarie Street. The brick and sandstone of Hyde Park Barracks, St James Church and the Old Supreme Court Building form a harmonious group on the site the governor envisaged as the city's civic centre.

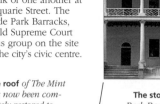

The Mint, *like its twin, Parliament House, has an unusual double-colonnaded, two-storeyed veranda.*

The roof *of The Mint has now been completely restored to replicate the original wooden shingles in casuarina (she-oak).*

The stone wall, *of Hyde Park Barracks' northwest pavilion still bears the marks of the convicts' chisels.*

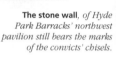

Hyde Park Barracks Café

THE MINT *(1816)*

by convict labour and designed to house 600 convicts who had previously been forced to find their own lodgings after their day's work. Subsequently, the building housed Irish orphans and then single female immigrants, before becoming courts and legal offices. Refurbished in 1990, it reopened as a museum with exhibits covering the the site and its occupants over the years.

The displays include a room reconstructed as convict quarters of the 1820s, as well as pictures, models and artifacts relating to this period of Australian history. Many of the objects recovered during archaeological digs at the site and now on display had been dragged away by rats to their nests; the scavenging rodents are acknowledged as valuable agents of preservation.

The Greenway Gallery on the first floor holds temporary exhibitions on history, ideas and culture. From the Barracks Café, which incorporates the original confinement cell area, the visitor can enjoy refreshment, gazing out over the now serene courtyard, once the scene of brutal convict floggings.

Detail from the Children's Chapel mural in the St James' Church crypt

St James' Church ⑭

173 King St. **Map** 1 B5. **Tel** 8227 1300.
🚇 St James, Martin Place. 🕙 10am–4pm Mon–Fri, 9am 1pm Sat, 7:30am–4pm Sun. **Free concerts** Mar–Dec Wed 1:15pm. www.sjks.org.au

This fine Georgian building, constructed with convict made bricks, was designed as a courthouse in 1819. The architect, Francis Greenway, was forced to convert it into a church in 1820, when plans to build a grand cathedral on George Street were abandoned.

Greenway unhappy about the change, designed a simple yet elegant church. Consecrated in 1824 by Samuel Marsden, the infamous "flogging parson", it is Sydney's oldest church. Many additions have been carried out, including designs by John Verge in which the pulpit faced towards high-rent pews, while convicts and the military sat behind the preacher where the service would have been inaudible. A Children's Chapel was added in 1930.

Prominent members of early 19th-century society, many of whom died violently, are commemorated in marble tablets. These tell the full and bloody stories of luckless explorers and shipwreck victims, among other untimely demises.

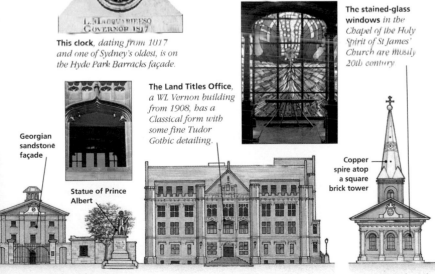

This clock, dating from 1817 and one of Sydney's oldest, is on the Hyde Park Barracks façade.

The Land Titles Office, a WL Vernon building from 1908, has a Classical form with some fine Tudor Gothic detailing.

The stained-glass windows in the Chapel of the Holy Spirit of St James' Church are mostly 20th century

Georgian sandstone façade

Statue of Prince Albert

Copper spire atop a square brick tower

HYDE PARK BARRACKS (1817–19) **LAND TITLES OFFICE** (1908–13) **ST JAMES'** (1820)

KINGS CROSS AND DARLINGHURST

S ituated on the eastern fringe of the city, Kings Cross, known as "The Cross", and Darlinghurst are a couple of Sydney celebrities. Their allure is tarnished – or enhanced, perhaps – by trails of scandal and corruption. Kings Cross, particularly, is still regarded as a hotbed of vice; both areas still bear the taint of 1920s gangland associations. In fact, both are now cosmopolitan areas – among the most densely populated parts of

Façade detail, Del Rio (see p119)

Sydney, famed as much for their street life and thriving café culture as for their unsavoury features. Kings Cross exudes a welcome breath of bohemia, in spite of the sleaze of Darlinghurst Road and the flaunting of its red light district. Darlinghurst comes brilliantly into its own every March, when the flamboyant Gay and Lesbian Mardi Gras parade, supported by huge crowds of spectators, makes its triumphant way along Oxford Street.

SIGHTS AT A GLANCE

Historic Streets and Buildings
Victoria Street ❷
Elizabeth Bay House ❸
Old Gaol, Darlinghurst ❻
Darlinghurst Court House ❼

Museums and Galleries
Sydney Jewish Museum ❺

Parks and Gardens
Beare Park ❹

Monuments
El Alamein Fountain ❶

GETTING THERE
Kings Cross railway station serves the area. Bus number 311 travels through Kings Cross and Darlinghurst, while the 324, 325 and 389 are also useful. Buses 378, 380 and 382 travel along Oxford Street.

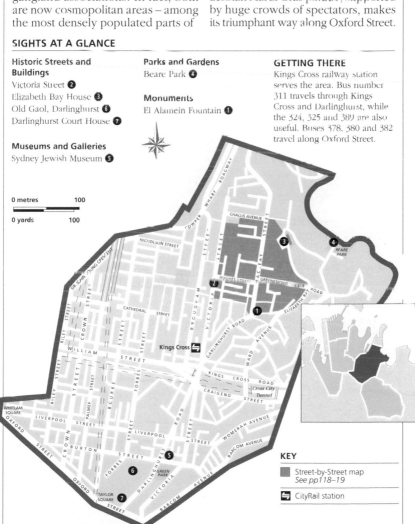

0 metres 100
0 yards 100

KEY

Street-by-Street map
See pp118–19

CityRail station

Street-by-Street: Potts Point

Beare Park fountain detail

The substantial Victorian houses filling the streets of this old suburb are excellent examples of the 19th-century concern with architectural harmony. New building projects were designed to enhance rather than contradict the surrounding buildings and general streetscape. Monumental structures and fine details of moulded stuccoed parapets, cornices and friezes, even the spandrels in herringbone pattern, are all integral parts of a grand suburban plan. (This plan included an 1831 order that all houses cost at least £1,000.) Cool and dark verandas extend the street's green canopy of shade, leaving an impression of cool drinks enjoyed on hot summer days in fine Victorian style.

The McElhone Stairs were preceded by a wooden ladder that linked Woolloomooloo Hill, as Kings Cross was known, to the estate far below.

Horderns Stairs

These villas, from the Georgian and Victorian eras, can be broadly labelled as Classical Revival and are fronted by leafy gardens.

★ Victoria Street
In 1972–4, residents of this historic street fought a sometimes violent battle against developers wanting to build high-rise office towers, motels and blocks of flats ❷

Kings Cross Station

Werrington, a mostly serious and streamlined building, also has flamboyant Art Deco detailing which is now subdued under brown paint.

STAR SIGHTS

★ Victoria Street

★ Elizabeth Bay House

Tusculum Villa was just one of a number of 1830s houses subject to "villa conditions". All had to face Government House, be of a high monetary value and be built within three years.

Challis Avenue is a fine and shady complement to nearby Victoria Street. This Romanesque group of terrace houses has an unusual façade, with arches fronting deep verandas and a grand ground-floor colonnade.

LOCATOR MAP
See Street Finder, map 2

Rockwall, a symmetrical and compact Regency villa, was built to the designs of the architect John Verge *(see p120)* in 1830–7.

Del Rio is a finely detailed high-rise apartment block. It clearly exhibits the Spanish Mission influence that filtered through from California in the first quarter of the 20th century.

Landmark Hotel

★ Elizabeth Bay House
A contemporary exclaimed over the beauty of the 1830s garden. "trees from Rio, the West Indies, the East Indies, China ... the bulbs from the Cape are splendid" ❸

The Arthur McElhone Reserve

Art Deco Birtley Towers

0 metres 50

0 yards 50

KEY

– – – Suggested route

Elizabeth Bay was part of the original land grant to Alexander Macleay *(see p120)*. He created a botanist's paradise with ornamental ponds, quaint grottoes and promenades winding all the way down to the harbour.

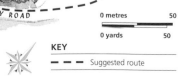

El Alamein Fountain, commemorating the World War II battle

El Alamein Fountain ❶

Fitzroy Gardens, Macleay St, Potts Point. **Map** 2 E5. 🚌 311.

This dandelion of a fountain in the heart of the Kings Cross district has a reputation for working so spasmodically that passers-by often murmur facetiously, "He loves me, he loves me not." Built in 1961, it commemorates the Australian army's role in the siege of Tobruk, Libya, and the battle of El Alamein in Egypt during World War II. At night, when it is brilliantly lit, the fountain looks surprisingly ethereal.

Victoria Street ❷

Potts Point. **Map** 5 B2. 🚌 311, 324, 325.

At the Potts Point end, this street of 19th-century ter- race houses, interspersed with a few incongruous-looking high-rise blocks, is, by inner-city standards, almost a boulevard. This gracious street was once at the centre of a bitter conservation struggle, one which almost certainly cost a prominent heritage campaigner's life.

In the early 1970s, many residents, backed by the "green bans" *(see p31)* put in place by the Builders' Labourers' Federation of New South Wales, fought to prevent demolition of old buildings for high-rise

development. Juanita Nielsen, publisher of a local newspaper and heiress, vigorously took up the conservation battle. On 4 July 1975, she disappeared without trace. A subsequent inquest into her disappearance returned an open verdict.

As a result of the actions of the union and residents, most of Victoria Street's superb old buildings still stand. Ironically, they are now occupied not by the low-income residents who fought to save them, but by the well-off professionals who eventually displaced them.

Elizabeth Bay House ❸

7 Onslow Ave, Elizabeth Bay. **Map** 2 F5. *Tel* 9356 3022. 🚌 *Sydney Explorer, 311.* ⏰ *9:30am–4pm Fri–Sun.* ⛔ *Good Fri, 25 Dec.* 🎟️ 📷 www.hht.net.au/museums

Elizabeth Bay House *(see pp24–5)* has the finest colonial interior on display in Australia. It is a potent expression of how the 1840s depression cut short the 1830s prosperous optimism. Designed in the fashionable Greek Revival style by John Verge, it was built for Colonial Secretary Alex- ander Macleay, from 1835–9. The domed oval saloon with its cantilevered staircase is recognized as Verge's masterpiece. The exterior is less satisfactory, as the intended colonnade and portico were not finished owing to a crisis in Macleay's financial affairs.

Juanita Nielsen

The present portico dates from 1893. The interior is furnished to reflect Macleay's occupancy from 1839–45, and is based on inventories drawn up in 1845 for the transfer of the house to Macleay's son, William Sharp. He took the house in return for payment of his father's debts, leading to a rift never to be resolved.

Macleay's original 22-hectare (54-acre) land grant was sub-divided for flats and villas from the 1880s to 1927. In the 1940s, the house itself was divided into 15 flats. In 1942, the artist Donald Friend, while standing on the balcony of his flat – the former morning room – saw the ferry *Kuttabul* hit by a torpedo from a Japanese midget submarine.

The house was restored and opened as a museum in 1977.

The sweeping staircase under the oval dome, Elizabeth Bay House

Beare Park ❹

Ithaca Rd, Elizabeth Bay. **Map** 2 F5. 🚌 311, 350.

Originally a part of the Macleay Estate, Beare Park is now encircled by a jumble of apartment blocks. A refuge from hectic Kings Cross, it is one of only a handful of parks serving a densely populated area. In the shape of a natural amphitheatre, the park puts Elizabeth Bay on glorious view.

The family home of JC Williamson, a famous theatrical entrepreneur who came to Australia from America in the 1870s, formerly stood at the eastern extremity of the park.

Star of David in the lobby of the Sydney Jewish Museum

Sydney Jewish Museum [5]

148 Darlinghurst Rd, Darlinghurst. **Map** 5 B2. ***Tel*** *9360 7999.* 🚌 *Sydney Explorer, Bondi & Bay Explorer, 311, 389.* 🕒 *10am–4pm Sun–Thu, 10am–2pm Fri.* ⛔ *Sat, Jewish hols.* 👂 ♿ ☞ 🛍 **www**.sydneyjewishmuseum.com.au

Sixteen Jewish convicts were on the First Fleet and many more were to be transported before the end of the convict era. As with other convicts, most would endure and some would thrive, seizing all the opportunities the colony had to offer for those wishing to make something of themselves.

The Sydney Jewish Museum relates stories of Australian Jewry within the context of the Holocaust. The ground floor display explores present-day Jewish traditions and culture within Australia. Ascending the stairs to mezzanine levels 1–6, the visitor passes through chronological and thematic exhibitions which unravel the history of the Holocaust.

From Hitler's rise to power and *Kristallnacht*, through the evacuation of the ghettos and the Final Solution, to the ultimate liberation of the infamous death camps and Nuremberg Trials, the harrowing events are graphically documented. This horrific period is recalled using photographs and relics, some exhumed from mass graves, as well as audiovisual exhibits and oral testimonies.

Holocaust survivors act as volunteer guides. Their presence, bearing witness to the recorded events, lends considerable power and moving authenticity to the exhibits.

Old Gaol, Darlinghurst [6]

Cnr Burton & Forbes Sts, Darlinghurst. **Map** 5 A2. ***Tel*** *9339 8744.* 🚌 *333, 378, 380, 389.* 🕒 *9am–5pm Mon–Fri.* ⛔ *public hols.* 📷 ♿

Originally known as the Woolloomooloo Stockade and later as Darlinghurst Gaol, this complex is now part the National Art School. It was constructed over a 20-year period from 1822.

Surrounded by walls almost 7 m (23 ft) high, the cell blocks radiate from a central roundhouse. The jail is built of stone quarried on the site by convicts which was then chiselled by them into blocks.

No fewer than 67 people were executed here between 1841 and 1908. Perhaps the most notorious hangman was Alexander "The Strangler" Green, after whom Green Park, outside the jail, is thought to have been named. Green lived near the park until public hostility forced him to live in relative safety inside the jail.

Some of Australia's most noted artists, including Frank Hodgkinson, Jon Molvig and William Dobell, trained or taught at the art school which was established here in 1921.

The former Governor's house, Old Gaol, Darlinghurst

Darlinghurst Court House [7]

Forbes St, Darlinghurst. **Map** 5 A2. ***Tel*** *9368 2947.* 🚌 *333, 378, 380.* 🕒 *Feb–Dec: 10am–4pm Mon–Fri & Sun.* ⛔ *mid-Dec–Jan, public hols.* ♿ ☞

Abutting the grim old jail, to which it is connected by underground passages, and facing tawdry Taylor Square, this unlikely gem of Greek Revival architecture was begun in 1835 by Colonial Architect Mortimer Lewis. He was only responsible for the central block of the main building with its splendid six-columned Doric portico with fine Greek embellishments. The balancing side wings were added in the 1880s.

The court house is still used by the state's Supreme Court mainly for criminal cases, and these are open to the public.

Beare Park, a quiet inner-city park with harbour views

PADDINGTON

Paddington is justly celebrated for its handsome terraces, but this "village in the city", as it is often dubbed, is also famed for its interesting speciality shops full of oddities and collectables, fine restaurants, small hotels, fashionable art galleries and antique dealers' shops. Paddington boasts a lively street culture, especially on Saturdays when people from far and wide flock to the famous weekly Paddington Markets, spilling out into the streets, pubs and cafés of the surrounding area. Stretching from the Victoria Barracks at its western end, along Oxford Street to the green haven of Centennial Park, Paddington slopes away

Clock tower on Paddington Town Hall

from this bustling central thoroughfare into the narrow lanes and elegant, leafy streets. The suburb has undergone a series of quite radical transformations. The first Paddington was built in the 1830s as a Georgian weekend retreat for the moneyed class. These gracious homes had a short life, before being knocked down and subdivided. The terraces succeeding them fell into ruin by the 1920s, but are now admired as finely restored Victorian homes with their distinctive wrought-iron "lace" verandas. The glimpses of harbour found in the quiet streets make Paddington one of Sydney's most sought-after residential areas.

SIGHTS AT A GLANCE

Historic Streets and Buildings
Paddington Street ❶
The Entertainment Quarter ❷
Five Ways ❹
Juniper Hall ❺
Paddington Town Hall ❻
Paddington Village ❼
Victoria Barracks ❽

Parks and Gardens
Centennial Park ❾

Markets
Paddington Markets ❸

GETTING THERE
The best way to travel to and around this area is by bus. Buses 378, 380 and 382 run along Oxford Street on their way between the city and beach suburbs, while bus 389 cuts through the back streets.

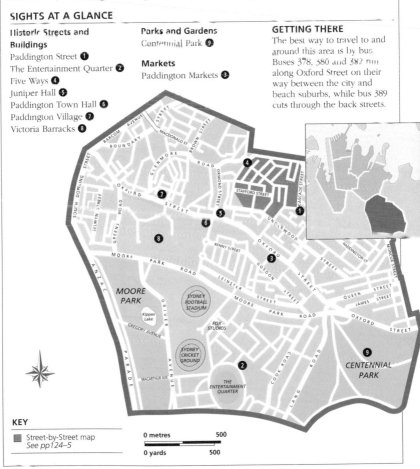

KEY

▪ Street-by-Street map
See pp124–5

0 metres   500

0 yards   500

◁ The front entrance to a lovingly restored Victorian terrace house in Paddington

Street-by-Street: Paddington

Paddington began to flourish in the 1840s, when the decision was made to build the Victoria Barracks. At the time much of it was "the most wild looking place… barren sandhills with patches of scrub, hills and hollows galore". The area began to fill rapidly, as owner builders bought into the area and built short rows of terrace houses, many extremely narrow

Victorian finial in Union Street

because of the lack of building regulations. After the Depression, most of Paddington was threatened with demolition, but was saved and restored by the large influx of postwar migrants.

★ Five Ways
This shopping hub was established in the late 19th century on the busy Glenmore roadway trodden out by bullocks ❹

Duxford Street's terrace houses in toning pale shads constitute an ideal of town planning: the Victorians preferred houses in a row to have a pleasingly uniform aspect.

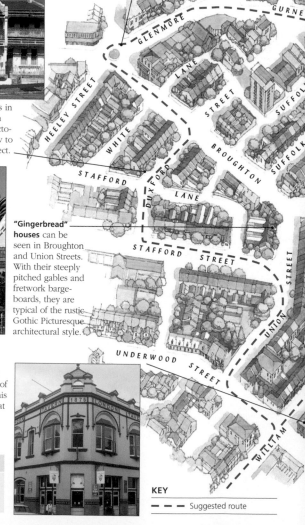

"Gingerbread" houses can be seen in Broughton and Union Streets. With their steeply pitched gables and fretwork bargeboards, they are typical of the rustic Gothic Picturesque architectural style. ❻

The London Tavern opened for business in 1875, making it the suburb's oldest pub. Like many of the pubs and delicatessens in this well-serviced suburb, it stands at the end of a row of terraces.

STAR SIGHTS

★ Five Ways

★ Paddington Street

KEY

- - - Suggested route

The Sherman Gallery is housed in a strikingly modern building. It is designed to hold Australian and international contemporary sculpture and paintings. Suitable access gates and a special in-house crane enable the movement of large-scale artworks, including textiles.

Paddington streets are a treasure chest of galleries, bars and restaurants.

LOCATOR MAP
See Street Finder, maps 5 & 6

Warwick, built in the 1860s, is a minor castle lying at the end of a row of humble terraces. Its turrets, battlements and assorted decorations, in a style somewhat fancifully described as "King Arthur", even adorn the garages at the rear.

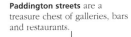

Windsor Street's terrace houses are, in some cases, a mere 4.5 m (15 ft) wide.

Street-making in Paddington's early days was often an expensive and complicated business. A cascade of water was dammed to build Cascade Street.

★ **Paddington Street**
Under the established plane trees, some of Paddington's finest Victorian terraces exemplify the building boom of 1860–90. Over 30 years, 3,800 houses were built in the suburb ❶

| 0 metres | 50 |
| 0 yards | 50 |

Paddington Street terrace house

Paddington Street ❶

Map 6 D3. 🚌 *333, 378, 380.*

With its huge plane trees shading the road and fine two-, three- and four-storey terrace houses on each side, Paddington Street is one of the oldest, loveliest, and at the same time most typical of the suburb's streets.

Paddington grew rapidly as a commuter suburb in the late 19th century and most of the terraces were built for renting to the city's artisans. They were cheaply decorated with iron lace (some of which had arrived in ships as ballast), as well as Grecian-style friezes, worked parapets, swagged urns, lions rampant, cornices, pilasters, scrolls and other fancy plastering. By the 1900s, these terraces had become unfashionable but in the 1960s, tastes changed again and Paddington experienced a renaissance.

Paddington Street now has a chic atmosphere where small art galleries operate out of quaint and grand shopfronts.

The Entertainment Quarter ❷

Lang Rd, Moore Park. **Tel** *8117 6700.* **Map** 5 C5. 🚌 *339, 355.* 🕙 *many retail shops open 10am– 10pm.* **www**.eqmoorepark.com.au

There's a vibrant atmosphere at the Entertainment Quarter, which is located next door to Fox Studios, which produced such well-known films as *The Matrix* and *Moulin Rouge.*

There are 16 cinema screens where you can watch the latest movies, and at the La Premiere cinema you can enjoy your movie with wine and cheese, sitting on comfort-able sofas. There are four live-entertainment venues which regularly feature the latest local and international acts. You can also enjoy bungy trampolining, bowling or seasonal ice-skating, and children love the three, well-designed playgrounds.

In addition to shops there are plenty of restaurants, cafés and bars offering a range of meals, drinks and snacks.

Every Wednesday and Saturday you can sample fresh produce at the Farmers Market or try a gourmet delicacy from one of the 40 stallholders. Many stalls offer free tastings. Sunday's market focuses on merchandise rather than food.

Shops are open until late, and there is a good selection – offering fashion, books and homewares. There is plenty of undercover parking and the complex is a pleasant stroll from Oxford Street.

Paddington Markets ❸

395 Oxford St. **Map** 6 D4. **Tel** *9331 2923.* 🚌 *333, 378, 380.* 🕙 *10am–4pm Sat.* 🔴 *25 Dec.* 📷 🚻 *See* **Shops and Markets** *p203.* **www**.paddingtonmarkets.com.au

This market, which began in 1973, takes place every Saturday, come rain or shine, in the grounds of Paddington Village Uniting Church and its neighbouring school. It is a place to meet and be seen as much as it is to shop. Stall-holders come from all over the world, and many young designers, hoping to launch their careers, display their wares. Among the offerings are jewellery, pottery, new and secondhand clothing and an array of other arts and crafts. Whatever you are looking for, you are likely to find it here, from designer bags and clothes or a tarot reading, to Oriental massages, bonsai trees and handmade soaps.

Five Ways ❹

Cnr Glenmore Rd & Heeley St. **Map** 5 C3. 🚌 *389.*

At this picturesque junction, a busy shopping hub develo-ped by the tramline that once ran to Bondi Beach. On the five corners stand Victorian and early 20th-century shops, one now a restaurant.

On another corner is the impressive Royal Hotel *(see p197),* built in 1888. This mixed Victorian and Classical Revival building, has a charac-teristic intricate cast-iron "lace" screen balcony offering stunning harbour views.

Juniper Hall ❺

250 Oxford St. **Map** 5 C3.**Tel** *9258 0123.* 🚌 *333, 378, 380.* 🔴 *to public.* **www**.nsw.nationaltrust.org.au

The emancipist gin distiller Robert Cooper built this superb example of Colonial Georgian architecture for his third wife, Sarah. He named it after the main ingredient of the gin that made his fortune.

Completed in 1824, it is the oldest building in Paddington still standing. It is probably also the largest and most extravagant. It had to be: he already had 14 children when he declared that Sarah would have the finest house in Sydney.

Juniper Hall was saved from demolition in the mid-1980s and restored in fine style. Now part of the National Trust, it is used as private office space.

Balcony of the Royal Hotel in the heart of Paddington

Paddington Town Hall

249 Oxford St (cnr Oatley Rd).
Map 5 C3. **Tel** 9265 9189. 🚌 *333, 378, 380.* ⬤ *10am–4pm Mon–Fri.*
⬤ *public hols.* 📷

The Paddington Town Hall was completed in 1891. An international competition which, in a spirit of Victorian self-confidence, was intended to produce the state's finest town hall, was won by local architect J.E. Kemp. His Classical Revival building, to which a clock tower was later added, still dominates the surrounding area, although it is no longer a centre of local government.

The lush green expanse of Centennial Park

The building now houses Chauvel Cinema, which is managed by the Australian Film Institute, Paddington Library, and a large ballroom that is available for hire.

Paddington Town Hall

Paddington Village

Cnr Gipps & Shadforth Sts. **Map** 5 C3. 🚌 *333, 378, 380.*

Paddington began its life as a working-class suburb. The community comprised the carpenters, quarrymen and stonemasons who supervised the convict gangs that built Victoria Barracks in the 1840s.

The artisans and their families occupied a tight huddle of spartan houses, a few of which still remain, crowded into the narrow streets nearby. Like the barracks, these dwellings and surrounding shops and hotels were built mainly of locally quarried stone.

Victoria Barracks

Oxford St. **Map** 5 B3. **Tel** 9339 3000. 🚌 *333, 378, 380.* **Museum** ⬤ *10am–12:30pm Thu, 10am–3:45pm Sun.* ⬤ *1 Jan, 25 & 26 Dec.* 📷 ♿ **Parade & tour:** *10am Thu.*

Victoria Barracks is the largest and best-preserved group of late Georgian architecture in Australia, covering almost 12 ha (29 acres). It is widely considered to be one of the best examples of a military barracks in the world.

Designed by the Colonial Engineer, Lieutenant Colonel George Barney, the barracks were built between 1841 and 1848 using local sandstone quarried by mainly convict labour. Originally intended to house 800 men, it has been in continuous military use ever since, and still operates as a centre of military planning, administration and command.

The main block is 225 m (740 ft) long and has symmetrical two-storey wings with cast-iron verandas flanking a central archway. The perimeter walls, which are designed to

The archway at the Oxford Street entrance to Victoria Barracks

repel surprise attacks, have foundations 10 m (40 ft) deep in places. In a former jail block, a museum traces New South Wales' military heritage.

Centennial Park

Map 6 F5. **Tel** 9339 6699. 🚌 *Clovelly, Coogee, Maroubra, Randwick, Bronte, City, Bondi Beach & Bondi Junction routes, Bondi Explorer Bus.* ⬤ *the park is open permanently; cars are permitted from sunrise* 🚻 ♿ *on request.* **www.** *centennialparklands.com.au*

Entering this 220-ha (544-acre) park through one of its sandstone and wrought-iron gates, the visitor may wonder how such an extensive and idyllic place has survived so close to the centre of the city.

Formerly a common, it was dedicated "to the enjoyment of the people of New South Wales forever" on 26 January 1888, the centenary of the foundation of the colony. On 1 January 1901, more than 100,000 people gathered here to witness the birth of the Commonwealth of Australia with the proclamation of the Federation of Australia. The striking Federation Pavilion marks the site of this event.

Today picnickers, painters, runners, horse riders, cyclists and in-line skaters enjoy this vast recreation area.

Once the source of Sydney's water supply, the swamps are now home to many waterbirds. Within the park are ornamental ponds, cultivated gardens, an Avenue of Palms, a sports ground and a café (*see p194*).

FURTHER AFIELD

Beyond the inner city, numerous places vie for the visitor's attention. Around the harbour foreshores are picturesque suburbs, secluded beaches, scenic outlooks and cultural and historic sights. Taronga Zoo is worth a visit as much for its incomparable setting as for its birds and animals. Manly, stretching between harbour and ocean, is the

Mr and Mrs Luna Park

city's northern playground, while Bondi is its eastern counterpart. In Balmain, Glebe and Surry Hills, the visitor can experience the character of the inner suburbs. Still further afield, out west at Parramatta, there are sights that recall and evoke the first days of European settlement and the colony's initially unsteady steps towards agricultural self-sufficiency.

SIGHTS AT A GLANCE

Historic Districts and Buildings
University of Sydney ❸
Balmain ❻
Kirribilli Point ❽
North Head ⓬
Vaucluse House ⓭
Watsons Bay ⓯
Macquarie Lighthouse ⓰
Captain Cook's Landing Place ⓲
Elizabeth Farm ⓴
Hambledon Cottage ㉑
Experiment Farm Cottage ㉒
Old Government House ㉔

16 km = 10 miles

Parks and Gardens
Nielsen Park ⓮

Museums and Galleries
Brett Whiteley Studio ❶
Nutcote ❾

Entertainment
Luna Park ❼
Taronga Zoo pp134–5 ❿
Sydney Olympic Park ⓳

Beaches
Manly ⓫
Bondi Beach ⓱

Restaurants and Pubs
Surry Hills ❷
Glebe ❹

Markets
Sydney Fish Market ❺

Cemeteries
St John's Cemetery ㉓

KEY

▦	Main sightseeing areas
▢	Park or reserve
✈	Airport
③	Metroad route
═	Freeway or motorway
▬	Major road
═	Minor road

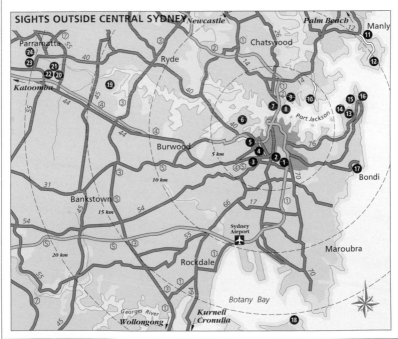

SIGHTS OUTSIDE CENTRAL SYDNEY

Brett Whiteley Studio ❶

2 Raper St, Surry Hills. **Map** 5 A4.
Tel 9225 1881. 🚌 343, 372, 393.
⏲ 10am–4pm Sat & Sun, or by
appointment on Thu & Fri. ◐ Easter
Sun, 25 Dec. ♿ partial access.

In June 1992, Brett Whiteley,
enfant terrible of Australian
contemporary art, died unex-
pectedly at the age of 53. An
internationally acclaimed and
prolific artist, he produced
some of the most sumptuous
images of Sydney and its distinctive harbour ever painted.

In 1985, Whiteley bought a
former factory and converted
it into a studio and residence.
The studio is now a public
museum and art gallery. It
features the work of Whiteley
and other artists. Visitors gain
an insight into Whiteley's life
and work through changing
exhibitions and displays of his
effects and memorabilia. The
studio is under the administration of the Art Gallery of New
South Wales *(see pp108–11).*

Surry Hills ❷

Map 5 A3. 🚌 301, 302, 303, 304,
339. See **Shops and Markets**
pp200–201.

This was once one of the
more depressed areas of the
inner city. In the 1920s, Surry
Hills was a haunt of the razor
gangs that terrorized inner-
city Sydney. The 1940s slums
were vividly described in Ruth
Park's celebrated novels *Poor
Man's Orange* and *The Harp*

Shop in Crown Street, Surry Hills

in the South. In the postwar
years, the low property and
rental prices attracted a large
number of new migrants to
the already-hectic district.

In recent decades, young
professionals have moved into
the area, lured by the charm
of its Victorian terraces and
closeness to the city. Many
of the suburb's traditional
inhabitants have since
been displaced.

Today Surry Hills
is a curious mixture
of fashion and seedi-
ness. Newly renovated
houses stand alongside
dilapidated dwellings,
while streets of elegant
Victorian terraces abut
modern high-rise flats and
factory warehouses.

For the visitor, the
suburb offers a wide
range of ethnic cuisines, often
at bargain prices. It is famed
for the Lebanese and Turkish
restaurants that cluster near
the intersection of Cleveland
and Elizabeth Streets. You will
also find Indian, Chinese, Thai,

French and numerous Italian
eateries scattered around the
suburb, along with smart and
casual cafés and stylish pubs.

Once the centre of Sydney's
garment trade, it still has factory outlets where clothing,
lingerie and haberdashery can
be purchased at below retail
prices. Alternative fashion and
retro clothing shops are found
at the Oxford Street end of
Crown Street. These boutiques
attract the street-smart crowd.

University of Sydney ❸

Parramatta Rd, Camperdown.
Map 3 B5. **Tel** 9351 2222. 🚌 343,
Parramatta Rd & City Rd routes.
⏲ daily. 📷 ♿ 🎧 phone 9351
2274 (book one week in advance).

Inaugurated in 1850, this is
Australia's oldest university.
The campus is a sprawling
hotchpotch of buildings
from different eras, of
often dubious architec-
tural merit. However,
the original Victorian
Gothic main building
still stands on its ele-
vated site, dominating
its surroundings. The
work of the Colonial
Architect Edmund
Blacket, it is scrupulously
modelled on the
architecture of Cam-
bridge and Oxford.

It features intricate stone
tracery, a clock tower with
carved pinnacles, gargoyles
(one, in the quadrangle, represents a crocodile) and a
cloistered main quadrangle.

The gem of the complex,
and probably Blacket's finest
work, is the Great Hall at the
main building's northern end.
This grandly sombre hall, with
its carved cedar ceiling and
stained-glass windows depicting famous philosophers and
scientists, is often used for
public concerts as well as for
university ceremonies.

The Nicholson Museum of
antiquities, the natural history
Macleay Museum and the War
Memorial Art Gallery, which
houses the university's art
collection, are all within the
grounds. They are open to the
public on most weekdays.

**Statue of Hermes,
Nicholson Museum**

Brett Whiteley Studio: former artist's studio, now a museum

Corner view of Badde Manors Café on Glebe Point Road, Glebe

Glebe ❹

Map 3 A4. 🚌 *431, 433. See* **Shops and Markets** *p203.*

The word "Glebe" means land assigned to a clergyman as part of his benefice. In 1789, Governor Phillip granted 162 ha (400 acres) to Richard Johnson, the First Fleet chaplain, and his wife Mary. Almost all of the present suburb was once part of that Glebe Estate. Many of its streets wind down to the working harbour and contain terrace houses with Sydney wrought-iron "lace" in varying states of repair.

The once-grand residences of the 19th-century élite were mostly towards the harbour end of Glebe Point Road, with workers' cottages clustered nearer Parramatta Road. Glebe is still partly a gentrified member of the café society, although its proximity to the Broadway shopping mall and its popularity with students from the nearby University of Sydney have given it a more bustling atmosphere.

It is densely populated and lively, with many restaurants and cafés in all price ranges, traditional and trendy pubs, good bookshops, an art-house cinema and shops selling everything from antique clocks to New Age goods and chattels. Glebe Market held every Saturday sells jewellery, second-hand clothing and bric-à-brac.

Sydney Fish Market ❺

Cnr Pyrmont Bridge Rd & Bank St, Pyrmont. **Map** 3 B2. **Tel** 9004 1100. 🚌 *443, 501.* ⏰ *7am–4pm daily.* ⭕ *25 Dec.* 🅿 ♿ 🛒 *Mon, Thu & Fri. Booking essential; phone 9004 1143.* www.sydneyfishmarket.com.au *See* **Shops and Markets** *pp202–3.*

Every weekday, about 200 seafood retailers and dealers arrive at this market's private auction to bid for the previous day's catch. It is sold by Dutch auction, with prices starting high and decreasing. The volume and variety of the catch, including fish and seafood makes this the most diverse fish market after Tokyo.

A fair amount of this catch ends up, later in the morning, in the fish market's six large retail outlets which, for the general public, are its main attraction. As well as fresh fish, these retailers sell smoked salmon and roe, sushi, marinated baby octopus and many other ready-to-eat delicacies.

Visitors watch the experts as they tenderize octopus and squid in concrete mixers. As well as fishmongers, there are a number of fresh food shops, several restaurants and a seafood school – cost includes tuition, seafood and wine.

Balmain ❻

🚌 *433, 434, 442. See* **Shops and Markets** *p203 and* **Four Guided Walks** *pp142–3.*

Balmain was once one of Sydney's most staunchly working-class areas, with shipyards, a dry dock and repair yards, a coal mine, numerous rough-and-ready pubs and an intimidating criminal element. Its late 19th-century town hall, post office, court house and fire station in Darling Street reflect the civic pride of the suburb in the Victorian era.

The many stone and timber cottages of what had become a slum have transformed into a charming, bustling suburb that still retains its village character, with interesting shops, galleries, cafés, restaurants and pubs.

The proximity of the Balmain peninsula to the city and its bohemian ambience may explain why many prominent writers – including novelist Kate Grenville and playwright David Williamson – have lived and worked here.

The Saturday market, held at St Andrew's Congregational Church in Darling Street, is one of Sydney's best. Antiques, estate jewellery and ingenious art and craft items are on sale.

Imposing entrance to Balmain court house on Darling Street

THE COLOURFUL FACES OF LUNA PARK

The gateway to Luna Park is the gaping mouth of a huge laughing face, flanked by two 36-m (129-ft) Art Deco towers. Between 1935 and 1945, four successive canvas, wire and plaster faces fell to the ravages of time. Built in the 1950s, the fifth face was replaced in 1973 with one designed by the Sydney artist Martin Sharp. The seventh, made in 1982, is now at the Powerhouse Museum *(see pp100–101)*. Today's face (1994) is made of polyurethane and fibreglass.

The gateway to Luna Park with its famous face

Luna Park's ferris wheel

Luna Park ❼

1 Olympic Drive, Milsons Point. *Tel* 9922 6644. ⬤ 11am–4pm Mon, 11am–10pm Fri & Sat, 10am–6pm Sun (additional hours during school & public hols). ⬛ Milsons Point. &. www.lunaparksydney.com

This famous fun fair, built on the site of former Harbour Bridge construction workshops, was modelled on Luna Park at Coney Island, New York. It opened in 1935 using rides from a short-lived Luna Park in South Australia. For the next 43 years it was one of the most conspicuous landmarks on the harbour foreshores. Except during the compulsory blackouts of World War II, its brilliant illuminations were a feature of the city's night scene.

In 1979, seven people were killed in a ghost train fire, a tragedy that led to the park's immediate closure. The park

has since reopened, and entry is free so you can just enjoy the atmosphere or buy a ticket and catch the views from the Ferris Wheel. Las Vegas glitz and 1940s Futurism are just two of the styles at one of Sydney's most treasured icons. The old-style fun house Coney Island, Crystal Palace and the gateway face are all heritage listed. The Big Top, a 2,000-seat venue, hosts music, dance and comedy acts.

Kirribilli Point ❽

Kirribilli Ave, Kirribilli. ⬛ Kirribilli North Sydney.

The two houses Occupying this prominent headland, in their delightful garden settings, are typical of the magnificent homes in sprawling grounds that once ringed the harbour. Most have been demolished

now and the land subdivided for apartment living. Kirribilli, meaning "place for fishing", is the most densely populated suburb in Australia.

The larger, more dominant of the two houses is Admiralty House, built as a single-storey residence in 1843. Between 1885 and 1913 it served as the residence of the commanding officer of Britain's Royal Navy Pacific Squadron, which was based in Sydney. Fortifications on the shoreline recall its military history. Now the official Sydney home of Australia's governor-general, it is said that even its shed could be considered the city's best address.

In 1855, the charming Gothic Kirribilli House, with its steep gables and decorative fretwork, was built in the grounds of Admiralty House. Today it is the official Sydney residence of Australia's prime minister.

Nutcote ❾

5 Wallaringa Ave, Neutral Bay. *Tel* 9953 4453. ⬛ Hayes Street, Neutral Bay. ⬤ 11am–3pm Wed–Sun. ⬤ some public hols. 🎫 📷 🛍

One of the classics of Australian children's literature, *Snugglepot and Cuddlepie*, was published in 1918. Since then, these two characters – known as the "gumnut" babies along with the cartoon characters Bib and Bub – have been loved by countless young Australians.

Nutcote was, for 44 years, the home of their creator, illustrator and author May Gibbs. Saved from demolition then

Admiralty House and Kirribilli House, near Sydney Harbour Bridge

Shop façades featuring decorative gables along Manly's Corso

restored and refurbished in the style of the 1930s, it opened in 1994 as an historic house museum. Visitors can view the author's painstakingly kept notebooks and other memorabilia (including the table at which she worked), as well as original editions of her books. There is a garden with views across the harbour and a shop that sells a range of May Gibbs' souvenirs.

May Gibbs' studio at Nutcote

Taronga Zoo ❿

See pp134–5.

Manly ⓫

🚢 *Manly.* **Oceanworld Manly**
West Esplanade. **Tel** *8251 7877.*
⭘ *10am–5:30pm daily.* ⬤ *25 Dec.*
🖼️ 📷 🚶 *See Four Guided Walks*
pp146–7. **www**.oceanworld.com.au

Long after Australia's conversion to the metric system, the slogan "seven miles from Sydney and a thousand miles from care" is still current. It refers to Manly and the 7-mile (11-km) journey from Circular Quay by harbour ferry. If asked

to suggest a single excursion to enjoy during your time in the city, most Sydneysiders would nominate a ferry ride to Manly. This narrow stretch of land lying between the harbour and ocean was named by Governor Phillip, even before the township of Sydney got its name, for the impressive bearing of the Aboriginal men.

As the ferry pulls in to Manly wharf you will notice on the right many shops, restaurants and bars and on the left, the tranquil harbourside beach known as Manly Cove.

At the far end of Manly Cove is Oceanworld Manly, where visitors can see reptiles, sharks and giant stingrays in an underwater viewing tunnel. You can also dive with sharks, and details of Shark Xtreme are on Oceanworld's website.

The Corso is a lively pedestrian thoroughfare of souvenir shops and fast food outlets, with a market held there on Sundays. The Corso leads to Manly's ocean beach, with its promenade lined by towering

pines. Nearby is a monument to a local newspaper proprietor who, in 1902, defied bans on daytime bathing and was promptly arrested.

Every October Manly hosts a great jazz festival *(see p48)*.

North Head ⓬

🚢 *Manly.* **Quarantine Station**
Ghost Tours *Bookings essential*
(starting times vary). **Tel** *9466 1500.*
www.qstation.com.au

The majestic cliffs of North Head afford the finest views in Sydney Harbour National Park, providing vistas along the coastline, across to Middle Harbour and towards the city. North Head is also the ideal place for observing the movements of harbour and seagoing craft and especially for seeing off the yachts at the start of the annual Sydney to Hobart race *(see p49)*.

The Quarantine Station nestles just above Spring Cove within the national park. Here, between 1832 and the 1960s, many ships, with their crews and passengers, were quarantined to protect Sydneysiders from the spread of epidemic diseases. More than 500 people died here, leading some to believe the area is haunted.

Now a five-star hotel called Q Station, the site, including its hospital, shower block and morgue, can be explored on a guided "ghost" tour. Countless migrants spent their first months in Australia in this place of splendid isolation. Many of its internees left poignant messages and poems carved in the sandstone.

First-class quarters at the Quarantine Station, North Head

Taronga Zoo [10]

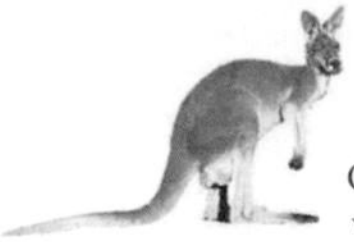

Red kangaroo

This famous harbourside zoo is home to almost 2,500 animals, with a special emphasis on unique Australian wildlife. Conspicuous bars and fences are absent, with moats used to separate the wandering public from the curious animal onlookers contained in environments closely resembling their natural habitat. The zoo is involved in the breeding of endangered animals, as well as in international efforts to ensure a sustainable future for wildlife.

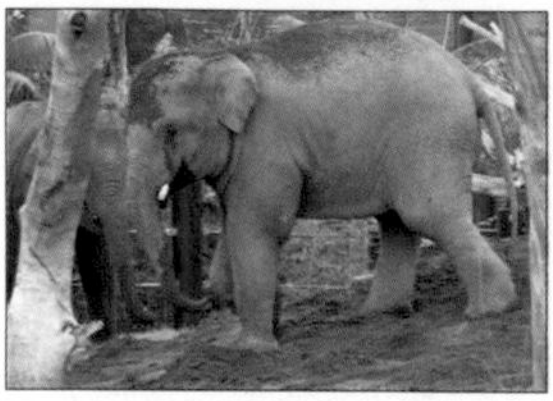

Elephant Breeding Facility
Endangered Asian elephants have been bred at Taronga since a small collection were brought over from Thailand in 2006. The precinct features a rainforest habitat with pools, mud wallows and scratching posts.

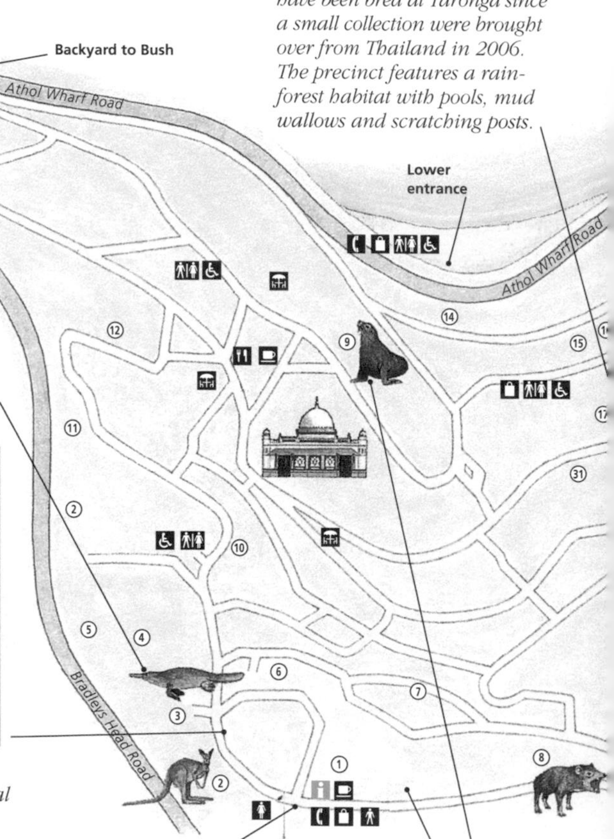
Backyard to Bush
Athol Wharf Road
Bradleys Head Road
0 metres 100
0 yards 100
Lower entrance
Athol Wharf Road
Bradleys Head Road
Upper entrance
Sky Safari Cable Car
Capral seal theatre

The platypus is one of only three species of egg-laying mammals.

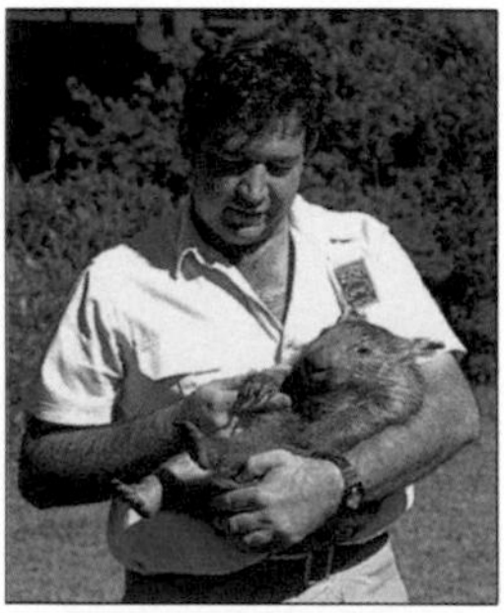

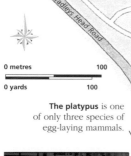

Common Wombat
This ground-dwelling animal is a powerful burrower able to move quickly if disturbed. It feeds on roots and has a pouch for carrying its young.

STAR DISPLAYS

- ★ Koala Walkabout
- ★ Orang-utan Rainforest
- ★ QBE Free Flight Bird Show

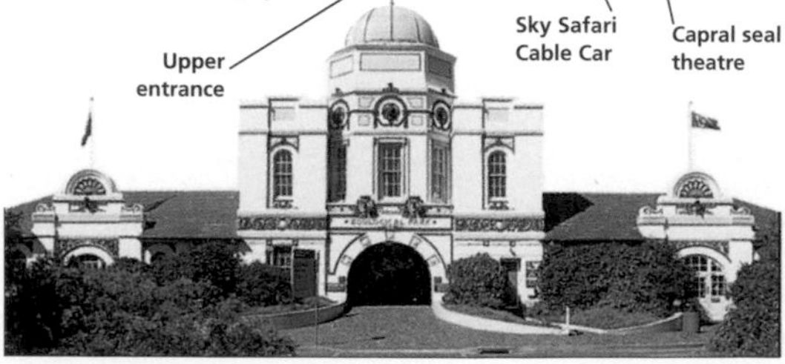

Upper Entrance
This edifice has greeted visitors since the opening in 1916. By 1917, more than half of Sydney's population had paid a visit.

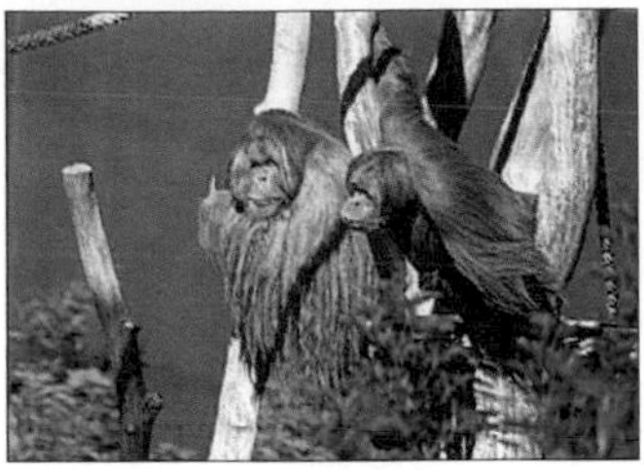

★ Orang-utan Rainforest
Threatened by widespread destruction of their natural habitat in the Sumatran and Borneo rainforests, these primates are on the world's endangered species list.

VISITORS' CHECKLIST

Bradleys Head Rd, Mosman. ***Tel*** *9969 2777.* 🚌 *238, 247, 250.* ⛴ *Taronga Zoo.* 🕐 *9am–5pm daily (last adm 4:30pm).*
📷 ♿ 🍴 ☕ 🛍
www.zoo.nsw.gov.au

★ QBE Free Flight Bird Show
In this spectacular display, birds fly free in an amphitheatre overlooking the harbour.

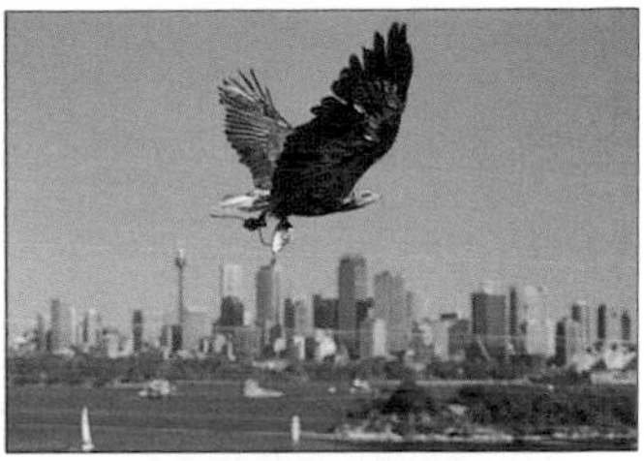

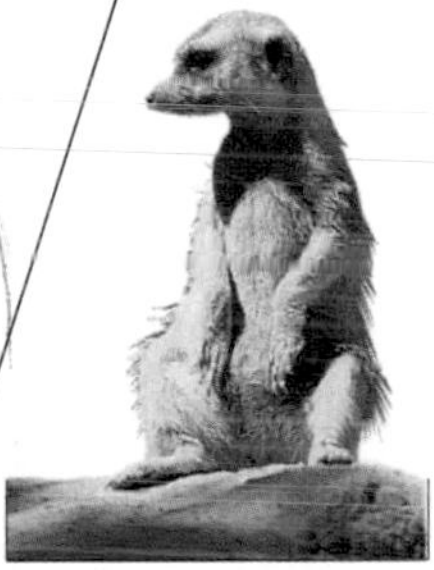

Meerkat
This southern African mongoose always forages in groups, with a guard alert for signs of danger.

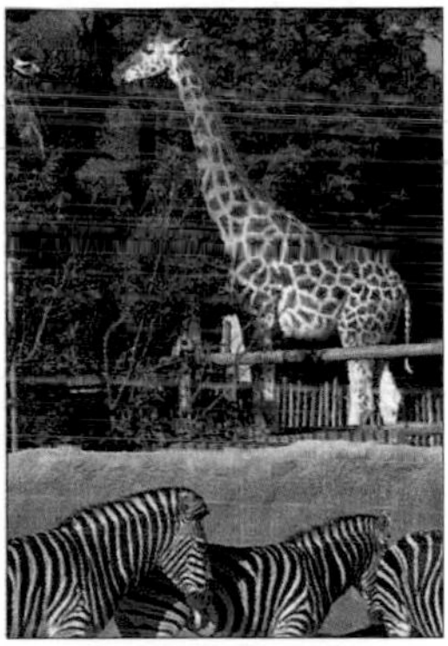

African Waterhole
The zoo re-creates the environment of savannah waterholes for giraffes, zebras and pygmi hippopotami.

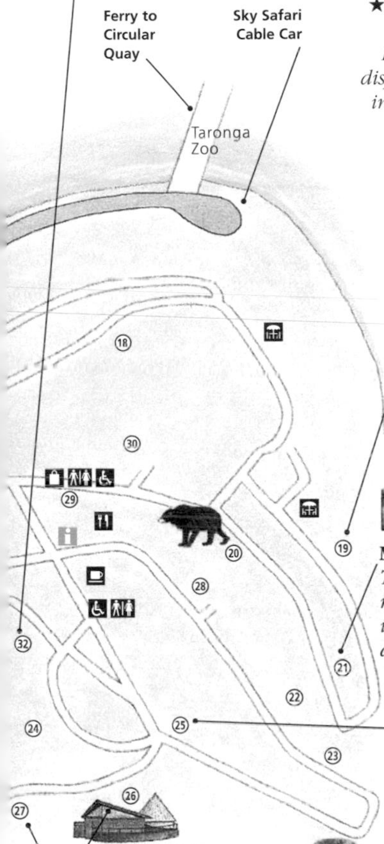
Ferry to Circular Quay
Sky Safari Cable Car
Taronga Zoo
18
30
29
20
19
28
21
32
22
24
25
23
26
27

Reptile World has amphibians, invertebrates and reptiles.

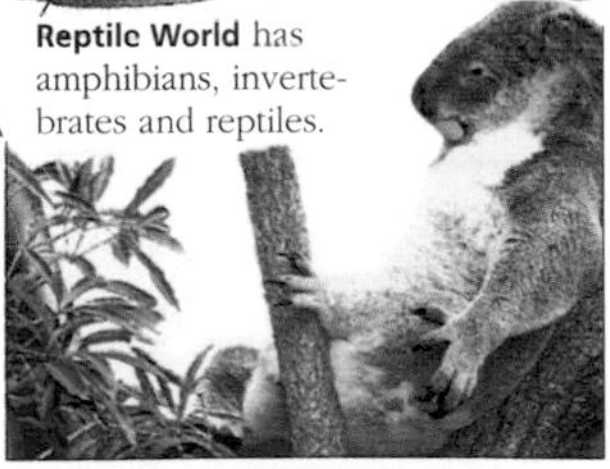

★ Koala Walkabout
Visitors can see the koalas in their eucalypt habitat at tree level. The spiral ramp allows you to get close to feeding and sleeping animals.

KEY TO ANIMAL ENCLOSURES

African Waterhole 25
Australia's Nightlife 6
Backyard to Bush 13
Bear 20
Chimpanzee Park 24
Creatures of the Wollemi 10
Elephant Breeding Facility 17
Free Flight Bird Show 19
Gorilla Forest 31
Great Southern Oceans 16
Himalayan Tahr 23
Jungle Cats 12
Koala Encounters 5
Koala Walkabout 27
Lion 28
Meerkat 21
Orang-utan Rainforest 32
Otter 18
Penguin 14
Platypus 3
Rainforest Aviary 7
Reptile World 26
Saltwater crocodile 9
Seals and sea-lions 15
Snow leopard 22
Taronga International Food Market 29
Tasmanian devil 8
Wetlands 1
Wild Asia 30
Wild Australia 2
Wombat 4
Yellow-footed rock wallaby 11

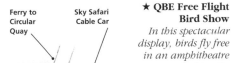

Façade of Vaucluse House, with its garden and fountain

Vaucluse House ⑬

Wentworth Rd, Vaucluse. **Tel** 9388 7922. 🚌 325. ⬤ 9:30am–4pm Fri–Sun (daily in Jan, NSW school hols & public hols). ⬤ Good Fri, 25 Dec. 🎥 📷 ♿ limited. 🎞

Tradition has it that the most riotous party colonial Sydney ever saw took place on the Vaucluse House lawns in 1831. WC Wentworth and 4,000 of his political cronies gathered there to celebrate the recall to England of Governor Ralph Darling, the arch-enemy.

WC Wentworth was a major figure in the colony, being one of the first three Europeans to cross the Blue Mountains *(see pp160–61)*. He was the son of a female convict and a physician forced to "volunteer" his services to the new colony in order to avoid conviction on a highway robbery charge.

The younger Wentworth became an author, barrister and statesman who stood for the Australian-born "currency" lads and lasses against the "sterling" English-born. He lived here with his family from 1829–53, during which time he drafted the Constitution Bill, giving self-government to the state.

Vaucluse House was begun in 1803 by Sir Henry Browne Hayes, a knight of the realm transported for kidnapping a Quaker heiress. Sitting comfortably in 11 ha (27 acres) of parkland, natural bush and cultivated gardens, this Gothic Revival house, with its many idiosyncratic additions, resembles a West Indian plantation house. The interior and grounds have been restored to 1840s style and the house contains furniture that belonged to the Wentworth family. A popular tea house is in the grounds.

Greycliffe House, in the tranquil grounds of Nielsen Park

Nielsen Park ⑭

🚌 325. ⬤ Sunrise–10pm daily.

Part of the Sydney Harbour National Park, Nielsen Park, with its grassy expanses, sandy beach and netted swimming pool, is the perfect spot for a family picnic. Here visitors can savour the unusual peace that descends on many harbour beaches on an endless sunny day. It is also an ideal vantage point from which to enjoy a pectacular summer sunset or simply to observe the coming and going of ferries and the meandering harbour traffic.

In the midst of this tranquil setting, enhancing its charm, stands Greycliffe House with its decorative gables and ornate chimney stacks. This Victorian Gothic mansion was completed in 1852 for WC Wentworth's daughter.

Watsons Bay ⑮

🚌 324, 325. ⛴ Watsons Bay. See **Four Guided Walks** pp148–9.

As the base for the boats that take the pilots out to arriving ships, this pretty bay has long been a vital part of the working harbour. It is also the home of Doyle's famous waterfront seafood restaurant, long a magnet for Sydneysiders and visitors alike.

Just up the hill and almost opposite the bay on the ocean side is The Gap, a spectacular cliff with tragic associations. Many troubled people have taken a suicidal leap from this rugged cliff on to the wave-lashed rocks below.

It was here that the ill-fated ship *Dunbar* was wrecked in 1857, with the loss of all but one of its 122 passengers and crew. Treacherous conditions had led to miscalculation of the ship's distance from the Heads. All hands were ordered

View over Watsons Bay, looking southwest towards the city

The crescent-shaped Bondi Beach, Sydney's most famous beach, looking towards North Bondi

on deck as The Gap's rock walls loomed. The recovered anchor is now set into the cliff near the shipwreck site.

The 1883 Macquarie Lighthouse overlooking the Pacific Ocean

Macquarie Lighthouse **16**

🚌 324, 325. 📷 ♿

This is the second lighthouse on this windswept site that is attributed to the convict architect Francis Greenway (see p114). He supervised the construction of the first tower, which was completed in 1818 and described by Governor Macquarie as a "noble magnificent edifice". The colony's first lighthouse, it replaced the previous system of bonfires lit up along the headland and earned Greenway a conditional pardon. When the sandstone

eventually crumbled away, the present lighthouse was built. Although designed by Colonial Architect James Barnet, it was based on Greenway's original and was illuminated for the first time in 1883.

Bondi Beach **17**

🚌 333, 380, 381. See **Four Guided Walks** pp144–5.

This long crescent of golden sand, so close to the city, has long been a mecca for the sun and surf set (see pp54–5). Throughout the year, surfing enthusiasts visit from far and wide in search of the perfect wave, and inline skaters hone their skills on the promenade. Despite a growing awareness of the dangers of sun exposure (see p223) and an expansion of other cultural preoccupations, beach life still defines the lives of many Australians, who regard it as healthier than ever.

People seek out Bondi for its trendy seafront cafés and cosmopolitan milieu as much as for the beach. The pavilion, built in 1928 as changing rooms, has been a community centre since the 1970s. Note that Bondi Beach itself is an alcohol-free zone.

BONDI SURF BATHERS' LIFE SAVING CLUB

The founding of the surf lifesaving club at Bondi Beach in 1906 gave impetus to the formation of other local clubs, and ultimately to a global movement. An early club member demonstrated his new lifesaving reel, designed using hair pins and a cotton reel. Now updated, it is standard equipment on beaches worldwide. In 1938, Australia's largest surf rescue was mounted at Bondi, when more than 200 people were washed out to sea by freak waves. Five died, but lifesavers rescued more than 180, establishing their highly dependable reputation.

Bondi surf lifesaving team at the Bondi Surf Carnival, 1937

Captain Cook's Landing Place

Captain Cook Drive, Kamay Botany Bay National Park, Kurnell. *Tel 9668 2000.* ▦ 987. **Toll Gate** ◯ *7am–7pm daily (to 5:30pm Jun–Jul).* **Visitor Centre** ◯ *9:30am–4:30pm daily.* ● *25 Dec.* 🖼️ 📷 ♿ www.nationalparks.nsw.gov.au

Although difficult to get to, visitors will find this place worth the effort. It is, after all, one of Australia's most important European historic sites. Here James Cook, botanists Daniel Solander and Joseph Banks and the crew of HMS *Endeavour* landed on 29 April 1770. Aboriginal peoples with spears were shot at. One, hit in the legs, returned with a shield to defend himself.

Nowadays people can cast a fishing line from the rock where the Europeans stepped ashore. Nearby are the site of

Cook's Obelisk, overlooking Botany Bay, Captain Cook's Landing Place

a well where, Cook recorded, a shore party "found fresh water sufficient to water the ship" and a monument which marks the first recorded European burial in Australia.

There are also monuments to Solander, Banks and Cook, but it is the peaceful ambience that is most impressive. Now part of Kamay Botany Bay National Park, Captain Cook's Landing Place has lovely walks, some accessible to wheelchairs, where visitors may roam and observe the flora which led to the naming of Botany Bay.

The Visitor Centre in the park focuses on a number of themes: the bay's wetlands and

the importance of their conservation; an interesting exhibition detailing Cook's exploration of the area; and an introduction to Aboriginal customs and culture.

Sydney Olympic Park ⑲

Homebush Bay. *Tel 9714 7958/7888.* ▦ Olympic Park. Visitors Centre (1 Showground Rd). ◯ *9am–5pm daily.* ● *1 Jan, Good Fri, 25 & 26 Dec.* 🖼️ ♿ ▯ ▦ www.sydneyolympicpark.com.au

Once host to the 27th Summer Olympic Games and Paralympic Games, Sydney Olympic Park is situated at Homebush Bay, 14 km (8.5 miles) west of the city centre. Visitors can follow a self-guided walk or buy a ticket for a guided tour to access venues such as the Showground and the Super-Dome. The interactive "ANZ Stadium Explore Tour" gives a taste of some of the stadium's best-loved sporting moments. For nature lovers, there is a tour of the five wetlands of the Bicentennial Park. You can buy tickets for tours at the Visitor's Centre.

Other facilities at the park include the Aquatic Centre, with a kids' waterpark, and the Tennis Centre, where you can play in the footsteps of such greats as Lleyton Hewitt. There are picnic areas and cafés throughout the park and on the fourth Sunday of every month you can sample fresh produce and gourmet food at the Boulevard Market.

Pampas grass and banana plants in the garden at Elizabeth Farm

Elizabeth Farm ⑳

70 Alice St, Rosehill. *Tel 9635 9488.* ▦ Parramatta. ▦ Parramatta or Granville. ◯ *9:30am–4pm Fri–Sun (daily in Jan, NSW school hols & public hols).* ● *Good Fri, 25 Dec.* 🖼️ 📷 ♿ ▯ 🛒 www.hht.net.au/museums

The discovery of fertile land at Parramatta, and the harvesting of its first successful grain crop in 1790, helped save the fledgling colony from starvation and led to the rapid development of the area.

This zone was the location of several of Australia's first colonial land grants. In 1793, John Macarthur, who became a wealthy farmer and sheep breeder, was granted 40 ha (100 acres) of land at Parramatta. He named the property after his wife and this was to be Elizabeth's home for the rest of her life. Macarthur was often absent from the farm as the centre of his wool operations had moved to Camden.

Part of the house, a simple stone cottage built in 1793, still remains and it is the oldest

John Macarthur, 1766–1834

European building in Australia. Over the next 50 years, it developed into a substantial home with many features of a typical Australian homestead. Simply furnished to the period of 1820–50, with reproductions of paintings and other possessions, it is now a museum that strongly evokes the original inhabitants' life and times.

The kitchen, Hambledon Cottage

Hambledon Cottage ㉑

Cnr of Hassall St & Gregory Place, Parramatta. *Tel* 9635 6924 🚃 *Parramatta.* 🕐 *11am–4pm Thu–Sun.* 🔴 *Good Fri, 25 & 26 Dec.* 🈲 ♿ 📷

This delightful cottage, with its walls of rendered and painted sandstock, was built in 1824 as the retirement home for Penelope Lucas, governess to the Macarthur daughters. It is set in a park containing trees brought to Australia from as early as 1817 by John Macarthur.

Visitors can see rooms restored to the period of 1820–50. An 1830 Broadwood piano is one of the furniture exhibits. The kitchen has walls of convict-made bricks and contains original appliances and utensils.

Experiment Farm Cottage ㉒

9 Ruse St, Parramatta. *Tel* 9635 5655. 🚃 *Harris Park.* 🕐 *10:30am–3:30pm Tue–Fri, 11am–3:30pm Sun & public hols.* 🔴 *Good Fri, 18–31 Dec.* 🈲 📷 ♿ 📷 *(groups must book in advance).* **www**.nationaltrust.com.au

When his sentence expired in 1789, convict farmer James Ruse was given 0.6 ha (1½

acres) of land at Parramatta on which to start a farm, along with a hut, grain for sowing, vital farming tools, two sows and six hens. He successfully planted and harvested a wheat crop with his wife Elizabeth's help. She was the first female convict to be emancipated in New South Wales. In 1791, they were rewarded with a grant of 12 ha (30 acres), the colony's first land grant. Arthur Phillip, governor of the day, called it Experiment Farm.

Medicine chest (c.1810), Experiment Farm

In 1793, Ruse sold this farm to surgeon John Harris for £40. The date of the cottage is not certain, but it is believed to be early 1830s. The woodwork is Australian red cedar and the cottage is furnished according to an 1838 inventory.

St John's Cemetery ㉓

O'Connell St, Parramatta. *Tel* 9635 5904. 🚃 *Parramatta.* 📷 ♿

This walled cemetery – the oldest European cemetery in Australia – houses the graves of many convicts and settlers who arrived on the First Fleet in 1788. The oldest grave that can be identified is the flat sandstone slab simply inscribed, "H.E. Dodd 1791". Henry Edward Dodd, known to be Governor Phillip's butler, was the tenth person buried in the cemetery, but the location

of the other nine graves is unknown. The first recorded burial was of a child on 31 January 1790. One prominent grave is that of churchman Samuel Marsden, who earned the title of the "flogging parson" during his time as magistrate general because of his harsh judgments. The merchant Robert Campbell (*see p66*) and the father of explorer William Charles Wentworth (*see p136*), D'Arcy Wentworth, are also buried here.

Old Government House ㉔

Parramatta Park (entry by Macquarie St gates), Parramatta. *Tel* 9635 8149. 🚃 *Parramatta.* 🕐 *10am–4.30pm Tue–Fri, 10:30am–4pm Sat, Sun & most public hols.* 🔴 *Good Fri, 25 Dec.* 🈲 ♿ *limited.* 📷 **www**.oldgovernmenthouse.com.au

The central block of Old Government House is the oldest intact public building in Australia. This elegant brick structure, plastered to resemble stone, was built by Governor Hunter in 1799 on the site of a cottage constructed in 1790 for Governor Phillip. Wings to the side and rear were added between 1812 and 1818. The Doric porch, added in 1816, has been attributed to Francis Greenway (*see p114*).

Australia's finest collection of early 19th-century furniture is now housed inside.

The drawing room of Old Government House, Parramatta

FOUR GUIDED WALKS

S ydney's temperate climate and natural beauty make it an ideal city for walking. The following walks have been chosen for their distinct character; they all capture a view of the essential Sydney. You can follow the paths that trace the headlands and inlets around Watsons Bay; enjoy an invigorating clifftop walk at Bondi; catch glimpses of the original landscape in Manly's unspoilt bushland; or explore the narrow streets of historic Balmain. Three of the walks incorporate ocean or harbourside beaches, so be prepared in warmer weather by packing a swimsuit, towel

Mural on a Manly surf shop

and hat and wearing a reliable sunscreen. In Sydney's national parks and bushland all the indigenous flora and fauna is protected. The best sign of appreciation is to leave the bush as you found it. The *Tips for Walkers* provide practical information about each walk, listing accessibility by bus, train or ferry and estimated distance of the walk, along with scenic rest areas, picnic spots, cafés and restaurants en route. Tourism NSW's Information Line *(see p221)* and www. sydneywalkingtours.com.au give details of the accompanied walking tours available throughout Sydney.

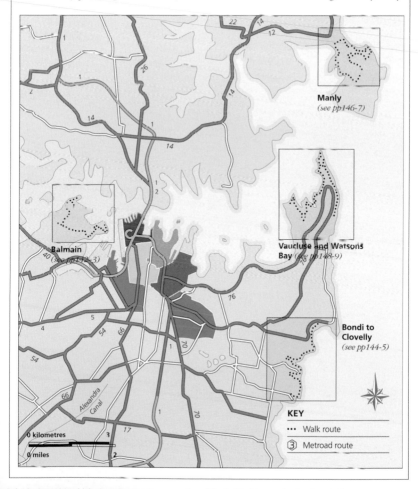

Manly
(see pp146-7)

Vaucluse and Watsons Bay *(see pp148-9)*

Balmain
(see pp142-3)

Bondi to Clovelly
(see pp144-5)

KEY

··· Walk route

③ Metroad route

0 kilometres 3

0 miles 2

◁ **A lookout rising high above the treacherous waters of the Pacific Ocean at the Gap** *(see p148)*

A Two-Hour Walk Around Balmain

Historic Balmain village was named after William Balmain, a ship's surgeon on the First Fleet. In 1800, he was granted rights to 223 ha (550 acres) of the peninsula, which he later sold for a paltry 5 shillings in a dubious business transaction. From the mid-1800s, much of the land was subdivided for housing to support the then flourishing mining and maritime industries. Today, grand colonial and Victorian buildings stand side by side with tiny workers' cottages, adding variety to every street.

Colourful shopfront on Darling Street, Balmain

The Waterman's Cottage ③

East Balmain

Begin from the Darling Street Wharf ①. By the 1840s, when the ferry service began, shipyards dotted these foreshores. The sandstone building at No. 10 Darling Street ②, once the Dolphin Hotel then the Shipwright's Arms, was a watering hole for sailors and ferrymen. On the opposite corer is The Waterman's Cottage (1841) ③, home to Henry McKenzie, whose boat ferried residents to and from Sydney Town.

Turn left into Weston Street and walk through the Illoura Reserve for views of the city and Darling Harbour. Leave the park via William and Johnston Streets, stopping in the latter to view Onkaparinga ④, the colonial residence at No. 12. When building started in 1860, mussel shells from Aboriginal feasts stood in mounds upon the harbour foreshore beyond.

Turn left onto Darling Street then right into Duke Street. Gilchrist Place then leads down to Mort Bay Reserve ⑤. Ship's propellers stand as monuments to the area's working past. A path leads up to The Avenue's timber workers' cottages.

Back on Darling Street, turn left down Killeen Street. Take the path across Ewenton Park to Ewenton ⑥ (c.1854). Past the park, Hampton Villa ⑦ at 12B Grafton Street was home to state premier Henry Parkes.

Turn right into Ewenton Street and then left into Wallace Street, with its variety of early Australian architecture. The rough stone home at No. 1 is called the Railway Station as its narrow frontage makes it resemble one. The charming Clontarf ⑧ is at No. 4, while Maitland House ⑨ has a symmetry worth a second glance. Return to Darling Street.

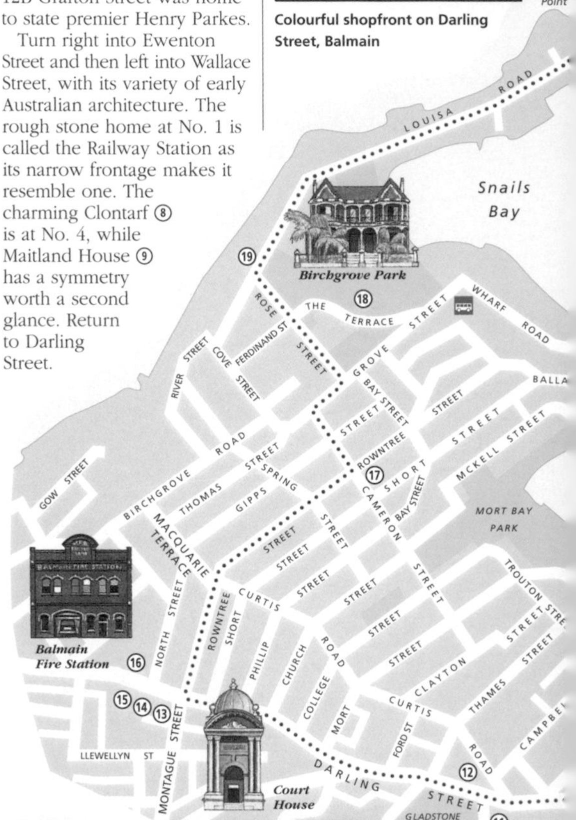

The domestic grandeur of Louisa Road

Historic Links

Sydney's oldest extant lock-up, The Watch House (1854) ⑩ at No. 179 Darling Street, has been restored, but a ghostly female form remains. Further along, enjoy a drink at The London Hotel (1870) ⑪, where the balcony stools are made of old-fashioned tractor seats.

After the roundabout, visit St Andrew's Church ⑫ before losing yourself to the bookshops, cafés and delicatessens of Balmain. Every Saturday, Balmain Market fills the churchyard *(see p203)*.

At the shops' far end, the Victorian Post Office (1887) ⑬ and neighbouring Court House ⑭ reflect 1880s Sydney's prosperity. The Town Hall ⑮ dome was removed during World War II for fear of air raids. Across the street is the Fire Station ⑯ (1894). Set on the crest of a hill, its horse-drawn vehicles always travelled downhill on their outward journey.

Distant views of the city and Sydney Harbour Bridge from Snails Bay

Balmain to Birchgrove

Retrace your steps to Rowntree Street. Turn left and wander down to Birchgrove (about 10 minutes' walk). From Birchgrove shops ⑰, take Cameron Street left and Grove Street right, to Birchgrove Park ⑱ and Snails Bay. Walk down Rose Street to Louisa Road. Two of the most notable homes are Nos. 12 and 14, Keba (1878) and Vidette (1876) ⑲, where deep verandas and iron-lace balconies hint at colonial opulence. A poem in praise of the nearby park is inscribed on a plaque at Keba's entrance. Amid Vidette's formal greenery, a deep well is still fed by a natural spring.

Balmain War Memorial

There is a wealth of interest in the homes that follow: a tiny porch, Victorian entrance tiles, ornate iron lace – plus occasional glimpses of water frontage and private moorings. At the road's end, the reserve at Yurulbin Point ⑳ marks the mouth of Parramatta River. A fishing nook on its eastern corner is a perfect vantage point for taking in the city skyline and passing harbour traffic.

Shops nestled in the quiet Birchgrove village ⑰

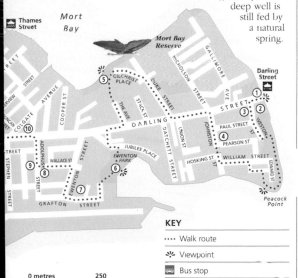

KEY

•••• Walk route

Viewpoint

Bus stop

Ferry boarding point

0 metres 250
0 yards 250

TIPS FOR WALKERS

Starting point: Darling Street Wharf.
Length: 5.5 km (3 1/2 miles).
Getting there: Ferries regularly leave Circular Quay for Darling Street Wharf. The 442 bus from the Queen Victoria Building stops in Darling Street. To return, there is a 15-minute ferry ride at hourly intervals from Birchgrove (pick up a schedule at Circular Quay). Alternatively, take Bus 441 from Grove Street (Snails Bay) back to the city (weekdays only).
Stopping-off points: Darling Street, in particular, has many good delicatessens, patisseries, restaurants and cafés. Places to picnic include Mort Bay Reserve, Gladstone Park, Birchgrove Park and Yurulbin Point.

A Two-Hour Walk from Bondi Beach to Clovelly

This invigorating oceanside and clifftop walk explores the beautiful shoreline and surfing beaches of eastern Sydney. The local colour along this scenic trail is at its most vibrant at weekends, when people flock to the cafés and beaches. The Victorian cemetery at the walk's end bears witness to Sydney's multicultural heritage.

Pool at North Bondi Beach

A Seaside Community

Walk north along Campbell Parade [1], passing a colourful array of hotels, beachwear shops and lively cafés that give the street a raffish atmosphere. The stylish Gelato Bar at No. 140 makes an indulgent pit-stop. Keep walking until the Hotel Bondi [2], the parade's most significant building and easily spotted by its pretty clock tower. Opened as a first-class hotel in 1920, it initially stood quite alone by what was then a bush-fringed beach. Turn right, crossing the road in front of the hotel, and walk down to Queen Elizabeth Drive leaving the traffic and noise of Campbell Parade behind as you reach Sydney's most famous beach, Bondi.

Statue of lifesaver near Bondi Pavilion

Bondi's popularity dates back to the 1880s. Although daylight bathing was banned at the time, the beach was considered a fashionable place to stroll. Bondi trams came into use shortly after and, by the time bathing restrictions were lifted in 1902, the red and white trams were filled with beach-goers. Just ahead you will see Bondi Pavilion [3]. Built in 1928 to replace a modest timber building, it was designed on a grand scale and originally housed a ballroom, gymnasium, restaurant, café, Turkish baths and open-air theatre. Although decidedly less glamorous today, the complex is still a thriving local community centre hosting cultural events. Photographs inside recall the romance of Bondi Beach in earlier times.

Next to the Pavilion is the home of arguably Australia's oldest surf life saving club, the Bondi Surf Bathers [4] *(see p137)*. Follow the sweep of the beach to its southern end.

Climb a flight of steps to continue on Notts Avenue, above Bondi Baths [5] and alongside the Bondi Icebergs clubhouse. Members of the Swimming Club must swim every Sunday during the winter regardless of the weather.

TIPS FOR WALKERS

Starting point: *Campbell Parade, southern end.*
Length: *4 km (21/2 miles).*
Getting there: *Take the train to Bondi Junction, then Bus 380 to Bondi Beach. Bus 339 runs from Clovelly Beach to Circular Quay. Waverley Cemetery is open from 8am to dusk every day.*
Stopping-off points: *Public toilets, showers and food and refreshments are available at Bondi, Tamarama and Bronte Beaches. Take-away cuisine can be bought along Bondi's Campbell Parade as the walk begins. Tamarama's beach café serves refreshing drinks. In warm weather, make the most of four of Sydney's best beaches by packing your swimming gear.*

Tamarama Surf Life Saving Club, at the beach's northern end

Bronte's swimming baths

Bondi to Bronte

Veer left off Notts Avenue as the path drops down and skirts sharp rock formations, the result of years of erosion. Take the steep steps to Mackenzies Point lookout [6] on the headland. The magnificent view stretches for 180 degrees from Ben Buckler in the north to Malabar in the distant south.

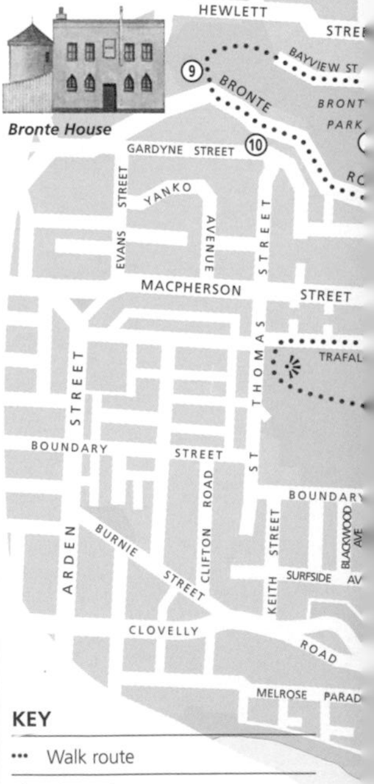

Bronte House

KEY

- ••• Walk route
- Viewpoint
- Bus stop
- [P] Parking

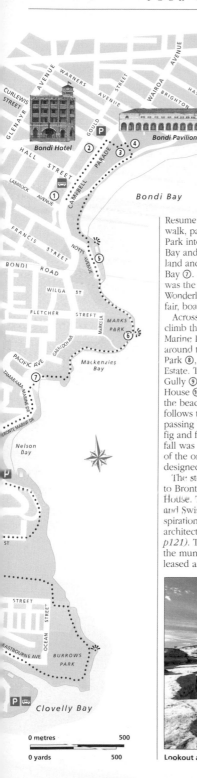

Bondi Hotel ②

Bondi Pavilion

Bondi Bay

Mackenzies Bay

Nelson Bay

Clovelly Bay

| 0 metres | 500 |
| 0 yards | 500 |

Bronte to Waverley

Continue down Bronte Road towards the southern end of Bronte Beach. After passing Bronte's cafés, walk through the car park and follow the road uphill, through a cutaway originally dug for trams. As the road winds through the cutting and veers right, take the steps through Calga Reserve. Walk down Trafalgar Street to the Waverley Cemetery ⑪.

In grand displays of Edwardian and Victorian monumental masonry, English, Italian and Irish residents have been laid to rest. Among notable Australians buried here are writers Henry Lawson and Dorothea Mackellar; Fanny Durack, the

Irish Memorial, Waverley Cemetery

first woman to win an Olympic gold medal (in 1912), and do the Australian crawl swimming stroke; and aeronautical pioneer Lawrence Hargrave.

The Irish Memorial honours the 1798 Irish Rebellion and its leader Michael Dwyer, who was transported to Australia for his part in the uprising.

Leave the cemetery at the southern end. Walk through Burrows Park, hugging the coast, to Eastbourne Avenue, which leads to the walk's end at Clovelly Beach ⑫.

Resume your walk, passing through Marks Park into rocky Mackenzies Bay and over the next headland and down to Tamarama Bay ⑦. In 1906-11, this beach was the unlikely home of Wonderland City – a rowdy fun fair, boasting a roller coaster.

Across the beach and park, climb the steps to Tamarama Marine Drive. Follow the road around to the slopes of Bronte Park ⑧, once part of Bronte Estate. To explore Bronte Gully ⑨, and glimpse Bronte House ⑩, continue away from the beach. Take the track that follows the creek into a valley, passing beneath a canopy of fig and flame trees. The waterfall was once a natural feature of the ornamental gardens designed for Bronte Estate.

The steps on your left lead to Bronte Road and Bronte House. The mixture of Gothic and Swiss styling was the inspiration of the original owner, architect Mortimer Lewis (see p121). Today it is owned by the municipal council and is leased as a private residence.

Lookout at Mackenzies Point, a popular spot for watching surfers ⑥

A Three-Hour Walk Around Manly

This walk takes in the holiday atmosphere of downtown Manly and its splendid surf beach, before passing along quieter shorelines and clifftop streets, and through unspoilt bushland replete with native flora and fauna. It features marvellous views, the commanding architecture of the historic building that was formerly St Patrick's Seminary, and the charm of Collins Beach and Fairy Bower.

Houses rising above Fairy Bower

Brass band plays in The Corso

From Harbour to Ocean

Start at Manly Wharf ①.This suburb was little more than a cosy fishing village until 1852, when entrepreneur Henry Gilbert Smith's vision of a resort similar to fashionable Brighton in his native England started to take shape. The ferry service began in 1855, operating from the same spot in use today.

Leaving Manly Cove, cross The Esplanade and walk down The Corso, a pedestrian mall. At the end of The Corso, to the left, stands the New Brighton Hotel ② in striking Egyptian Classical Revival Style. In 1926, it replaced the original New Brighton, built in 1880 as the resort's first attraction.

Head towards the rolling surf and sweeping sands of Manly Beach ③ then continue south along the promenade. From the 1950s-style Surf Pavilion, follow Marine Parade walkway around to Cabbage Tree Bay. The pretty area around the rock pool was named Fairy Bower ④ for the delicate wildflowers and maidenhair ferns that once grew on the hillside. Beyond the rock pool, continue on the pathway around to Shelly Beach ⑤, a secluded scuba diving and snorkelling spot, which is also ideal for child swimmers. The 1920s beach kiosk has now been stylishly restored and converted into the smart Le Kiosk restaurant.

Detail on the New Brighton Hotel

Shelly Beach to the former St Patrick's Seminary

Across the park, take the steps to your left to Shelly Beach Headland. A path further left loops around the headland. Viewing platforms ⑥ overlook the vast South Pacific Ocean.

Take the carpark exit into Bower Street. Follow the road as it rounds high above Fairy Bower, passing by homes of diverse architectural styles, from Spanish Mission to Neo-Georgian. Turn left into College Street, then right into Reddall Street, and left again

TIPS FOR WALKERS

***Starting point**: Manly Wharf*
***Length**: 7.5 km (41/2 miles).*
***Getting there**: Regular ferry and Manly Fast Ferry services depart from Circular Quay.*
***Stopping-off points**: The wide range of fresh food counters at Manly Pier make it an ideal place to stock up on picnic fare. Restaurants and cafés line The Corso and Manly Beach Promenade. Le Kiosk at Shelly Beach offers the choice of a smart restaurant, barbecue or snack bar. In warm weather, come prepared with a swimsuit, hat, towel and sunscreen.*

The clear waters of sheltered Shelly Beach ⑤

into Addison Road. Opposite the Victorian buildings at Nos. 97–99 and 95, a lane into Fairy Bower Road leads to views of the former St Patrick's Seminary, now the International College of Tourism and Hotel Management ⑦. Both Romanesque and Neo-Gothic architecture are in evidence in this 1885 edifice, built only after much deliberation by an essentially Protestant government.

Leave Fairy Bower Road by Vivian Street to turn left into Darley Road and arrive at the seminary building. Just opposite, the site of the former Archbishop's House, once known as the Cardinal's Palace, is being redeveloped.

The former St Patrick's Seminary, now the International College of Tourism ⑦

North Head Reserve
At the top of Darley Road, turn right beneath the Parkhill Sandstone Arch ⑧ into North Head

Reserve. Follow the right-hand fork (leading to the Institute of Police Management) onto Collins Beach Road down through bushland alive with bird calls and native lizards. Paperbarks, smooth-barked apple trees and banksias are some of the native flora growing in abundance.

At the road's end, follow the track to your right across two footbridges, then down steps to Collins Beach ⑨. A stone cairn between the second footbridge and the beach marks where Governor Arthur Phillip was speared by the Aboriginal Wil-ee-ma-rin after a misunderstanding. The quiet waterfall and dense bushland make it possible to imagine this beach in pre-colonial days.

Leave via a small set of stone steps at the right-hand end of the beach which lead to a footpath, then out into Stuart Street.

Back to the Present
For memorable harbour views, follow the direction of Stuart Street through Little Manly Point Reserve, passing by the baths of Little Manly Cove ⑩. If you are reluctant to end this charming walk, turn left and proceed to the end of Addison Road. Manly Point Peace Park offers a quiet place to take in a panorama of the distant city.

Return down Addison Road, making your way back to the wharf via Stuart Street and the East Esplanade. With its boat sheds and bleached timber yacht clubs, the East Esplanade Park has a nautical atmosphere and is a relaxing place to meander. Continue past the attractions of the amusement pier to Manly Wharf, which was your starting point.

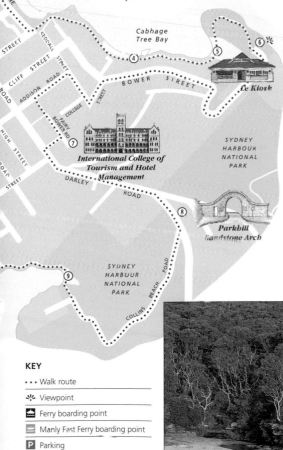

KEY

• • • Walk route

☆ Viewpoint

⛴ Ferry boarding point

⛴ Manly Fast Ferry boarding point

P Parking

0 metres   250

0 yards   250

Collins Beach ⑨ on the edge of Sydney Harbour National Park

A Three-Hour Walk in Watsons Bay and Vaucluse

Tracing the perimeters of spectacular South Head, this walk touches on the area's colonial connections and takes in a variety of ocean and harbourside terrain, from headlands with sweeping views and crashing waves, to secluded coves, white sandy beaches and the streets of one of Sydney's most desirable neighbourhoods.

Signal Station [2] at Dunbar Head

Macquarie Lighthouse to Camp Cove

The start of this walk is majestic Macquarie Lighthouse (1883) [1]. A copy of the country's first lighthouse built in 1818 *(see p137)*, it stands on the same site.

Take the walk northwards, passing by the Signal Station [2] following Old South Head Road. Before the station was built in 1848, a flag was hoisted to warn the colony of ships entering the harbour.

Continue along the footpath, where a plaque marks the location of Australia's worst maritime disaster. It was here that the migrant ship *Dunbar* crashed onto the rocks in a gale in 1857 *(see pp136–7)*. The only survivor was hauled to safety up the treacherous cleft in the cliff face known as Jacob's Ladder [3]. From here, follow the descending path, arriving at the jutting stony ledges of The Gap [4]. The *Dunbar's* anchor is here set into concrete, while salvaged personal effects are displayed at the Australian National Maritime Museum *(see pp94–5)*.

Taking the steps down from The Gap, bear right into the entrance of Sydney Harbour National Park. This single-lane roadway leads through natural bushland into HMAS *Watson* Military Reserve. Follow the road up to visit the Naval Memorial Chapel [5]. A large clear window inside the chapel offers spectacular views of North Head and the Pacific Ocean. Resume your walk by taking the road out of the reserve, and then turn right into Cliff Street. Passing a row of weatherboard cottages on your left, follow the street to its end and onto Camp Cove Beach [6]. It was here in 1788 that Captain Arthur Phillip first stepped ashore after leaving Botany Bay to explore the coastline.

Bust, Macquarie Lighthouse [1]

Camp Cove to Watsons Bay

Take the wooden steps at the northern end of the cove to make the 40-minute return walk to South

Nudist Lady Bay Beach

Doyle's well-known restaurant at Watsons Bay [8]

6
12
10
11
Vaucluse House
KEY
Walk route
Viewpoint
Bus stop
Ferry boarding point

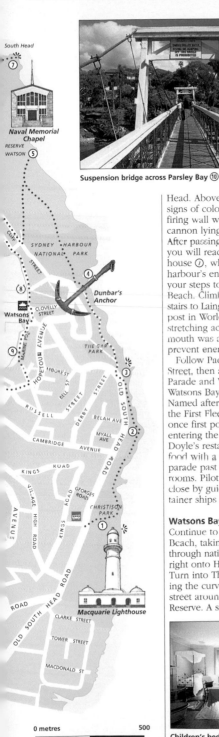

Suspension bridge across Parsley Bay ⑩

onto a suspension bridge hung across the waters of tranquil Parsley Bay ⑩. Crossing the bridge, follow the pathway between two houses to arrive on Fitzwilliam Road. Continue right along Fitzwilliam Road, turning left into Wentworth Road to reach the extravagant Vaucluse House ⑪, surrounded by exotic gardens (see p136).

To finish your walk, make your way along Coolong Road to Nielsen Park (see p136) and Shark Bay ⑫. Protected from its namesake by a netted enclosure, the natural setting and safe waters of this beach make it a favourite for picnics.

Head. Above the steps are signs of colonial defences: a firing wall with rifl slots; a cannon lying further along. After passing Lady Bay Beach, you will reach Hornby Lighthouse ⑦, which marks the harbour's entrance. Retrace your steps to Camp Cove Beach. Climb the western-end stairs to Laings Point, a defence post in World War II. A net stretching across the harbour mouth was anchored here to prevent enemy ships entering.

Follow Pacific Street to Cove Street, then along to Marine Parade and Wharf Beach in Watsons Bay ⑧ (see pp136–7). Named after Robert Watson of the First Fleet's Sirius, this was once first port of call for ships entering the harbour. Nearby, Doyle's restaurant offers seafood with a view. Follow the parade past the baths and tea rooms. Pilot boats ⑨ moored close by guide cruise and container ships into the harbour.

Watsons Bay to Vaucluse
Continue to secluded Gibsons Beach, taking the footpath left through native shrubbery, then right onto Hopetoun Avenue. Turn into The Crescent, tracing the curve of this exclusive street around to Parsley Bay Reserve. A short descent opens

Children's bedroom, one of the exhibits at Vaucluse House ⑪

Dramatic rock cleft known as Jacob's Ladder ③ near The Gap

TIPS FOR WALKERS

Starting point: *Macquarie Lighthouse.*
Length: *8 km (5 miles).*
Getting there: *Take Bus 324 from Circular Quay, or Bus 387 from Bondi Junction. Return by Bus 325 from Nielsen Park.*
Stopping-off points: *There are public toilets and showers at Camp Cove, Watsons Bay, Parsley Bay and Nielsen Park. Food and refreshments are available throughout the walk at Watsons Bay, Parsley Bay, Vaucluse and Nielsen Park. The tea rooms at Vaucluse House offer views of the gardens, and the café at Nielsen Park sells homemade fare in generous portions. The walk covers several harbour beaches where you can swim safely. In warm weather, bring a swimsuit, towel, hat and sunscreen, and allow time for swimming, sunbathing and picnicking.*

BEYOND SYDNEY

Exploring Beyond Sydney

To the east, Sydney is bounded by the Pacific Ocean; to the west, by the Great Dividing Range. To the north and south, within easy distance of the city, are superb beaches and stretches of coastal scenery, while inland, you will encounter waterfalls, deep valleys and fascinating flora and wildlife. On the Hawkesbury River, to the north and west of the city, are settlements of historical as well as scenic interest while, further north, the Hunter River meanders through sloping vineyards. The excursions on pages 154–65 offer the visitor the chance to sample the rich variety of Sydney landscapes from the exhilarating to the tranquil.

Cable car ride over the Blue Mountains

Façade of Hope Estate in the Hunter Valley

SIGHTS AT A GLANCE

Blue Mountains **4**

Hawkesbury Tour **2**

Hunter Valley **3**

Pittwater and Ku-ring-gai Chase
   National Park **1**

Royal National Park **6**

Southern Highlands Tour **5**

GETTING AROUND

All the areas covered in these excursions can be easily reached by road from Sydney. Freeways and motorways take travellers part of the way to the Southern Highlands, Blue Mountains and Hunter Valley, while the other areas are accessible on sealed, well-signposted major roads. A number of tour operators offer guided one-day, or longer, tours to the Blue Mountains, Hunter Valley, Southern Highlands and South Coast, and parts of the Hawkesbury region. CityRail has regular train services to the Blue Mountains, Royal National Park and to parts of the area covered by the Southern Highlands Tour. Ferries offer access to some parts of the Hawkesbury River.

0 kilometres   50

0 miles   25

Grand old house in Kiama, near the Southern Highlands

Mudgee
Glen Davis
Capertree
86
Cullen Bullen
Portland
Bathurst
Meadow Flats
Orange, Dubbo
Walang
32
Lithgow
Zig Zag Railway
Tarana
Berambing
Mount Victoria
Hampton
Blackheath
BLUE MOUNTAINS
4
Oberon
Katoomba
Black Springs
Jenolan Caves
Blue Mountains National Park
Porters Retreat
Natta
Richlands
Bullio
Taralga
Myrtleville
Bowral
Chatsbury
Moss Vale
Tarlo
Brayton
SOUTHERN
31
Canberra
Bungonia
Morton National Park
Nerriga
Sassafras
Conjola
Bega

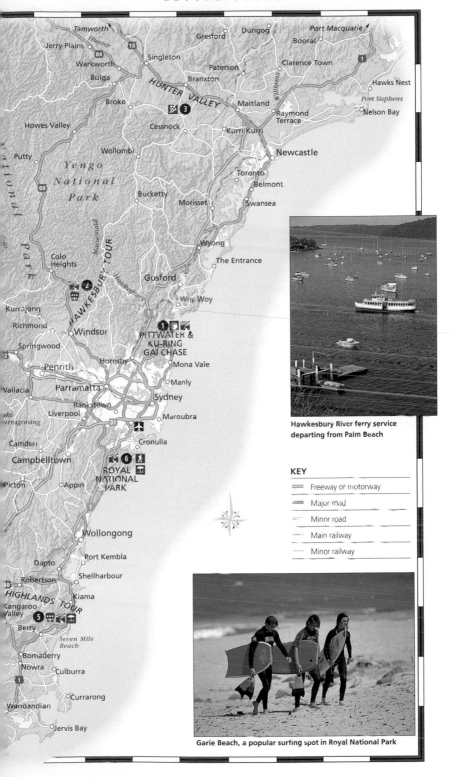

Hawkesbury River ferry service departing from Palm Beach

KEY

Freeway or motorway
Major road
Minor road
Main railway
Minor railway

Garie Beach, a popular surfing spot in Royal National Park

Pittwater and Ku-ring-gai Chase ❶

Pittwater and the adjacent Ku-ring-gai Chase National Park lie on Sydney's northernmost outskirts. They are bounded to the north by Broken Bay, at the mouth of the Hawkesbury River *(see pp156–7)*. Sparkling waterways and golden beaches are set against the unspoiled backdrop of the national park.

Barrenjoey Lighthouse

Picnicking, bushwalking, surfing, boating, sailing and windsurfing are popular pastimes with visitors. The Hawkesbury River system curls around an ancient sandstone landscape rich in Aboriginal rock art, and flora and fauna.

Coal and Candle Creek

The pretty inlet is typical of eroded valleys formed during the last Ice Age. Water melted from the ice caps flooded the valleys to form the bays and creeks of Broken Bay.

Akuna Bay

The isolated marina, general store and café serve the Hawkesbury River boating fraternity.

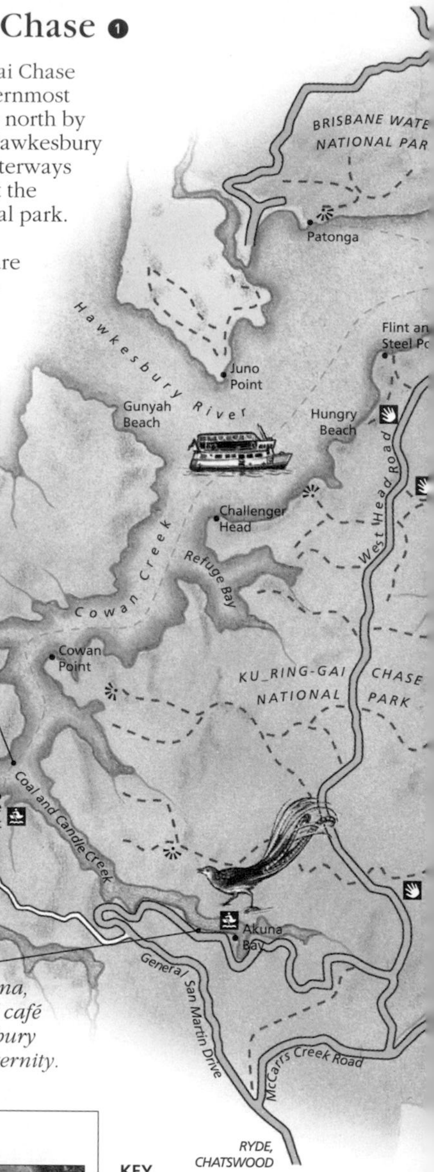

ABORIGINAL ART IN KU-RING-GAI CHASE

Ku-ring-gai Chase has literally hundreds of Aboriginal rock art sites, providing an insight into one of the world's oldest cultures. The most common are rock engravings, generally made in groups with as many as 100 individual figures. They include whales up to 8 m (26 ft) long, fish, sharks, wallabies, echidnas and Ancestral Spirits such as Daramulan, who created the land, its people and animals.

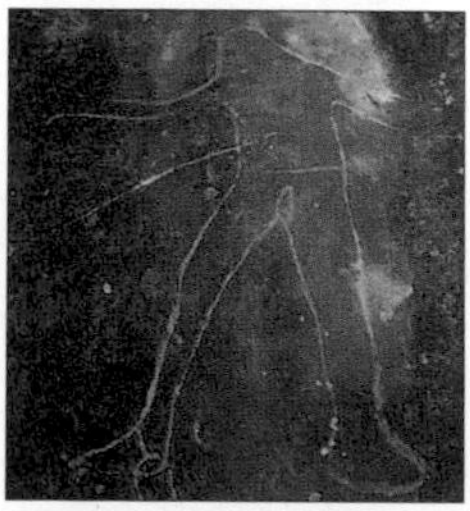

Aboriginal rock art near the Basin, Ku-ring-gai Chase

KEY

■	Major road
▭	Secondary road
—	Minor road
▢	National Park
- - -	Ferry route
---	Walk route
⚓	Boat hire
◪	Aboriginal rock art
✲	Viewpoint

Map labels: BRISBANE WATER NATIONAL PARK, Patonga, Hawkesbury River, Juno Point, Flint and Steel Point, Gunyah Beach, Hungry Beach, Challenger Head, West Head Road, Cowan Creek, Refuge Bay, Cowan Point, Coal and Candle Creek, Cottage Point, Smitts Creek, KU-RING-GAI CHASE NATIONAL PARK, Akuna Bay, General San Martin Drive, McCarrs Creek Road, RYDE, CHATSWOOD

Palm Beach Wharf

Palm Beach, a haven for sea birds such as pelicans, is popular with sun-seekers. It is also the base for the boats that visit and deliver supplies to the isolated communities on Pittwater and the Hawkesbury.

Pittwater

This graceful finger of water separates Palm Beach from Ku-ring-gai Chase. Pittwater boasts secluded beaches, picnic areas and several hamlets that can only be reached by water.

Whale Beach

Spectacular houses seem to hug the cliffs overlooking this fine surf beach. The Palm Beach Peninsula's beaches are often less congested than those closer to the city.

0 kilometres 2

0 miles 1

TIPS FOR TRAVELLERS

Distance from Sydney: About 30 km (19 miles). **Duration of journey:** About 45 minutes to Mona Vale Beach. **Getting there:** Take Military Rd on the city's North Shore and cross the Spit Bridge. Follow Pittwater Rd to Mona Vale Beach. **When to go:** The Christmas holiday period is the peak season and beaches can be crowded. Ku-ring-gai Chase offers everything from shoreline to bushwalks and can be enjoyed year round. **Where to stay and eat:** Contact the visitors' information centre for full details of facilities. **Tourist information:** NPWS N. Region Info Centre. **Tel** 9472 8949. ◯ 9am–5pm Mon–Fri. ⬤ Christmas Day. www.npws.nsw.gov.au

Bilgola Beach

A small community of residents backs this patrolled surf beach set against a pretty rainforested valley. Wooden steps lead down from the ridge above through coastal heathland.

Hawkesbury Tour [2]

Australia's longest eastward-flowing river, the Hawkesbury–Nepean, forms Sydney's northern and western boundaries. It was at first thought to be two separate rivers until further exploration revealed that they were in fact one. The section known as the Hawkesbury runs from the Colo River Valley to Broken Bay in the north *(see pp154–5)*.

Settled in 1794, by 1799 the Hawkesbury Valley's small farms produced three-quarters of the colony's grain. Its riverscape is little changed since then and much of the area remains a quiet backwater. It is an area rich in relics of the early colonial period, including towns and villages established during the Macquarie era of 1810–19 *(see p24)*. It is also a place of great scenic grandeur, with magnificent vistas of one of Australia's most beautiful rivers.

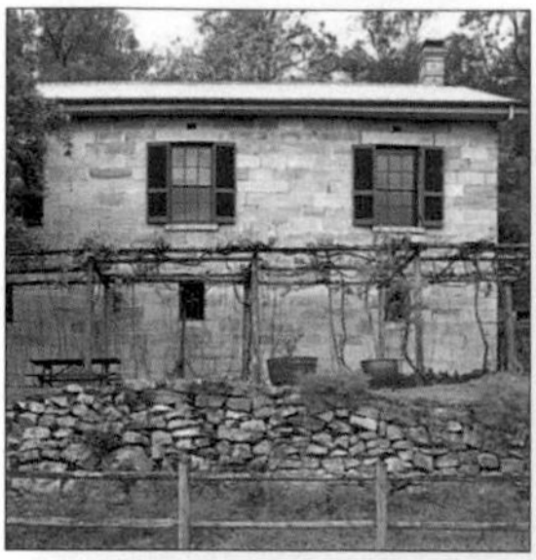

Tizzana Winery [5]
A touch of Tuscany on the banks of the Hawkesbury, this sandstone winery was built in 1887 by Dr Thomas Fiaschi. It is open to visitors on weekends and public holidays.

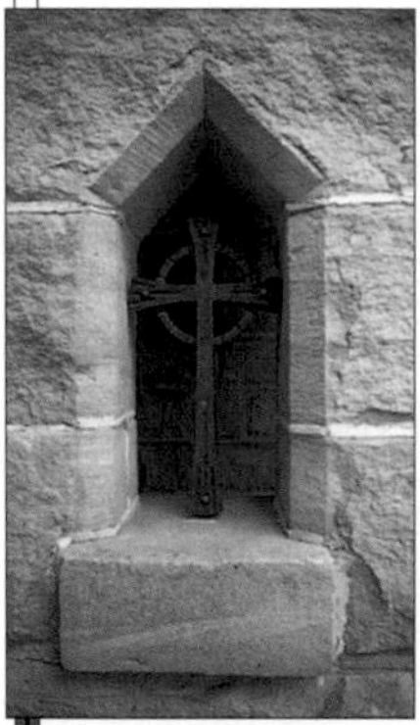

Ebenezer Uniting Church [4]
Built in 1809, the church and its 1817 schoolhouse have been superbly restored. The tree under which services were first held still stands.

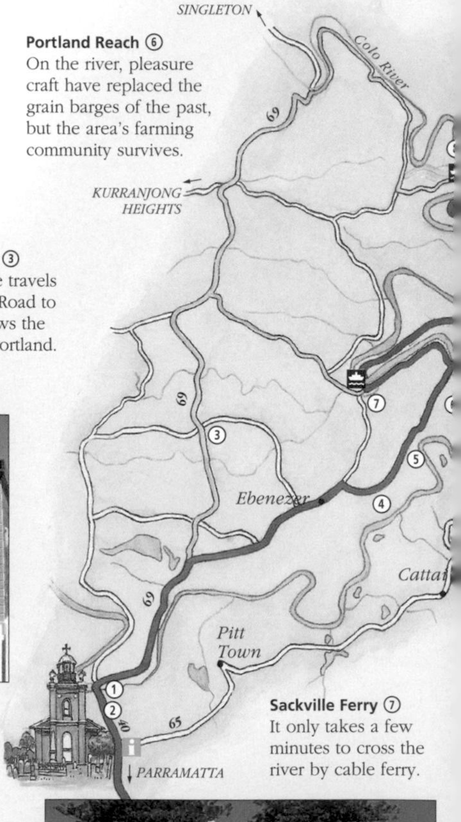
SINGLETON
Colo River
69
KURRANJONG HEIGHTS
69
Ebenezer
69
Pitt Town
65
40
PARRAMATTA

Portland Reach [6]
On the river, pleasure craft have replaced the grain barges of the past, but the area's farming community survives.

Colo River Drive [3]
This pretty route travels along the Putty Road to Colo, then follows the river to Lower Portland.

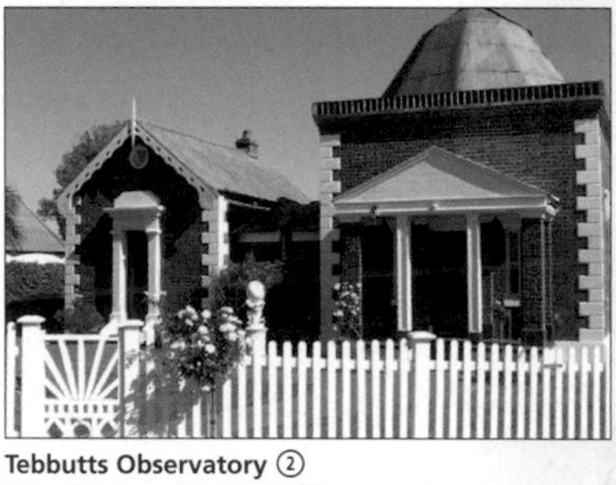

Tebbutts Observatory [2]
John Tebbutt (1834–1916), an early amateur astronomer, built this observatory in Windsor in 1854, where he studied the solar system and discovered a comet in 1861.

Sackville Ferry [7]
It only takes a few minutes to cross the river by cable ferry.

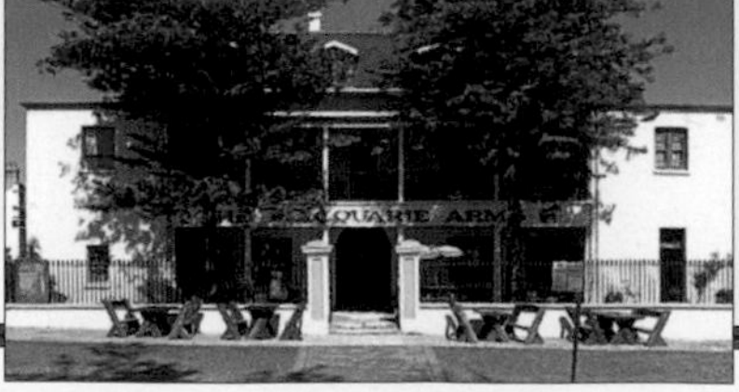

Windsor [1]
Built in 1815, the Macquarie Arms Hotel is just one of Windsor's fine early colonial buildings. Many others, including several by architect Francis Greenway *(see p114)*, remain from the town laid out in 1810.

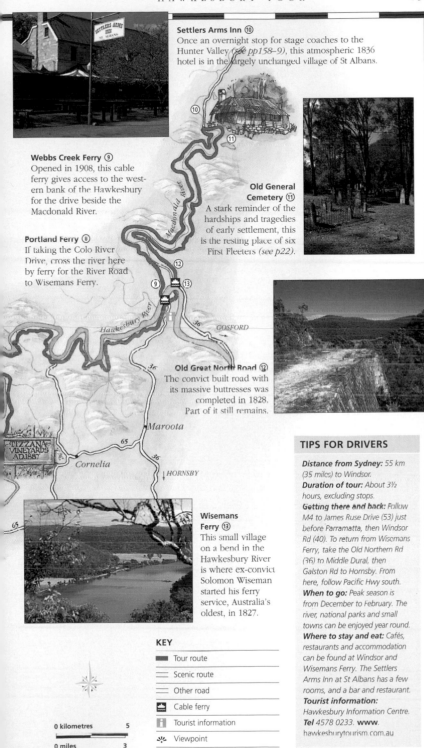

Settlers Arms Inn ⑩
Once an overnight stop for stage coaches to the Hunter Valley (see pp158–9), this atmospheric 1836 hotel is in the largely unchanged village of St Albans.

Webbs Creek Ferry ⑨
Opened in 1908, this cable ferry gives access to the western bank of the Hawkesbury for the drive beside the Macdonald River.

Portland Ferry ⑧
If taking the Colo River Drive, cross the river here by ferry for the River Road to Wisemans Ferry.

Old General Cemetery ⑪
A stark reminder of the hardships and tragedies of early settlement, this is the resting place of six First Fleeters (see p22).

Old Great North Road ⑫
The convict built road with its massive buttresses was completed in 1828. Part of it still remains.

Maroota

Cornelia

↓ HORNSBY

GOSFORD

Wisemans Ferry ⑬
This small village on a bend in the Hawkesbury River is where ex-convict Solomon Wiseman started his ferry service, Australia's oldest, in 1827.

KEY

▬	Tour route
═	Scenic route
═	Other road
⛴	Cable ferry
ℹ	Tourist information
☀	Viewpoint

0 kilometres   5
0 miles   3

TIPS FOR DRIVERS

Distance from Sydney: 55 km (35 miles) to Windsor.
Duration of tour: About 3½ hours, excluding stops.
Getting there and back: Follow M4 to James Ruse Drive (53) just before Parramatta, then Windsor Rd (40). To return from Wisemans Ferry, take the Old Northern Rd (36) to Middle Dural, then Galston Rd to Hornsby. From here, follow Pacific Hwy south.
When to go: Peak season is from December to February. The river, national parks and small towns can be enjoyed year round.
Where to stay and eat: Cafés, restaurants and accommodation can be found at Windsor and Wisemans Ferry. The Settlers Arms Inn at St Albans has a few rooms, and a bar and restaurant.
Tourist information:
Hawkesbury Information Centre.
Tel 4578 0233. **www.**
hawkesburytourism.com.au

Hunter Valley ❸

Some of the earliest vineyards
to be planted in Australia were
on the fertile flats of the Hunter
River in the 1830s, developing a
thriving industry in fortified wine.
Since the 1970s, it has evolved
into a premium wine district

**Cheese made by
local producer**

(see pp182–3). With some 90
wineries the area is a popular weekend trip
from Sydney. Hot air ballooning, golf and
horse riding supplement vineyard visits. The
Jazz in the Vines festival takes place in October.
Many wineries open daily but it is best to
phone ahead and check.

Brokenwood

*Under the ownership
of Ian Riggs, this
medium-sized
winery has
produced some of
the region's finest
Shiraz from the
Graveyard vineyard,
as well as an
excellent Semillon.*

Lindemans

*In 1842, Dr Henry John
Lindeman resigned his
naval commission to
establish a vineyard in
the Hunter Valley. His
company has been a
major producer in the
Australian wine
industry ever since.*

SINGLETON,
UPPER HUNTER

Sweetwater Creek

Old North Road

TERRACE
RANGE

Hermitage Road

Rothbury Creek

🏁 Hunter Estate

Marsh Estate

Sutherland

Deaseys Road

ROSEMOUNT
ESTATE, UPPER
HUNTER

Mary Anne's Creek

Broke Road

Brian
McGuigan

Tyrrell's
Wines

Brokenwood

Tamburlaine

Tulloch

Pokolbin

Debeyers Road

Pokolb

Lungerford
Hill

Draytons

Drayton
Family Estate

Oakey Cree

McWilliam's

Marrowbone

BROKEN BACK RANGE

Petersons

PERSONALITIES OF THE HUNTER VALLEY

The wine industry seems to attract or create
larger-than-life characters. Among the
legends was the great Len Evans, writer,
wine judge, *bon vivant* and founder of the
ambitious Hope Estate and
Evans Family Wines, as
well as Tower Estate. His
contemporaries included
Max Lake, a Sydney surgeon
who started Lake's Folly as
a weekend winery, and the
late Murray Tyrrell, patriarch
of a wine-making family that
produced its first Hunter
vintage in 1864 and proudly
retains its independence.

Len Evans checking grape vines

Hope Estate

On the site of the late Len Evans' former winery, The Rothbury Estate, Hope Estate hosts dinners and concerts in the winery's cask hall.

Pepper's Convent

A restored 1909 convent is now an elegantly appointed guest house, with the Pepper Tree vineyard and winery and Robert's Restaurant only a short walk away.

Lake's Folly

Australian growers stopped planting Cabernet Sauvignon vines in the 19th century. But in the 1960s, former owner Max Lake reintroduced the variety.

Golden Grape Estate

A popular coach stop, the winery has a vine gallery showing grape varieties found around the world. There is also a museum which features early wine making equipment.

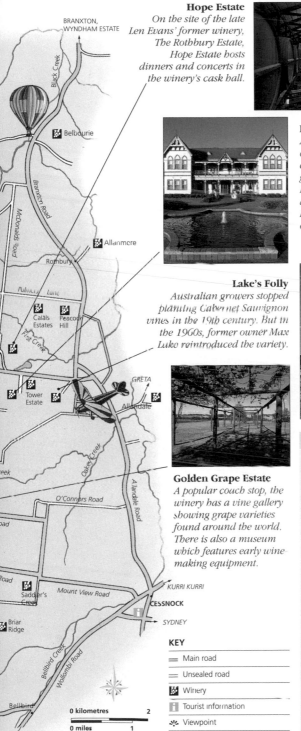

KEY

═══	Main road
──	Unsealed road
🏰	Winery
ℹ	Tourist information
☀	Viewpoint

0 kilometres   2
0 miles   1

TIPS FOR TRAVELLERS

Distance from Sydney: 160 km (100 miles).

Duration of journey: About 2 hours from the centre of Sydney.

Getting there and back: Take the Sydney–Newcastle F3 freeway north of Sydney and follow the signs to Cessnock. Another route is through the picturesque Wollombi Valley. Allow about 3 hours as there are unsealed roads.

When to go: Year round. Vintage is Jan–Mar.

Where to stay and eat: There is a wide variety of motels, guesthouses, self-catering cottages and cabins, cafés and restaurants.

Visitor information: Hunter Valley Wine Country Tourism, 455 Wine Country Drive, Pokolbin. **Tel** 4990 0900. www.winecountry.com.au

Further afield: The Upper Hunter vineyards are about 40 minutes by car northwest of Pokolbin.

Blue Mountains ❹

The Blue Mountains, now a World Heritage area, prevented westward expansion of the European colony until 1813, when explorers Gregory Blaxland, William Lawson and William Charles Wentworth found a way across. The magnificent scenery, characterized by rugged cliffs and rock formations, ravines and waterfalls, is best appreciated on the bushwalks that wind along cliff tops and through valleys. The restaurants, cafés and antique shops in the centre of Katoomba will tempt the less energetic. The mountains are named for the blue haze, caused by light striking eucalyptus oil particles in the air.

Zig Zag Railway
A steam train travels through cuttings and tunnels, and over three impressive viaducts built from 1866–9.

Grose Valley from Govetts Leap
Considered by many to be the most imposing view in the Blue Mountains, a great panorama with a series of ridges stretches into the far distance.

The Grose River flows between the two roads crossing the mountains.

Victoria Falls

Mount York

JENOLAN CAVES

ZIG ZAG RAILWAY

Three Sisters
This giant rock formation near Echo Point takes its name from an Aboriginal legend. The story tells of three sisters turned to stone by their witch-doctor father to keep them safe from an evil bunyip or monster.

JENOLAN CAVES

About 55 km (34 miles) south-west of Mount Victoria is a magical series of spectacular underground limestone caves with icy blue rivers and fleecy limestone formations. They are surrounded by an extensive wildlife reserve. People have been making the trek here since the caves were discovered in 1838, staying originally in the Grand Arch cave and later in the Edwardian splendour of Jenolan Caves House, which still operates today.

The vividly coloured Pool of Cerberus at Jenolan Caves

KEY

▬▬	Major road
	Other road
•••	Suggested walk
🚶	Starting points for other walks
⛺	Campsite
🏕	Picnic area
ℹ	Tourist information
☼	Viewpoint

Mount Wilson
A picturesque village with cultivated gardens and exotic trees, it has been called a "little corner of the northern hemisphere". Some gardens are open to the public in spring and autumn.

The **Cathedral of Ferns** is a remnant of the temperate rainforest that once covered this area.

Mount Tomah Botanic Gardens
This superbly landscaped garden, specializing in cool-climate plants, has sweeping views over the Grose Valley.

RICHMOND

Mount Banks

Norman Lindsay Gallery and Museum
The stone cottage is home to a collection of works by artist and writer Norman Lindsay (1879–1967).

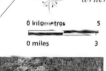

0 kilometres   5
0 miles   3

Kings Tableland

Jamison Valley

Wentworth Falls
An impressive double water-fall is the starting point for the National Pass track, a challenging four-hour return walk to the next valley.

Leura village is classified by the National Trust. Nearby are Leura Cascades, floodlit at night and one of the prettiest sights in the mountains.

TIPS FOR TRAVELLERS

Distance from Sydney: About 105 km (65 miles).
Duration of journey: About 90 minutes to Wentworth Falls.
Getting there and back: Follow Metroad route 4 and the Great Western Highway. Return by Bells Line of Road to Windsor. State Rail has regular services to the area. An Explorer Bus runs from Katoomba train station at 9:30am on weekends and public holidays.
When to go: Year round. Always be prepared for the cold, especially when hiking, as the weather can change rapidly in all seasons.
Where to stay and eat: Contact the visitor information centre.
Tourist information: Blue Mountains Visitors' Information Centre, Echo Point, Katoomba. **Tel** 1300 653 408. **www.** visitbluemountains.com.au

Southern Highlands Tour ⑤

This easily accessible area to the south of Sydney is often said to be more typical of Great Britain, than Australia. It is actually a delightful combination of both: Australian high country and coastal hinterland with many European qualities. It is a land of abrupt hills and valleys, waterfalls and streams; of quaint villages, cosy restaurants, antique shops and elegant places to stay. The tour takes in spectacular Seven Mile Beach and the pretty town of Berry before heading to Kangaroo Valley, sleepy Bundanoon and the antique shops and wineries of Berrima and Bowral. An exhilarating adjunct to the tour is nearby Minnamurra Falls with its boardwalk through rainforest.

Common wombat

Bowral ⑧
This highlands town holds a famous spring tulip festival every year and is home to cricket's Bradman Museum.

Berrima ⑦
By-passed by the railway in the 19th century, the only Georgian village in the highlands remains one of the most picturesque.

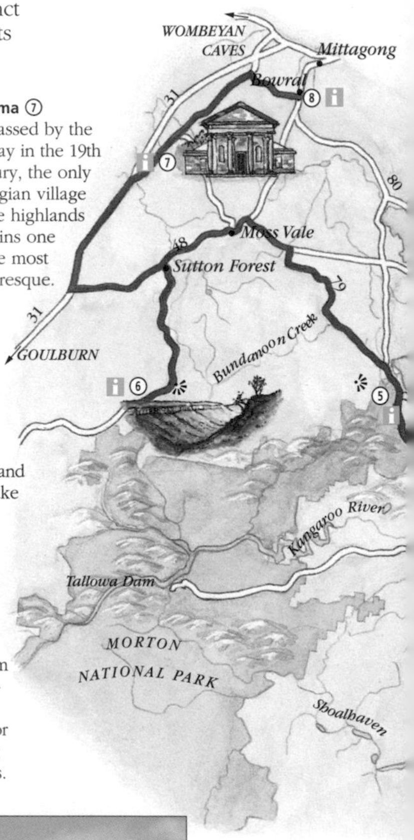

Bundanoon ⑥
Romantic guesthouses and a glow-worm cave make this town a popular weekend destination.

Fitzroy Falls ⑤
Part of Morton National Park, the falls plunge 80 m (262 ft) into the subtropical rainforest below. The falls lookout has access for the disabled and walking trails with stunning views.

| 0 kilometres | 10 |
| 0 miles | 5 |

KEY

- ▬ Tour route
- ═ Scenic route (alternative)
- ─ Other roads
- 🅷 Tourist information
- ❀ Viewpoint

Kangaroo Valley ④
Hampden Bridge, a castellated suspension bridge, crosses the Kangaroo River at this small village. The river is an idyllic place for canoeing.

Map labels: WOMBEYAN CAVES, Mittagong, Bowral ⑧, Berrima ⑦, Moss Vale, Sutton Forest, GOULBURN, Bundanoon Creek, Bundanoon ⑥, Kangaroo River, Tallowa Dam, MORTON NATIONAL PARK, Shoalhaven

BERRIMA GAOL
Completed in 1839 by convict labour, this Georgian sandstone jail is featured in Rolf Boldrewood's classic 1888 bushranging novel, *Robbery Under Arms*. The fictitious character Captain Starlight, who escapes from Berrima, describes it as "the largest, most severe, the most dreaded of all prisons in New South Wales".

Kiama ①
The historic town began life in the 1820s as a port for shipping cedar. Its blowhole can spurt water as high as 60 m (200 ft).

Seven Mile Beach ②
Part of a national park and best seen from Gerroa's Black Head, the beach is flanked by dunes and hardy coastal vegetation, including forest and swamp. It is a great fishing, swimming and picnicking spot.

TIPS FOR DRIVERS

Distance from Sydney: 120 km (75 miles).
Duration of tour: About 3½ hours, excluding stops.
Getting there and back: Take Metroad route 1, then follow the F3 freeway and Princes Hwy (1) to Kiama. Return via the F5 freeway (31) from Mittagong, then Metroad route 5 into the city.
When to go: Year round. The beaches are best in summer, the gardens in spring and autumn. History buffs and antique-lovers will enjoy the towns.
Where to stay and eat: Eating places, hotels and guesthouses are found all over the area.
Tourist information: Kiama Visitors Centre, Blowhole Point, Kiama. **Tel** 4232 3322. **www.** kiama.com.au Southern Highlands Visitors Information Centre, 62–70 Main St, Mittagong. **Tel** 4871 2888. **www.**visitsouthern highlands.com.au

Berry ③
This town, surrounded by lush dairy country, is well known for its main street lined with shady trees, antique and craft shops, tea rooms and historic buildings. The Berry Museum, built in 1886, is in a former bank.

Royal National Park ❻

Designated as a national park in 1879, the "Royal" is the oldest national park in Australia. It covers 16,000 ha (37,100 acres) of landscape typical of the Sydney Basin sandstone. To the east, waves from the Pacific Ocean have undercut the sandstone and produced majestic coastal cliffs broken occasionally by small creeks and some spectacular beaches. Streams flowing north and east have incised deep river valleys. Heath vegetation on the plateaux merges with woodlands on the upper slopes. The park is ideal for bushwalking, picnicking, camping, swimming and birdwatching.

Waratah

Hacking River
Boating, fishing and canoeing are common water sports.

Audley
A popular picnic area since the Edwardian era, it has a pavilion that was built in 1901. Look out for the 1920s dance hall also in the park.

Heathcote

Lady Carrington Drive
Named after a governor's wife and now closed to vehicles, the road is crossed by 15 creeks and is delightful to walk or cycle. It also leads to the track to Palona Cave.

KEY

▬	Main road
	Walking track
⇄	CityRail station
⚓	Ferry boarding point
▦	Picnic area
▲	Campsite
≋	Swimming
P	Parking
⁎	Viewpoint

The Forest Path follows a circular route, passing through subtropical rainforest.

Garie Beach is a popular surf beach accessible by road.

Werrong Naturist Beach

Figure Eight Pool

0 kilometres   4

0 miles   2

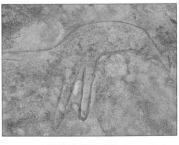

Bundeena

Enclosed by national park on three sides, the small settlement at the mouth of the Hacking River may be reached by ferry from Cronulla or by road through the national park.

Cronulla

Jibbon Head

Guided tours of the Jibbon Head Aboriginal rock engravings site may be arranged.

Jibbon Lagoon

Deer Pool

One of many freshwater pools in the park, this sheltered spot is on the track from Bundeena Drive to Marley and Little Marley.

Little Marley Beach

Wattamolla Lagoon

This pretty picnic spot has a lagoon with a waterfall at its edge and a protected ocean beach.

Curracurrang

This rock formation is about halfway along the two-day Coast Walk. Sea eagles and terns nest in caves at the base of this rocky cove which also has a secluded swimming hole and waterfall.

TIPS FOR TRAVELLERS

Distance from Sydney: *34 km (21 miles).*

Duration of journey: *About 1 hour from the centre of Sydney.*

Getting there: *Follow Metroad route 1 south to Sutherland, then the signs to Heathcote and Wollongong. The turn-off to Farnell Avenue and the park entrance is shortly after Sutherland.*

When to go: *Year round, but conditions for walking in summer can be hot so allow for this. If bushwalking, carry fresh water at all times and check on the fire danger at the Visitors' Centre.*

Where to stay and eat: *There are kiosks at Audley, Garie Beach and Wattamolla. Camping information can be obtained at the Visitors' Centre.*

Tourist information: *Royal National Park Visitors' Centre, Farnell Ave, Audley.* **Tel** *9542 0648.* **www.**npws.nsw.gov.au

Guided Tours: *The Coast Track* **Tel** *0424 546 921.* **www.** royalcoastwalks.com.au

TRAVELLERS' NEEDS

WHERE TO STAY

With Australia's emergence as a major tourist destination, the urgent need for more high-quality and good-value accommodation became apparent. Previously, most Sydney hotels and guesthouses had been regarded as expensive and of varying standard. There has since been an enormous improvement in both quality and value, and there are excellent choices for visitors ranging from five-star luxury to the homeliness of a small, unpretentious hotel. In addition to hotels, Sydney has

Sydney hotel doorman

self-catering apartments, homestay accommodation and budget and backpacker hostels for those travelling on a budget. Information on these alternatives is given below. From a survey of various types of accommodation in different areas and varying price brackets, we have selected those offering good value for money. Detailed descriptions of each hotel can be found on pages 172–7. Included with each hotel review is a list of symbols indicating the full range of facilities on offer there.

Façade of the Hilton Sydney Hotel
(see p174)

WHERE TO LOOK

Most of the expensive hotels are in or near the city centre, but it is possible to find accommodation within most price ranges throughout Sydney. The city centre has the advantage of having many of the larger theatres, galleries and shops at hand, as well as easy transport access to more distant sights and attractions.

Cheaper accommodation can be found in the vibrant Kings Cross district. Choices here range from backpacker hostels to the small "boutique" hotels where the emphasis is on quality and personal service.

In The Rocks area, with its beautifully restored colonial buildings, you can choose from bed and breakfast in a traditional Sydney pub or the opulence of a five-star luxury hotel with good views of the Sydney Opera House.

The hotels around Darling Harbour and Chinatown offer good value for shoppers and are also within easy reach of

the city centre. Paddington has smaller hotels and self-catering apartments, while to the east are the upmarket hotels of Double Bay. On the other side of Sydney Harbour Bridge, the leafy North Shore provides a more relaxed look at Sydney, and you can travel to and from the city centre by ferry.

The popular beachside suburbs of Bondi and Manly are a little way out of the centre of Sydney, but some visitors may like the opportunity to be close to superb beaches and yet still be reasonably near to the city.

You should also remember that in Australia a hotel can be a pub or a place to drink *(see pp196–7)*. Pubs do not always provide accommodation.

HOW TO BOOK

It is advisable to book well in advance, especially for the Christmas school holidays in December and January, the Gay and Lesbian Mardi Gras

Festival in February and Mardi Gras Parade in early March, the Easter holidays and July and September school holidays.

Bookings can be made by letter, phone, fax, e-mail or through your local international travel agent. A credit card number or bank cheque in Australian dollars is usually required to secure your booking. Check cancellation requirements and reconfirm before you arrive in Sydney.

The **Sydney Visitors Centre** books certain hotels and will send a brochure pack. **Australian Accommodation Services** does not charge for bookings. If you belong to a motoring association, ask your travel agent to check which NRMA- (National Roads and Motorists' Association-) affiliated hotels offer a discount. **Countrylink** agencies at major railway stations offer a comprehensive service and AFTA travel agencies will book most hotels. Some travel

One of the elegant guestrooms at the Swissôtel *(see p173)*

Curvilinear shape of the Four Points By Sheraton *(see p174)*

agencies specialize in specific areas. Tourist information centres can also offer valuable advice about where to stay in Sydney.

DISCOUNT RATES

With fewer visitors staying in Sydney from April to October (except during the school holiday periods), some more expensive hotels may be willing to negotiate a better rate. This is particularly so if they think you will look elsewhere for accommodation. It is always worth asking for the corporate rate at which hotels give discounts for group or company bookings. Most hotels give these without question.

At the weekend there are fewer business clients around, so this is the time when prices are frequently cheaper in the top hotels. Money can also be saved by booking for a week at a time. Asking for a room without a harbour or ocean view is another good way of reducing the costs.

The **Travellers Information Service** in the city can often arrange up to 50 per cent off the price of regular hotel accommodation rates (this does not normally apply to budget hotels) to those who book in person on the day a room is required.

Stained glass at Simpsons hotel *(see p176)*

HIDDEN EXTRAS

Breakfast is usually charged on top of the room rate in the more expensive hotels. It is best to avoid consuming any of the contents of the mini-bar until you have checked the price. Alcohol is usually much more expensive here than in shops. Also, be wary of the telephone charges. There will almost certainly be a considerable mark-up on any calls you make from your room. In general, tipping is not widespread, but it is expected in the more expensive hotels. You should make a note of the check-out time when you arrive, or negotiate a late check-out, as a surcharge may be incurred if you stay late.

SPECIAL OFFERS

Hotels often cooperate with airlines, rail services, bus companies, theatres and entertainment promoters to provide package deals that include discounted accommodation. Booking agencies will have brochures with details of these seasonal offers, or ask the hotel for information on any special deals.

"Special occasion" packages (such as for anniversaries or honeymoons) are available at the top end of the market.

DISABLED TRAVELLERS

The information regarding wheelchair access that is given on pages 172–7 relies very much on each hotel's own assessment of its facilities. **Spinal Cord Injuries Australia** supplies a booklet called *Access Sydney* for people with mobility problems. It details accessible locations around Sydney and is available from their office in Little Bay, or it can be delivered by post. Their website is also worth visiting.

TRAVELLING WITH CHILDREN

It is worth inquiring about special rates or deals that allow children to stay in their parents' room for no extra cost. Most hotels in Sydney welcome children, although you should ask about special facilities before booking.

SELF-CATERING FLATS

Accommodation including full kitchen and laundry facilities offers the traveller greater independence. Such self-catering apartments are the latest accommodation trend in Australia. In addition to comfort, they also provide good value because the living space is larger than standard hotel rooms and the prices are competitive: although rates can vary, they are generally on a par with the major chain hotels.

The choice ranges from one- to three-bedroom luxury apartments in the inner city to basic flats at the beach. Some apartments cater for business travellers, complete with fax and other communications amenities. They are also ideal for families, especially those with young children, who appreciate not only the greater amount of space but also the flexibility provided by self-catering.

All the "apartment" hotels in the listings on pages 172–7 offer self-catering facilities. In addition, Sydney has several agencies that can help visitors to arrange self-catering accommodation *(see p170)*.

A luxurious room at the Regents Court hotel in Potts Point *(see p175)*

PRIVATE HOMES

European-style bed-and-breakfast accommodation in a private home can be an ideal way to experience a city. It is fast becoming a popular alternative to more impersonal hotel rooms for many people who choose to visit Sydney.

People from all walks of life offer rooms in a wide variety of house styles and locations. Agencies such as **Bed and**

Breakfast **Sydney Central** and the **Homestay Network** make every effort to match the host and guest if possible, so ring to discuss any preferences before making a reservation.

BUDGET ACCOMMODATION

As a favoured destination for many young travellers, Sydney has a large number of hostels that cater specifically for their needs. Despite fierce competition, standards vary widely. At their best, hostels offer excellent value.

While it is necessary to book in advance at some hostels, others do not take bookings and beds are on a first come, first served basis. Apartments,

DIRECTORY

DISCOUNT AGENCIES

Travellers Information Service
Sydney Coach Terminal, Eddy Ave, Sydney NSW 2000. **Map** 4 E5.
Tel 9281 9366.
Fax 9281 0123.

USEFUL BOOKING ADDRESSES

Australian Accommodation Services
Tel 9974 4884.
Fax 9974 1692.
www.tourist.net

Countrylink
Central Railway Station.
Map 4 E5. *Tel 132 232.*

Sydney Visitors Centre
Cnr Argyle & Playfair sts, The Rocks NSW 2000.
Map 1 A4.
Tel 1800 067 676.
www.sydney.com

DISABLED ASSISTANCE

Ideas Incorporated
81 Caper St, Tumut NSW 2720.
Tel 1800 029 904, 6947 3377.
www.ideas.org.au

Spinal Cord Injuries Australia
1 Jennifer St, Little Bay NSW 2036. *Tel 9661 8855, 1800 819 775.*
Postal Address PO Box 397, Matraville NSW 2036. www.scia.org.au

SELF-CATERING AGENCIES

Medina
359 Crown St, Surry Hills NSW 2010. **Map** 5 A3.
Tel 1300 633 462.
www.medina apartments.com.au
Also nine other locations.

Pacific International Hotels
Sydney, Chatswood and Parramatta. *Tel 1300 987 604.* www.pacific inthotels.com

HOMESTAY AGENCIES

Bed and Breakfast NSW
Tel 1300 888 862.
www.bedandbreakfast nsw.com.au

Bed and Breakfast Sydney Central
139 Commonwealth St, Sydney NSW 2000.
Tel 9211 9920.
www.bedandbreakfast sydney.com.au

Homestay Network
5 Locksley St, Killara NSW 2071. *Tel 9498 4400.*
www.homestaynetwork. com.au

HOSTELS

Backpackers World Travel
477 Kent St, Sydney NSW 2000. *Tel 9262 7277.*

Blue Parrot Backpackers
87 Macleay St, Potts Point NSW 2011.
Tel 9356 4888.
www.blueparrot.com.au

G'day Backpackers
153 Forbes St, Woolloomooloo NSW 2011. **Map** 5 B1. *Tel 9358 4327.*

Pink House
6-8 Barncleuth Sq, Kings Cross NSW 2011. **Map** 5 C1. *Tel 1800 806 385.*
www.pinkhouse.com.au

Sydney Central YHA
Cnr Pitt St & Rawson Pl, Sydney NSW 2000.
Tel 9218 9000.
www.yha.com.au

University of Sydney
International House
Tel 9950 9800. St John's College *Tel 9394 5200.*
Sancta Sophia. *Tel 9577 2100.*

Wesley College
Tel 9565 3333.
Women's College
Tel 9517 5000.

Wake Up! Sydney Central
509 Pitt St. **Map** 4 E5.
Tel 9288 7888.
www.wakeup.com.au

YHA Australia
422 Kent St, Sydney NSW 2000. **Map** 4 D3. *Tel 9261 1111.* www.yha.com.au

GAY AND LESBIAN ACCOMMODATION

Gay and Lesbian Tourism Australia
www.galta.com.au

IGLTA
PO Box 20891, World Square NSW. *Tel 9575 4869.* www.iglta.org

CAMPING

Blue Mountains National Park
Tel 4787 8877.

Jenolan Caravan Park
Tel 6336 0344.

Ku-ring-gai Chase National Park
Tel 9472 8949.

Royal National Park
Tel 9542 0648.

Interior of boutique hotel Medusa, Darlinghurst (see p176)

rooms and dormitories are all available, but dormitories are often mixed sex; check before arriving. The backpacker scene changes quickly, so ask other travellers for the latest developments. Kings Cross and Glebe have the largest concentration of cheap accommodation.

Wake Up! Sydney Central backpacker hostel is one of the best of the bunch, with clean, modern facilities, including a bistro, café, bar and Internet connection. It is well located right next to Central Railway Station and offers a free orientation morning to all guests. Staff can also provide a list of suitable employment agencies for those who would like to work during their stay in Sydney.

G'day Backpackers and **Pink House** are smaller hostels offering good facilities in restored buildings close to Kings Cross. Pink House also provides plenty of help if you need to find work in Sydney.

Sydney Central combines modern facilities, such as a swimming pool, sauna and 24-hour security access, with old-world charm and is very conveniently situated right opposite Sydney Central Railway Station.

Blue Parrot Backpackers is situated in a converted mansion in the quieter end of Potts Point and only a short walk from the Harbour. Choose between the huge sunny garden courtyard with its tall trees or the large, cosy common room complete with fireplace.

YHA Australia is a useful source of information when planning your trip, offering advice about travel deals as well as helping you decide on your itinerary and find places to stay. Two other useful online sources that provide lists of budget hostels in Sydney are **hostels.com** and **hostelworld.com**.

HALLS OF RESIDENCE

Student rooms, with shared bathroom facilities, are available at the University of Sydney over the summer break from December to February. The university is conveniently close to the city and to public transport, and the moderate price includes breakfast.

GAY AND LESBIAN ACCOMMODATION

Lesbian and gay visitors are welcome in all of Sydney's hotels. In fact, quite a number of places cater primarily, if not exclusively, for same-sex couples. Many of the small hotels in the inner city areas of Darlinghurst, Paddington, Newtown and Surry Hills are geared specifically towards gay and lesbian visitors, although most of them also welcome heterosexual guests.

At the **IGLTA** (International Gay and Lesbian Travel Association) and the **Gay and Lesbian Tourism Australia** websites you can search for gay or gay-friendly travel-related businesses, including hotels, guesthouses and tours.

CAMPING

Although not an option in the city itself, camping is available in several national parks close to Sydney. This can be a cheap and idyllic way of enjoying the natural beauty and wildlife of the bushland.

The **Royal National Park** (see pp164–5) has a campsite with facilities at Bonnie Vale, just outside Bundeena. Advance booking is required all year round. Free bush or "walk-in" camping is allowed in several other places, but you should ring the park in advance to obtain the necessary camping permit.

At The Basin in **Ku-ring-gai Chase National Park** (see pp154–5), bookings should be made and all fees paid before your stay or on arrival. There are toilets, cold showers, barbecue facilities and a phone.

There are basic campsites near Glenbrook, Woodford, Blackheath and Wentworth Falls in the **Blue Mountains National Park** (see pp160–61). **Jenolan Caravan Park** in Oberon has cabins and caravans for hire as well as camping pitches with and without electric hook-ups. You will need to book if you want to camp at the Euroka Clearing near Glenbrook, but this is not necessary for the other sites. Bush camping is also permitted in the park, but there are some restrictions. Contact the national park for more details before you visit.

Manly Pacific (see p177), overlooking Manly's ocean beach

Choosing a Hotel

These hotels have been selected across a wide price range for their good value, excellent facilities and location. This chart lists the hotels by area in the same order as the rest of the guide. Entries are listed alphabetically within each price category, from the least to the most expensive. Restaurant listings are on pages 184–93.

PRICE CATEGORIES
For a standard double room per night including service (prices in Australian dollars):

$ under A$120
$$ A$120–A$200
$$$ A$200–A$280
$$$$ A$280–A$380
$$$$$ over A$380

THE ROCKS AND CIRCULAR QUAY

Mercantile Hotel 🍴 $
25 George St, The Rocks ***Tel*** *9247 3570* ***Fax*** *9247 7047* ***Rooms*** *15* — ***Map*** *1 B2*

Its George Street location means that all of the Rocks attractions are nearby, including the Argyle Cut and Garrison Church. The hotel boasts spacious rooms with period fittings and marble fireplaces. Some even have Jacuzzis. The basic rate is for a room with a shared bathroom. Rate includes breakfast. **www.mercantilehotel.citysearch.com.au**

Lord Nelson Brewery Hotel 🍴 $$
19 Kent St, The Rocks ***Tel*** *9251 4044* ***Fax*** *9251 1532* ***Rooms*** *9* — ***Map*** *1 A2*

The top floor of the celebrated pub, famous for its home brews, offers cosy bedrooms with stonewalls and rustic furnishings. There are two basic rooms with shared bathrooms; for those not on a tight budget en suite rooms are available. Located close to Circular Quay. Rate includes breakfast. **www.lordnelsonbrewery.com**

Rendezvous Stafford ❄ [P] 🏊 👪 🏋 $$
75 Harrington St, The Rocks ***Tel*** *9251 6711* ***Fax*** *9251 3458* ***Rooms*** *61* — ***Map*** *1 B2*

At this unusual boutique hotel most rooms are studio and one-bedroom apartments but suites are available in the seven charmingly restored 1870s terrace houses nearby. Rooms have kitchen facilities and there are business , a spa and sauna, plus Continental breakfasts available. **www.rendezvoushotels.com/sydney**

The Russell 🍴 $$
143A George St, The Rocks ***Tel*** *9241 3543* ***Fax*** *9252 1652* ***Rooms*** *29* — ***Map*** *1 B2*

This lovely old-fashioned hotel sits above a historic 19th-century pub, the Fortune of War. There is a quaint sitting room, well-stocked library and sunny rooftop garden overlooking the busy Quay. The interior is decorated with country-style antiques. Some rooms have shared bathrooms. Rate includes breakfast. **www.therussell.com.au**

Sydney Harbour YHA ❄ 👪 💼 ♿ $$
110 Cumberland St, The Rocks ***Tel*** *8272 0900* ***Rooms*** *106* — ***Map*** *1 B2*

This environmentally sensitive budget accommodation includes double, family and dormitory rooms and an archaeology education centre. Its star attraction, however, is its location and there is a rooftop terrace with loungers and unobstructed harbour views. Kitchen facilities available. **www.yha.com.au**

Harbour Rocks Hotel 🍴 👪 💼 [P] ♿ $$$
34 Harrington St, The Rocks ***Tel*** *8220 9999* ***Fax*** *8220 9998* ***Rooms*** *55* — ***Map*** *1 B2*

This is a charming boutique hotel with elegant foyer, intimate feel and a bar overlooking cobblestone lanes. The site of Sydney's first hospital, built by 28 men including 12 convict carpenters, today is a "home away from home" with personalised service. Complimentary movies are available from its DVD library. **www.harbourrocks.com.au**

Old Sydney Holiday Inn ❄ [P] 🍴 🏊 👪 ♿ $$$$
55 George St, The Rocks ***Tel*** *9252 0524, 1800 669 562* ***Fax*** *9251 2093* ***Rooms*** *175* — ***Map*** *1 B2*

Big enough to offer all the facilities of a grand establishment, this hotel is also small enough to provide personal attention. Great location in the historic Rocks area and close to Circular Quay and the Sydney Opera House. The view from the sparkling blue rooftop pool is spectacular. There is also a sauna and a whirlpool. **www.holiday-inn.com**

Shangri-La ❄ [P] 🍴 🏊 🏋 ♿ $$$$
176 Cumberland St, The Rocks ***Tel*** *9250 6000* ***Fax*** *9250 6250* ***Rooms*** *563* — ***Map*** *1 A3*

This hotel spent A$40 million on a complete refurbishment and it shows. The spacious rooms are decorated in neutral tones with rich gold brocade highlights, and all offer lovely views of the harbour. On the top floor, Altitude restaurant and the blu horizon bar are popular dining and nightspots. **www.shangri-la.com**

Park Hyatt Sydney ❄ [P] 🍴 🏊 🏋 ♿ $$$$$
7 Hickson Rd, The Rocks ***Tel*** *9241 1234* ***Fax*** *9256 1555* ***Rooms*** *158* — ***Map*** *1 B1*

Many rooms in this six-star hotel have Opera House views, as does the rooftop swimming pool. Walking up the road for a few minutes takes you to the small park beneath the Harbour Bridge, a few minutes in the other direction to Circular Quay. Well-equipped for business travellers and offers high-speed Internet. **http://sydney.park.hyatt.com**

Key to Symbols *see back cover flap*

Quay Grand
⬚ P ⬚ ⬚ ⬚ $$$$$
61 Macquarie St **Tel** *9256 4000* **Fax** *9256 4040* **Rooms** *68*   **Map** *1 C3*

Next door to the Opera House at one of Sydney's premiere addresses, the hotels' bedroom apartments are tastefully furnished. Features include spa baths, kitchen and laundry facilities, televisions and stereos. There is grocery service available, or try Quadrant Restaurant or ECQ, the hotel's dress-circle bar. **www.mirvachotels.com**

WALSH BAY The Sebel Pier One
⬚ P ⬚ ⬚ ⬚ $$$$$
11 Hickson Rd, Walsh Bay **Tel** *8298 9999* **Fax** *8298 9777* **Rooms** *161*   **Map** *1 A2*

This is Sydney's first over-the-water hotel, built on a 1912 finger wharf in the Walsh Bay World Heritage precinct, beside the Harbour Bridge. The hotel's luxurious rooms combine original features with contemporary design. An extensive room service menu is available, and all the rooms have Internet access. **www.sebelpierone.com.au**

CITY CENTRE

Railway Square YHA
⬚ ⬚ ⬚ $
8–10 Lee St **Tel** *9281 9666* **Fax** *9281 9688* **Rooms** *64*   **Map** *4 E5*

Located in a historic 1904 building, this YHA hostel adjoins Central Station's Platform Zero. Some rooms are inside converted railway carriages, while others are in the main building. Features modern design and a timber deck for sunbathing beside the over-sized spa pool. There is an Internet cafe and a tour desk. **www.yha.org.au**

Wake Up! Sydney Central
⬚ ⬚ ⬚ $
509 Pitt St **Tel** *9288 7888* **Fax** *9288 7889* **Beds** *approx. 500*   **Map** *4 E5*

If your plan for Sydney is all action, this is the place for you. It is a party hostel, and here large mixed dorms are more popular than the smaller, single-sex ones. Some hotel-style double rooms with en suites are available. Offers laundry and kitchen facilities, a lounge room with TV and a video library. **www.wakeup.com.au**

Y Hotel Hyde Park
⬚ P ⬚ ⬚ $
5–11 Wentworth Ave **Tel** *9264 2451* **Fax** *9285 6288* **Rooms** *121*   **Map** *4 F3*

This budget hotel caters for everyone. It has a range of rooms, including backpacker dorms and modern, stylish private rooms with en suite bathrooms. There are also studios available that have self-catering facilities. Coffee, tea and Continental breakfast included in the price. **www.yhotel.com.au**

Castlereagh Boutique Hotel
⬚ ⬚ ⬚ $$
169–171 Castlereagh St **Tel** *9284 1000, 1800 801 576* **Fax** *9284 1045* **Rooms** *82*   **Map** *1 B5*

Full of character, this hotel has a plush old-fashioned dining room, decorated with chandeliers and elaborate paint and plasterwork. The rooms, furnished with period pieces and patterned upholstery, offer essentials such as TVs, bars, fridges and tea and coffee facilities. **www.thecastlereagh.com.au**

Hotel Pensione
⬚ ⬚ ⬚ ⬚ $$
631–635 George St **Tel** *9265 8888* **Fax** *9211 9825* **Rooms** *68*   **Map** *4 E4*

Many features of this heritage building survived its transformation into a hotel, including an old staircase and wood-panelled elevator. All rooms have stylish mosaic-tiled en suites, phones, dataports, cable TV and air conditioning. Quad rooms are fabulous value. Breakfast boxes are also available. **www.pensione.com.au**

Rydges World Square
⬚ P ⬚ ⬚ ⬚ $$
389 Pitt St **Tel** *9268 1888* **Fax** *9283 5899* **Rooms** *443*   **Map** *4 E3*

Close to Town Hall station and the monorail stop at World Square, this hotel offers comfortable, reasonably priced rooms. The hotel's gallery includes work by Australian luminaries such as Peter Kingston and John Coburn, as well as important indigenous art. **www.rydges.com**

The Grace
⬚ P ⬚ ⬚ ⬚ ⬚ ⬚ $$$
77 York St **Tel** *9272 6888* **Fax** *9299 8189* **Rooms** *382*   **Map** *1 A4*

You could not be closer to the action than at The Grace as General Douglas Macarthur used the building as a base during World War II. The hotel dates from the 1930s and its restoration has retained the building's original Art Deco style. Rooms are well equipped and there is a choice of three restaurants and bars. **www.gracehotel.com.au**

Regis on Castlereagh
⬚ P ⬚ ⬚ ⬚ ⬚ $$$
317 Castlereagh St **Tel** *8217 6200* **Fax** *9211 1323* **Rooms** *75*   **Map** *1 B4*

A choice of one-, two- and three-bedroom self-contained apartments make this high-rise hotel an affordable option in a central location. Suitable for both leisure and business travellers, facilities include a heated indoor pool and spa, a fitness room and secure underground parking (for a fee; book in advance). **www.regisoncastlereagh.com.au**

Swissôtel
⬚ ⬚ ⬚ ⬚ ⬚ ⬚ P ⬚ $$$
68 Market St **Tel** *9238 8888* **Rooms** *359*   **Map** *4 E2*

This deluxe, family-friendly hotel in the heart of the city will set up your room with cuddly toys, children's DVDs and bright bed linen, and put milk and chocolate in the mini-bar for the little ones. If you or they tire of the room or view, there is an outdoor heated pool and spa. **www.swissotel.com/EN**

Waldorf Apartment Hotel

$$$

57 Liverpool St **Tel** *9261 5355* **Fax** *9261 3753* **Rooms** *48*

Map *4 E3*

This hotel is a short stroll from the city shopping centres and cinemas and a slightly longer one to Darling Harbour attractions like Tumbalong Park, the Chinese Gardens and IMAX Theatre. The apartments are spacious, with kitchen facilities and balconies overlooking the city. Has a rooftop pool and free in-house movies. **www.waldorf.com.au**

The York

$$$

5 York St **Tel** *9210 5000* **Fax** *9290 1487* **Rooms** *120 apartments*

Map *1 A3*

There is an understated elegance throughout this centrally located hotel. Each of its apartments is individually designed and has a balcony, fully-equipped kitchen and large bathroom. Apartments vary in size from studios to executive two-bedroom penthouses. Close to The Rocks and Circular Quay. **www.theyorkapartments.com.au**

Establishment Hotel

$$$$

5 Bridge Lane **Tel** *9240 3100* **Fax** *9240 3101* **Rooms** *31*

Map *1 B3*

One of the most fashionable places in town. Its rooms, including two penthouses, have lively or tranquil colour schemes, and marble or stone bathrooms. The hotel is in the same building as four bars, two restaurants and a nightclub, though it is secluded from them. **www.establishmenthotel.com**

Meriton World Tower

$$$$

91 Liverpool St **Tel** *9287 2890, 1800 214 822* **Fax** *9261 5722* **Rooms** *114*

Map *4 E3*

Some serviced apartments are available short term in this vertical village, the tallest residential building in Sydney. Spacious two-bedroom apartments with kitchens can sleep up to five. Everything guests might need is just a short stroll away. Facilities include a child-minding centre, DVD players and more. **www.meritonapartments.com.au**

Park8 Hotel

$$$$

185 Castlereagh St **Tel** *9283 2488* **Fax** *9283 2588* **Rooms** *36*

Map *1 B4*

An intimate boutique hotel in the heart of the CBD, Park8 offers spacious rooms oozing old-world charm. Close to public transport and attractions, it is a peaceful oasis from the hustle and bustle outside. Guests can make use of a complimentary pass to a nearby gym and have takeaway meals delivered by Food 2 Go. **www.park8.com.au**

Sheraton on the Park

$$$$

161 Elizabeth St **Tel** *9286 6000* **Fax** *9286 6686* **Rooms** *557*

Map *1 B5*

Arriving at this hotel's very grand entrance, guests can expect all the complete luxuries of a five-star hotel. Amenities include marble bathrooms, stylish furnishings, dataports, 24-hour room service, helpful concierges, babysitting services and lounges. Many rooms have views over the trees of Hyde Park. **www.sheraton.com**

Hilton Sydney

$$$$$

488 George St **Tel** *9266 2000* **Fax** *9265 6065* **Rooms** *577*

Map *1 B5*

An enormous renovation was carried out on this hotel, with the aim of setting new standards in luxury. The slick design is immediately apparent and upgraded features include stylish interiors, quality furniture, LCD TVs and avant-garde Internet Protocol technology phones. Guests have access to the health clubs. **www.hiltonsydney.com.au**

DARLING HARBOUR

Citigate Central Sydney

$$$

169–179 Thomas St, Haymarket **Tel** *9281 6888* **Fax** *9281 4237* **Rooms** *251*

Map *4 D5*

Located near Paddy's Market in Chinatown, this hotel is close to many city attractions. Part of the Citigate is made up of the original 1902 Infants' Hospital Building. All rooms and suites are large and guest facilities include a rooftop pool, barbecue area and garden. The hotel specializes in arranging theatre tickets. **www.mirvachotels.com.au**

Four Points By Sheraton

$$$

161 Sussex St **Tel** *9290 4000* **Fax** *9290 4040* **Rooms** *630*

Map *4 D2*

With 630 rooms, the contemporary Four Points is Sydney's largest hotel. Located on the CBD side of Darling Harbour, it is close to the restaurant and entertainment precincts including King Street and Cockle Bay wharfs. The hotel is also an easy walk from the Queen Victoria Building and Town Hall station. **www.starwoodhotels.com**

Holiday Inn Darling Harbour

$$$

68 Harbour St, Darling Harbour **Tel** *9291 0200, 1800 669 562* **Fax** *9281 1212* **Rooms** *304*

Map *4 D3*

The location is great and so is the heritage-listed wool store that houses this hotel. The Holiday Inn has good facilities for business travellers with special executive suites. The restaurant offers à la carte and casual dining plus a breakfast buffet. Children eat for free. **www.holidayinn.com**

Novotel Darling Harbour

$$$

100 Murray St, Pyrmont **Tel** *9934 0000* **Fax** *9934 0099* **Rooms** *525*

Map *3 C2*

These superstructure towers above the Harbourside centre at Darling Harbour are close to the Powerhouse and Maritime Museums. The four-star quality rooms are available in many different ranges and have views across the city. In cooler weather, guests avoid the unheated pool and play tennis instead. **www.noveteldarlingharbour.com.au**

BOTANIC GARDEN AND THE DOMAIN

Hotel InterContinental

⬚ P 🔢 ≋ 🏊 📺 ♿ $$$$

117 Macquarie St **Tel** *9253 9000* **Fax** *9240 1240* **Rooms** *509*   **Map** *1 C3*

The foyer and lower stories of this luxurious hotel are made up of part of the old 1851 Treasury Building. Small music ensembles frequently perform in the lobby, where guests and visitors indulge in high tea, served on tiered cake stands. Well-equipped rooms have window seats, chaise lounges and fine views. **www.sydney.intercontinental.com**

Sir Stamford Circular Quay

⬚ P 🔢 ≋ 📺 ♿ $$$$

93 Macquarie St **Tel** *9252 4600* **Fax** *9252 4286* **Rooms** *105*   **Map** *1 C3*

There is a refined but relaxed air in this intimate hotel. The decor is built around the hotel's collection of fine art and 18th-century antiques. Paying a little extra per night allows guests access to the Quay Lounge, and with it a host of benefits including complimentary breakfast, tea/coffee, drinks and faxes. **www.stamford.com.au/sscq**

KINGS CROSS AND DARLINGHURST

Formule 1

⬚ P ♿ $

191–201 William St **Tel** *9326 0300* **Fax** *9326 0155* **Rooms** *115*   **Map** *5 B1*

You can count on rooms being spick and span at this reliable budget motel chain. Located just down the hill from the famous Coke sign at the top of Kings Cross, it is close to the action. Rooms can accommodate two, three or four people for the flat room rate. Do not expect much here, they only have TV. Limited parking. **www.formule1.com.au**

The Chelsea

P ♿ $$

49 Womerah Ave, Darlinghurst **Tel** *9380 5994* **Fax** *9332 2491* **Rooms** *13*   **Map** *5 C1*

At this beautiful guesthouse, decorated in French Provincial and contemporary styles, your stay is made tranquil by attentive hosts and a quiet street. Particularly popular with businesswomen, the property is gay and lesbian friendly. On-street parking is available nearby. Breakfast included in the price. **www.chelsea.citysearch.com.au**

The Diamant Hotel Sydney

⬚ 🔢 🏊 📺 🔲 P ♿ $$

14 Kings Cross Rd, Potts Point **Tel** *9295 8888* **Fax** *9295 8899* **Rooms** *76*   **Map** *5 B1*

A contemporary boutique hotel featuring all the latest high-tech gadgets, including iPod docks, 42-inch plasma TVs with in-built Internet and Wi-Fi. Second floor rooms have big walled terraces and cane outdoor loungers. The sensual interiors feature sleek black decor while maintaining an airy sense of space. **www.diamant.com.au**

L'otel

🔢 $$

114 Darlinghurst Rd **Tel** *9360 6868* **Fax** *9331 4536* **Rooms** *16*   **Map** *5 A2*

This large terrace house has been converted into a designer hotel, with small but lovely rooms decorated in white French-Provincial style with painted furniture and art pieces. There is a hip bar and restaurant downstairs, and the hotel is close to Oxford Street's cafés and bars. The concierge can arrange tours. **www.lotel.com.au**

Morgan's Boutique Apartment Hotel

⬚ 🔢 $$

304 Victoria St, Darlinghurst **Tel** *9360 7955* **Fax** *9360 9217* **Rooms** *26*   **Map** *2 E5*

This gay-friendly boutique Art Deco hotel is set in a leafy location in the café district. A rooftop terrace with glimpses of the Opera House and Harbour Bridge add to the hotel's charm. Rooms have cable TV and fully equipped kitchens, and some can accommodate a third person for an extra charge. **www.parklodgesydney.com**

Regents Court

⬚ P 🔲 ♿ $$

18 Springfield Ave, Potts Point **Tel** *9356 6900* **Fax** *9356 6999* **Rooms** *30*   **Map** *2 E5*

An innovative team transformed this Art Deco gentlemen's chambers into a stylish boutique hotel, favoured by artists, actors and writers. Spacious and well-equipped, all studios have queen beds. A rooftop garden has lush plants and great views of the city. Cots and child-minding available. **www.8hotels.com/regentscourt**

Blue Sydney

⬚ P 🔢 ≋ 📺 ♿ $$$

6 Cowper Wharf Rd, Woolloomooloo **Tel** *9331 9000* **Fax** *9331 9031* **Rooms** *100*   **Map** *2 D5*

This hotel's glamour and reputation as the coolest in Sydney makes up for the far from spacious rooms. Guests enjoy luxury robes and Serendipity bath products, a fabulous cocktail bar and a row of great restaurants below on the finger wharf. All rooms are equipped with business technology and 27-inch TV screens. **www.tajhotels.com**

Hotel Altamont

🔲 $$$

207 Darlinghurst Rd **Tel** *9360 6000* **Fax** *9332 2499* **Rooms** *14*   **Map** *5 A2*

In a past life, this hotel had Mick Jagger as a guest. Now this fun budget hotel has rooms with king- or queen-sized beds and solid, comfy wooden furniture. There are discounted weekly rates and a few good quality backpacker rooms: they fill up quickly so book early. Formerly a Georgian mansion. **www.altamont.com.au**

Simpsons of Potts Point
P 🚶 ♿ | $$$

8 Challis Ave, Potts Point **Tel** *9356 2199* **Fax** *9356 4476* **Rooms** *12* **Map** *2 E4*

A charming B&B at the "Paris" end of Potts Point, where the complimentary breakfast is served in a glass-roofed conservatory. Built in 1892 as a family residence, the hotel has been exquisitely restored and boasts elegantly designed rooms. Guests staying in the romantic Cloud Suite enjoy a private spa bath. **www.simpsonshotel.com.au**

Medusa
🍴 | $$$$

267 Darlinghurst Rd, Darlinghurst **Tel** *9331 1000* **Fax** *9380 6901* **Rooms** *18* **Map** *5 B1*

Medusa makes its own rules as only a boutique hotel can. An old Victorian row house has been transformed into a brightly coloured miracle of modernism, with inspiration from Caravaggio's *Medusa*. Lindt chocolates and Aveda toiletries are complimentary, as is use of a neighbouring gym. **www.medusa.com.au**

PADDINGTON

Arts Hotel
🛏 P 🍴 ♨ 🚶 🍴 | $$

21 Oxford St, Paddington **Tel** *9361 0211* **Fax** *9360 3735* **Rooms** *64* **Map** *5 B3*

Standard rooms at this friendly, family-owned hotel face the bustle of Oxford Street. It is worth paying a tiny bit more for a garden room that overlooks the courtyard and has free Wi-Fi. The breakfast room, with its windows looking out onto the street, is great for people-watching. All rooms are non-smoking. **www.artshotel.com.au**

Hart's Homestay Paddington
♿ | $$

91 Stewart St, Paddington **Tel** *9380 5516* **Fax** *9332 2860* **Rooms** *4* **Map** *6 D4*

This historic, 19th-century Gothic-style cottage has a central courtyard and is located in a quiet residential heritage precinct. A short stroll away are the shops and cafés of busy Oxford Street and Paddington's popular Saturday art and craft markets. Rate includes breakfast. **www.bbbook.com.au**

Hughenden Hotel
P 🍴 🚶 ♿ | $$$

14 Queen St, Woollahra **Tel** *9363 4863* **Fax** *9362 0398* **Rooms** *35* **Map** *6 E4*

This rambling old building, once a 19th-century family home, is restored to its original grandeur with beautifully carved staircases and marble fireplaces. Rooms are comfortably furnished and the restaurant is very good. Writers groups meet and artists exhibit their work here. Breakfast included in the price. **www.thehughenden.com.au**

Kathryn's on Queen Boutique Bed & Breakfast
📖 | $$$

20 Queen St, Woollahra **Tel** *327 4535* **Fax** *9327 4535* **Rooms** *3* **Map** *6 E4*

This charming National Trust-listed Victorian terrace offers comfort and convenience in one of Sydney's most beautiful streets for window-shopping – fashion, antique and gourmet food stores as well as small galleries are all found here. Bedrooms feature antique furniture, luxury linen and balconies. Rate includes breakfast. **www.kathryns.com.au**

FURTHER AFIELD

Dive
$$

234 Arden St, Coogee **Tel** *9665 5538* **Fax** *9665 4347* **Rooms** *16*

A stylish hotel featured in design magazines, with rooms that feature polished floorboards, high ceilings and designer bathrooms. Rooms also have kitchen facilities. This is a great sanctuary from the backpacker madness of Coogee Beach. Complimentary breakfast and unlimited tea and coffee are available. **www.divehotel.com.au**

Lane Cove River Tourist Park
P 🚶 🍴 📖 ♿ | $$

Plassey Rd, North Ryde **Tel** *9888 9133* **Fax** *9888 9322* **Rooms** *28*

Just 10 km (6 miles) from the city centre, this bushland ecotourism campground has fully serviced en suite cabins complete with TV, lounge and towels. It offers bushwalking, nocturnal animal spotting and stargazing tours and has boat and mountain bike hire. Kitchen facilities available. **www.lcrtp.com.au**

Periwinkle Manly Cove
P 🚶 | $$

18–19 East Esplanade, Manly **Tel** *9977 4668* **Fax** *9977 6308* **Rooms** *18*

A striking Federation-era mansion has been converted into a B&B, with antique furniture and colour schemes. Rooms with a view attract only a small premium. Features high ceilings, wrought-iron verandahs and a leafy courtyard. Also has private outdoor areas. Breakfast included in the price. **www.periwinkle.citysearch.com.au**

Rydges Camperdown Hotel
🛏 P ♨ 🚶 📖 ♿ | $$

9 Missenden Rd, Camperdown **Tel** *9516 1522* **Fax** *9519 4020* **Rooms** *144*

In a good location on the city fringe and a five-minute walk to the eclectic restaurants, shops and entertainment venues of King Street. Rooms are comfortable and many offer city views. There is a swimming pool and a wading pool for children. Nearby Parramatta Road is on bus routes into the city centre. **www.rydges.com/camperdown**

Key to Price Guide *see p172* **Key to Symbols** *see back cover flap*

Adina Apartment Hotel Sydney, Crown Street

359 Crown St, Surry Hills **Tel** *8302 1000* **Fax** *9361 5965* **Rooms** *85*

Map *5 A1*

Close to the groovy Crown Street shops and restaurants, SCG and the Fox Studios, this hotel is a favourite with visiting rock bands. It is also right above the restaurants bills, Marque and Billy Kwong. Charge-to-the-room facilities are established at all three. Apartments are spacious and have full kitchens. **www.medina.com.au**

Bundeena Beach Bed & Breakfast

75 Bundeena Drive, Bundeena **Tel** *9527 9977* **Rooms** *1*

Step off the front lawn and onto the beach at this luxurious accommodation with spa bath for two and separate open shower. Explore the Royal National Park and Aboriginal rock carvings, go bushwalking, cycling or just relax. Rooms have kitchen facilities and rate includes breakfast. **www.beachbedandbreakfast.com.au**

Manly Pacific

55 N Steyne, Manly **Tel** *9977 7666* **Fax** *9977 7822* **Rooms** *213*

Manly's ocean beach is one of Sydney's most famous. It plays host to iron man competitions and triathlons, along with herds of surfers, tourists and locals just after a suntan. Situated right on the beach, this hotel has unbeatable views of sand and surf. All rooms are light and spacious with balconies. **www.novotelmanlypacific.com.au**

Meriton Bondi Junction

95–97 Grafton St, Bondi Junction **Tel** *9287 2890 or 1800 214 822* **Fax** *9261 5722* **Rooms** *140*

Built above the Bondi Junction bus and train interchange, the two-bedroom apartments have views of Sydney Harbour and the ocean. Great features include full-sized kitchens and laundries, tennis and basketball courts and virtual golf. Close to a giant, luxury shopping centre and cinema complex. **www.meritonapartments.com.au**

Ravesi's

Cnr Campbell Parade & Hall Sts, Bondi Beach **Tel** *9365 4422* **Fax** *9365 1481* **Rooms** *12*

This lovely boutique hotel has been refurbished and epitomizes the relaxed style of beach life at Bondi. Split-level suites cost more but are gorgeous, opening onto private terraces with ocean views. Ravesi's has a restaurant downstairs and popular bar, which is packed with a mix of tourists and funky locals. **www.ravesis.com.au**

Swiss Grand

Cnr Campbell Parade & Beach Rd, Bondi Beach **Tel** *9365 5666* **Fax** *9365 5330* **Rooms** *203*

This luxurious all-suite hotel is a kitsch take on the style of the French Riviera. Its exterior of terraces and creamy decorative balustrades looks a little like a giant wedding cake. Inside, marble adorns the lobby's surface. The hotel's beachfront location is unbeatable, with full facilities, a rooftop pool and restaurants. **www.swissgrand.com.au**

BEYOND SYDNEY

BOWRAL, SOUTHERN HIGHLANDS Berida Manor

6 David St, Bowral **Tel** *4861 1177* **Fax** *4861 1219* **Rooms** *56*

Adjacent to the Royal Bowral Golf Course, this restored manor house is walking distance from the cafés and antique stores of Bowral town. Equally good for romantic weekends or families, there is plenty to keep children occupied, including tennis, billiards and bikes. Expensive on weekends. Includes breakfast. **www.beridamanor.com.au**

KATOOMBA, BLUE MOUNTAINS Carrington Hotel

15–47 Katoomba St, Katoomba **Tel** *4782 1111* **Fax** *4782 7033* **Rooms** *66*

A popular weekend retreat, this hotel offers old-world charm in the heart of Katoomba. The basic rate is for a budget room with shared bathroom, en suite rooms are more. The Yindi Day Spa specializes in hydrotherapy and various facial, massage and body treatments. Breakfast included in the price. **www.thecarrington.com.au**

KATOOMBA, BLUE MOUNTAINS Lilianfels

Lilianfels Ave, Katoomba **Tel** *4780 1200* **Fax** *4780 1300* **Rooms** *85*

Overlooking the Jamison Valley and a short walk from the Three Sisters in the Blue Mountains, this hotel is listed among the Small Luxury Hotels of the World. It boasts a cosy lounge, first-class indoor and outdoor heated pools, open fires and a library. Staff can arrange personal tours and gourmet picnic baskets. **www.lilianfels.com.au**

POLKOBIN, HUNTER VALLEY Peppers Guest House

Ekerts Rd, Pokolbin **Tel** *4993 8999* **Fax** *4998 7739* **Rooms** *48*

In the heart of the Hunter Valley wine district, Peppers is a luxury lodge with lovely gardens and excellent facilities. There is also a swimming pool, spa, sauna, tennis court and *boules*. Friendly staff can arrange trips to nearby wineries or a leisurely tour of the area. Breakfast included in the price. **www.peppers.com.au**

WHALE BEACH, PITTWATER Jonah's

69 Bynya Rd, Palm Beach **Tel** *9974 5599* **Fax** *9974 1212* **Rooms** *7*

Originally built in 1929 as a roadhouse, Jonah's has long been one of Sydney's most desirable destinations. Rooms have been refurbished with king-size beds, hand-crafted furniture and limestone bathrooms with spa baths. The restaurant is acclaimed and the suites share its amazing views of the oceans. Breakfast included. **www.jonahs.com.au**

RESTAURANTS, CAFES AND PUBS

Sydneysiders are justifiably proud of their dining scene. Australia's largest city has been populated by successive waves of migrants, all of whom have added something of their home countries to the communal table. These influences have spilled over into contemporary cuisine, which is often called "Modern Australian". This term covers just about any ethnic style the chef may fancy, loosely based on French cuisine. The result is that, in terms of ethnic diversity, Sydney is

Fresh seafood, Chinese style

able to offer many dining options. From a survey of different types of restaurant in varying price brackets, we have selected those offering good value for money. Detailed descriptions of each restaurant can be found in the listings on pages 184–93. Casual eating places, where you can often enjoy food that is as good as at a restaurant but cheaper, are featured on pages 194–7; here you will also find mention of pubs that have recommended bistros and dining areas.

WHERE TO EAT

Circular Quay, The Rocks, Darlinghurst, Potts Point, Surry Hills and Paddington are the areas where you will find the widest choice of places to eat. Just outside the city centre, and not covered in depth in these listings, are the inner-city "eat streets" of Glebe Point Road, Glebe *(see p131)*, and King Street, Newtown.

On the lower North Shore is Military Road, which extends from Neutral Bay to Mosman. It would be difficult to walk along any of these streets and not find a café or restaurant to suit your taste and budget.

All of the major hotels have at least one restaurant and a few of these offer beautiful surroundings, too.

To enjoy a spectacular view while you dine, start with drinks at the Horizon Blu bar at the Shangri-La hotel *(see p172)*, followed by any of

the restaurants at the Opera Quays or at one of Sydney's best restaurants, Quay *(see p185)*, at the Overseas Passenger Terminal.

Many restaurants at Darling Harbour, Cockle Bay and King Street Wharf have outside tables, so diners can enjoy the atmosphere of the lights, the water and the boats.

HOW MUCH TO PAY

Compared with other major world capitals, dining out in Sydney is relatively inexpensive. The cost of a three-course meal in an average restaurant is probably 25 per cent lower than its equivalent in, say, New York or London. The cost is further reduced if you choose a BYO restaurant where you can avoid paying the marked-up price of restaurant wine by taking your own alcohol. However, there will usually be a "corkage" cost per drinker.

Main dining room of the Rockpool Bar & Grill *(see p186)*

OPENING TIMES

Most restaurants serve lunch from noon to 3pm and dinner from 6pm to about 11pm, though last orders are often at 10:30pm. Cheap and cheerful ethnic kitchens may close around 9:30pm, but this largely depends on demand. Outside the city centre, restaurants may close one day a week, usually Monday. Many restaurants close on some, if not all, public holidays *(see p51)*.

RESERVATIONS

Booking is recommended in most places – earlier in the day is usually adequate. If, you want to be sure of a table for Friday or Saturday in a spot that is currently fashionable, however, you may need to make a reservation up to one month in advance. If a restaurant says it's full, it is worth asking about an early table, around 6pm, or whenever the place opens. Many

Hugo's at Manly Wharf *(see p192)*

casual brasseries and bistros are open all through the day and, as they aren't the sort of place where people linger over their meal, they do not take bookings. You may have to wait a few minutes for a table if you arrive at a busy time.

LICENSING LAWS

Sydney restaurants must be licensed to sell food, but when a place is described as licensed, this usually refers to its licence to sell alcohol. BYO (bring your own) restaurants are not licensed to sell liquor and you will need to buy it beforehand if you want to drink alcohol with your meal. A small amount will probably be charged for "corkage", either per person or per bottle. It will be more at expensive restaurants, which can reduce the cost benefit of taking your own wine.

BYO restaurants not only reduce the cost of dining out, but also allow wine buffs to choose exactly the wines they wish to drink with their meal.

Bondi Icebergs Dining Room and Bar (see p193)

Relaxing in a café at the top end of Oxford Street, Paddington

DRESS CODES AND SMOKING

Dress standards in Sydney restaurants are really quite relaxed, even in the more up-market establishments. Most restaurants will draw the line, however, at patrons in beach wear and flip flops.

Neat and tidy is the general rule. Smart-casual dress is the safest option when considering what to wear. Jackets and ties are a rare sight unless the wearer has come straight from the office or is conducting a business meeting over a meal.

In line with health trends the government has imposed a non-smoking policy for indoor areas of all restaurants, pubs and clubs. However, many venues now provide an outdoor area for smokers.

TAX AND TIPPING

A 10 per cent GST is inclusive in prices, although it can be listed separately on the final receipt. While tipping is not compulsory, 10 to 15 per cent of the total bill is customary as a reward for good service. You can leave a cash tip after you have paid or add it to the total if paying your bill by credit card.

EATING WITH CHILDREN

Most restaurants accept children who can sit still throughout a meal, although you may feel more comfortable in either Chinese restaurants or the cheap pasta eateries in East Sydney, where children are always welcome. Harry's Café de Wheels (see p195) is a roadside pie shop next to the Finger Wharf that is a cheap and cheerful lunch option. Eat outdoors beside the harbour where kids can make as much noise as they want.

The Harbourside and Market City food courts in Darling Harbour are another inexpensive option. Here, there is a variety of eating places in one complex, including Mexican and Chinese food outlets, pasta and salad bars, all with a central seating area. For families who prefer to dine out rather than snack, chains such as Pizza Hut and the Black Stump steakhouses offer special menus for children but they also serve alcohol for the adults.

Perhaps the best locations to dine out with children are those where they can play safely outside after they have eaten. The Bathers' Pavilion Restaurant (see p193) is right on Balmoral Beach (see pp54–5), a sheltered harbour beach which has a netted swimming pool. Centennial Parklands Dining (see p194) is also a great place for families being within supervisory range of grassy lawns and a children's playground.

CREDIT CARDS

Many restaurants will accept credit cards, but you should ask if in doubt. Visa, Master-Card and Japanese Credit Bureau are widely accepted; Amex and Diners Club are less commonly accepted, so always check before ordering a meal. Some restaurants also now offer EFTPOS transactions (electronic money transfers direct from your bank account) as an alternative method of payment, which may be more convenient.

The Flavours of Sydney

The city of Sydney surrounds its famous harbour, and countless bars, restaurants and cafés have views of sparkling sunlit water. Taking advantage of the mild climate, outdoor eating – from morning coffee to dinner – is the norm. The cutting-edge food scene is often categorized with New York, London and Paris, and Sydney's top-class chefs are admired the world over. Sydney is cosmopolitan, multicultural and vibrant, with the laid-back atmosphere of the beach always nearby. Sydneysiders are passionate about socializing and, whether eating out or cooking at home, food is always central to a good time.

Wattleseed, pepperberry and lemon myrtle

Fresh seafood dishes at one of the city's many upmarket restaurants

NATIVE INGREDIENTS

There are many native foods in Australia that have been used by aborigines for thousands of years, and which are now becoming widely popular. Fruits and vegetables with distinctive colours, flavours and textures include quandong, munthari, bush tomato, wild limes, warrigal greens and rosellas. All of them are still primarily wild-harvested by aboriginal communities. Although native Australians never used seasonings in their campfire cooking, modern Australians have discovered the exciting flavours of such indigenous herbs and spices as lemon myrtle, wattleseed, mountain pepperleaf, pepperberry, forest berry and akudjura. Native meats such as kangaroo and emu are also being used more frequently, although don't expect to see witchity grubs on many menus. These native meats sit alongside a vast and impressive array of beef, lamb and, of course, seafood. Fish native to Australia include barramundi, trevalla and blue eye trevalla. The popular native shellfish, yabbies and moreton bay bugs, are similar to, but smaller than, lobster. Also worth a mention are the lovely fragrant honeys that are produced out of native Australian forests.

Samphire   Snapper   Lobster
Scallops   Red mullet   Oysters

Selection of seafood available in Sydney's restaurants and food shops

LOCAL DISHES AND SPECIALITIES

There's nowhere better in the world to enjoy fish and chips than sitting on a Sydney beach. As well as the standard choice of hake fillets, you may find more unusual fish on offer, such as wild barramundi or John Dory.

Alongside traditional Asian restaurants serving yum cha, dim sum curries and noodles, there is plenty of modern cuisine, fusing Asian flavours with local produce, such as a Thai-style salad of kangaroo with peanuts and lime. And you can rest assured that just about every other cuisine in the world will be represented in Sydney in some way.

Anzac biscuits

Sandwiches and burgers are often made with Sydney's favourite "Turkish" bread – light and fluffy, and great toasted with Vegemite or for dipping in olive oil.

Kangaroo pizza *This Italian classic is given a modern Australian spin with the addition of seared lean fillet.*

Diners enjoying an outdoor meal on the harbour at Circular Quay

THE WORLD ON A PLATE

Having one of the most eclectic populations on earth means great things for food (or "tucker"). Australians are happy with olive oil in one hand and fresh chilies in the other, so no rules apply – you can be sure of great flavours using the best produce.

Farming plays a very important role in Australia, the world's largest producer of beef. The lush pastures on the coast are particularly good for farming, and milk-fed lamb from New South Wales is as wonderful as the brie produced in South Australia. King Island, off the coast of Victoria, is dedicated to dairy produce, selling their amazing cheeses and creams all around the country. Alongside the rapidly growing wine industry is olive oil and balsamic vinegar production, examples of which you are likely to find at the cellar door of many vineyards.

Australia has one of the most diverse marine faunas in the world, due to its range

Fresh fruit on sale at Paddy's Market in Chinatown

of habitats, from the warm tropical northern waters to the sub-Antarctic Tasman sea, as well as its geographical isolation. A total of 600 marine and freshwater species are caught in Australian waters, providing chefs with plenty of inspiration *(see p202)*.

Every kind of fruit and vegetable is grown in Australia. Pineapples and mangoes are widely grown in Queensland, apples in Victoria, strawberries in New South Wales and rambutans in the Northern Territory. Exotic and notoriously hard to farm, truffles are cultivated in several areas, including Tasmania, highlighting how versatile Australia's land is.

FOOD ON THE RUN

Sushi Major cities are dotted with tiny counters offering fresh sushi to grab on the go.

Juice bars This booming industry is found on most city streets, serving delicious, cool blends of fruits.

Milk bars As well as milk-shakes, ice creams and salads, these sell a wide range of deep-fried foods.

Coffee & cake Little cafés everywhere also sell Italian-style cakes and pastries.

Pubs Most pubs serve a decent steak sandwich.

Pies An Aussie institution, pies are readily available. Look out for gourmet versions.

Grilled barramundi *Served on ginger and bok choy risotto, this is a great mix of local seafood and Asian flavours.*

Prawn Laksa *This spicy coconut noodle soup can be found all over the country in noodle bars, cafés and pubs.*

Lamingtons *These little Victoria sponge cakes are coated in chocolate icing and shredded coconut.*

What to Drink in Sydney

Semillon Chardonnay

Australia has one of the world's finest cuisines and part of its enjoyment is the marriage of the country's wine with great food. Australians have a very relaxed attitude to food and wine mixes, so red wine with fish and a cold, dry Riesling as an apéritif can easily be the order of the day. Also, many of the restaurants in the wine regions offer exclusive brands, or offer rare wines so these are worth seeking out. Australians also enjoy some of the best good-value wine in the world. It is estimated that there are 10,000 different Australian wines on the market at any one time. Australians do love their beer, and it remains a popular drink, with a wide range of choices available. While the health-conscious can choose from a variety of bottled waters and select-your-own, freshly squeezed fruit juices. Imported wines, beers and spirits are also readily available.

SPARKLING WINE

Domaine Chandon in the Yarra Valley produces high-quality sparkling wines

Australia is justly famous for its sparkling wines, from Yalumba's Angas Brut to Seppelts Salinger. Tasmania has showed considerable promise in producing some high quality sparkling wines, particularly Pirie from Pipers Brook. However, the real hidden gems are the sparkling red wines – the best are made using the French *Méthode Champenois*, matured over a number of years and helped by a small drop of vintage port. The best producers of red sparkling wines are Rockford and Seppelts. These sparkling wines are available throughout Sydney from "bottle shops", which sell alcohol.

Angus Brut premium

WHITE WINE

Australian Riesling   Botrytis Semillon

The revolution in wine making in the 1970s firmly established dry wines made from international grape varieties on the Australian table. Chardonnay, Sauvignon Blanc, and more recently Viognier and Pinot Gris are all popular. However, there has also been a renaissance and growing appreciation for Riesling, Marsanne and Semillon, which age very gracefully. Australia's other great wines are their fortified and dessert wines. Australian winemakers use *botrytis cinera*, or noble rot, to make luscious dessert wines such as De Bortoli's "Noble One".

Some of the vines in Australia are the oldest in the world.

GRAPE TYPE	STATE	BEST REGIONS	BEST PRODUCERS
Chardonnay	VIC	Geelong, Beechworth	Bannockburn, Giaconda, Stoniers
	NSW	Hunter Valley	Lakes Folly, Rosemount, Tyrrell's
	WA	Margaret River	Leeuwin Estate, Pierro, Cullen
	SA	Barossa Valley, Eden Valley	Penfolds, Mountadam
Semillon	NSW	Hunter Valley	Brokenwood, McWilliams, Tyrrell
	SA	Barossa Valley	Peter Lehmann, Willows, Penfolds
	WA	Margaret River	Moss Wood, Voyager, Evans & Tate
Riesling	SA	Clare Valley and Adelaide Hills	Grosset, Pikes, Petaluma, Mitchells
	SA	Barossa Valley	Richmond Grove, Leo Buring, Yalumba
	TAS	Tasmania	Piper's Brook
Marsanne	VIC	Goulburn Valley	Chateau Tahbilk, Mitchelton

RED WINE

Vineyards of Leeuwin Estate, Margaret River

Australia's benchmark red is Grange Hermitage, the creation of the late vintner Max Schubert in the 1950s and 1960s. Due to his work, Shiraz has established itself as Australia's premium red variety. However, there is also plenty of diversity with the acknowledged quality of Cabernet Sauvignon produced in the Coonawarra. Recently, there has also been a re-appraisal of traditional "old vine" Grenache and Mourvedre varieties in the Barossa Valley and McLaren Vale.

Shiraz   **Pinot Noir**

GRAPE TYPE	BEST REGIONS	BEST PRODUCERS
Shiraz	Hunter Valley (NSW)	Brokenwood, Lindmans, Tyrrells
	Great Western, Sunbury (VIC)	Bests, Seppelts, Craiglee
	Barossa Valley (SA)	Henschke, Penfolds, Rockford, Torbreck
	McLaren Vale (SA)	Hardys, Coriole, Chapel Hill
	Margaret River, Great Southern (WA)	Cape Mentelle, Plantagenet
Cabernet Sauvignon	Margaret River (WA)	Cape Mentelle, Cullen, Moss Wood
	Coonawarra (SA)	Wynns, Lindemans, Bowen Estate
	Barossa, Adelaide Hills (SA)	Penfolds, Henschke, Petaluma
	Yarra Valley, Great Western (VIC)	Yarra Yering, Yerinberg, Bests
Merlot	Yarra Valley, Great Western (VIC)	Bests, Yara Yering
	Adelaide Hills, Clare Valley (SA)	Petaluma, Pikes
Pinot Noir	Yarra Valley (VIC)	Coldstream Hills, Tarrawarra
	Gippsland, Geelong (VIC)	Bass Philip, Bannockburn, Shadowfax

BEER

Most Australian beer is vat fermented, or lager, and consumed chilled. Full-strength beer has an alcohol content of about 4.8 per cent, mid-strength beers have around 3.5 per cent while "light" beers have less than 3 per cent. Traditionally heat sterilized, cold filtration is now popular. Fans of real ale should seek out one of the city's pub breweries. Beer is ordered by glass size and brand: a schooner is a 426 ml (15 fl oz) glass and a middy is 284 ml (10 fl oz).

Bluetongue Lager   **Cascade Premium Lager**

Middy   **Schooner**

FRUIT JUICES

With the fabulous fresh fruit at their disposal year round, cafés concoct an astonishing array of fruit-based non-alcoholic drinks. They include frappés of fruit pulp and juice blended with crushed ice; smoothies of fruit blended with milk or yoghurt; and pure juices, extracted from everything from carrots to watermelons.

Pear and kiwi frappé   **Banana smoothie**   **Strawberry juice**

COFFEE

Sydney's passion for coffee means that short black, macchiato, caffe latte, cappuccino and flat white (with milk) are available at every neighbourhood café.

Flat white coffee   **Caffe latte**

OTHER DRINKS

Tap water in Sydney is fresh and clean, but local and imported bottled water is fashionable. The cola generation has graduated to alcoholic soft drinks and soda drinks. One brand, Two Dogs alcoholic lemonade, was born when a glut of lemons flooded the fruit market.

Spring water

Choosing a Restaurant

The restaurants in this section have been selected for their exceptional food and good value. Within each area, entries are listed alphabetically within each price category, from the least to the most expensive. Details of *Light Meals and Snacks* are on pages 194–5 and for Sydney's best *Pubs and Bars* see pages 196–7.

PRICE CATEGORIES
For a three-course meal for one person including service and cover charge (prices in Australian dollars):

Ⓢ under A$40
ⓈⓈ A$40–A$65
ⓈⓈⓈ A$65–A$90
ⓈⓈⓈⓈ A$90–A$120
ⓈⓈⓈⓈⓈ over A$120

THE ROCKS AND CIRCULAR QUAY

The Australian Heritage Hotel
Ⓢ
100 Cumberland St, The Rocks **Tel** *9247 2229*

Map *1 B2*

This pub specializes in topping pizzas with surprising combinations, including kangaroo, emu and crocodile meat. They also offer an all-day breakfast pizza, salads and pies. During lunch it is packed with office workers jostling for a table so it is best to take an early or late lunch or for an evening meal.

Vintage Cafe on the Rocks
Ⓢ
Shop R2, Nurses Walk, The Rocks **Tel** *9252 2055*

Map *1 B2*

Tucked away in a little cobble-stoned courtyard, in the earliest-settled part of Sydney, this sweet diner is a great place for a quick lunch or afternoon pitstop. Pierce Brosnan and Princess Anne were both spotted here when in town, though it is unknown whether they were dining on sandwiches or Devonshire tea. Big all-day breakfasts too.

City Extra
ⓈⓈ
Shop 4, East Podium, Circular Quay **Tel** *9241 1422*

Map *1 C3*

Located in the heart of Circular Quay with views of the water, this light and airy restaurant serves meals around the clock, from hearty cooked breakfasts, to light snacks and salads, through to popular steak, pasta and burger dishes. Close to public transport links, it makes a great budget choice in a prime location any time of day or night.

East Chinese
ⓈⓈ
Shop 8, 1 Macquarie St, East Circular Quay **Tel** *9252 6868*

Map *1 C2*

There is no secret Chinese menu at this busy restaurant, just a range of dishes from the familiar to the adventurous. Native Australian meats, including kangaroo, emu and crocodile, are on the menu, as well as a bevy of seafood treats, fresh from the tank. It's the best Chinese restaurant for people-watching.

Heritage Belgian Beer Café
ⓈⓈ
135 Harrington St, The Rocks **Tel** *9241 1775*

Map *1 A3*

There are other options listed on the menu but for anyone in the know, mussels provide the only authentic Belgian experience, cooked one of eight ways and served in a pot. Other entrées include duck pâté, oysters and a selection of Belgian Ardennes charcuterie. Of course, there are Belgian beers on tap and an amazing range of artisan brews.

Nelson's Brasserie
ⓈⓈ
19 Kent St, The Rocks **Tel** *9251 4044*

Map *1 A2*

The best of old and new Australia combine in this restaurant with its crisp white linen and 18th-century sandstone walls located in the heart of The Rocks. The modern Australian food is easily washed down with a beer which has been brewed on the premises.

Opera Bar
ⓈⓈ
Lower Concourse Level, Sydney Opera House, Bennelong Point **Tel** *9247 1666*

Map *1 C2*

This is a great place for a refreshing stop on the way to or from the Opera House and an excellent destination in its own right. Bar food is available from noon until 11pm, with good-value tasting plates. There are also pre-theatre, lunch and dinner menus. Nightly entertainment sees DJs and jazz, soul and funk bands.

Sailors Thai Canteen
ⓈⓈ
Sailors' Home, 106 George St, The Rocks **Tel** *9251 2466*

Map *1 B2*

In the historic Sailors' Home building *(see p67)*, diners sit at a long, zinc communal table, or on one of the small tables on the sunny balcony, and tuck into bowls of Thai street food. This informal restaurant makes an ideal pitstop in a busy part of the city. There is also a more formal restaurant downstairs *(see p185)*.

Young Alfred
ⓈⓈ
31 Alfred St, Circular Quay **Tel** *9251 51 92*

Map *1 B3*

From the former owners of one of Sydney's all-time favourite pizza places comes modern Italian fare and wonderfully named pizzas dished up near the harbour, in the historic Customs House building. Try the TNT, Betty Boston and the "surprise". What's on it? It depends on the chef's mood – but it's always delicious.

Key to Symbols *see back cover flap*

Café Sydney   ⓢⓢⓢ

Level 5, Customs House, 31 Alfred St, Circular Quay **Tel** *9251 8683*   **Map** *1 B3*

This buzzing restaurant, on the top floor of historic Customs House, has sweeping views. The terrace is delightful; in winter, gas heaters keep diners warm and special resin lamps make each table glow. The kitchen's tandoor oven, wood-fired grill, wok and rotisserie turn out a great variety of food. There is live jazz on Sunday afternoons.

Sailors Thai   ⓢⓢⓢ

106 George St, The Rocks **Tel** *9251 2466*   **Map** *1 B3*

Located at the historic Sailors' Home, chef and Thai food expert David Thompson continues to oversee the menu at this restaurant. Highly recommended are the crispy fish and green papaya salad, and braised beef ribs spiked with chilli. The cheaper Sailors Thai Canteen, upstairs *(see p184)*, is open for lunch and dinner too.

The Wharf Restaurant   ⓢⓢⓢ

Sydney Theatre Company, Harbour end of Pier 4, Hickson Rd, Walsh Bay **Tel** *9250 1761*   **Map** *1 A1*

A wonderful setting in a restored wharf offering an unusual view of the Harbour Bridge. Directly opposite, Luna Park provides an glittering backdrop of night-lights. Try the braised duck leg with rice noodle rotollo and Asian greens. Plan to dine after 8pm to avoid the theatre crowd. Disabled access should be arranged in advance.

Wildfire   ⓢⓢⓢ

Ground Level, Overseas Passenger Terminal, West Circular Quay **Tel** *8273 1222*   **Map** *1 B2*

This glamorous restaurant has views of the Opera House when there is no cruise ship in port. Great for a big night out or a snack after a show. Enjoy a range of offerings from the wood-fired Brazilian *churrasco* grill or pull up a seat at the Sea Bar. Mixologists create some of Sydney's best cocktails at the intimate bar, Ember.

Altitude   ⓢⓢⓢⓢ

Level 36, Shangri-La Hotel Sydney, 176 Cumberland St, The Rocks **Tel** *9250 6000*   **Map** *1 A3*

One of the few places in Sydney that requires guests to look smart, anything less would clash with the super slick decor. Those who arrive early might sip on one of a great range of apéritif cocktails in the blu horizon bar before supper. Altitude serves modern Australian cuisine inspired by European influences.

Aria   ⓢⓢⓢⓢⓢ

1 Macquarie St, East Circular Quay **Tel** *9252 2555*   **Map** *1 C2*

With uninterrupted panoramic views of Sydney Harbour, the Opera House and the Bridge, there are many options here, from a seven-course *dégustation* to a set price one, two- or three-course lunch, pre-theatre meal or supper. Fish and seafood star in many dishes.

Guillaume at Bennelong   ⓢⓢⓢⓢⓢ

Sydney Opera House, Bennelong Point **Tel** *9241 1999*   **Map** *1 C2*

You cannot beat the excitement of dining in the Opera House, especially in such a romantic, elegant space. An emphasis on seafood produces dishes such as the steamed Murray cod served on braised baby endive. A cheaper way to taste chef Guillaume Brahimi's food is by ordering tapas-style served from the cocktail bar.

Quay   ⓢⓢⓢⓢⓢ

Upper Level, Overseas Passenger Terminal, West Circular Quay **Tel** *9251 5600*   **Map** *1 B2*

Another spectacular view, and food to match, with star chef Peter Gilmore making magic out of the best and freshest produce and combining ingredients in suprising ways. Try the confit of pure-bred Suffolk lamb. The famous chocolate cake is to die for.

Rockpool   ⓢⓢⓢⓢⓢ

107 George St, The Rocks **Tel** *9252 1888*   **Map** *1 B3*

Neil Perry opened his Sydney fine-dining institution in 1989 and invented modern Australian cuisine with his fusion of European and Asian flavours. In a stunning building with big marble columns, high ceilings and decorated in olive greens and golds, choose between a *dégustation* menu of nine courses, a set course menu or à la carte.

Yoshii   ⓢⓢⓢⓢⓢ

115 Harrington St, The Rocks **Tel** *9247 2566*   **Map** *1 A3*

Ryuichi Yoshii is one of Sydney's top sushi chefs and the author of a sushi cookbook. His restaurant serves dinner in the *kaiseki* style, a series of unique small dishes that gradually warm the stomach like a small stone (a Japanese precursor to the hot water bottle). Though pricey, this is excellent value. Lunchtime bento boxes are cheaper.

CITY CENTRE

Bodhi in the Park   ⓢ

Cook & Phillip Park, 2–4 College St **Tel** *9360 2523*   **Map** *1 C5*

This is a wonderful place to come for lunch on a sunny day, or for dinner on a summer's night, when you can sit outside. You will be amazed by the realistic vegan versions of fish and chicken. The *sang choy bau* (not-pork) is excellent, as is the signature dish, a skin-and-all vegan Peking duck. There is also a good wine and cocktail list.

Indochine Café ♿ ↗ $

Shop 14, 111 Elizabeth St ***Tel*** *9233 1088* ***Map*** *4 F2*

Creative, authentic-tasting Vietnamese food served in a first-floor location. Watch the rush on the busy street below or just take in the sunlight streaming through the floor-to-ceiling glass windows. This is a popular weekday lunch choice for city workers and is also open for dinner Friday and Saturday.

Mother Chu's Vegetarian Kitchen 👶 $

367 Pitt St ***Tel*** *9283 2828* ***Map*** *4 E3*

A cheap and cheerful restaurant that offers big servings of hearty food by blending the flavours of Taiwan, China and Japan. It's often full of students and arty types enjoying the warm Buddhist hospitality. They offer delicious stir-fries and curries you can trust are really vegetarian. Do not be put off by the canteen decor.

Diethnes 👶 $$

336 Pitt St ***Tel*** *9267 8956* ***Map*** *1 B5*

A Sydney institution, Diethnes has been in the same basement spot for 35 years, and you can tell. But get past the kitsch decor, and you will find huge portions of hearty meals. With dozens of meat dishes, pastas, rice, salads and traditional Greek fare such as *tzaziki* and *spanakopita*, there is something for everyone.

Encasa ♿ ↗ $$

423 Pitt St ***Tel*** *9211 4257* ***Map*** *4 E4*

Near Central Station, this casual Spanish restaurant is one of Sydney's best. If you intend to try their signature dish, Romesco de Peix, a Catalan seafood stew, it is best to let them know in advance. Served in an earthenware bowl, the prawns, squid and fish swim in a traditional, hazelnut sauce. Their standards of tapas, paella and sangria are great.

GPO Woodfired Pizza ♿ 👶 $$

Lower Ground Floor, GPO, 1 Martin Place ***Tel*** *9229 7722* ***Map*** *1 B4*

Serving a regular pizza for $15 makes this city diner fabulous value, meaning you can dine in the restored GPO building for a fraction of the cost of neighbours Prime and Post. The pizzas have crispy bases and the freshest toppings. Try a salame piccante with classic toppings of tomato, mozzarella, salami and olives.

Slip Inn ♿ ⛱ $$

111 Sussex St ***Tel*** *8295 9999* ***Map*** *1 A4*

This is the gentrified pub where Australia's Mary Donaldson met her husband, Crown Prince Frederik of Denmark. During the day, two menus offer modern Australian and Thai fare, best devoured in the sunny courtyard. At night, a short and sweet selection of pizzas keeps the customers happy.

Sushi e ♿ $$

Level 4, Establishment, 252 George St ***Tel*** *9240 3041* ***Map*** *1 B3*

Located inside the exclusive Hemmesphere Bar, there are so many magnificent sushi and sashimi dishes on offer here; it is impossible to list them. Ordering the set of little Asian spoons, each with a different delicious morsel, is a good idea. You might follow this with a nigiri sushi set or test your taste buds with a chilli-loaded dynamite sushi roll.

Glass Brasserie ♿ 👶 $$$

Hilton Sydney, Level 2, 488 George St ***Tel*** *9265 6068* ***Map*** *1 B5*

Located in the snazzy Hilton Sydney *(see p174)*, this restaurant aims to find a happy medium between the comfort and familiarity of a hotel bistro and the quality and excitement of chef Luke Mangan's previous restaurant, Salt. The menu is filled with classics such as steak tartare.

Machiavelli $$$

123 Clarence St ***Tel*** *9299 3748* ***Map*** *1 A4*

A Sydney dining institution where deals are done over lunch and dinner, this is where the city's politicians, lawyers and business leaders come to eat and be seen while enjoying traditional, hearty Italian food made with passion. The Italian trattoria decor features air-dried meats hanging from the ceiling. Closed Sat and Sun.

Rockpool Bar & Grill [D] $$$

66 Hunter St ***Tel*** *8078 1900* ***Map*** *4 F1*

Taking steakhouse to new heights in a heritage-listed Art Deco building is this 2009 addition to the renowned Rockpool stable. Premium beef is dry-aged on the premises and fish filleted in a purpose-built room. Choose the main dining room, or offerings like Wagyu beef burgers from the less formal bar menu.

Bécasse $$$$

Level 5, Westfield Sydney, Pitt St Mall ***Tel*** *9283 3440* ***Map*** *1 A5*

Once a tiny bistro, Bécasse is now located in the Westfield Sydney shopping mall. Chef Justin North does wonderful things with less popular cuts of meat, as well as luxe updates of classics. Choose either the 10-course *dégustation* or the à la carte for dinner or the good value "Producers Lunch". Luckily, the very rich food is served in small portions.

Bistrode CBD $$$$

Level 1, 52 King Street Sydney ***Tel*** *8297 7010* ***Map*** *4 E1*

A stylish restaurant popular with the young business lunch crowd, serving up an innovative take on modern British cuisine with an emphasis on meat including steak and offal. The buzzy dining room features large windows, Grecian columns and photographic portraits of chefs.

Key to Price Guide *see p184* **Key to Symbols** *see back cover flap*

est.
⬛ $$$$$

Level 1, Establishment, 252 George St **Tel** *9240 3010* **Map** *1 B3*

A former winner of the Best Restaurant in Australia AHA. Head chef Peter Doyle is widely regarded as a founding father of modern Australian cuisine, with a career spanning over 30 years, he has been referred to as a "home-grown legend". The menu features fresh, local seafood and beef from Rangers Valley.

Spice Temple
⬛ $$$$$

10 Blight St **Tel** *8078 1888* **Map** *4 F1*

Open the video-screen door and enter a modern Chinese marvel that draws inspiration from provinces throughout China. Chillies feature in every form – fresh, dried, salted, pickled, brined and fermented. The innovative cuisine is served in a dark, moody basement space decorated with Chinese lanterns and red table lamps.

Tetsuya's
⬛ $$$$$$

529 Kent St **Tel** *9267 2900* **Map** *4 E3*

Internationally revered and widely considered Australia's best restaurant, Tetsuya's serene space puts the emphasis on the food and wine. The *dégustation* menus fuse Japanese flavours with French technique. Wines can be matched to each course and vegetarian *dégustations* are available on request. Ask to meet the chef for a tour

DARLING HARBOUR

BBQ King
$

18–20 Goulburn St **Tel** *9267 2586* **Map** *4 E4*

A large eatery with abrupt service and non-existent decor. Despite this it has long held cult status. To understand why, try dining late at the end of a big night and you will discover just how welcome this hearty food can be. Almost everyone orders the same thing, barbecued duck and Chinese beer. Open until 2am on weekends.

Chat Thai
$

20 Campbell St **Tel** *9211 1808* **Map** *4 E4*

In the busy Chinatown food district, this Thai restaurant stands out in a mainly Chinese dining area. An interesting, authentic menu features daily specials and a few spicy dishes for those who like it hot. Food is prepared at the shop front window, which entertains the queue of guests waiting for a table in the bustling dining room.

Pasteur
$

709 George St, Haymarket **Tel** *9212 5622* **Map** *4 F4*

Finish your A$9 bowl of beef and rice noodle soup and you may not need dinner. *Pho* is a Vietnamese speciality, which may come with chicken or beef. These float in fragrant broth, served with a pile of mint and basil leaves, chilli and fish sauce. Fresh spring rolls are another delicious snack, filled with pork and prawns, which you can order here.

Zibar
$

Cnr Druitt & Sussex sts, Darling Harbour **Tel** *9268 0222* **Map** *4 E2*

A small restaurant/café conveniently located between the city centre and Darling Harbour. The food is consistently good and the coffee is arguably the best in the area. It is a busy and friendly place often filled with hotel guests from next door and "suits" from nearby office towers.

Zilver
$

Level 1, 477 Pitt St **Tel** *9211 2232* **Map** *4 E4*

Classic Chinese cuisine is complemented by modern presentation, ambience and service, with interesting and delicious food choices and complementary fruit. *Yum cha* draws the crowds at lunchtime, while the à la carte menu ensures a more relaxed dinner. The legendary custard tarts are a must-have at any time.

Chinta Ria: The Temple of Love
$$

The Roof Terrace, Cockle Bay Wharf, 201 Sussex St, Darling Harbour **Tel** *9264 3211* **Map** *4 D2*

Feelings of happiness are brought into this lively restaurant by the giant Buddha that takes centre stage. Its reasonable prices and fun atmosphere make it popular with a young crowd. The fresh and spicy Malaysian food is great for sharing and may be an aphrodisiac. Bookings are not taken for dinner, so expect long queues.

Golden Century
$$

393–399 Sussex St **Tel** *9212 3901* **Map** *4 E4*

The menu is huge, the staff are friendly and the selection of live seafood, including crab, abalone, lobster, parrot fish, barramundi and coral trout, is enormous. But what is truly amazing about this restaurant is that its kitchen stays open until 4am. It is not unusual to find the place full of other chefs relaxing after work.

The Malaya
$$

39 Lime St, King Street Wharf **Tel** *9279 1170* **Map** *4 D1*

For more than 45 years, this Sydney institution has been serving up Malaysian cuisine that packs a punch. With feisty, flavour-filled favourites and contemporary dishes, this harbourside establishment offers excellent variety. The seafood dishes are particularly recommended.

Marigold
Levels 4 & 5, 683–689 George St **Tel** *9281 3388*   **Map** *4 D4*

A truly enormous restaurant, covering two floors atop a shopping arcade, and long considered to serve Sydney's best *yum cha* (a meal of dumplings served with tea at lunchtime). At dinner, groups of six or more can choose from banquet menus, which offer excellent value dishes such as king prawns with vegetables and crispy-skinned chicken.

Oscars Restaurant and Lounge
84 Union St, Pyrmont **Tel** *9660 5933*   **Map** *3 B2*

Just a short walk from Darling Harbour is this light and airy restaurant with an earthy decor and a modern look. Good hearty "pub" food with a contemporary twist is served, complemented by a great selection of wines and draught and bottled beers.

Taste on Sussex Lane
Unit 10, 275 Kent St **Tel** *9299 0888*   **Map** *4 D1*

East meets west with Vietnamese styling complementing the French food at this popular destination. There is an à la carte and a bar menu, so you can choose to dine in the bistro or the swankier, pricier restaurant. Either way, the food is great. Diners without a booking should be prepared to queue.

Zaaffran
Level 2, 345 Harbourside Shopping Centre, Darling Harbour **Tel** *9211 8900*   **Map** *3 C2*

The pick of Darling Harbour's eateries, this Indian restaurant is heaven for vegetarians. The food goes beyond the standards, to offer eggplant and okra with coconut and tamarind. Carnivores will be satisfied by an aromatic lamb shank stew, chicken biryani or the excellent tandoori baby snapper. There are also good value set menus.

Coast
The Roof Terrace, Cockle Bay Wharf, 201 Sussex St **Tel** *9267 6700*   **Map** *4 D2*

Eating fresh local seafood by the water is a quintessential Sydney experience. Business lunches by day and big groups at night pack this popular spot on the city side of Darling Harbour. The Italian-leaning menu focuses on seafood and the best of Australian and Italian produce.

Kobe Jones
29 Lime St, King St Wharf, Darling Harbour **Tel** *9299 5290*   **Map** *4 D1*

Decorated in stylish black and red, this modern Japanese restaurant avoids being too touristy, despite front-row views of Darling Harbour. A large menu includes signature dishes such as a trio of oyster shooters, each with a distinctive flavour, and seared smoked salmon marinated in green tea with wasabi mash and nori cream. Great cocktails too.

Nick's Bar & Grill
The Promenade, Cockle Bay Wharf, Darling Harbour **Tel** *9279 0122*   **Map** *4 D2*

Nick's offers a menu full of crowd-pleasers and a fabulous spot to bask in Sydney's sunshine. At night, Darling Harbour's lights sparkle on the water. There is a cheap kids' menu of fish, calamari or chicken with chips, followed by vanilla ice cream. Grown-ups might try char-grilled tuna or octopus, served with chips and salad.

BOTANIC GARDEN AND THE DOMAIN

The Hyde Park Barracks
Queens Sq, Hyde Park Barracks, Macquarie St **Tel** *9222 1815*   **Map** *1 C5*

A quiet retreat within the walls of the Hyde Park Barracks Museum. This café serves modern Australian fare with a European slant (mainly traditional French and Italian), such as crispy-skinned barramundi fillet served on a bed of buttered potatoes, tomatoes and kalamata olives.

Pavilion on the Park
1 Art Gallery Rd, The Domain **Tel** *9232 1322*   **Map** *2 D4*

Close to the city centre yet serene and enchanting, the Pavilion on the Park is the ideal location to escape and enjoy a leisurely meal on its expansive terrace surrounded by lush parkland. Open seven days a week for breakfast, lunch and light meals.

The Art Gallery Restaurant
The Art Gallery of New South Wales, Art Gallery Rd, The Domain **Tel** *9225 1819*   **Map** *2 D4*

Open only for lunch daily and also for brunch on weekends, this restaurant provides a sophisticated place to discuss the latest exhibition. The menu is small but should please most. There is also a more casual café on the lower level, which is great for kids, offering little cardboard boxes with sandwiches, a drink and a chocolate.

Botanic Garden Restaurant
Royal Botanic Garden, Mrs Macquaries Rd **Tel** *9241 2419*   **Map** *2 D4*

Set among the lush greenery, this excellent value lunch venue opens on to a terrace, letting in the sounds of the garden, even the squawks of the famous bats. Serious gourmets might try the delicious braised lamb shoulder, eggplant purée and harissa sauce. Weekend brunch is lovely too, and there is a café next door.

Key to Price Guide *see p184* **Key to Symbols** *see back cover flap*

KINGS CROSS AND DARLINGHURST

Bill and Toni's ♿ 🚸 ⛱ 🍴 [$]

74 Stanley St, East Sydney ***Tel*** *9360 4702* **Map** *5 A1*

A Sydney stalwart loved for its strong coffee and old-fashioned feel with their famous red tablecloths. Upstairs you will find basic but delicious home-style Italian fare like spaghetti Bolognese and *bistecca*, and fast, friendly service. Afterwards, head downstairs for *macchiato* and *gelato*. An excellent place to bring kids with its pinball machines.

Govinda's 🚸 🍴 [$]

112 Darlinghurst Road, Darlinghurst ***Tel*** *9380 5155* **Map** *5 B1*

Dining at this Indian vegetarian restaurant means piling up a plate of delicious curries, breads and salads from the all-you-can-eat buffet. Many of the dishes are Indian, but pastas and casseroles are available too. For a little extra you can see a film in the upstairs movie room, and it is best to eat afterwards to avoid drifting off in the comfy couches.

Fishface ♿ 🚸 ⛱ 🍴 [$][$]

132 Darlinghurst Rd, Darlinghurst ***Tel*** *9332 4803* **Map** *5 B2*

In a tiny space which seats just 26, this restaurant offers the best value fish in town. The beer-battered fish and hand-cut chips are famous, and there is also a sushi bar. The menu is full of appealing choices, including the signature dish of blue-eye trevalla topped with thin rounds of potato shaped into scales. No bookings after 7pm.

Mahjong Room [$][$]

312 Crown St, Surry Hills ***Tel*** *9361 3985* **Map** *5 A2*

This modern Chinese restaurant, packed with a young crowd, is very different from the big Chinatown diners. Dishes such as crispy San-Dong chicken in light ginger vinegar sauce are served at mahjong tables in a series of small rooms. Double the experience by sharing the reasonably priced dishes.

Pink Peppercorn ⛱ 🍴 [$][$]

122 Oxford St, Darlinghurst ***Tel*** *9360 9922* **Map** *5 A2*

The simple, fresh flavours of Lao cuisine can be enjoyed at this inner city restaurant with a modern, upmarket atmosphere. Try the *taam som* (green papaya salad). The restaurant is decorated with three large murals depicting scenes from Lao life.

Tilbury Hotel ♿ 🍴 [$][$]

12–18 Nicholson St, Woolloomooloo ***Tel*** *9368 1955* **Map** *2 D5*

The Tilbury Hotel has been refurbished and transformed into one of the trendiest pubs in Sydney. The restaurant offers excellent Italian fare, and the daily menu might include lamb rack with peas, pancetta and mint. Also has a café serving wraps, bagels and coffees.

Yellow Bistro ♿ 🚸 ⛱ 🍴 [$][$]

57 Macleay St, Potts Point ***Tel*** *9357 3400* **Map** *2 E4*

Van Gogh yellow walls make this, one of the most famous buildings in the Cross, stand out. In the 1970s it was an artists' commune, which housed Brett Whiteley. Today creative genius is obvious in the food. The brunch menu is lovely but nothing beats the celebrated date tart created by pastry chef, Lorraine Godsmark (if on the menu).

a Tavola ⛱ [$][$][$]

348 Victoria St, Darlinghurst ***Tel*** *9331 7871* **Map** *5 B1*

The centerpiece of this stylish Italian trattoria's long, narrow dining room is a 10-m (32-ft) pink marble table for communal dining. The menu is determined when the day's pasta is made and fresh ingredients are in the chef's hands. Innovative cuisine or a simple bowl of spaghetti, you can get it all.

Bayswater Brasserie 🚸 🍴 [$][$][$]

32 Bayswater Rd, suburb of Kings Cross ***Tel*** *9357 2177* **Map** *5 B1*

This veteran of Kings Cross is famous for its freshly shucked oysters and friendly service. The modern Australian menu changes with the availability of the best produce, which may include blue swimmer crab lasagne with tomato *beurre blanc* or rhubarb *crème brûlée*. Everything is handmade here, such as bread, pasta and ice cream.

Jimmy Liks ♿ 🍴 [$][$][$]

186–188 Victoria St, Potts Point ***Tel*** *8354 1400* **Map** *2 E5*

The no-bookings policy at this buzzing, modern Asian joint means you can count on a lengthy wait for a seat at the communal table. Those who stick it out dine on Southeast Asian treats such as betel leaves with chicken and smoked eggplant and good sized mains. The adjoining bar offers 25 Asian-inspired and award-winning cocktails.

Lotus Bar & Bistro 🍴 [$][$][$]

22 Challis Ave, Potts Point ***Tel*** *9326 9000* **Map** *2 E4*

This sophisticated bistro with soft lighting and unique decor provides a chic atmosphere of warmth and simplicity. The award-winning head chef, Lauren Murdoch, has produced a menu that features home-style influences with fresh Mediterranean flavours.

Manta   ⓢⓢⓢ
Wharf 9, 6 Cowper Wharf Rd, Woolloomooloo **Tel** *9332 3822*   **Map** *2 D4*

The impressive menu at Manta changes daily to ensure that only the freshest seafood of the highest quality is included. Look out for the steamed Tasmanian black mussels, fregola and roasted shellfish broth. As many as six types of oyster may be available, including, in season, the superb native Angasis, Sydney Rock and Pacific.

Otto   ⓢⓢⓢ
Area 8, The Wharf, 6 Cowper Wharf Rd, Woolloomooloo **Tel** *9368 7488*   **Map** *2 D4*

Otto is a piece of Melbourne brought to Sydney's waterfront and is so appreciated that it often draws celebrities, from footballers to Kylie Minogue, to its dark and handsome surrounds. Italian fare is jazzed up with local ingredients, such as twice-cooked pork belly, salsify, roasted garlic, olives, thyme and mugolio.

PADDINGTON

Paddington Inn   ⓢ
338 Oxford St, Paddington **Tel** *9380 5913*   **Map** *6 D4*

This perennially popular pub in the heart of the Paddington strip is especially busy on weekend afternoons, when hip locals meet over beers and tapas-style plates. Pub classics such as bangers and mash and fish and chips are given a restaurant touch. There are also plenty of lighter meals, such as salt and pepper prawns. Great for lunch.

Phamish   ⓢ
50 Burton St, Darlinghurst **Tel** *9357 2688*   **Map** *5 B2*

Its no-fuss attitude means Phamish offers no wine, desserts, lunches, bookings or website. Never mind, hordes of diners still flock here for the excellent, cheap food. You can bring your own wine, devour the large servings of fresh and spicy modern Vietnamese food and then walk up the hill to Victoria Street for a mouth-cooling *gelato*.

Big Mama's   ⓢⓢ
51 Moncur St, Woollahra **Tel** *9328 7629*   **Map** *6 E4*

A great alternative to all the pub-dining choices that abound in Paddington. It can get noisy and crowded, but that gives it the home-style Italian atmosphere that is as enjoyable as the honest, hearty comfort food. The menu consists of traditional Italian cuisine. Try the home-made *Limoncello* for the full experience.

Buzo   ⓢⓢ
3 Jersey Rd, Woollahra **Tel** *9328 1600*   **Map** *6 D4*

Buzo is another piece of evidence showing that bistro food is booming in Sydney. Bookings are essential at this restaurant, just off Oxford Street. Carnivores will delight in the meaty menu, offering roast lamb, char-grilled steak and even various offal dishes. You will need to order some side dishes to accompany your main.

Vamps Bistro   ⓢⓢ
227 Glenmore Rd, Paddington **Tel** *9331 1032*   **Map** *5 B3*

This small, traditional French restaurant is situated in the heart of Paddington at The Five Ways and is a favourite with the locals, providing as it does good food and a relaxed atmosphere. It is BYO (which is fast becoming a rarity in Sydney), so remember to take a bottle of good Australian wine.

Bistro Moncur   ⓢⓢⓢ
The Woollahra Hotel, 116 Queen St, Woollahra **Tel** *9327 9713*   **Map** *6 E4*

A stroll down Queen Street from the main strip, Bistro Moncur in the Woollahra Hotel has been an eastern suburbs favourite for more than a decade. The menu lists such French classics as sirloin café de Paris and French onion soufflé gratin. No bookings, so arrive early or to start with a drink in the bar, where top jazz bands play on Sunday evenings.

Bistro Moore   ⓢⓢⓢ
Olympic Hotel, 308 Moore Park Rd, Paddington **Tel** *9361 6315*   **Map** *5 C4*

Across the road from the Sydney Football Stadium and the Sydney Cricket Ground, this bistro serves excellent modern Australian food. There are just six entrées, pastas, mains and desserts on the seasonal menu, but you will feel spoilt for choice as each dish is so appealing. The pasta is handmade, the coffee spot on, and puddings delicious.

Four In Hand   ⓢⓢⓢ
105 Sutherland St, Paddington **Tel** *9362 1999*   **Map** *6 E3*

An eye-catching painting of a giant squid greets diners to this hotel restaurant, which is now under the supervision of chef Colin Fassnidge who produces excellent French provincial cuisine. His small but superbly constructed menu combines French bistro with a modern touch.

Buon Ricordo   ⓢⓢⓢⓢ
108 Boundary St, Paddington **Tel** *9360 6729*   **Map** *5 C2*

Ask a Sydney chef where he goes on nights off and the answer is likely to be this small restaurant. The emphasis of the menu is Roman and Neapolitan dishes, which sees the signature dish of fettuccine with Parmesan, cream and truffled egg tossed at your table. Dishes here are said to be better than at most places in Italy.

Lucio's ♿ $$$$

47 Windsor St, Paddington ***Tel*** *9380 5996* ***Map*** *6 D3*

Lucio's is right in the middle of the area of Sydney's art galleries and the walls of the restaurant display a collection of contemporary Australian artists such as John Olsen, John Coburn, Gary Shead and Tim Storrier. There is art on the plate too, the expertly cooked Italian food varies according to what is in season.

Claude's ♿ ⛱ $$$$$

10 Oxford St, Woollahra ***Tel*** *9331 2325* ***Map*** *6 D4*

A Sydney icon for over thirty years, this intimate restaurant in a converted terrace house seats just 40 people. Choose between the set-price menu or the eight-course tasting menu. Dishes sound simple on paper but are actually as close to works of art as food can get. Bookings recommended. Ring the doorbell when you arrive.

FURTHER AFIELD

Café Mint ⛱ 🏪 $

579 Crown St, Surry Hills ***Tel*** *9319 0848*

This café is tiny and can seem crammed, but it's worth the "cosy" feeling when the food is this good. The coffee is excellent and food is fabulous value, particularly at lunch. For a rainbow of dips and pickles, try the large meze plate. The Lebanese *fattoush* salad with garlicky, crunchy pitta bread is great.

The Crabbe Hole 📖 ♿ 🚸 🏪 $

1 Notts Ave, Bondi Beach ***Tel*** *0450 27723*

Tiny in size but big on views, this café in a peaceful spot away from the crowds of Campbell Parade serves great coffee, as well as juices, smoothies, fruit bread, sandwiches and snacks. Tables shaded by umbrellas are next to the famous Bondi Iceberg Baths and overlook Bondi Beach. Open 7am 5pm daily.

Il Baretto ♿ 🚸 ⛱ 🏪 $

496 Bourke St, Surry Hills ***Tel*** *9361 6163*

Diners wishing to sup at this crammed café often face the longest waits in Sydney, so it is lucky the pasta is so good, and that there is a pub across the road. Very basic pastas, such as a penne arrabiata, laced with enough chillies to make your tongue tingle, start at $12. The duck ragu and hand-rolled gnocchi are loved by many.

Manly Wharf Hotel ♿ 🚸 🏪 $

Manly Wharf East Esplanade, Manly ***Tel*** *9977 1266*

Not much beats sharing a seafood platter packed with oysters, prawns, salt and pepper squid, octopus, scallops and fish, while looking out over Sydney Harbour. Even better, this is a pub you can bring your kids to, keeping them happy with one of the well-priced offerings from the kids' menu. Perfect after a long day at the beach.

Maya 🚸 ⛱ $

470 Cleveland St, Surry Hills ***Tel*** *9699 8663*

Even almost broke vegetarians in board shorts and thongs do well at this sweet and chaat house, popular with a diverse crowd, including students, hippies, Indian taxi drivers and foodies. Authentic treats such as thali plates of assorted curries and breads and the famous masala dosai are promptly delivered. Finish off with some Indian fudge.

Rowda-Ya Habibi 🚸 ⛱ [D] $

101 King St, Newtown ***Tel*** *9557 5368*

Many Sydneysiders rely on Lebanese restaurants for consistently good, healthy, fresh food. Though some of the delicacies here are deep-fried, there are more than enough salads and vegetables to make up for that bit of oil. Servings are large and feel even bigger if you have filled up on dips and pitta first. Belly dancing on weekend nights.

Sushi Suma 🚸 ⛱ $

425 Cleveland St, Surry Hills ***Tel*** *9698 8873*

The number of Japanese crammed around tables in this neighbourhood restaurant tells you how authentic the food is. The servings here are enormous so many people leave with doggy bags. When it is busy, and that is most of the time, orders are taken from the queue and food arrives as guests are seated. Great tempura too.

Alhambra ♿ 🚸 ⛱ 🏪 $$

1/54 West Esplanade Manly ***Tel*** *9976 2975*

Hugely popular on Friday and Saturday nights, when flamenco dancers add to the din, this casual restaurant has views of the Manly Wharf. The Moroccan chef cooks Moorish and Spanish food. A meal might begin with tapas followed by a Moroccan tagine of chicken and preserved lemon or lamb and date.

Alio ♿ 🚸 ⛱ $$

5 Baptist St, East Redfern ***Tel*** *8394 9368*

Alio is just off the main drags of Crown and Cleveland Streets and worth seeking out, particularly because of the warm room, good service and excellent food. Home-made breadsticks are a good start and mains are rich and filling. The chef here is a good friend of Jamie Oliver's, who dines (and sometime cooks) here when in town.

Bird Cow Fish

Shops 4 & 5, 500 Crown St, Surry Hills **Tel** *9380 4090*

Bird Cow Fish is the perfect blend of a café and bistro. A great place to drop in for just a coffee or for a more leisurely lunch or dinner. Modern Australian regional dishes produced in a Mediterranean style. Bistro food at its best with generous helpings and a lively atmosphere.

Blue Orange

49 Hall St, Bondi Beach **Tel** *9300 9885*

You could spend your whole day here, starting with smoked salmon pancakes for breakfast, followed by chilli linguini and chicken for lunch. By night the casual café, loved by locals and tourists alike, transforms into an intimate restaurant with a menu drawing on African and Middle Eastern flavours. Best of all, there is jazz on Sunday nights.

Bodega

216 Commonwealth St, Surry Hills **Tel** *9212 7766*

Spanish and South American food with all their flavours are celebrated in this restaurant with its striking mural of a matador and a large bull. The decor is modern, combining Scandinavian furniture and Italian design. There is an excellent wine list of Spanish and South American wines.

Bondi Trattoria

34 Campbell Parade, Bondi Beach **Tel** *9365 4303*

Every table here (inside and outside) has a spectacular view of the beach which makes this place popular with both locals and tourists. It is a café by day and a restaurant at night, serving a fusion of traditional Italian and modern Australian cuisine.

Hugo's at Manly Wharf

Shop 1, Manly Wharf, East Esplanade, Manly **Tel** *8116 8555*

This long-time favourite offers a great mix of modern cuisine, seafood and pizza with equally great views of the water and ferries arriving at the restaurant's doorstep on Manly wharf. Soak up the sun or watch it set in chic, beach house-style surroundings.

Longrain

85 Commonwealth St, Surry Hills **Tel** *9280 2888*

Chilli and ginger turn up the spice at Sydney's hippest restaurant, where the giant communal tables were one of the first in town. The Thai food lends itself well to sharing, with dishes such as mango and sweet pork, and spiced curry of duck with peanuts and mandarin juice. It has a great bar as well.

Mohr Fish

202 Devonshire St, Surry Hills **Tel** *9318 1326*

The many devotees of this classy fish and chip shop cram into its tiny space. Those who cannot find a table wait in the neighbouring pub, the Shakespeare Hotel, or thanks to the amiable relations between the two establishments order their fish to take away and eat next door. The legendary chips are wide, hand cut and golden. No bookings.

Pompei's

126 Roscoe St, Bondi Beach **Tel** *9365 1233*

It is a mystery how the residents of Bondi survived Sydney's long hot summers before the arrival of this pizzeria and gelateria. Thin-based pizzas are scattered with the freshest toppings and although the *gelato* kicked off a city-wide craze, it is still the best in town. Seasonal flavours include Granny Smith apple, nectarine and roasted almond.

Uchi Lounge

15 Brisbane St, Darlinghurst **Tel** *9261 3524*

Map *4 F4*

A small bar that specialises in *saketinis*, and a long room with warm but minimal design, provide excellent environs for French-Japanese fusion food. The menu offers many small courses, including the chrysanthemum sushi and wagyu beef with wasabi mash dishes.

3 Weeds Restaurant

197 Evans St, Rozelle **Tel** *9818 2788*

The Sydney bistro burst onto the inner West scene when this refurbished pub dining room opened. Off Rozelle and Balmain's main drag of Darling Street, the vibe is casual and comfortable. The food, whether bar snacks or a three-course meal, is excellent.

Aqua Dining

Cnr Paul and Northcliff Sts, Milsons Point **Tel** *9964 9998*

Floor to ceiling windows afford fine views of the harbour and the Olympic pool immediately below. The often luxurious menu allows the produce to shine and includes dishes such as smoked fillet of King Island beef tenderloin. Extensive wine list and weeknight dinner deals are of great value.

Billy Kwong

355 Crown St, Surry Hills **Tel** *9332 3300*

Map *5 A3*

If the long queues are not a dead giveaway then the smell when you walk in the door will tell you that this place is special. Run by Kylie Kwong, one of Sydney's latest celebrity chefs, it specializes in traditional Chinese family food, souped up with a modern edge. Banquets are good value and there are always beautiful flowers.

Garfish

2/21 Broughton St, Kirribilli **Tel** *9922 4322*

This is the best fishy place on the North side. Not many places offer breakfasts as exciting as spanner crab omelette with sweet chilli, masala spice and raita. Diners are able to customize their dishes by selecting a type of fish, how they would like it cooked and can even select its garnish. Very busy during weekends.

Icebergs Dining Room and Bar

1 Notts Ave, Bondi Beach **Tel** *9365 9000*

The first really swish restaurant to hit the surf at Bondi, this dining room is above the famous swimming pool. The decor gives a glamourous beach feel with a palette of ocean blues, giant rustic chandeliers and a scattering of silk cushions. Food is simple, modern Italian, such as *Brodetto all'Anconetena* (thick fish soup).

Orso Bayside Restaurant

79 Parriwi Rd, Mosman **Tel** *9968 3555*

This luxurious waterfront restaurant is destined to impress, with freshest seafood and splendid views of the harbour. Take a seat on Orso's private jetty and be greeted by schools of fish and ducks as you enjoy seared Tasmanian mussels followed by warm melting chocolate cake.

Red Lantern

545 Crown St, Surry Hills **Tel** *9698 4355*

A relaxed atmosphere and fiery red interior add to the enjoyment in this converted terrace. Most people, however, visit Red Lantern because they have heard of its high standards of fresh and spicy Southern Vietnamese food. For extra fun, order one of the "at the table" dishes you assemble yourself from rice paper or crêpes. Bookings essential.

Restaurant Balzac

141 Belmore Rd, Randwick **Tel** *9399 9660*

This local bistro, with its sandstone walls and thick white tablecloth, is luxurious and yet relaxed. It has earned a reputation with gourmands for its excellent Anglo French food, reasonable prices and great service. *Dégustation* menus and special deals are available. Also try treats from the tasting plate of tiny petit fours. Booking is essential.

Sean's Panaroma

270 Campbell Parade, Bondi Beach **Tel** *9365 4924*

Like an oversized family dining room, Sean's is intimate and friendly. Serving a small range of seasonal dishes, with a few constants such as linguine with shredded arugula, lemon, chilli and Parmesan, and the famous white chocolate and rosemary nougat. Bookings essential.

Bathers' Pavilion Restaurant

4 The Esplanade, Balmoral Beach **Tel** *9969 5050*

This classic restaurant is housed in the historic beachside changing rooms. The atmosphere is relaxed and there's a sea view from every table. Flavours vary from Chinese to Greek, Middle Eastern to French, sometimes all in one dish. Great set-price lunch deals during the week. The accompanying café has vegetarian options and good breakfasts.

The Boathouse on Blackwattle Bay

End of Ferry Rd, Glebe **Tel** *9518 9011*   **Map** 3 A3

Housed in the upper level of a boatshed, it looks out at the fish markets and busy traffic of trawlers and pleasure crafts. The menu changes daily, but the chef keeps his signature dish of salt and pepper mud crab. Also famous for their wide range of freshly shucked oysters.

Catalina Rose Bay

1 Sunderland Ave, Lyne Park, Rose Bay **Tel** *9371 0555*

It has been described as Sydney's veranda and this restaurant, which hangs over the harbour's edge, certainly has one of the best views. High-flyers snooze at lunchtime, while dinner at Catalina is a classic Sydney big night out. The flavoursome modern Australian food offers plenty of variety including the roast snapper signature dish.

Flying Fish

Lower Deck, Jones Bay Wharf, 19–21 Pirrama Rd, Pyrmont **Tel** *9518 6677*   **Map** 3 C1

Glam meets clams, with fabulous modern Australian and Sri Lankan flavours, and a sculpture of 500 lights. Australian soldiers embarked for World War II from this Wharf and train tracks remain along its length. History evaporates as you stare out at the harbour views.

Pier

594 New South Head Rd, Rose Bay **Tel** *9327 6561*

This restaurant is one long, timber-panelled room which runs the length of a small pier and juts out into the harbour. Yachts moored in the marina float all around and you would feel like you were on one if the food was not quite so good. Good quality fish is cooked to perfection in dishes such as carpaccio of John Dory and roasted barramundi.

Marque

355 Crown St, Surry Hills **Tel** *9332 2225*   **Map** 5 A3

Choose between the eight-course *dégustation* menu, which can also be vegetarian, or the à la carte menu. The dishes here are complex and with flavours you would never have imagined. The signature dish is a beetroot tart served with a frothy horseradish cream.

Light Meals and Snacks

The mercurial nature of Sydney's dining scene is visible in the multitude of establishments that open and close each year. With cafés, this situation is magnified and, as a result of this competition, the standards are high. Coffee is of good quality across Sydney and almost every eatery has its own espresso machine. A surge in the popularity of tea has made many places switch from teabags to boutique, loose-leaf black teas, tisanes and herbal brews. Tipping is unnecessary at takeaways. While it is not essential at cafés, many have a jar on the counter where patrons leave their change as a gratuity.

CAFES

Coffee culture was introduced to Sydney by Italian migrants, who flooded in after World War II. **Bar Coluzzi**, with its boxing pictures on the walls, has long been the capital of Darlinghurst's caffeine kingdom. Media types, lawyers and taxi drivers throng here both for the company and the coffee. **Toby's Estate**, a latecomer on the scene, imports, roasts and grinds its own beans. Bondi Beach's bookshop-cum-café **Gertrude & Alice** is named after Gertrude Stein and Alice B Toklas. The vegetarian **Badde Manors** in Glebe is frequented by students.

Nothing revives quite like a good pot of tea. **The Tea Centre** is an oasis of calm in a city shopping centre and can serve you a pot of any of the dozens of teas they import. In the Rocks, the **Gumnut Café** serves traditional Devonshire tea with scones and jam. Those looking for a chocolate fix might try **Max Brenner** or the **Lindt Chocolat Café**, where treats come as dark, milk or white, and in both solid and liquid forms.

Most cafés offer a menu of sandwiches, salads, cakes and muffins throughout the day. The fabulous food at **Danks Street Depot** presents a serious challenge to some of Sydney's top restaurants. The Depot shares a converted warehouse in a rapidly gentrifying industrial area with a handful of galleries, and is more than worth the cab fare. As well as excellent food, **Yellow Bistro** (see p189)

serves some of the best pastries in town, and their food store is a great place to buy supplies. The French **Café Sel et Poivre** is very popular, while **Sloanes** in Paddington is a great pit stop for those weary after a day of treading the Oxford Street strip and Saturday's markets (see p126).

Cafés at attractions vary, but generally, those at art galleries and museums are of a high standard, while those at sporting venues are not. **Opera Bar** (see p184) on the Sydney Opera House concourse is hard to beat (see pp74–7). The **Museum of Sydney Café** (see p85) is also very good. Its shaded outdoor tables look out on the museum's paved forecourt and office workers striding by. The **Art Gallery Café** is a smart eatery at the **Art Gallery of New South Wales** (see pp108–11) that serves delicious sandwiches, good coffee and wine, and special lunchboxes for children. There is also a restaurant on the ground floor (see p188). Coveted outdoor tables offer a view over the Woolloomooloo fingerwharf. The **Sailor's Thai Canteen**, in the former Sailor's Home building (see p67), is an easy and economical, drop-in noodle bar.

Lunch amid lush greenery is possible at the **Botanic Garden Café** (see pp104–5), attached to the lovely restaurant (see p188), and at the breezy **Centennial Parklands Dining** (see p127), which also has a takeaway kiosk next door, a favourite of mothers with prams.

BEST BREAKFASTS

Many believe that, as the showpiece of celebrity chef Bill Granger, **bills** serves the official best breakfast. Tuck into his famous ricotta hotcakes with honeycomb butter and a healthy sunrise juice. At Darlinghurst stalwart **Le Petit Crème**, breakfast consists of Parisian options, including traditional bowls of café au lait and *croque monsieur*. For the ultimate Sydney start to the day, you have to head to the water. Watch the surfers at Bronte's **Swell**, or the swimmers at the **Icebergs Bistro** at Bondi Icebergs Club. At the **Marina Kiosk Café**, where the excitement is in the location more than the food, sit on the edge of the pier and dangle your feet over the harbour.

TAKEAWAY FOOD

All kinds of cuisine, such as Thai, Turkish, Afghani and Albanian, can be found in this very multicultural city. Most cheap local restaurants offer takeaway. Connoisseurs of ethnic cuisines might want to catch a train or bus and explore the areas specialising in them. While Leichhardt is Italian, you'll find Greek and Vietnamese restaurants in Marrickville, and Kosher cafés in Bondi. A cluster of Indian restaurants can be found on Cleveland Street in Surry Hills. At lunchtime, the food courts of city shopping centres offer a wide variety of quick, cheap meals. Try **Westfield Sydney** and **Sydney Central Plaza**. Above **Paddy's Markets** (see p99) at Haymarket, **Market City** offers a selection of Chinese, Japanese, Korean and Thai food. The famous Food Hall at **David Jones** (see p199) has the best supplies for any picnic, snack, sweet treat or takeaway dinner.

If you're craving fast food, try a Bondi burger from **Oporto**, a Portuguese chicken chain that has shops across Sydney, including one in Kings Cross and another in Galeries Victoria. Takeaway can be healthy too: top fish (maybe without the chips) comes from **A Fish Called Coogee**, where side dishes include barbecued corn on the cob and wok-fried greens. One of many sushi outlets, **Sushi Train** only serves the freshest fish and seafood. Juice bars, such as **Boost Juice**, have sprung up all over town, and most can add a shot of vitamins or wheatgrass

to your drink. Macrobiotics has become popular too. At **Iku** the food is flavourful as well as nutritious.

LATE-NIGHT SNACKS

Drop in to the long-standing **Harry's Café de Wheels** to sample an Aussie meat pie from the stand-up bar. Having satisfied the midnight cravings of locals and visitors for

decades, it is particularly popular with sailors from the adjacent naval dockyard.

BBQ King *(see p187)* is open until 2am most nights, as is noodle chain **Wagamama** on weekends.

For real night owls, **City Extra** is open 24 hours. **Café Hernandez**, also open throughout the day, is famous for its Spanish short black tortillas and cakes.

DIRECTORY

CAFES

Art Gallery Café
Art Gallery Rd,
The Domain.
Map 2 D4.
Tel 9225 1819.

Badde Manors
37 Glebe Point Rd,
Glebe. **Map** 3 B5.
Tel 9660 3797.

Bar Coluzzi
322 Victoria St,
Darlinghurst. **Map** 5 B1.
Tel 9380 5420.

Botanic Garden Café
Royal Botanic Garden,
Mrs Macquaries Rd.
Map 2 D4.
Tel 9241 2419.

Café Sel et Poivre
263 Victoria St
Darlinghurst. **Map** 5 B2.
Tel 9361 6530.

Centennial Parklands Dining
Cnr Grand & Parkes
Drives, Centennial Park.
Map 6 E5.
Tel 9380 9350.

Danks Street Depot
1/2 Danks St, Waterloo.
Tel 9698 2201.

Gertrude & Alice
46 Hall St, Bondi Beach.
Tel 9130 5155.

Gumnut Café
28 Harrington St,
The Rocks. **Map** 1 B3.
Tel 9247 9591.

Lindt Chocolat Café
53 Martin Place.
Map 1 B4.
Tel 8257 1600.

Max Brenner
437 Oxford St,
Paddington. **Map** 6 D4.
Tel 9357 5055.

Museum of Sydney Café
Cnr Bridge and Phillip sts.
Map 1 B3.
Tel 9241 3636.

Opera Bar
Sydney Opera House,
Bennelong Point.
Map 1 C2.
Tel 9247 1666.

Sailor's Thai Canteen
Upper level,
106 George St,
The Rocks. **Map** 1 B3.
Tel 9251 2466.

Sloanes
312 Oxford St,
Paddington.
Map 5 C3.
Tel 9331 6717.

The Tea Centre
Shop 4005, The Glass
House, 135 King St.
Map 4 E2.
Tel 9223 9909.

Toby's Estate
6/81 Macleay St,
Potts Point.
Map 2 E5.
Tel 8356 9264.

Yellow Bistro
57 Macleay St, Potts Point.
Map 2 E4.
Tel 9357 3400.

BEST BREAKFASTS

bills
355 Crown St,
Surry Hills.
Map 5 A3.
Tel 9360 4762.

Icebergs Bistro
Bondi Icebergs Club,
1 Notts Ave, Bondi Beach.
Tel 9130 3120.

Le Petit Crème
118 Darlinghurst Rd,
Darlinghurst,
Map 5 B1.
Tel 9361 4738.

Marina Kiosk Café
Rose Bay Marina, 594 New
South Head Rd, Rose Bay.
Tel 9362 3555.

Swell
465 Bronte Rd, Bronte.
Tel 9386 5001.

TAKEAWAY FOOD

A Fish Called Coogee
229 Coogee Bay Rd,
Coogee. *Tel 9664 7700.*

Boost Juice
98 Bathurst St.
Map 4 E3.
Tel 9264 4007.

David Jones
Cnr Market and
Castlereagh sts.
Map 1 B5.
Tel 9266 5544.

Iku
62 Oxford St, Darlinghurst.
Map 5 B3
Tel 9360 5351.

Market City
9–13 Hay St, Haymarket.
Map 4 D4.
Tel 9288 8900.

Oporto
3C Roslyn St,
Kings Cross.
Map 5 C1.
Tel 9380 2975.

Sushi Train
570 George St.
Map 1 B3
Tel 9283 1622.

Sydney Central Plaza
450 George St.
Map 1 B5.
Tel 8274 2000.

Westfield Sydney
Pitt St Mall.
Map 1 B5.
Tel 8236 9200.

LATE-NIGHT SNACKS

BBQ King
18–20 Goulburn St.
Map 4 E4.
Tel 9267 2586.

Café Hernandez
60 Kings Cross Rd,
Potts Point **Map** 5 C1.
Tel 9331 2343.

City Extra
Shop E4, East Podium,
Circular Quay.
Map 1 B3.
Tel 9241 1422.

Harry's Café de Wheels
Cowper Wharf Rd,
Woolloomooloo.
Map 2 E5.
Tel 9357 3074.

Wagamama
49 Lime St,
King Street Wharf.
Map 4 D1.
Tel 9299 6944.

Sydney Pubs and Bars

Confusingly for the overseas visitor, Australian pubs and bars are also known as hotels. This is because licensing laws originally required any place serving alcohol to provide accommodation too. In the cities, at least, hotels have changed radically and what were once the domains of beer-swilling males have now evolved into far more civilized spots. Pub menus have also undergone a metamorphosis. In place of the former meat pie and sauce, most pubs now offer hearty snacks at remarkably low prices. All pubs serve beer, basic mixed spirit-based drinks and wine by the glass, but cocktails tend to be the preserve of the more up-market venues. Pubs are also often good venues for live music (see pp214–15) and for watching telecasts of major international and local sporting matches.

RULES AND CONVENTIONS

The pubs and bars across Sydney operate under various licensing schemes. In general, those located in quiet neigh-bourhoods close at 10pm on weekdays and midnight on Friday and Saturday nights. Many pubs in busy tourist areas such as Darlinghurst, Kings Cross and near Central Station stay open much later; some of these even have 24-hour licences.

You must be at least 18 years of age to buy or consume alcohol, or to even enter many bars. Anyone under 30 should carry photo ID such as a driver's licence or passport. Children and teenagers under 18 are often allowed to join their parents in outdoor beer gardens and pub restaurants. It is also against the law for a hotel to serve alcohol to someone who is inebriated. The management can refuse service and may not allow people who seem drunk to enter a bar.

Dress requirements vary and these too are at the discretion of the publican. Upmarket bars might require patrons to look stylish, sometimes banning sneakers, though very few insist on suit jackets. Local pubs might refuse entry to those in flip flops or shorts.

One aspect of traditional pub culture is the custom of "shouting", or buying drinks for your companions. When someone buys you a drink, it is considered bad form if you do not return the favour. How-ever, it can become tricky if you are on a budget. Explain that you are only staying for one drink.

HISTORIC PUBS

Hotels have been part of Sydney life since the early days of the colony. Many of the town's old pubs are in The Rocks and while you will spot some on George Street, others are hidden in backstreets. The **Hero of Waterloo** (see p69), built in 1843, has a maze of stone cellars underneath. First licensed in 1841, the **Lord Nelson** (see p172) now brews its own ales. It offers a bistro and a few guest rooms. **The Australian Heritage Hotel** (see p184) boasts a pizza menu that features crocodile, kangaroo and emu meat, making it a favourite with locals and visitors. The **London Tavern** (see p124), the oldest pub in Paddington, opened in 1875. Underneath the glamorous Hilton Sydney hotel (see p174) the ornate **Marble Bar** is much as it was when built in 1893.

BARS WITH VIEWS

In a city built around one of the world's most beautiful harbours, it will not be out of the ordinary to find a plethora of bars with magnif-icent views. Many restaurants have compact bars attached. The bar at **Guillaume at**

Bennelong is a destination in its own right. Another favourite venue is **Opera Bar** (see p184) with its spectacular views of the city and indoor and outdoor seating. On level 36 of the Shangri-La Hotel (see p172), **blu horizon** is a flamboyant bar offering a range of cocktails as well as extraordinary views over the harbour, airport and city lights. The **Manly Wharf Hotel** (see p191) occupies a prime position in the ferry building. It is a great spot for a relaxed drink with friends and serves excellent food. Established in 1870, the **London Hotel** (see pp131, 142–3) in Balmain enjoys the reputation of being the most atmospheric pub in Sydney. Those arriving early can grab a tractor seat on the balcony and sip local Red Back beer while soaking up the most unusual view.

STYLISH BARS

Sydney has no lack of beautiful people, or of places for them to play. Those who wish to dive into the social scene might head to the pricey **Hugo's Lounge, Mint Bar and Dining** at the luxurious Hotel InterContinental (see p175), **Water Bar** at Blue Sydney (see p175) or **Zeta** at the Hilton Sydney (see p174). Overlooking Taylor Square, **Middle Bar** at Kinsela's is hip yet relaxed, as is **Longrain** (see p192). The smart little bar at the tiny **Lotus Bar & Bistro** (see p189) continuously wins awards for the best cocktails in Sydney. Darling-hurst's **The Victoria Room** feels like an estate in colonial Singapore, and serves tapas-style food. In the CBD, the fashionable **Establishment Hotel** (see p174) is home to several bars, including the eponymous ground-floor spot, a post-work favourite for city suits. Also on the hotel grounds is the exclusive **Hemmesphere**, decorated like a Moroccan lounge. Contemporary chan-deliers, chairs suspended from the ceiling, a scattering of silk cushions and endless ocean views make the ultra swish **Icebergs Dining Room and Bar** (see p193) the best of the lot.

LOCAL FAVOURITES

Join the locals at city nightspot, **Arthouse Hotel**, which hosts life-drawing classes and live music on some nights, DJs on others. The lovely Art Deco **Civic Hotel**, with a small cocktail bar and a large main bar, is low-key in the early evening, but turns into a club on weekend nights. Paddington has a surfeit of pubs and some of the best are the **Royal Hotel** at

Five Ways *(see p126)*, the busy **Paddington Inn** *(see p190)* and, at the top of Oxford Street, the **Light Brigade Hotel**. The renovated **Tilbury Hotel** *(see p189)* is another trendy pub in town and plays jazz on Sunday afternoons. The crowd here and at the **Green Park Hotel** is usually a mix of gay and straight. The **Bank Hotel** in Newtown hosts lesbian nights every Wednesday. In Bondi, suntanned locals frequent

Ravesi's. Even after most other bars close, **Baron's** in Kings Cross offers drinks and backgammon long into the night.

TOURIST CENTRAL

Those who enjoy being surrounded by fellow travellers should try the **Bondi Hotel**, **Cargo Bar** in Darling Harbour, The **Coogee Bay Hotel** or Irish pub **Scruffy Murphy's**. **Forrester's** in Surry Hills is famed for its $7 steaks.

DIRECTORY

HISTORIC PUBS

The Australian Heritage Hotel
100 Cumberland St,
The Rocks **Map** 1 B2.
Tel 9247 2229.

Hero of Waterloo
81 Lower Fort St,
Millers Point.
Map 1 A2.
Tel 9252 4553.

London Tavern
85 Underwood St,
Paddington.
Map 6 D3.
Tel 9331 3200.

Lord Nelson
19 Kent St, Millers Point
Map 1 A2.
Tel 9251 4044.

Marble Bar
Level B1, Hilton Sydney,
488 George St.
Map 1 B5.
Tel 9265 6072.

BARS WITH VIEWS

blu horizon
Shangri-La Hotel Sydney,
176 Cumberland St.
Map 1 A3.
Tel 9250 6250.

Guillaume at Bennelong
See p185.

London Hotel
234 Darling St, Balmain.
Tel 9555 1377.

Manly Wharf Hotel
Manly Wharf Esplanade.
Tel 9977 1266.

Opera Bar
Sydney Opera House,
Bennelong Point.
Map 1 C2.
Tel 9247 1666.

STYLISH BARS

Establishment Hotel and Hemmesphere
Levels 1 and 4, 252
George St. **Map** 1 B3.
Tel 9240 3000.

Hugo's Lounge
33 Bayswater Rd,
Potts Point. **Map** 5 B1.
Tel 9357 4411.

Icebergs Dining Room and Bar
1 Notts Ave,
Bondi Beach.
Tel 9365 9000.

Longrain
85 Commonwealth St,
Surry Hills. **Map** 4 F4.
Tel 9280 2888.

Lotus Bar & Bistro
22 Challis Ave, Potts Point.
Map 2 E4.
Tel 9326 9000.

Middle Bar
Kinsela's, 383 Bourke St,
Darlinghurst.
Map 5 A5.
Tel 9331 3100.

Mint Bar and Dining
Hotel InterContinental,
cnr Bridge & Phillip sts.
Map 1 C3.
Tel 9240 1220.

The Victoria Room
231a Victoria St,
Darlinghurst.
Map 5 B2.
Tel 9357 4488.

Water Bar
Blue Sydney,
6 Cowper Wharf Rd,
Woolloomooloo.
Map 2 D5.
Tel 9331 9000.

Zeta
Level 4, Hilton Sydney,
488 George St.
Map 1 B5.
Tel 9265 6070.

LOCAL FAVOURITES

Arthouse Hotel
275 Pitt St.
Map 4 E2
Tel 9284 1200

Bank Hotel
324 King St, Newtown.
Tel 8568 1988.

Baron's
5 Roslyn St, Kings Cross.
Map 5 C1.
Tel 9358 6131.

Civic Hotel
388 Pitt St
(Cnr Goulburn St).
Map 4 E4.
Tel 8080 7000.

Green Park Hotel
360 Victoria St,
Darlinghurst.
Map 5 B2.
Tel 9380 5311.

Light Brigade Hotel
2 A Oxford St, Woollahra.
Map 6 D4.
Tel 9331 2930.

Paddington Inn
338 Oxford St,
Paddington.
Map 6 D4.
Tel 9380 5913.

Ravesi's
118 Campbell Pde,
Bondi Beach.
Tel 9365 4422.

Royal Hotel
237 Glenmore Rd,
Paddington.
Map 5 C3.
Tel 9331 2604.

Tilbury Hotel
12–18 Nicholson St,
Woolloomooloo.
Map 2 D5.
Tel 9368 1955.

TOURIST CENTRAL

Bondi Hotel
Cnr Campbell Parade and
Curlewis St, Bondi Beach.
Tel 9130 3271.

Cargo Bar
52–60 The Promenade,
King St Wharf.
Map 4 D2.
Tel 9262 1777.

The Coogee Bay Hotel
Cnr Coogee Bay Rd and
Arden St, Coogee.
Tel 9665 0000.

Forrester's
336 Riley St,
Surry Hills.
Map 4 F5.
Tel 9211 2095.

Scruffy Murphy's Hotel
43–49 Goulburn St.
Map 4 E4.
Tel 9212 0874.

SHOPS AND MARKETS

The shopping options in Sydney are wide and the quality of merchandise is usually good. The inner city has innumerable elegant arcades and shopping galleries, with plenty of nooks and crannies to explore. The range of goods on offer is enormous – most international labels, Gucci, Vuitton and

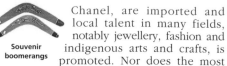

Souvenir boomerangs

Chanel, are imported and local talent in many fields, notably jewellery, fashion and indigenous arts and crafts, is promoted. Nor does the most interesting shopping stop at the city centre; there are several "satellite" alternatives. Some of the best shopping areas are highlighted on pages 200–1.

A typical junk-shop-cum-café in Balmain *(see p131)*

SHOPPING HOURS

Most shops are open from 9am–5:30pm each day of the week, though some may close early on Sundays. High-end boutiques open from 10am–6pm. On Thursdays, most shops stay open until 9pm. Most shops in Chinatown are open late every evening and on Sundays.

HOW TO PAY

Major credit cards are accepted almost everywhere. You will need identification, such as a passport or driver's licence,

when using traveller's cheques. Department stores will exchange goods or refund your money if you are not satisfied, provided you have kept your receipt. Other stores will only refund if an item is faulty. There is also a 10 per cent Goods and Services Tax (GST) which by law must be displayed in the marked price.

SALES

Many shops conduct sales all year round. The big department stores of **David Jones** and **Myer** have two gigantic and chaotic clearance sales each year. The post-Christmas sales start on 26 December, lasting into January. The other major sale time is during June, in the lead up to the end of the financial year.

TAX-FREE SALES

Duty-free shops are found in the city centre as well as at Kingsford Smith Airport *(see p228)*. You can save 10 per cent on goods such as perfume, jewellery, watches and perhaps up to 30 per cent on alcohol at duty-free shops but you must show

your passport and onward ticket. Some stores will also deliver your goods to the airport to be picked up on departure. Duty-free items must be kept in their sealed bags until you leave the city.

You can claim back the GST paid on most goods, purchased for (or in a single transaction of) A$300 or more, at the airport.

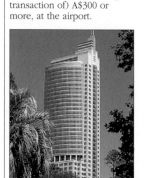

Chifley Tower, with the Chifley Plaza shopping arcade at its base

ARCADES AND MALLS

The **Queen Victoria Building** *(see p82)* is Sydney's most palatial shopping space. Four levels contain more than 200 shops. The top level, Victoria Walk, is devoted to merchandise such as silver, antiques, designer knitwear and high-quality souvenirs. The **Strand Arcade** *(see p84)* was originally built in 1892. Jewellery, chocolates, coffee shops and tea rooms are its stock in trade.

Pitt Street Mall has several shopping centres. **Westfield Sydney** features numerous local and international designer brand stores, including Zara, Escada, Gucci and Gap.

Next door to the Hilton, the **Galeries Victoria** houses

Inside Gleebooks, popular with students and locals in Glebe *(see p131)*

the fantastic Kinokuniya bookstore, which sells a variety of both Australian and American imprints as well as Chinese and Japanese language, anime art books and stationery. The Mooks store is packed with designer streetwear for men and women from the eponymous Australian label, as well as international brands such as G-Star and Camper.

Further down George Street, **World Square** shopping centre houses more than 90 speciality stores, from electronics to Australian menswear label Jack London.

The **MLC Centre**, which faces onto Castlereagh Street, and **Chifley Plaza** also cater to the prestige shopper. Gucci, Cartier, Tiffany & Co., MaxMara and Kenzo are just some of the shops here.

The **Harbourside Shopping Centre** has dozens of shops, plus several waterfront restaurants. The atmosphere is festive and the merchandise includes fine arts, jewellery, duty-free shopping, beachwear and Australiana.

DEPARTMENT STORES

The **David Jones** and **Myer** chains compete fiercely, each snaring exclusive rights to stock various local design talents and international labels. The David Jones in Sydney, or DJs, is legendary for its spring floral displays, as well as for its luxurious perfumery and cosmetics hall on the ground floor. The

Greengrocer's display of fresh fruit and vegetables

magnificent store spreads out in two buildings, across the road from each other on Market and Elizabeth streets. The food hall on the lower ground floor is famous for its gourmet fare and fine wines. The first David Jones store opened in 1838, and they claim to have the oldest department store in the world still trading under its original name. Myer now operates 60 stores across Australia, and their first store opened in 1900. The Myer store here in Sydney has a ground floor packed with make-up and accessories, including a large MAC counter. Both the Sydney stores of these famous chains sell women's clothing, lingerie, menswear, baby goods, children's clothes, toys, stationery, kitchenware, furniture, china, crystal and silver

SHOPPING FURTHER AFIELD

Good shopping areas outside central Sydney are Balmain, for village-style shopping; Double Bay, with its chic, though pricey, boutiques; the enormous mega-mall **Westfield Bondi Junction** which is only a short train journey away and has over 447 shops; and Left Bank-style student haunts of Newtown and Glebe. Bargains can be found at the factory outlets in Redfern, **Market City** and at Birkenhead Point. **Shopping Spree Tours** arrange day trips to a number of little-known factory outlets in their minibus, with lunch provided.

Part of the spring floral display, David Jones department store

DIRECTORY

Chifley Plaza
2 Chifley Square. **Map** 1 B4.
Tel 9221 6111.

David Jones
Cnr Elizabeth & Market sts.
Map 1 B5. *Tel* 9266 5544.
Also. Cnr Market & Castlereagh sts. **Map** 1 B5. *Tel* 9266 5544.

Galeries Victoria
500 George St. **Map** 1 B5.
Tel 9265 3888.

Harbourside Shopping Centre
Darling Harbour. **Map** 3 C2.
Tel 9281 3999.

Market City
9–13 Hay St, Haymarket.
Map 4 D4. *Tel* 9288 8900.

MLC Centre
19–29 Martin Place.
Map 1 B5. *Tel* 9224 8333.

Myer
436 George St. **Map** 1 B5.
Tel 9238 9111.

Queen Victoria Building
455 George St. **Map** 1 B5.
Tel 9264 9209.

Shopping Spree Tours
Tel 1300 558 353.

Strand Arcade
412–414 George St. **Map** 1 B5.
Tel 9232 4199.

Sydney Central Plaza
100 Market St. **Map** 4 E2.
Tel 8224 2000.

Westfield Bondi Junction
500 Oxford St, Bondi Junction.
Map 4 F3. *Tel* 9947 8000.

Westfield Sydney
Pitt St Mall. **Map** 4 E2.
Tel 8236 9200.

World Square
680 George St. **Map** 4 E3.
Tel 8669 6900.

Sydney's Best: Shopping Streets and Markets

Sydney's best shopping areas range from galleries, arcades and department stores selling expensive gifts and jewellery *(see pp198–9)*, to boutiques of extroverted or elegant cutting-edge fashion and its accessories. The range of styles is impressive – both international couture brands and acclaimed local designer labels *(pp204–5)*. The city's hip fringe areas are alive with street fashion and its accoutrements.

Colourful markets are a delight for collectors and bargain-hunters alike *(p203)*, while those who seek out the quirky and one-off items are well catered for, as are those looking to take home quality craft and indigenous art as mementos of their visit. Specialist browsers will find a tempting selection of book and music shops *(pp206–7)* from which to choose.

The Rocks Market
At weekends, the stalls offer affordable arts and crafts and jewellery. (See p203.)

THE ROCKS AND
CIRCULAR QUAY

CITY
CENTRE

Queen Victoria Building
This elegant shopping gallery offers four floors of designer wear, gifts, and speciality stores amid cafés.

Darling Harbour
Quality Australiana, surf and beach wear, souvenir ideas, children's clothes, colourful knits and art and craft shops abound.

DARLING
HARBOUR

Sydney Fish Market
You can buy fresh seafood daily in the colourful fishmongers' halls or order from the cafés which spill out on to the sunny terrace alongside the marina. (See p202.)

Chinatown
This is the place to find discounts on watches, gold jewellery, opals and even fabrics. There are also Chinese butchers' shops, herbalists and supermarkets.

| 0 metres | 500 |
| 0 yards | 500 |

City Centre
Dazzling shopping arcades and smart malls are dotted throughout the city centre, notably Pitt Street Mall, Strand Arcade and Westfield Sydney.

Castlereagh Street
The city's designer row is home to Chanel, Gucci, Hermès and others. The most exclusive names cluster near the King Street intersection.

BOTANIC
GARDEN AND
THE DOMAIN

KINGS CROSS AND
DARLINGHURST

Darlinghurst and Surry Hills
These suburbs are the youth culture barometer: young designers, leather à la mode, gay fashion, hot music and gifts for those who love quirky collectables.

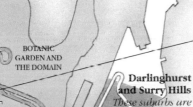

PADDINGTON

Paddington Markets
Considered by many to be Sydney's best market and a showcase for the up-and-coming fashions, it is held every Saturday. (See p203.)

Paddington and Woollahra
Upmarket clothing, shoes, homeware and gourmet food are on show here, while cafés and galleries add to the allure. Queen Street, Woollahra, is the antique shop strip.

Sydney Fish Market

Each day, 65 tonnes (tons) of fresh fish and other seafood are sold at the Fish Market's Dutch Clock auction. According to this system, prices start high, and gradually descend on a computerized "clock", until a buyer puts in a bid. At this point,

Balmain bug

no other bids are accepted, and the deal is made. This unusually quiet auction starts at 5:30am every Monday to Friday, and runs for two to three hours until all the seafood is sold. Members of the public can follow the auction proceedings from a viewing area.

The waterfront cafés *offering fine seafood at reasonable prices make dining here a rare treat.*

Blue swimmer crabs *have a mild flavour and are found all around the Australian coastline.*

About 30 wholesalers, *many of them family concerns, buy bulk quantities of the day's catch; some also have retail outlets at the market itself.*

Local fishermen *send their fish to the market anytime between 4pm the previous day and 8am on the day of the auction. Most of the catch is from the far coasts of New South Wales.*

SELECTING YOUR FISH

SHELLFISH

| Freshwater crayfish | Cuttlefish | Blue swimmer crab | Tiger prawn |

FRESHWATER FISH

| Rainbow trout | Golden perch | Murray cod | Barramundi |

SALTWATER FISH

| Coral trout | Blue-eyed trevalla | John dory | Flounder |

| Opah | Ocean perch | Leatherjacket | Red emperor |

Markets

Scouring markets for the cheap, the cheerful and the chic has become a popular weekend pastime in Sydney. Weekly or monthly markets that suit both the bargain-hunter and the serious shopper have sprung up all over the suburbs. Caps, souvenir t-shirts, leather jackets, high-class art – there is something to suit every taste. Even more popular are the Sydney Fish Market and the produce markets, which teem with people from early in the morning and have turned shopping into a big event.

BALMAIN MARKET

Cnr Darling St and Curtis Rd, Balmain. ▦ 442, 434.
Open 8:30am–4pm Sat.

Held in the grounds of St Andrews Congregational Church in the shade of a fig tree said to be more than 150 years old, this compact market attracts both locals and tourists. Fees from stallholders contribute to the ongoing restoration of the church, which was built in 1853. As well as stalls selling children's wear, second hand books, contemporary and antique jewellery, arty mirrors, recycled stationery, stained-glass mobiles and Chinese healing balls, there is a food hall where you can find fresh and aromatic Japanese, Thai, Indian and specialist vegetarian dishes in the making.

BONDI BEACH MARKET

Bondi Beach Public School, Campbell Parade, North Bondi. ▦ 333, 380.
Open 10am–5pm Sun in summer; 4pm in winter.

Many Sydney fashion labels start off here, as did current darlings **Sass & Bide** (see p204). There are also lots of second-hand clothing buys; funky 1970s gear is particularly popular. Arrive early as some of the stalls are all set up by 9am. The best bargain clothes are near the back of the market. Expect to see the odd actor or rock star among the browsers.

THE ENTERTAINMENT QUARTER

Lang Rd, Moore Park. **Map** 5 C5.
▦ Oxford St or Anzac Pde routes.
Open 10am–3:30pm Wed, Sat, 10am–4pm Sun. (See p126.)

There is plenty of fresh produce and gourmet delicacies to sample at the Farmers Produce Market every Wednesday and Saturday, located next to the working Fox Studios, where films such as *Mission Impossible 2* and the *Star Wars* prequels were shot. There is a Merchandise Market on Sunday.

GLEBE MARKET

Glebe Public School, Glebe Point Road, Glebe. **Map** 3 B5. ▦ 431, 433.
Open 10am–4pm Sat.

A treasure trove for the junk shop enthusiast and canny scavenger, this market is bright, changeable and popular with the inner-city grunge set. Best buys are bric-à-brac and crafts made from recycled wood, metal and glass. Get there early for bargain porcelain and, if you are lucky, the odd undervalued lithograph. A few fashion students also sell their creations. You will also find handmade bags, hats and jewellery. Second-hand clothes are a good buy here, as are leather wallets, silver rings and pendants, books, CDs and records.

THE GOOD LIVING GROWERS' MARKET

Pyrmont Bay Park, opposite Star City Casino. **Map** 3 C1. ▦ light rail from Central. **Open** 7–11am first Saturday of every month.

Get in early; by 8am long lines snake back from each of the stalls selling coffee, bread and pastries. This is the place to find native Australian bushfoods, such as lemon myrtle linguini, dried bush tomatoes, nutty wattleseed and pepperberries. There is everything you will need to cook a gourmet feast, including poultry, beef, pork and venison from around NSW; lesser-found vegetables such as wild mushrooms, cavolo nero and golden beetroot; and delicacies such as honey, cheese and fudge. Fresh flowers are available too.

PADDINGTON MARKETS

(See p126.)

From nouveau to novelties, there is always something tempting here, and it is unlikely you will come away empty-handed. Silver jewellery is abundant, so prices are very competitive; there are also children's clothes, leather goods, unusual buckles, belts and accessories, stationery, candles, and oddities such as babies' baseball caps and rubbery novelty masks.

PADDY'S MARKETS

(See p99.)

In the 19th century, Paddy's in the Haymarket was the city's fringe market and also the location of fairgrounds and circuses. Today, it has between 500 and 1,000 stalls under one roof. Early birds will get the best flowers, fruit, vegetables and seafood. There are also good buys in caneware, luggage, leather goods, tools, homewares, ornaments, souvenirs and toys.

THE ROCKS MARKET

George St, The Rocks. **Map** 1 B2.
▦ 431, 432, 433, 434.
Open 10am–5pm Sat & Sun.

At weekends, rain or shine, a sail-like canopy is erected at the top end of George Street, transforming the area into an atmospheric marketplace. Get there early to beat the afternoon crowds. There are about 140 stalls, whose wares are unique rather than inexpensive. Quality is a priority here. Look out for wind chimes, pewter picture frames, pub poster prints, oils, leather goods, wooden toys, gold-plated bush leaves, and jewellery made from wood, shell, silver or crystal. Every Friday in November the Rocks Market hosts "Markets by Moonlight", a combination of night markets, live music and outdoor bars and food stalls.

SYDNEY FISH MARKET

(See p131.)

Sydney is famous for its fresh seafood and the Sydney Fish Market is the ideal place to buy it. The displays of seafood are arresting, with coral reds, marble pinks, greys, blacks and iridescent yellows to take your mind off the sloshy floors and the smell of the sea. The market also has a sushi bar, fish cafés, a bakery, a gourmet deli, a poultry and game specialist, a bottle shop, and a vegetable shop. The Sydney Seafood School operates above the market, offering lessons in preparing and serving seafood.

SYDNEY OPERA HOUSE MARKET

Western Boardwalk, Sydney Opera House. **Map** 1 C2. ▦ 438.
Open 9am–5pm Sun & public hols.

Under calico market umbrellas, you will find arts and crafts in a spectacular setting. Some call this a distillation of the market, and certainly you will not find T-shirts and cheap souvenirs, but rather goods that have been either handmade or hand-finished.

Clothes and Accessories

Australian style was once an oxymoron. Sydney now offers a plethora of chic shops as long as you know where to look. Top boutiques sell both men's and women's clothing, as well as accessories. The city's "smart casual" ethos, particularly in summer, means there are plenty of luxe but informal clothes available.

AUSTRALIAN FASHION

A number of Sydney's fashion designers have attained a global profile, including **Collette Dinnigan** and **Akira Isogawa**. Dinnigan's is filled with lacy evening gowns whereas Japanese-born Isogawa makes artistic clothing for women and men.

Young jeans labels such as **Ksubi** (for men and women) and **Sass & Bide** (women only) have also shot to fame, with celebrities wearing their denims. **Scanlan & Theodore** is another stalwart of the Australian fashion scene.

For retro women's and children's clothes head to **Dragstar**. **Jack London** stocks upscale, trendy menswear; their suits are particularly popular. The quirky **Capital L** boutique houses the hottest names in Aussie fashion, while **Zimmermann** offers women's and girls' clothes and is famous for its swimwear. **Lisa Ho** is the place to go for a frock, with designs ranging from pretty sundresses to glam gowns. Head to **Farage Man & Farage Women** for quality suits and shirts.

High-street clothing can be found in and around Pitt Street Mall and Bondi Junction. Here you will find both international and homegrown fashion outlets. **Sportsgirl** sells funky clothes that appeal to both teens and adult women. The **Witchery** stores are a favourite among women for their stylish designs. **Just Jeans** doesn't just sell jeans; it stocks the latest trends for men and women.

General Pants has funky street labels like One Teaspoon and Just Ask Amanda. Surry Hills is the place for discount and vintage clothing; check out **Zoo Emporium**. New designers try out their wares in Bondi, Glebe and Paddington markets.

INTERNATIONAL LABELS

Many Sydney stores sell designer imports. For the best ranges, visit **Belinda** – a men's and women's boutique – as well as others in Double Bay, and the MLC Centre. In **Robby Ingham Stores** you will find women's and men's ranges including Chloé, Paul Smith and Comme des Garçons. For shoe addicts, **Cosmopolitan Shoes** stocks labels such as Dolce & Gabbana, Sonia Rykiel, Dior and Jimmy Choo. **Hype DC** also offers all the latest ranges. New Zealand designers **Zambesi** offer their own designs for women and men as well a range of Martin Margiela pieces.

LUXURY BRANDS

Many visitors like to shop for international labels such as **Louis Vuitton**, which you will find located in Castlereagh Street, along with **Chanel**. The Queen Victoria Building is home to **Bally**, and Martin Place has resident A-listers such as **Prada** and **Giorgio Armani**. **Diesel** is further afield on Oxford Street.

SURF SHOPS

For the latest surf gear, look no further than Bondi where the streets are lined with shops selling clothing, swimwear and boards of all sizes to buy and hire. Serious surfers and novices should check out **Between the Flags** and **Bondi Surf Co**. Besides stocking its own beachwear label, **Rip Curl** also sells Australian brands such as Tigerlily and Billabong. **Labyrinth** and **The Big Swim** are hugely popular swimwear shops packed with bikinis by designers such as Jet and Seafolly.

CLOTHES FOR CHILDREN

Department stores, **David Jones** and **Myer** (see pp198–9), are one-stop shops for children's clothes, from newborn to teenage. Look out for good quality

SIZE CHART

Women's clothes

Australian	6	8	10	12	14	16	18	20
American	4	6	8	10	12	14	16	18
British	6	8	10	12	14	16	18	20
Continental	38	40	42	44	46	48	50	52

Women's shoes

Australian	6–6½	7	7½–8	8½	9–9½	10	10½–11	
American	5	6	7	8	9	10	11	
British	3	4	5	6	7	8	9	
Continental	36	37	38	39	40	41	42	

Men's suits

Australian	44	46	48	50	52	54	56	58
American	34	36	38	40	42	44	46	48
British	34	36	38	40	42	44	46	48
Continental	44	46	48	50	52	54	56	58

Men's shirts

Australian	36	38	39	41	42	43	44	45
American	14	15	15½	16	16½	17	17½	18
British	14	15	15½	16	16½	17	17½	18
Continental	36	38	39	41	42	43	44	45

Men's shoes

Australian	7	7½	8	8½	9	10	11	12
American	7	7½	8	8½	9½	10½	11	11½
British	6	7	7½	8	9	10	11	12
Continental	39	40	41	42	43	44	45	46

Australian labels such as Fred Bare and Gumboots. Mambo, Dragstar and Zimmermann (see above) also sell fun and unusual kidswear.

ACCESSORIES

The team behind **Dinosaur Designs** are some of Australia's most celebrated designers. They craft chunky bangles, necklaces and rings, and also bowls, plates and vases, from

jewel-coloured resin. **Collect**, the retail outlet of Object Gallery, is another place to look for handcrafted jewellery, scarves, textiles, objects, ceramics and glass by leading and emerging Australian designers. At trendy **Family Jewels**, unique silver creations feature Australian pearls, nautilus shell and crystals. They also showcase international designers. In her plush store, **Jan Logan** sells exquisite

jewellery, using precious and semi-precious stones.

Australian hat designer, **Helen Kaminski**, uses fabrics, raffia, straw, felt and leather to make hats and bags. In a different style, **Crumpler** uses high-tech fabrics to make bags that will last a century. And in a street of designer names, **Andrew McDonald's** little studio shop doesn't cry for attention, but he does sell handcrafted shoes for men and women.

DIRECTORY

AUSTRALIAN FASHION

Akira Isogawa
12A Queen St, Woollahra.
Map 6 E4. Tel 9361 5221.
Level 2, Strand Arcade.
Map 1 B4. Tel 9232 1078.

Capital L
333 South Dowling St,
Darlinghurst. **Map 5 A3.**
Tel 9361 0111.

Collette Dinnigan
33 William St,
Paddington. **Map 6 D3.**
Tel 9360 6691.

Dragstar
535a King St, Newtown.
Tel 9550 1243.

Farage Man & Farage Women
Shops 54 & 79, Level 1
Strand Arcade. **Map 1 B5.**
Tel 9231 3479.

General Pants
Queen Victoria Building.
Map 4 E2. Tel 9264 2840.

Jack London
World Square Shopping
Centre, 680 George St.
Map 4 E3. Tel 9261 2012.

Just Jeans
Mid City Centre, Pitt St.
Map 4 E2. Tel 9223 8349.

Ksubi
16 Glenmore Rd,
Paddington. **Map 5 B3.**
Tel 9361 6291.

Lisa Ho
43 Queen St, Woollahra.
Map 6 D4. Tel 9327 6300.

Sass & Bide
132 Oxford St,
Paddington. **Map 5 B3.**
Tel 9360 3900.

Scanlan & Theodore
122 Oxford St,
Paddington. **Map 5 B3.**
Tel 9380 9388.

Sportsgirl
Level 2, Shop 2047,
Westfield Sydney,
Pitt St Mall. **Map 1 B5.**
Tel 9223 8255.

Witchery
Sydney Central Plaza &
Pitt St. **Map 4 E2.**
Tel 9231 1245.

Zimmermann
Shop 2, 2–16 Glenmore
Rd, Paddington. **Map 5
B3. Tel** 9357 4700.

Zoo Emporium
180b Campbell St,
Surry Hills. **Map 5 A2.**
Tel 9380 5990.

INTERNATIONAL LABELS

Belinda
39 William St,
Paddington. **Map 6 D3.**
Tel 9380 8728.

Cosmopolitan Shoes
Cosmopolitan Centre,
Knox St, Double Bay.
Tel 9362 0510.

Hype DC
Cnr Market St & Pitt St
Mall. **Map 1 B5.**
Tel 9221 5688.

Robby Ingham Stores
424–428 Oxford St,
Paddington. **Map 6 D4.**
Tel 9332 2124.

Zambesi
5 Glenmore Rd.
Tel 9331 1140.

LUXURY BRANDS

Bally
Ground floor, Queen
Victoria Building.
Map 1 B5. Tel 9267 3887.

Chanel
70 Castlereagh St.
Map 1 B5. Tel 9233 4800.

Diesel
408–410 Oxford St,
Paddington. **Map 6 D4.**
Tel 9331 5255.

Giorgio Armani
4 Martin Place.
Map 1 B4.
Tel 8233 5800.

Gucci
Level 3, Westfield Sydney,
Pitt St Mall. **Map 1 B5.**
Tel 9221 8999.

Louis Vuitton
63 Castlereagh St. **Map 1
B5. Tel** 1300 883 880.

Prada
44 Martin Place. **Map 1
B4. Tel** 9231 3929.

SURF SHOPS

Between the Flags
152–158 Campbell
Parade, Bondi Beach.
Tel 9365 5611.

The Big Swim
74 Campbell Parade,
Bondi Beach.
Tel 9365 4457.

Bondi Surf Co.
72–76 Campbell Parade,
Bondi Beach.
Tel 9365 0870.

Labyrinth
30 Campbell Parade,
Bondi Beach.
Tel 9130 5091.

Rip Curl
82 Campbell Parade,
Bondi Beach.
Tel 9130 2660.

CLOTHES FOR CHILDREN

David Jones
Cnr Elizabeth & Market
sts. **Map 1 B5.**
Tel 9266 5544.

Myer
436 George St.
Map 1 B5.
Tel 9238 9111.

ACCESSORIES

Andrew McDonald
58 William St, Paddington.
Map 6 D3.
Tel 9358 6793.

Collect
417 Bourke St, Surry Hills.
Map 5 A3. Tel 9361 4511.

Crumpler
The Strand Arcade.
Map 1 B5.
Tel 9222 1300.

Dinosaur Designs
See pp206–7.

Family Jewels
393A Oxford St,
Paddington. **Map 5 D3.**
Tel 9331 3888.

Helen Kaminski
Shop 3, Four Seasons
Hotel, 199 George St.
Map 1 B3. Tel 9251 9850.

Jan Logan
36 Cross St, Double Bay.
Tel 9363 2529.

Specialist Shops and Souvenirs

Sydney offers an extensive range of gift and souvenir ideas, from unset opals and jewellery to Aboriginal art and hand-crafted souvenirs. Museum shops, such as at the Museum of Sydney *(see p85)* and the Art Gallery of NSW *(see pp108–11)*, often have specially commissioned items that make great presents or reminders of your visit.

ONE-OFFS

Specialist shops abound in Sydney – some practical, some eccentric, others simply indulgent. **Ausfurs** sells everything from luxurious sheepskin coats and jackets to pure wool handknits and mohair rugs.

Wheels & Doll Baby is a powder-room, 1950s chic, a mixture of rock 'n' roll heaven and Hollywood glamour. **The Hour Glass** stocks traditional-style watches, while designer sunglasses such as Armani and Jean Paul Gaultier can be found at **The Looking Glass**.

For a touch of celebrity glamour, **Napoleon Perdis Cosmetics** sells a huge array of make-up and bears the name of Australia's leading make-up artist to the "stars". Or, for some eclectic fashion and homewares, try a branch of **Orson & Blake**, the one in Surry Hills has a good café.

AUSTRALIANA

Australiana has become more than just a souvenir genre; it is now an art form in itself.

Done Art and Design has distinctive prints by Ken and Judy Done on a wide range of clothes, swimwear and accessories, while at **Weiss Art** you will find tasteful, minimalist designs on clothes, umbrellas, baseball caps and cups. The shop at the **Art Gallery of New South Wales** stocks a wide range of art books, posters, prints and gifts. The Queen Victoria Building's Victoria Walk *(see p82)* is dominated by shops selling Australiana: souvenirs, silver, antiques, art and crafts.

The **Australian Museum** *(see pp88–9)* has a shop that sells unusual gift items such as native flower presses, bark paintings and Australian animal puppets, puzzles and games.

BOOKS

The large **Dymocks** chain has a good range of guide books and maps on Sydney. For more eclectic browsing, try **Abbey's Bookshop, Ariel** and **Gleebooks**, while **Berkelouw Books** has three floors of new, second-hand and rare books. **The Bookshop Darlinghurst** specializes in gay and lesbian fiction and non-fiction. The **State Library of NSW** *(see p112)* bookshop has a good choice of Australian books, particularly on history. The **ABC Shop** stocks TV tie-in titles, many of them on cookery and music.

MUSIC

Several specialist music shops of international repute can be found in Sydney. **Red Eye Records** is for the streetwise, with its stock of collectables, rarities, alternative music and concert tickets. **Central Station Records and Tapes** has mainstream grooves, plus rap, hip hop, and cutting edge dance music. **Birdland** has a massive selection of blues, jazz, soul and avant-garde. **Folkways** specializes in world music, **Waterfront** in world and left-of-centre, and **Utopia Records** has an impressively comprehensive stock of hard rock and heavy metal. **Michael's Music Room**, which sells classical music only, specializes in both historical and contemporary opera recordings.

ABORIGINAL ART

Traditional paintings, fabric, jewellery, boomerangs, cards and carvings can be bought at the **Aboriginal and Pacific Art**. You can find tribal artifacts from Aboriginal Australia at several shops in the Harbourside Shopping Centre,

Darling Harbour. The **Coo-ee Aboriginal Art Gallery** boasts a large selection of limited edition prints, hand-printed fabrics, books and Aboriginal music. The **Kate Owen Gallery & Studio** in Rozelle features a wide range of contemporary Aboriginal art displayed over three floors. With works by numerous indigenous artists, it has been voted one of Sydney's best Aboriginal art galleries. Works by urban indigenous artists are found at the **Boomalli Aboriginal Artists' Cooperative**.

OPALS

Sydney offers a variety of opals in myriad settings. **Flame Opals** is a family-run store, selling stones from all the major Australian opal fields. At **Opal Fields** you can view a museum collection of opalised fossils, before buying from the wide range of gems. **Giulian's** has unset opals, including blacks from Lightning Ridge, whites from Coober Pedy and boulder opals from Quilpie.

JEWELLERY

Long-established Sydney jewellers with 24-carat reputations include **Fairfax & Roberts, Hardy Brothers** and **Percy Marks**. World-class pearls are found in the waters off the northwestern coast of Australia. Rare and beautiful examples can be found at **Paspaley Pearls**.

Bill Hicks Jewellery's award-winning owner can create unique one-off pieces according to your designs. Alternatively, browse their ready-made collection. **Dinosaur Designs** made its name with colourful, chunky resin jewellery, while at **Love & Hatred**, jewelled wrist cuffs, rings and crosses recall lush medieval treasures. **Jan Logan** is an iconic Australian jewel-lery designer, with stores in Melbourne, Hong Kong, and London. Choose from beautiful and unusual contemporary pieces, otherwise the shop also carries antiques.

DIRECTORY

ONE-OFFS

Ausfurs
10 Charles St,
Chipping Norton.
Tel 0402 115 712.

The Hour Glass
142 King St.
Map 1 B5.
Tel 9221 2288.

The Looking Glass
Queen Victoria Building.
Map 1 B5.
Tel 9264 3696.

**Napoleon Perdis
Cosmetics**
74 Oxford St,
Paddington. *Tel 9331
1702.* **Map** 5 A2. **www**.
napoleoncosmetics.com

Orson & Blake
83–85 Queen St,
Woollahra. **Map** 6 E4
Tel 9326 1155.
Also at:
483 Riley St, Surry Hills.
Map 4 F5.
Tel 8399 2525. **www**.
orsanandblake.com.au

Wheels & Doll Baby
336 Crown St,
Darlinghurst.
Map 5 A2.
Tel 9361 6255.

AUSTRALIANA

**Art Gallery of New
South Wales Shop**
Art Gallery Rd.
Map 2 D4.
Tel 9225 1700.

**Australian
Museum Shop**
6 College St. **Map** 4 F3.
Tel 9320 6150.

**Done Art
and Design**
123 George St, The Rocks.
Map 1 B2.
Tel 9251 6099.
One of several branches.

Weiss Art
85 George St, The Rocks.
Map 1 B2.
Tel 9241 3819.

BOOKS

Abbey's Bookshop
131 York St.
Map 1 A5.
Tel 9264 3111.

ABC Shop
Shop 48, Queen
Victoria Building.
Map 1 B5.
Tel 9286 3726.

Ariel
42 Oxford St, Paddington.
Map 5 B3.
Tel 9332 4581.

Berkelouw Books
19 Oxford St, Paddington.
Map 5 B3.
Tel 9360 3200.
Also at:
70 Norton St, Leichhardt.
Tel 9560 3200.
www.berkelouw.com.au

**The Bookshop
Darlinghurst**
207 Oxford St,
Darlinghurst.
Map 5 A2.
Tel 9331 1103.

Dymocks
424 George St.
Map 1 B5.
Tel 9235 0155.
One of many branches.

Gleebooks
49 Glebe Point Rd, Glebe.
Map 3 B5.
Tel 9660 2333.

**Lesley Mackay's
Bookshop**
Queens Court, Queens St,
Woollahra.
Map 6 E4.
Tel 9328 2733.

**State Library
of NSW Shop**
Macquarie St.
Map 1 C4.
Tel 9273 1611.

MUSIC

Birdland
Suite 909/45 Market St.
Map 1 A5.
Tel 9267 6811.

**Central Station
Records and Tapes**
46 Oxford St, Darlinghurst.
Map 4 F4.
Tel 9361 5222.

Fish Records
350 George St.
Map 1 B3.
Tel 9233 3371.

Folkways
282 Oxford St,
Paddington.
Map 5 C3.
Tel 9361 3980.

**Michael's
Music Room**
Shop 17, Town Hall
Square.
Map 4 E3.
Tel 9267 1351.

Red Eye Records
66 King St, Sydney.
Map 1 B5.
Tel 9299 4233.

Utopia Records
233 Broadway,
Broadway.
Map 3 C5.
Tel 9571 6662.

ABORIGINAL ART

**Aboriginal and
Pacific Art**
2 Danks St, Waterloo.
Tel 9699 2211.

**Boomalli Aboriginal
Artists' Cooperative**
191 Parramatta Rd,
Annandale.
Map 3 A5.
Tel 9560 2541.

**Coo-ee Aboriginal
Art Gallery**
31 Lamrock Ave,
Bondi Beach.
Tel 9300 9233.

**Kate Owen Gallery
& Studio**
680 Darling St, Rozelle.
Map 3 A1.
Tel 9555 5283.

OPALS

Flame Opals
119 George Street,
The Rocks.
Map 1 B2.
Tel 9247 3446.

Giulian's
2 Bridge St.
Map 1 B3.
Tel 9252 2051.

Opal Fields
190 George St, The Rocks.
Map 1 B2.
Tel 9247 6800.
One of two branches.

JEWELLERY

Bill Hicks Jewellery
Suite 1005/155 King St.
Map 4 E1.
Tel 9231 0994.

**Dinosaur
Designs**
Strand Arcade.
Map 1 B5.
Tel 9223 2953.
One of two branches.

Fairfax & Roberts
44 Martin Place.
Map 1 B4.
Tel 9232 8511.

Hardy Brothers
60 Castlereagh St.
Map 1 B5.
Tel 9232 2422.

Jan Logan
36 Cross St,
Double Bay.
Tel 9363 2529.

Love & Hatred
Strand Arcade.
Map 1 B5.
Tel 9233 3441.

Paspaley Pearls
2 Martin Place.
Map 1 A4.
Tel 9232 7633.

Percy Marks
60–70 Elizabeth St.
Map 1 B4.
Tel 9233 1355.

ENTERTAINMENT IN SYDNEY

A Wharf Theatre production poster

Sydney has the standard of entertainment and nightlife you would expect from a cosmopolitan city. Everything from opera and ballet at Sydney Opera House to open-air productions in the Botanic Garden is on offer. Venues such as the Capitol and the Theatre Royal play host to the latest musicals, while Sydney's many smaller theatres are home to interesting fringe theatre, modern dance and rock and pop concerts. Pub rock thrives in the inner city and beyond; and there are many nightspots for jazz, dance and alternative music. Movie buffs are well catered for with film festivals, art-house films and foreign titles, as well as the latest Hollywood blockbusters. One of the features of harbourside living is the free outdoor entertainment so children will find that a visit to Sydney can be especially memorable.

Sydney Theatre (see p210) on Hickson Road, Walsh Bay

INFORMATION

For details of events in the city, you should check the daily newspapers first. They carry cinema, and often arts and theatre, advertisements daily. The most comprehensive listings appear in the *Sydney Morning Herald*'s "Metro" guide every Friday. The *Daily Telegraph* has a gig guide daily, with opportunities to win free tickets to special events. The *Australian*'s main arts pages appear on Fridays and all the papers review new films in weekend editions.

Tourism NSW information kiosks have free guides and the quarterly *What's on in Darling Harbour*. Kiosks are at Town Hall, Circular Quay and Martin Place. *Where Magazine* is available at the airport and the Sydney Visitor Centre at The Rocks. Hotels offer free guides, or try **www. sydney.citysearch.com.au**.

Music fans are well served by the free weekly guides *Drum Media* and *3-D World* and *Brag,* found at video and music shops, pubs and clubs.

Many venues have leaflets about forthcoming attractions, while the major venues have information telephone lines and websites.

BUYING TICKETS

Some of the most popular operas, shows, plays and ballets in Sydney are sold out months in advance. While it is better to book ahead, many theatres do set aside tickets to be sold at the door on the night.

You can buy tickets from the box office or by telephone. Some orchestral performances do not admit children under seven, so check with the box office before buying. If you make a phone booking using a credit card, the tickets can be mailed to you. Alternatively, tickets can be collected from the box office

half an hour before the show. The major agencies will take overseas bookings.

Buying tickets from touts is not advisable if you are caught with a "sold on" ticket you will be denied access to the event. If all else fails, hotel concierges have a reputation for being able to secure hard-to-get tickets.

CHOOSING SEATS

If booking in person at either the venue or the agency, you will be able to look at a seating plan. Be aware that in the State Theatre's stalls, row A is the back row. In Sydney, there is not as much difference in price between stalls and dress circle as in other cities.

If booking by phone with one of the agencies, you will only be able to get a rough idea of where your seats are. The computer will select the "best" tickets.

The annual New Mardi Gras Festival's Dog Show (see p49)

BOOKING AGENCIES

Sydney has two main ticket agencies: **Ticketek** and **Ticketmaster**. Between them, they represent all the major entertainment and sporting events. Ticketek has more than 30 outlets throughout NSW and the ACT, open from 9am to 5pm weekdays, and Saturdays from 9am to 4pm. Opening hours vary between agencies and call centres, so check with Ticketek to confirm. Phone bookings: 9am–9pm, Monday to Saturday, and 9am–7pm Sundays. For Internet bookings, visit their website.

Ticketmaster outlets are open 9am–5pm Monday to Friday – some are open later. Phone bookings: 9am–9pm Monday to Saturday and 10am–5pm Sunday. Agencies accept traveller's cheques, bank cheques, cash, Visa, MasterCard and American Express. Some agencies do not accept Diners Club. A booking fee applies, plus a postage and handling charge if tickets are mailed out. There are generally no refunds (unless a show is cancelled) or exchanges. If one agency has sold out its allocation for a show, it is worth checking with another.

DISCOUNT TICKETS AND FREE ENTERTAINMENT

Tuesday is budget-price day at most cinemas. Some independent cinemas have special prices throughout the week. The Sydney Symphony Orchestra and Opera Australia *(see p212)* offer a special Student Rush price to full-time students under 28 but only if surplus tickeTs are available. These can be bought on the day of the performance, from the box office at the venue.

Outdoor events are especially popular in Sydney, and many are free *(see pp48–51)*. Sydney Harbour is a splendid setting for the fabulous New Year's Eve fireworks, with a

The Spanish firedancers Els Comediants at the Sydney Festival

display at 9pm for families as well as the midnight display.

The Sydney Festival in January is a huge extravaganza of performance and visual art. Various outdoor venues in the Rocks, Darling Harbour and in front of the Opera House feature events to suit every taste, including musical productions, drama, dance, exhibitions and circuses. The most popular free event are the symphony and jazz concerts held in the Domain. Also popular are Darling Harbour's Hoopla over Easter and the food and wine festival held in June at Manly Beach.

A busker at Circular Quay

DISABLED VISITORS

Many older venues were not designed with the disabled visitor in mind, but this has been redressed in most newer buildings. It is best to phone the box office beforehand to request special seating and

other requirements, or call **Ideas Inc**, who can provide a list of Sydney's most wheelchair-friendly venues. The **Sydney Opera House** has disabled parking, wheelchair access and a loop system in the Concert Hall for the hearing impaired. A brochure, *Services for the Disabled*, is also available.

(see p212)

DIRECTORY

USEFUL NUMBERS

CitySearch
www.sydney.citysearch.com.au

Ideas Inc
Tel 1800 029 904.

Sydney Opera House
Information Desk
Tel 9250 7111

Disabled Information
Tel 9250 7175.

Sydney Visitor Centre
Tel 1800 067 676 or 9240 8788.
www.sydney.com

Tourism NSW
Tel 132 077.
www.visitnsw.com.au

TICKET AGENCIES

Ticketek
Tel 132 849.
www.ticketek.com.au

Ticketmaster
Tel 136 100.
www.ticketmaster.com.au

The highly respected Australian Chamber Orchestra *(see p212)*

Theatre and Film

Sydney's theatrical venues are well known for their atmosphere and quality. There is a stimulating range of productions, from musicals, classic plays and Shakespeare by the Sea to contemporary, fringe and experimental theatre. Comedy is also finding a strong niche as a mainstream performance art. Prominent playwrights include David Williamson, Debra Oswald, Brendan Cowell, Stephen Sewell and Louis Nowra.

Australian film-making has also earned an excellent international reputation. A rich variety of both local and foreign films are screened throughout the year, as well as during eagerly anticipated annual film festivals.

The Sydney Opera House regularly has performances for children.

In the suburb of Killara, the **Marian St Theatre for Young People** stages the occasional theatrical production. With luck, you may even be able to see a performance by the incredibly athletic **Flying Fruit Fly Circus**. This troupe of boys and girls, aged from eight to 18, excels in aerial gymnastics.

THEATRE

Sydney's larger, mainstream musicals, such as those of Andrew Lloyd Webber, are staged at the **Theatre Royal**, the opulent **State Theatre** (see p82) and the **Capitol Theatre** (see p99). **The Star** entertainment and casino complex boasts two theatres, the Showroom, and the first-rate Lyric Theatre for musical productions and stage shows.

Smaller venues also offer a range of interesting plays and performances. These include the **Seymour Theatre Centre**, which has three theatres; the **Belvoir Street Theatre**, which has two; the **Ensemble Theatre**, a theatre-in-the-round by the water; and the **Footbridge Theatre**. The **Griffin Theatre** specialises in works by new Australian playwrights, while the **Parade Theatre** at the National Institute of Dramatic Arts (NIDA) showcases work by NIDA's acting, directing and production students throughout the year. It also hosts shows by other theatre groups and is part of the Festival of Sydney (see p49).

The well-respected **Sydney Theatre Company** (STC) has introduced an ensemble of actors, employed full time, who perform a minimum of two plays each season. Most STC productions are at **The Wharf** or the **Sydney Theatre** at Walsh Bay, though some are staged in the Drama Theatre of the **Sydney Opera House** (see pp74–7).

The **Bell Shakespeare Company** interprets the Bard with an innovative slant without tampering with the original text. Its productions are ideal for young or wary theatre-goers. While venues vary, there are two seasons in Sydney – one at the beginning of summer and one in autumn.

Street performances and open-air theatre are popular during the summer months when life in Sydney moves outdoors. The **Australian Shakespeare Company** puts on open-air productions in the Botanic Garden in January.

For the adventurous, the **Sydney Festival** (see p49) offers a celebration of original, often quirky, Australian theatre, dance, music and visual arts. Once considered somewhat frivolous, it has now developed the reputation of having serious artistic depth, while maintaining its unique flavour of Sydney in the summer.

CHILDREN'S THEATRE

Sydney thrives on spectacles that delight children, and their parents. You will often find jugglers, mime artists, buskers and magic shows at Circular Quay and around Darling Harbour (see p91).

FILM

The city's main commercial cinema, **Greater Union Complex**, is in George Street, just one block south of Town Hall, and screens the most recent film releases. Similar multiplexes, such as **Hoyts at Broadway**, can be found in the Entertainment Quarter on Driver Avenue, and in Bondi Junction in the Westfield Shopping Centre. The **IMAX Theatre** (see p92) in Darling Harbour has a giant, 8-storey screen and shows 2D and 3D films made specifically for the large screen. Many of these are suitable for children.

Cinephiles flock to the **Palace Norton St Cinema** at Norton Street, and to the **Dendy Cinemas** at Newtown and Opera Quays. **Cinema Paris** shows arthouse and indie films, and often screens Bollywood movies as well. The **Reading Cinema** regularly shows the latest Chinese films. Foreign films are usually screened in the original language with English subtitles.

For a movie and a meal, **Govinda's** (see p189), which is also an Indian restaurant, screens films that have just finished their run at the cinemas. The admission price includes a tasty vegetarian buffet dinner.

The latest screenings are usually at 9:30pm, although most major cinema complexes run shows up to as late as midnight. Commercial cinema houses offer half-price tickets on Tuesday, while Palace and Dendy do so on Monday.

FILM CENSORSHIP RATINGS

G For general exhibition
PG Parental guidance recommended for those under 15 years
M 15+ Recommended for mature audiences aged 15 and over
MA 15+ Restricted to people 15 years and over
R 18+ Restricted to adults 18 years and over

FILM FESTIVALS

The **Sydney Film Festival** is a highlight of the city's calendar (see p51), screening some 200 new features, shorts and documentaries from all over the globe. Tribute sessions and retrospectives are also presented. The main venue is the State Theatre but other venues hold satellite screenings.

The **Flickerfest International Short Film Festival** (see p49) is held at the Bondi Pavilion Amphitheatre at Bondi Beach in early January. It screens shorts and animation films from around the world. In February, **Tropfest** (see p49) shows local short films that can be no longer than seven minutes. Each must feature the special Tropfest signature item, which in past years has included a rock, a pickle and a match.

Run by Queer Screen, the **New Mardi Gras Film Festival** (see p49), starts mid-February and continues for 15 days. Films dealing with issues relevant to the lesbian, gay and transgender community are shown at various inner-city venues.

COMEDY

Sydney's most established comedy venue, the **Comedy Store** is known for performances by the best of the touring comedians and is owned by the same people who organise the Sydney Comedy Festival. Monday is comedy night at **The Old Manly Boatshed**, where both local and visiting comics perform. The **Roxbury Hotel** hosts comedy several nights a week. Newcomers to the stage mix with seasoned professionals.

DIRECTORY

THEATRE

Australian Shakespeare Company
Tel 1300 122 344
www.australian
shakespearecompany.
com.au

Bell Shakespeare Company
Tel 8298 9000. www.
bellshakespeare.com.au

Belvoir Street Theatre
25 Belvoir St, Surry Hills.
Tel 9699 3444.
www.belvoir.com.au

Capitol Theatre
13 Campbell St,
Haymarket. **Map** 4 E4.
Tel 9320 5000.
Box office tel 1300 136
166. www.capitoltheatre.
com.au

Ensemble Theatre
78 McDougall St, Kirribilli.
Tel 9929 8877. **Box
office tel** 9929 0644.
www.ensemble.com.au

Footbridge Theatre
University of Sydney,
Parramatta Rd, Glebe.
Map 3 A5. *Tel* 9351 2222.

Griffin Theatre
10 Nimrod St, Kings Cross.
Map 5 B1. *Tel* 9361 3817.

Parade Theatre
215 Anzac Parade,
Kensington. **Map** 5 B4.
Tel 9697 7613.

Seymour Theatre Centre
Cnr Cleveland St and
City Rd, Chippendale.
Tel 9351 7940. www.
seymourcentre.com.au

The Star
80 Pyrmont St, Pyrmont.
Map 3 B1. *Tel* 9777 9000.

Lyric Theatre Box office
Tel 9777 9000.
www.starcity.com.au

State Theatre
49 Market St. **Map** 1 B5.
Tel 9373 6852. www.
statetheatre.com.au

Sydney Festival
Tel 8248 6500. www.
sydneyfestival.org.au

Sydney Theatre
22 Hickson Rd, Walsh Bay.
Map 1 A2. *Tel* 9250 1999.

Sydney Theatre Company
Tel 9250 1777. www.
sydneytheatre.com.au

Theatre Royal
MLC Centre, King St.
Map 1 B5. *Tel* 9224 8444.

The Wharf
Pier 4, Hickson Rd,
Walsh Bay. **Map** 1 A1.
Tel 9250 1777.

CHILDREN'S THEATRE

Flying Fruit Fly Circus
Tel 6021 7044.
www.fruitflycircus.com.au

Marian St Theatre for Young People
2 Marian St, Killara.
Tel 9498 3166.

FILM

Cinema Paris
Entertainment Quarter,
Driver Ave, Moore Park.
Map 5 C5. *Tel* 9332 1633.

Dendy Cinemas
Newtown
261–263 King St,
Newtown. *Tel* 9550 5699.
Opera Quays
Shop 9/2, East Circular
Quay. *Tel* 9247 3800.

Govinda's
112 Darlinghurst Rd. **Map**
5 A2. *Tel* 9380 5155.
www.govindas.com.au

Greater Union Complex
505–525 George St.
Map 4 E3. *Tel* 9273 7431.
www.greaterunion.com.au

Hoyts at Broadway
Broadway Shopping
Centre, 3 Bay St.
Map 3 C5. *Tel* 9211 1911.
www.hoyts.com.au

IMAX Theatre
Southern Promenade,
Darling Harbour.
Map 4 D3.
Tel 9281 3300.
www.imax.com.au

Palace Norton St Cinema
99 Norton St, Leichhardt.
Tel 9550 0122. www.
palacecinemas.com.au

Reading Cinema
Level 3, Market City,
9 Hay St, Haymarket.
Map 4 E4.
Tel 9280 1202.
www.readingcinemas.
com.au

FILM FESTIVALS

Flickerfest International Short Film Festival
Tel 9365 6888.
www.flickerfest.com.au

New Mardi Gras Festival
Tel 9332 4938. www.
queerscreen.com.au

Sydney Film Festival
Tel 9318 0999. www.
sydneyfilmfestival.org

Tropfest
Tel 9368 0434.
www.tropfest.com

COMEDY

Comedy Store
Entertainment Quarter,
Driver Ave, Moore Park.
Map 5 C5. *Tel* 9357 1419.
www.comedystore.
com.au

The Old Manly Boatshed
40 The Corso, Manly.
Tel 9977 4443.

The Roxbury Hotel
182 St Johns Rd, Glebe.
Tel 9692 0822.
www.roxbury.com.au

Opera, Classical Music and Dance

Music buffs cannot possibly visit Sydney without seeing an opera or hearing the city's premier orchestra perform in the Sydney Opera House. And that is just the start. Since the 1970s, music played in Sydney has considerably broadened its base, opening the door to all manner of influences from Asia, Europe and the Pacific, not to mention local compositions. For the visitor, there is a wealth of orchestral, choral, chamber and contemporary music to choose from.

OPERA

Australia has produced a number of world-class opera singers, including Joan Sutherland, and eminent conductors such as Sir Charles Mackerras, Simone Young and Stuart Challender. The first recorded performance of an opera in Sydney was in 1834. For 120 years, most opera was performed by visiting international companies.

In 1956, the Australian Opera (now called **Opera Australia**) was formed. It presented four Mozart operas in its first year. But it was the opening of the **Sydney Opera House** (see pp74–7) in 1973 that heralded a new interest in opera. Opera Australia's summer season is held from early January to early March; the winter season from June to the end of October. Each season usually includes one accessible opera in English as well as more challenging shows. Every year at the hugely popular Opera in The Domain (see p49), members of Opera Australia perform excerpts from famous operas.

ORCHESTRAL MUSIC

Much of Sydney's orchestral music and recitals are the work of the famous **Sydney Symphony Orchestra** (SSO). Numerous concerts are given, mostly in the Opera House Concert Hall, the **City Recital Hall** and the **Sydney Town Hall** (see p87). A Tea and Symphony series is held mid-year on Friday mornings at the Sydney Opera House.

The renovated Conservatorium of Music (see p106), set in the Royal Botanic Garden, provides a wonderful atmosphere and location. It holds a number of concerts, where you can enjoy symphony and chamber orchestras, or jazz big bands.

Formed in 1973, the **Sydney Youth Orchestra**, is praised for its talent, enthusiasm and impressive young soloists. With a loyal following, it stages several performances in major concert venues throughout the year. Aficionados of Baroque and classical music should try to catch a performance by the **Australian Brandenburg**

Orchestra. Australia's first period instrument orchestra, this popular group appears regularly in Sydney's major concert halls.

CONTEMPORARY MUSIC

The first concert held by **Musica Viva** was in 1945, at the NSW Conservatorium of Music. Originally specializing in chamber music, it now also presents string quartets, jazz, piano groups, percussionists, soloists and international avant-garde artists. Concerts take place at the Opera House and the City Recital Hall.

Synergy is one of Australia's foremost percussion quartets. The group commissions works from all over the world and gives its own concert series at the Sydney Opera House and at Sydney Town Hall. It also collaborates with dance and theatre groups.

Eastside Arts, held, like Paddington Markets (see p126), in the Uniting Church, hosts Café Carnivale every Friday night, showcasing some of the best world music, including rembetika, Indian, African, percussion, gypsy, salsa and tango music.

Fourplay is a group of classically trained musicians who play electric string quartet versions of popular music at various venues.

CHAMBER MUSIC

Under director Richard Tognetti, the **Australian Chamber Orchestra** has won high acclaim for its creativity and interesting choice of venues, including museums, churches and even wineries. Its main concerts are held at the Opera House and the City Recital Hall, Angel Place.

The **Australia Ensemble** is the resident chamber music group at the University of New South Wales. It performs six times a year at the Sir John Clancy Auditorium and also appears for Musica Viva. Many choral groups and ensembles like to book **St James' Church** because of its atmosphere and acoustics.

FREE CONCERTS

Throughout the year, festivals provide free live music (see pp48–51). These are mostly held outdoors, to take advantage of Sydney's warm weather. During the Sydney Festival the city's favourite outdoor concerts take place, including Opera in the Park, Symphony in the Domain and the Australia Day Concert, all held in The Domain, as well as Latin music in the Aquadome at Darling Harbour and events in the Sydney Opera House forecourt.

The Conservatorium of Music holds a weekly series of inexpensive concerts in their Verbrugghen Hall (see p106) at 1:10pm each Wednesday during the university semester, entry is by gold coin (A$1 or A$2) donation. Staff and students present classical, modern and jazz music in ensemble, soloist and chamber performances. Each January the renowned choir of St James' (see p115 and p213) presents two orchestral masses to the congregation and entry is free.

CHORAL MUSIC

Comprised of four choirs: the 300-member Festival Chorus, the 100-member Symphony Chorus, the 32-member Chamber Singers and the 25-member Vox, the **Sydney Philharmonia Choirs** are the city's finest. They perform at the Opera House. December is the focal point of Sydney's choral scene, with regular massed choir performances of Handel's *Messiah*.

The **Australian Youth Choir** is booked for many private functions, but if lucky, you may catch one of their major annual performances.

One of Sydney's most impressive vocal groups is the **Café of the Gate of Salvation**, described as an "Aussie blend of *a capella* and *gospel*."

The choir of St James' Church is an excellent choral group. The orchestral masses performed in January, such as those by Mozart, Haydn and Schubert, usually fill the church to capacity so arrive early. Former choir members who are now professional soloists also occasionally perform.

DANCE

There is an eclectic variety of dance on offer in Sydney. The **Australian Ballet** has two seven-week Sydney seasons at the Opera House: one in March/April, the other in November/December. The company's repertoire spans traditional through to modern, although it is perhaps most noted for classical ballets such as *Swan Lake* and *Giselle*.

Sydney Dance Company is the city's leading modern dance group, often combining its vigorous productions with innovative musical scores. The company has performed in Italy, New York, London and China. Productions are mostly staged at the Sydney Opera House, but are, on occasion, held at The Wharf or the new Sydney Theatre *(see pp210–11)*. Rafaela Bonachela was appointed artistic director in 2009.

The **Performance Space**, which is now located at the CarriageWorks, is very popular for its experimental dance and movement theatre. Artists with backgrounds in everything from dance, mime and circus work to Butoh and performance art are likely to appear here.

Bangarra Dance Theatre uses traditional Aboriginal and Torres Strait Islander dance and music as its inspiration, infused with contemporary elements. It makes outback interstate and international tours, but is based in Sydney.

The startling and original **Legs on the Wall** are a physical theatre group who work all over the world, combining circus and aerial techniques with dance and narrative to form a heady mix. Their spectacular performances take place in intimate theatres or use dramatic settings such as skyscrapers from which the performers are suspended.

The smaller experimental companies rely on year-to-year funding or community-based work. These include **Reel Dance**, established in 2008 after eight years as a side project of the now defunct One Extra Dance Company.

DIRECTORY

OPERA

Opera Australia
Tel 9318 8200. **www.** opera-australia.org.au

ORCHESTRAL MUSIC

Australian Brandenburg Orchestra
Tel 9328 7581. **www.** brandenburg.com.au

Sydney Symphony Orchestra
Tel 8215 4600. **www.** sydneysymphony.com

Sydney Youth Orchestra
Tel 9251 2422. www.syo.com.au

CONTEMPORARY MUSIC

Eastside Arts
395 Oxford St, Paddington. *Tel 9331 2646.* **www.**paddingtonuca. org.au/ea

Fourplay
www.fourplay.com.au

Musica Viva
www.mva.org.au

Synergy
www.synergypercussion. com

CHAMBER MUSIC

Australian Chamber Orchestra
www.aco.com.au

Australia Ensemble
Tel 9385 4872. www.ae.unsw.edu.au

CHORAL MUSIC

Australian Youth Choir
www.niypaa.com.au

Café of the Gate of Salvation
www.cafeofthegateof salvation.com.au

Sydney Philharmonia Choirs
Tel 9251 2024. www.sydneyphilharmonia. com.au

DANCE COMPANIES

Australian Ballet
Tel 9252 5500. www.australianballet. com.au

Bangarra Dance Theatre
Tel 9251 5333. www.bangarra.com.au

Legs on the Wall
Tel 9560 9479. www.legsonthewall. com.au

Reel Dance
www.reeldance.org.au

Sydney Dance Company
www. sydneydancecompany.com

CONCERT AND DANCE VENUES

City Recital Hall
Angel Place. **Map** 1 B4. *Tel 8256 2222.* www.cityrecitalhall.com

Performance Space
245 Wilson St, Everleigh. *Tel 8571 9111.* **www.** performancespace.com.au

St James' Church
173 King St. **Map** 1 B5. *Tel 9232 3022.* www.sjks.org.au

Sydney Opera House
Bennelong Point. **Map** 1 C2. *Tel 9250 7111.* www.sydneyoperahouse. com

Sydney Town Hall
483 George Street. **Map** 4 E2. *Tel 9265 9333.*

Music Venues and Nightclubs

Sydney attracts some of the biggest names in modern music all year round. Venues range from the cavernous Sydney Entertainment Centre to small and noisy back rooms in pubs. Visiting international DJs frequently play sets at Sydney clubs. Some venues cater for a variety of music tastes – rock and pop one night, jazz, blues or folk the next. There are several free weekly gig guides available, including *Drum Media*, *3-D World* and *Brag (see p208)*, which tell you what is on.

GETTING IN

Tickets for major shows are available through booking agencies such as Ticketek and Ticketmaster *(see p208)*. Prices vary considerably, depending on the shows that are going to take place. You may pay from $30 to $70 for a gig at the Metro, but over $150 for seats for a Rolling Stones concert. Moshtix also sells tickets for smaller venues across Sydney and their website gives a good idea of the various venues and what is on. Buying online also prevents you from having to queue early for tickets from the door.

You can also pay at the door on the night at most places, unless the show is sold out. Nightclubs often have a cover charge, but some venues will admit you free before a certain time in the evening or on weeknights.

Most venues serve alcohol, so shows are restricted to those at least 18 years of age. This is the usual case unless a gig is specified "all ages". It is advisable that people under 30 years old carry photo identification, such as a passport or driver's licence, because entry to some venues is very strict. You are also not allowed to carry any kind of bottle into most nightclubs or other venues. Similarly, any cameras and recording devices are usually banned.

Dress codes vary, but generally, shorts (on men) and flip flops are not welcome. Wear thin layers which you can remove when you get hot instead of a coat, and avoid carrying a big bag, because many venues do not have a cloakroom. For more information on rules and conventions, which are followed in Sydney bars and pubs see pages 196–7.

ROCK, POP AND HIP HOP

Pop's big names and famous rock groups perform at the **Sydney Entertainment Centre**, **Hordern Pavilion**, and sports grounds such as the Aussie Stadium at **Sydney Olympic Park** *(see p138)* in Homebush Bay. More intimate locations include the **State Theatre** *(see pp210–11)*, **Enmore Theatre** and Sydney's best venue, **The Metro Theatre**. Hip hop acts usually play in rock venues rather than in nightclubs. You are almost as likely to find a crew rapping or a band strumming and drumming at the Metro Theatre, the **Gaelic Club**, the **Macquarie Hotel** or **Notes in Newtown**. It is not unusual to catch a punk, garage or electro-folk band at **Spectrum** or the **Annandale Hotel** on Parramatta Road.

Pub rock is a constantly changing scene in Sydney. Weekly listings appear on Fridays in the "Metro" section of the *Sydney Morning Herald* and in the entertainment press *(see p208)*. Music stores are also full of flyers and gigs by international acts and popular Australian bands, on every week at the Metro Theatre and Gaelic Club, usually sell out.

JAZZ, FOLK AND BLUES

For many years, the first port of call for any jazz, funk, groove or folk enthusiast has been **The Basement**. Visiting luminaries play some nights, talented but struggling local musicians others, and the line-ups now also include increasingly popular world music and hip hop bands.

Slide, in a converted Art Deco bank building on Oxford Street, is a combination of a Parisian-style nightclub and a New York-style lounge bar. It plays host to both local and international performers. Experimental jazz is offered on Fridays and Saturdays at the **Seymour Theatre Centre** *(see pp210–11)*. **The Vanguard** also offers dinner and show deals, as well as show-only tickets, and has been drawing an excellent roster of jazz, blues and roots talent. Annandale's **Empire Hotel** is Sydney's official home of the blues, and the **Cat & Fiddle Hotel** in Balmain of acoustic music and folk.

HOUSE, BREAKBEATS AND TECHNO

Sydney's only super club, **Home Sydney** in Cockle Bay features three levels and a gargantuan sound system. Friday night is the time to go, as the DJs present house, trance, drum and bass, and breakbeats. A mainstream crowd flocks to the nearby **Bungalow 8** on King Street Wharf with its fresh seafood dishes and great views of the Harbour. Once the sun has set, house DJs turn the place into a club. At the swank **Tank** on Bridge Lane, the emphasis is on pure house music and the decor is a throwback to Studio 54 in New York. **36° Bar**, at The Star casino complex, is another mainstream house club.

For something a little more hip, try the underground **Candy's Apartment** with its bunker-style bar on Bayswater Road, or the buzzy **World Bar** on the same street. Based in a converted Victorian terrace, World Bar is known for serving its cocktails in teapots designed for sharing. Down the road, **Q Bar** on Oxford Street, Darlinghurst, has arcade games for when you need a breather. Or try the low-ceilinged **Chinese Laundry** on Sussex Street tucked under the gentrified pub, Slip Inn *(see p186)*.

GAY AND LESBIAN PUBS AND CLUBS

Sunday night is the big night for many of Sydney's gay community, although there is plenty of action throughout the week. A number of venues have a gay or lesbian night on one night of the week and attract a mainstream crowd on the other nights. Wednesday is lesbian night at the stylish **Bank Hotel** in Newtown and some Sundays are queer nights at Darling Harbour's Home Sydney.

ARQ on Flinders Street is the largest of the gay clubs, with pounding commercial house music. The main dance floor is overlooked by a mezzanine for watching the writhing mass of bodies below. This is a world-class venue with great facilities, from the cutting-edge sound systems to the state-of-the-art lighting shows. **Midnight Shift** on Oxford Street is for men only, and **Stonewall** plays camp anthems and is patronized mostly by men and their straight female friends.

The **Colombian** is the best and one of the most popular of the Oxford Street bars, with a mock-Central American jungle decor self-styled as "South American chic" and with large windows that open out to the street. The **Oxford Hotel** and its upper-level cocktail bars are popular too. Some of Sydney's most entertaining drag shows can be found in the Cabaret Bar of the **Imperial Hotel** where shows are staged most nights of the week.

DIRECTORY

ROCK, POP AND HIP HOP

Annandale Hotel
17–19 Parramatta Rd,
Annandale.
Tel 9550 1078. **www.**
annandalehotel.com

Enmore Theatre
130 Enmore Rd,
Newtown.
Tel 9550 3666. **www.**
enmoretheatre.com.au

The Gaelic Club
64 Devonshire St, Surry
Hills. *Tel* 9211 1687.
www.thegaelic.com

Hordern Pavilion
Driver Ave, Moore Park.
Map 5 C5.
Tel 9921 5333.
www.playbillvenues.com

Macquarie Hotel
42 Wentworth Ave,
Surry Hills. **Map** 1 D4.
Tel 8262 8888.

The Metro Theatre
624 George St. **Map** 4 E3.
Tel 9550 3666. **www.**
metrotheatre.com.au

Moshtix
Tel 1300 438 849.
www.moshtix.com.au

Notes in Newtown
75 Enmore Rd, Newtown.
Tel 9557 5111.
www.noteslive.com.au

Spectrum
34 Oxford St,
Darlinghurst. **Map** 4 F4.
www.exchangehotel.biz

State Theatre
49 Market St. **Map** 1 B5.
Tel 9373 6852
www.statetheatre.com.au

Sydney Entertainment Centre
Harbour St, Haymarket.
Map 4 D4.
Tel 9320 4200.

Sydney Olympic Park
Homebush Bay.
Tel 9714 7888.
www.sydneyolympicpark.
nsw.gov.au

JAZZ, FOLK AND BLUES

The Basement
29 Reiby Place.
Map 1 B3.
Tel 9251 2797. **www.**
thebasement.com.au

Cat & Fiddle Hotel
456 Darling St, Balmain.
Tel 9810 7931.
www.thecatandfiddle.net

Empire Hotel
Cnr Johnston St &
Parramatta Rd, Annandale.
Tel 9557 1701.
www.empirelive.com.au

Seymour Theatre Centre
Cnr Cleveland St and City
Rd, Chippendale.
Tel 9351 7940.

Slide
41 Oxford St, Darlinghurst.
Map 4 F4.
Tel 8915 1899.
www.slide.com.au

The Vanguard
42 King St, Newtown.
Tel 9557 7992. **www.**
thevanguard.com.au

HOUSE, BREAKBEATS AND TECHNO

36° Bar
The Star, Pirrama Rd,
Pyrmont. **Map** 3 C1
Tel 9566 4755.

Bungalow 8
The Promenade,
King St Wharf.
Tel 9299 4660.

Candy's Apartment
22 Bayswater Rd,
Kings Cross. **Map** 5 B1.
Tel 9380 5600.

Chinese Laundry
Slip Inn, 111 Sussex St.
Map 1 A3. *Tel* 8295 9950.

Home Sydney
Wheat Rd, Cockle Bay,
Darling Harbour.
Map 4 D2.
Tel 9266 0600.
www.homesydney.com

Q Bar
Level 2, 44 Oxford St,
Darlinghurst.
Map 4 F4.
Tel 9360 1375.

Tank
3 Bridge Lane.
Tel 9240 3000.

The World Bar
24 Bayswater Rd,
King's Cross. **Map** 5 C1.
Tel 9357 7700.

GAY AND LESBIAN CLUBS AND PUBS

ARQ
16 Flinders St,
Taylor Square.
Map 5 A2.
Tel 9380 8700.
www.arqsydney.com.au

Bank Hotel
324 King St, Newtown.
Tel 8568 1900.
www.bankhotel.com.au

Colombian
Cnr Oxford & Crown sts,
Surry Hills.
Map 5 A2.
Tel 9360 2151.
www.colombian.com.au

Imperial Hotel
35 Erskineville Rd,
Erskineville.
Tel 9519 9899.

Midnight Shift
85 Oxford St, Darlinghurst.
Map 5 A2
Tel 9360 4319. **www.**
themidnightshift.com

Oxford Hotel
134 Oxford St,
Darlinghurst.
Map 5 A2.
Tel 9331 3467. **www.**
theoxfordhotel.com.au

Stonewall
175 Oxford St,
Darlinghurst.
Map 5 A2.
Tel 9360 1963. **www.**
stonewallhotel.com

SURVIVAL
GUIDE

PRACTICAL INFORMATION

Sydney has become a popular destination for international tourists. Located on one of the world's most beautiful harbours, the city offers exciting nightlife, excellent sporting activities, interesting culture and the opportunity to just relax and enjoy the spectacular views. As expected of a major city, Sydney has first-rate facilities, good service and a comprehensive range of hotels and restaurants to suit most budgets and requirements. Public transport is reliable and inexpensive, especially if

Koala

you take advantage of the composite travel cards that offer combined bus, ferry, train and light rail (tram) travel *(see p230)*. Cash dispensers (ATMs) are plentiful, with bureaux de change found in the more tourist-frequented areas *(see pp224–5)*, and credit cards are accepted in most hotels, restaurants and shops. Visitors will find Sydney a safe, clean and welcoming city. They should encounter few practical problems as long as they follow a few common-sense guidelines about personal security *(see pp222–3)*.

WHEN TO GO

The best times to travel are during autumn (March–May) and spring (September–November), when the weather is warm to mild. The summer months tend to be hot and steamy, particularly February. However, if you can stand the humidity then some of the best deals often occur during this period when children are back at school. Winter (June–August) is rarely very cold, and temperatures can be as high as 20° C (68° F).

VISAS AND PASSPORTS

All visitors to Australia must hold a valid passport and, with the exception of New Zealand, must either have an Electronic Travel Authority (ETA) or a tourist visa (depending on your country of origin). Citizens of the UK, the USA, France, Spain, Ireland, Germany, Denmark and several other countries qualify for an ETA, which allows entry to Australia for up to three months. The ETA can be applied for online or through a travel agent, airline or an Australian Visa Office, and has a service fee of A$20. Visitors who are not eligible for an ETA, want to stay longer or enter on a working holiday, should check the requirements through the **Department of Immigration and Citizenship**. All visitors must also have an onward ticket and proof they have sufficient funds for their visit.

CUSTOMS INFORMATION

The customs allowance per person over 18 entering Australia is up to the value of A$900 plus 2.25 litres (3.75 pints) of alcohol and a carton of 250 cigarettes or 250 grams (0.5 pounds) of cigars/tobacco.

Australia's quarantine regulations are strict and all people entering the country at Sydney Airport will be given a customs form to fill in on the plane. Visitors must declare all foods – it is illegal to bring in fruit, vegetables, seeds, live plants and plant products, and any endangered species or animal products. Packaged food such as biscuits and chocolates are usually allowed but must still be declared. There are severe penalties for bringing in illegal drugs. Because of these restrictions, personal luggage and hand luggage may be x-rayed before you can leave the baggage reclaim area and

often customs officers with sniffer dogs will check luggage both near the baggage carousel and along the queues of exiting passengers from the airport.

Australia levies a departure tax on all passengers aged 12 or over. This is included in the cost of your airline ticket.

TOURIST INFORMATION

To obtain information about Sydney and the rest of Australia before leaving home, travellers should look at the **Tourism Australia** website, where there are lists of specialist Australian travel agents, who can provide the latest information.

Once in Australia, Sydney's principal tourist information points are the **Sydney Visitor Centres** at The Rocks and Darling Harbour. Both centres can book tours as well as accommodation at certain listed hotels. Information

Visitor information kiosk inside Central Railway Station

booths can also be found at **Central Railway Station**, **Circular Quay** and **Town Hall**, as well as at Sydney's major attractions and main beaches. These booths have free maps, brochures and entertainment listings *(see p208).*

For visitors arriving by air, there are free Sydney visitor booklets available on stands just before the duty free shops and customs area. Once in the arrivals hall (terminal 1) you will see the **Travel Concierge** desk *(see p228).* As part of this complimentary service, staff can make accommodation, car hire, restaurant and event bookings. They also sell shuttle bus tickets to the domestic airport and international phone cards, and can provide additional travel information. Visitors have access to a bank of self-help computers where they can browse for themselves.

Art Gallery of New South Wales

ADMISSION PRICES

Most of Sydney's museums, galleries and historic houses charge an admission fee, usually from A$8–12. The Art Gallery of New South Wales *(see pp108–11)* is free, but there is a charge for special exhibitions. Family-oriented attractions, such as zoos, aquariums and wildlife parks are more expensive, often costing between A$20 and A$40. However, cheaper family passes are usually available on the company's website, and in some cases combination attraction deals are on offer.

Student and senior concessions are available at many attractions on presentation of an official international ID card.

If visiting several attractions, it is worth considering the

Public toilets with a colourful exterior

Sydney Attractions Pass, which offers free admission to more than 40 attractions for a one off fee. The card is available for periods of two, three and seven days, and can be combined with a travel pass.

OPENING HOURS

Although opening hours vary, the majority of museums and galleries are open 10am–5pm daily, except on Christmas Day and Good Friday. Smaller galleries are usually closed on Mondays. Museums, galleries and other attractions are often at their busiest on weekends.

ETIQUETTE AND SMOKING

While Sydney society is generally laid back, there are a few rules to follow. Eating and drinking is prohibited on public transport, and is also frowned upon when travelling in taxis. Dress codes are generally smart casual, but are more relaxed in summer – although people do go all out for formal occasions. Topless bathing is accepted on many beaches, but not at public swimming pools.

Smoking is banned in all public venues, restaurants, pubs and bars, but many clubs have covered outdoor areas (often attached to the indoors via corridors) where smoking is allowed.

ACCESSIBILITY TO PUBLIC CONVENIENCES

Free public toilets can be found in Sydney's galleries

and museums, department stores and all bus and railway stations. They are generally well serviced and clean. Baby changing facilities are also quite common, particularly in department stores and major museums and galleries.

Clean drinking fountains can be found throughout the city. Spring, or distilled, water is also often freely available from dispensers in waiting areas of chemist shops, travel agents and offices.

TAXES AND TIPPING

Sydney has a 10 per cent Goods and Services Tax (GST), but it is often included within the price, especially for clothing and restaurant bills. If travellers spend more than A$300 in one store and get a single tax invoice, they can claim back the GST when they leave Australia – this is known as the Tourist Refund Scheme (TRS). Refunds are available at the airport and at cruise line terminals. All goods must either be carried as hand luggage or worn (unless they are liquids, which must be packed in your checked baggage). It is advisable to allow extra time at the airport or port to make your claim. For more information, check the **Australian Customs and Border Protection** website.

Although tipping is optional, it is the custom to leave about 10 per cent for good service in cafés and restaurants *(see p179),* to tip hotel porters *(see p169)* and to leave any small change for bartenders and taxi drivers.

TRAVELLERS WITH SPECIAL NEEDS

Sydney has made much-needed advances in catering for the disabled. As old buses go out of service the State Transit Authority (the government body that manages buses and ferries) is purchasing new buses with doors at pavement level and ramps that allow people in wheelchairs access to the vehicle. There is also priority seating for those with a disability, and bus handrails and steps are marked with bright yellow paint to assist visually impaired passengers.

Many of the CityRail stations, including Circular Quay railway station, are completely accessible to wheelchair users, while several other stations have wide entrance gates and most have ramps installed.

Metro Light Rail and Monorail trams and stations are all wheelchair accessible. The **Transport Infoline** *(see p233)* has details on disabled access at each station and bus stop.

Museums, many hotels and some major sights cater to the less mobile, including those in wheelchairs, as well as people with other disabilities. You are strongly advised to phone all sights in advance to check on facilities.

For detailed information on accessible services and venues, *Access Sydney* is available from Spinal Cord Injuries Australia *(see p170)*. A map and directory for those with limited mobility can be obtained from the **Sydney City Council One-Stop Shop** behind Sydney Town Hall.

SYDNEY TIME

Sydney is in the Australian Eastern Standard Time zone (AEST). Daylight saving in New South Wales starts on the last Sunday in October and finishes on the last Sunday in March. The Northern Territory, Queensland and Western Australia do not observe daylight saving, so check time differences when you are there.

City and Country	Hours + or − AEST
Adelaide (Australia)	−½
Brisbane (Australia)	same
Canberra (Australia)	same
Darwin (Australia)	−½
Hobart (Australia)	same
Melbourne (Australia)	same
Perth (Australia)	−2
London (UK)	−9
Los Angeles (USA)	−17
Singapore	−2
Toronto (Canada)	−14

TRAVELLING WITH CHILDREN

Sydney is an easy city to explore with children. There are many beaches, several wildlife parks (two either in or very near the city centre) and plenty of fun attractions to keep families entertained. Public transport and most attractions offer cheaper tickets for children and many offer discount family tickets. There are numerous free festivals and events held in the city and tourist areas, like The Festival of Sydney *(see p49)* and Sculpture by the Sea *(see p48)*, that appeal to families. Details can be obtained from the **Sydney Visitors Centre** *(see p218)* and are often publicised in the *Sydney Morning Herald* newspaper and the free publication, *Sydney's Child*.

STUDENT TRAVELLERS

Student travellers carrying the International Student Identity Card (ISIC) are eligible for discounts in many museums, theatres and cinemas, as well as a 40 per cent reduction on internal air fares and 15 per cent off interstate coach travel. Students receive cheaper fares on Great Southern Rail trips – The Ghan and Indian Pacific trains – when booking the budget "red service".

Overseas visitors who are full-time students in Australia can purchase an ISIC card (which comes with a guide book) for $25 from Sydney branches of **STA Travel**.

GAY AND LESBIAN TRAVELLERS

Sydney is an ultra gay-friendly city with many gay bars and nightclubs. It also hosts the annual Gay Mardi Gras festival which attracts thousands of international visitors and a vast TV audience. The hub of Sydney's gay community is Oxford Street, Darlinghurst (on the city's eastern fringe, *see pp116–21*). There are several gay newspapers including the *Sydney Star*

Entrance gates with wheelchair access at Circular Quay railway station

Gay pride event, Sydney harbour

Observer and *Lesbians on the Loose*. A well known gay travel agency is **Out Travel** in Elizabeth Bay.

ELECTRICITY

Australia's electrical current is 240–250 volts AC. Electrical plugs can have either two or three pins. Most good hotels will provide 110-volt shaver sockets and hair dryers, but a flat, two or three-pin adaptor will be necessary for other appliances. These can be bought from electrical stores and also from airports.

CONVERSION TABLE

Imperial to Metric
1 inch = 2.54 centimetres
1 foot = 30 centimetres
1 mile = 1.6 kilometres
1 ounce = 28 grams
1 pound = 454 grams
1 pint = 0.6 litres
1 gallon = 4.6 litres

Metric to Imperial
1 centimetre = 0.4 inches
1 metre = 3 feet, 3 inches
1 kilometre = 0.6 miles
1 gram = 0.04 ounces
1 kilogram = 2.2 pounds
1 litre = 1.8 pints

RESPONSIBLE TOURISM

Many Sydney hotels have adopted power-saving and recycling practices. At least 10 city hotels have been bench-marked by the **EarthCheck** organization for their efficient energy plans, including the Hotel InterContinental *(see p175)*. The purpose-built Harbour View YHA (youth hostel) also has a strong eco focus *(see p172)*.

Increasing numbers of restaurants are making a point of using produce from local growers or their own farms. **Farmers' Markets** have sprung up in the city and main tourist areas, including Eveleigh (near Redfern railway station), the Sydney Morning Herald Growers' Market at Prymont Bay Park and the Bondi Beach Farmers' Market. These offer an opportunity to buy fresh, local produce, which can make a delicious, cheap picnic with less packaging.

DIRECTORY

EMBASSIES AND CONSULATES

Canada
Level 5, 111 Harrington St.
Map 1 B3. *Tel 9364 3000*. www.canada international.gc.ca

New Zealand
Level 10, 55 Hunter St.
Map 1 B4.
Tel 1300 559535.
www.nzembassy.com/ australia

Republic of Ireland
Level 26, 1 Market St.
Map 4 E2. *Tel 9264 9635.*
www.irishconsulate sydney.net

United Kingdom
Level 16, Gateway Building, 1 Macquarie Place. **Map** 1 B3.
Tel 9247 7521.
http://ukinaustralia.fco. gov.uk

USA
Level 10, MLC Centre, 19–29 Martin Place.
Map 1 B4. *Tel 9373 9200*. http://sydney. usconsulate.gov

VISAS AND PASSPORTS

Department of Immigration and Citizenship
www.immi.gov.au

TOURIST INFORMATION

Central Railway Station
Sydney Terminal.
Map 4 E5.
🕑 6am–10pm daily.

Circular Quay
Cnr of Pitt & Alfred Sts, Circular Quay.
Map 1 B3.
🕑 9am–5pm daily.

Darling Harbour Sydney Visitor Centre
Next to IMAX Theatre, Darling Harbour.
Map 3 D2.
Tel 9240 8788.
🕑 9:30am–5:30pm daily.

Sydney Airport International
Tel 9667 9111.

Sydney Visitor Centre
Cnr Argyle & Playfairs Sts, The Rocks, NSW 2000.
Map 1 B2. *Tel 9240 8788.*
🕑 9:30am–5:30pm daily.

Tourism Australia
www.australia.com
www.tourism.australia. com

Town Hall
George St, Sydney.
Map 4 E2.
🕑 9am–5pm daily.

Travel Concierge Sydney Airport
Tel 1300 402060.
www.gnconcierge.com

ADMISSION PRICES

Sydney Attractions Pass
http://seesydneypass. iventurecard.com

TAXES AND TIPPING

Australian Customs & Border Protection
www.customs.gov.au

TRAVELLERS WITH SPECIAL NEEDS

Sydney City Council One-Stop Shop
Town Hall House, Sydney Square. **Map** 4 E3.
Tel 9265 3333. www cityofsydney.nsw.gov.au

STUDENT TRAVELLERS

STA Travel
www.statravel.com.au

GAY AND LESBIAN TRAVELLERS

Out Travel
47 Elizabeth Bay Road.
Map 2 F5. *Tel 8667 3336.*
www.out-travel.com.au

Pride Centre
http://pridecentre.com.au

RESPONSIBLE TOURISM

EarthCheck
www.earthcheck.org

Farmers' Markets
www.farmersmarkets. org.au

Personal Security and Health

Street crime in Sydney is less prevalent than in many other large cities, but it does exist, particularly late at night in some popular entertainment areas. You can minimize any risks by exercising reasonable caution and following the advice given below. Members of Sydney's police patrol the city's streets and public transport system in pairs. Mobile police stations are set up at crowded tourist areas and at public events. Further afield, the surf beaches and natural bushland can present dangers of their own, and the following information offers some practical advice for coping with environmental hazards.

Police officers patrolling on motorbikes

POLICE

Sydney has a strong police force with more than 700 officers stationed in the city centre, The Rocks and Kings Cross. To report emergencies, major crimes and fires call 000 from any phone. Victims of non-life threatening crimes such as personal theft, car theft, breaking and entering, and malicious damage should call the Police Assistance Line on 131 444. There are 24-hour police stations at **The Rocks**, **Kings Cross** and **Day Street**, Sydney.

WHAT TO BE AWARE OF

Leave valuables and important documents in your hotel safe, and don't carry large sums of cash with you. Try to avoid carrying all of your credit and debit cards with you. Leave one of your cards in the hotel safe as a backup if your wallet is stolen. It is also worth photocopying vital documents in case of loss or theft.

Be on guard against purse snatchers and pickpockets in big crowds. Prime areas for theft are tourist areas, beaches, markets, sporting venues and on public transport.

Never carry your wallet in an outside pocket and wear shoulder bags and cameras with the strap across your body and the bag or camera in front. If you have a car, always try to park in well-lit, reasonably busy streets. It is also important not to leave any valuables or property visible inside the car.

Sydney has no definite off-limit areas during the day, but it is probably wise to avoid the more unsavoury side streets and lanes of areas such as Kings Cross. At night, stay clear of deserted, poorly-lit streets and toilets in parks.

When travelling by train at night, travel in the carriage near the guard's compartment; wait for the train on the part of the platform marked "Nightsafe".

Taxis are probably the safest means of travel at night, especially for shorter journeys or for women on their own. Ten secure taxi ranks in the city centre are manned by security guards on Friday and Saturday nights.

Two secure bus services run between Circular Quay and Parramatta suburb, and between The Rocks and Town Hall on weekends.

IN AN EMERGENCY

The number to call for all emergencies – police, fire and ambulance – is 000. If you witness suspicious activity, report it to the National Security Hot Line 1800 123400.

LOST AND STOLEN PROPERTY

If you lose anything on public transport or in a taxi you should report it immediately, providing the transport route you were travelling on. **State Rail** and **CityRail** trains have one number. **Sydney Ferries** has a separate number, while bus passengers should call the individual **Sydney Buses** depots. For anything left in a taxi, call the taxi company.

If your passport is stolen report it to your embassy or consulate (see p221). Lost or stolen credit or debit cards should also be reported to your card provider so that your account can be blocked.

HOSPITALS AND PHARMACIES

Sydney has excellent medical services. If you are in need of urgent medical attention, dial

Police car

Fire engine

Intensive care ambulance

Surf lifesaving sign indicating a dangerous undertow or "rip"

000 for an ambulance or go to the emergency department of the nearest main public hospital. **Sydney Hospital** and **St Vincent's Hospital** both have emergency departments. For less urgent treatment, look under "Medical Centres" in the Yellow Pages of the Sydney telephone directory or at www.yellowpages.com.au.

The **King's Cross Travellers' Clinic** and the **International Travel Vaccinations Centre** offer treatment for travel-related illnesses and vaccinations.

For non-urgent dental treatment, look under "Dentists" in the Yellow Pages. **The Gentle Dentist** can be contacted after hours for urgent cases. The **Dental Hospital** is open from 8am–4:30pm Mon–Fri.

Pharmacies are generally known as "chemists" and can be found throughout the city and suburbs. They sell a wide range of drugs and medical supplies over the counter. A handful of city, Kings Cross and Bondi Beach chemists stay open until around 10pm.

TRAVEL AND HEALTH INSURANCE

It is a good idea to buy travel insurance before arriving in Australia. Most overseas visitors are not covered by Australia's "Medicare" government health scheme, and medical, dental and ambulance costs are expensive.

British and New Zealand passport holders (and nationals from eight other European countries) are entitled to free basic emergency medical and hospital treatment.

ENVIRONMENTAL HAZARDS

When swimming at an ocean beach, check that there are lifesavers on patrol and swim within the "flagged" areas. In their red and yellow caps, volunteer surf lifesavers keep an eye out for changing surf conditions, people in difficulty and surfers close to areas set aside for swimmers only. Lifeguards from district councils are dressed in blue (see p54). Look out for signs on the beach indicating that it is dangerous to swim, and do not go in under any circumstances.

If you plan to bushwalk, do not hike alone. Always tell someone where you are going and when you will be back. Take a map, a basic first-aid kit, food and fresh water, and warm, waterproof clothing. It is very unlikely that you will encounter any poisonous snakes or spiders, but you should wear substantial footwear, keep a close eye on where you step, and check around logs and rocks before sitting on them.

PROTECTING YOUR SKIN

Australia has the world's highest rates of skin cancer, caused by the harmful effects of ultraviolet rays. The risk of skin damage is high, even on cloudy days, and particularly between 10am and 2pm (11am and 3pm in daylight saving). Always wear a good SPF 30+ sun screen and cover up with protective clothing, hat and sunglasses. The **Cancer Council** has more information.

DIRECTORY

POLICE

Day Street
192 Day St, Darling Harbour.
Map 4 D3. **Tel** 9265 6499.

Kings Cross
Cnr of Elizabeth Bay Road, Kings Cross. **Map** 2 E5. **Tel** 8536 0099.

The Rocks
132 George St, The Rocks.
Map 1 B2. **Tel** 8220 6399.

IN AN EMERGENCY

Police, Fire and Ambulance
Tel 000 from any phone. Calls are free (24-hour phone line).

LOST AND STOLEN PROPERTY

State Rail and CityRail
Tel 9379 3341

Sydney Buses
Randwick depot **Tel** 9298 6725.
Waverley depot **Tel** 9298 6625.

Sydney Ferries
Tel 8113 3002.

HOSPITALS AND PHARMACIES

Blake's Pharmacy
20 Darlinghurst Rd, Potts Point.
Map 5 C1. **Tel** 9358 6712.

Dental Hospital
2 Chalmers St, Surry Hills.
Map 4 E5. **Tel** 9293 3488.

The Gentle Dentist
Suite 5, 377 Sussex St, Sydney.
Map 4 F3. **Tel** 9191 3964.

International Travel Vaccinations Centre
Level 10, 35 Bligh Street, Sydney.
Map 1 B4. **Tel** 1300 557070.

King's Cross Travellers' Clinic
Suite 1, 13 Springfield Ave, Potts Point. **Map** 2 E5. **Tel** 9358 3376.

St Vincent's Hospital
Victoria St (cnr Burton St), Darlinghurst. **Map** 5 B2. **Tel** 8382 1111.

Sydney Hospital
Macquarie St (near Martin Place).
Map 1 C4. **Tel** 9382 7111.

PROTECTING YOUR SKIN

Cancer Council
www.cancer.org.au

Banking and Local Currency

Sydney is Australia's financial capital. In the central business district (CBD) are the imposing headquarters of several of the country's leading banks, as well as the Australian head offices of major foreign banks. Visitors will find local, state and national bank branches dotted at convenient intervals throughout the city and suburbs.

There is no limit to the amount of personal funds that visitors can bring into Australia, but they must declare amounts over A\$10,000 on their entry form. Most currencies can be exchanged on arrival at the airport. Banks generally offer the best exchange rates, but money can also be changed at bureaux de change and hotels.

High street bank logos

BANKS AND BUREAUX DE CHANGE

Bank trading hours are usually from 9:30am–4pm Monday to Thursday, and 9:30am–5pm on Fridays. Some branches are also open to midday on Saturdays. Major city banks open 8:30am–5pm on weekdays.

Most bureaux de change are open Monday to Saturday from 9am–5:30pm, and some are open on Sundays. Many advertise they don't charge commissions or fees, but their exchange rates may be lower than those offered at banks. The current exchange rates, which can vary considerably from day to day, are displayed in the windows or foyers of banks and bureaux de change.

Traveller's cheques are a safe way to carry large sums of money, but they are rarely accepted by hotels or shops; if stores take them, they will display a sign. A valid passport or another form of photographic ID is usually needed if you are cashing traveller's cheques.

ATMS

Automatic teller machines (ATMs) can be found in most bank lobbies or on an external wall near the bank's entrance. They are also found in the foyers of some clubs and pubs, and at some convenience stores in tourist areas. Ask your home bank or credit card provider which Sydney banks and cash dispensers will accept your debit and credit cards, and what the transaction charges will be. Using an ATM is not only convenient, but may also provide a better exchange rate than cash transactions.

Automatic cash dispenser

CREDIT AND DEBIT CARDS

All well-known international credit cards are widely accepted in Australia, as well as debit cards issued by major foreign banks. Use your card to book and pay for hotel rooms, airline tickets, car hire and entertainment tickets. Visa and MasterCard (Access) are the most widely accepted cards, and American Express is also taken by many retailers and travel providers. You can use credit cards to withdraw cash from ATMs at most banks.

Credit cards are a convenient way to make phone bookings and avoid the need to carry large sums of cash. They can be especially useful in emergencies or if you need to fly home at short notice.

Carry the phone number of your credit card issuer in case your card is lost or stolen.

WIRING MONEY

Money can only be transferred to a person travelling in Australia if that person has set up a bank account in Australia. Transfer fees, which may average around £10, are charged by UK banks and the Australian bank may also charge a fee. The **ANZ Bank** has a branch in London where travellers can set up an Australian account before they leave home. It can take up to five days for the money to arrive. A quicker way is via **Western Union** and other similar operators.

DIRECTORY

BANKS AND BUREAUX DE CHANGE

American Express
60 Martin Place. **Map** 1 B4.
50 Pitt St. **Map** 1 B3.
275 & 341 George St. **Map** 1 B4.
296 & 673 George St. **Map** 1 B3.
Tel 1300 132 639.

ANZ Bank
68 Pitt St. **Map** 1 B4.

The Change Group
Jetty 6, Circular Quay. **Map** 1 B3.
Shop 2, Opera Quays, East Circular Quay. **Map** 1 C2. *Tel 9247 2081.*
◻ 9am–7pm daily.

Citibank
2 Park St. **Map** 4 E2.
55–57 Pitt St. **Map** 1 B3.
695 George St. **Map** 4 E4.
Tel 1800 637 642.

Commonwealth Bank
48 Martin Place. **Map** 1 B4.

National Australia Bank
343 George St. **Map** 1 B4.

Travelex
28 Bridge St. **Map** 1 B3.
570 George St. **Map** 1 B5.

Westpac Bank
341 George St. **Map** 1 B4.

WIRING MONEY

ANZ Bank UK
40 Bank St, Canary Wharf,
London, E14 5EJ, UK.
Tel 0203 229 2121

Western Union
www.westernunion.co.uk

CURRENCY

The Australian currency is the Australian dollar ($ or A$), which breaks down into 100 cents (c).

Single cents may still be used for some prices, but as the Australian 1c and 2c coins are no longer in circulation, the total amount to be paid will be rounded up or down to the nearest five cent amount.

It can be difficult to get A$50 and A$100 notes changed, so avoid using them in smaller shops and cafés and, more particularly, when paying for taxi fares. If you do not have change, it is always wise to tell the taxi driver before you start your journey to avoid any misunderstandings. Otherwise, when you arrive at your destination, you may have to find change at the nearest shop or automatic cash dispenser.

To improve security, as well as increase their circulation life, all Australian bank notes have now been plasticized.

Bank Notes

Australian bank notes are produced in denominations of A$5, A$10, A$20, A$50 and A$100. All bank notes are made of plastic. Paper notes have been phased out and are no longer legal tender.

A$100 note

A$50 note

A$20 note

A$10 note

A$5 note

5 cents (5c)

10 cents (10c)

20 cents (20c)

50 cents (50c)

1 dollar (A$1)

2 dollars (A$2)

Coins

Coins currently in use are 5c, 10c, 20c, 50c, A$1 and A$2 (shown here at actual sizes). There are several 20c, 50c and $1 coins in circulation; all are the same shape, but have different commemorative images. The 10c and 20c coins are useful for local telephone calls (see p226).

Media and Communications

Sydney's public payphones are generally maintained in good working order and are plentiful in the city. Alternatively, hire a mobile phone or bring your own phone and buy an Australian SIM card for it on arrival. Internet cafés are easily found and offer another means of communication. Australia's postal service is efficient, and there's an express delivery option. Several different newspapers and magazines are also readily available.

Telstra public telephone booths

INTERNATIONAL AND LOCAL PHONE CALLS

Local calls (those with the 02 area code) are untimed and cost 50 cents. Credit card public phones have a minimum charge of A$1.20 making them uneconomical for local calls. It's better to find a public phone that takes phonecards.

Long-distance calls are cheaper if you dial without the help of an operator. **Telstra** sells pre-paid phonecards in denominations of A$5, A$10 and A$20. You can buy cards from newsagents, chemists and other retail outlets. A cheaper option is to buy an international calling card for the country you will be calling. These are available at newsagents and supermarkets.

MOBILE PHONES

Mobile phones are used extensively in Australia. You can rent one from **Vodafone** at their shop in the airport international arrivals hall (open 6am–10pm). It costs A$4–10 a day to rent the phone and calls are extra. You'll need a credit card and your passport. Other rental companies are

listed in the Yellow Pages telephone directory under "Mobile Telephones".

Another option is to buy an Australian SIM card to use in your mobile phone – the rates are much cheaper than roaming charges using your own service plan. SIM cards are available from **Optus**, **Telstra**, **Virgin** and Vodafone. You must have an unlocked compatible international phone, if in doubt, ask your service provider about whether your mobile phone will work in Australia. Online companies such as **Telestial** sell Australian SIM cards for about $9 each.

PUBLIC TELEPHONES

Most payphones accept coins and phonecards, although some operate solely with phonecards and credit cards.

Phonecards can be bought from selected newsagents and news kiosks displaying the Telstra sign. All public telephones have a hand receiver and 12-button keypad, though they may vary in shape and colour, as well as instructions (in English only). They are easy to use: lift the receiver,

wait for the dial tone and then insert coins, a phonecard or a credit card. Dial the number. When finished any unused coins will be refunded. Only put 50 cents in for a local call – if you insert a A$2 coin you won't receive change. If making an international call or a call to a mobile using coins, don't overload the phone with change; just insert your money when the phone prompts you to do so. If using a pre-paid phonecard, the amount to be debited will appear on the phone screen.

INTERNET

Internet cafés provide relatively cheap Internet access and can be found throughout the city; one of the most popular is **Global Gossip**, which also offers fax and scanning services. Wireless (Wi-Fi), which allows you to connect to the Internet using your own laptop, is increasingly common in Sydney and is available for free in some public places, including Gloria Jean's cafés and McDonalds. Hotels also provide Wi-Fi and broadband Internet, but often charge for it, although some boutique hotels offer Wi-Fi for free. A list of free Wi-Fi hotspots is available at www.freewifi.com.au.

POSTAL SERVICES

All domestic mail is first class and usually arrives within one to four days, depending on distance. Be sure to include the postcode in the address to avoid delays in delivery.

Computer terminals at a Global Gossip Internet café

REACHING THE RIGHT NUMBER

• To ring Sydney from the UK, dial 0061 2, then the local number.
• To ring Sydney from the USA and Canada, dial 011 61 2, then the local number.
• For long-distance direct-dial calls outside your local area code, but within Australia (STD calls), dial the appropriate area code, then the number, e.g. for Melbourne dial 03 first.
• For international direct-dial calls (IDD calls): dial 0011, followed by the country code (USA and Canada: 1; UK: 44; New Zealand: 64), then the city or area code (omit initial 0) and then the local number.
• International directory enquiries: dial 1225.
• Local directory enquiries: dial 1223.
• Call Connect: dial 12455 (call connection charges apply).
• International operator assistance: dial 1225.
• International reverse charge call 1800 801 800 to access operator in home country.
• Numbers beginning with 1800 are toll-free numbers.
• Ten-digit numbers beginning with 04 are mobile phones.
• See also Emergency Numbers, *p223*.

Express Post, for which you need to buy one of the special yellow and white envelopes sold in post offices, guarantees next-day delivery in designated areas of Australia. International airmail takes from 5 to 10 days to reach most countries.
There are two types of international express mail. Express Courier International is the fastest service and will reach nearly all overseas destinations within two to four days, with its delivery tracked from door-to-door. Alternatively, items sent via Express Post International will reach most destinations throughout the world in three to seven days.

Standard and express postboxes

If you want to ensure the addressee receives the letter or parcel, use Registered Post International where the recipient signs for the item on delivery.
Sydney has red and yellow postboxes. The red boxes are for the normal postal service; the yellow boxes are for Express Post within Australia.
Post offices are open 9am–5pm week days. Almost all post offices offer a wide range of services, including fax, money orders, money transfer and telegrams, as well as stamps, envelopes, packaging, stationery and postcards. Stamps can also be bought from hotels and shops where postcards are sold, and from some newsagents.
Address **Poste Restante** letters to c/- Poste Restante, GPO Sydney, NSW 2000, but collect them from 310 George St, Hunter Connection Building, opposite Wynyard Station. You will need to show your passport or other proof of identity.

NEWSPAPERS AND MAGAZINES

Sydney's chief daily morning newspaper is the *Sydney Morning Herald*. It includes a comprehensive listing of local entertainment on Fridays and Saturdays. The other Sydney daily is the *Daily Telegraph*.
The *Australian* is the country's only daily national paper with the most comprehensive coverage of overseas news; the *Australian Financial Review* largely reports on business and international monetary matters. *Time* magazine is Australia's leading international news magazine and covers Australia, New

Zealand and the South Pacific. Major foreign newspapers and magazines are available at many newsstands.

TELEVISION AND RADIO

Sydney has two state-run television networks, ABC (Channel 2) and SBS. There are also commercial networks: Channels 7, 9 and 10. ABC provides news and current affairs coverage, children's programmes and local and international dramas. The Special Broadcasting Service (SBS) caters to Australia's many cultures with foreign-language programmes. Commercial channels offer a variety of entertainment from sport and news to soap operas.
Sydney has several AM and FM radio stations and 20 digital stations. ABC stations cater for various musical tastes, as well as providing news and magazine-style programmes.

TRAVEL INFORMATION

Travelling to Sydney can involve a long and tiring flight. Visitors from Europe can take advantage of stopovers in Asia; those from the United States could break their journey in Hawaii or one of the other Pacific Islands. A

Blue and yellow Indian Pacific train

break can mean the difference between arriving in Sydney jet-lagged or stepping off the plane refreshed and ready to take in the sights. Sydney is linked to Australia's other state capitals

by efficient air, rail and coach connections. Long-distance coach travel is comfortable and relatively inexpensive; interstate trains are more expensive, but they are generally a great deal faster. People travelling by coach should consider taking one of the scenic routes with stopovers offered by some coach companies. Car travellers can also plan their journey to Sydney to pass through scenic areas.

ARRIVING BY AIR

The main gateway to the city is **Sydney Airport**, which has three terminals. T1 is the international terminal, and is 3 km (2 miles) from the two domestic terminals – T2 and the Qantas-only T3. The international and domestic terminals are connected by a shuttle bus (fare A$5.50) and train line (fare A$5). Taxis are also available.

T1 can get busy at peak times (usually early morning), which can sometimes result in delays in immigration and baggage collection. There is a large duty-free shop for arriving passengers and a stand with free Sydney guidebooks. The arrivals lounge has a concierge desk whose staff can book hotels, tours and other tourist services (*see p219*). T1 also has a range of shops, a bureau de change, Internet facilities, ATMs and several car hire desks.

Qantas Airways, **Virgin Australia** and **Jetstar**, which are Australia's major international and domestic carriers, link Sydney with other cities and tourist destinations in

Australia from T2 and T3. Other regional carriers, including **REX**, which connects Sydney to New South Wales, use T2 also.

TICKETS AND FARES

International flights to Sydney are expensive and are often heavily booked, especially from December to February. December is the pinnacle of peak season, and therefore the most expensive time to fly. From February to mid-April tickets are much cheaper.

APEX fares are often the best priced. Some stipulate set arrival and departure dates, or carry penalties if you cancel your flight. Round-the-world fares can offer good value and are popular, as are flight comparison websites such as skyscanner.com.

ON ARRIVAL

International airline passengers are issued with an Incoming Passenger Card to be filled in before passport control. This card is presented to immigration and customs officials, along with your passport,

Taxis lining up to take passengers at Sydney Airport

who will mark and return it. Keep the card safe, because you must hand it to another customs officer once you have collected your luggage and are exiting the customs area. Packaged food, wooden items and other goods deemed to be a risk must be declared (*see p218*).

GETTING INTO THE CITY

Sydney airport is about 9 km (5 miles) from the CBD. The **Airport Link** rail line (a private line that links with CityRail), takes 15 minutes to get into the city and costs A$15.80 from T1. Shuttle bus companies, such as **KST Sydney Airporter**, run from the airport to hotels in the city, Darling Harbour and Kings Cross. Tickets cost around A$12 one way.

Catch buses and taxis from outside the terminals or take the train from the underground station at each terminal. A State Transit bus (Metro route 400) stops at the airport. It travels to Bondi Junction and the western suburb of Burwood (but not the city). A taxi from the airport to the city costs A$25–30.

Qantas flight arriving at Sydney Airport

A passenger ship berthed at Circular Quay

ARRIVING BY SEA

Undoubtedly, the most delightful way to arrive in Sydney is by ship. Passenger ships berth at terminals at **Circular Quay** and **Barangaroo Wharf 5**. The Circular Quay site (known as the Overseas Passenger Terminal) is in The Rocks, with the information booths, tour booking centres, buses, trains, ferries, taxis and water taxis all close at hand. Barangaroo Wharf 5, just north of Darling Harbour, is a temporary facility. Despite this the terminal still has many facilities. It is a five-minute taxi ride to The Rocks and an uphill walk to the city centre.

A second permanent cruise passenger terminal is being built at Little Bay to the west of the CBD. The port will mainly serve domestic cruise lines and is due to open in early 2013.

ARRIVING BY TRAIN

All interstate and regional trains arrive at **Central Railway Station**. Australia's nationwide rail network is known by a different name in each state, but it still operates cohesively. **Countrylink** is the New South Wales regional rail network. Its reservations line answers queries and takes bookings (6:30am–10pm daily) for train services throughout Australia.

The city train operator, CityRail (see p232), also has slower but cheaper services to some country areas such as Newcastle and Wollongong, but seats cannot be booked in advance on these trains. The Transport Infoline (see p236) has information about CityRail's country services.

ARRIVING BY COACH

Most long-distance bus or coach services arrive at the **Sydney Coach Terminal** at Central Railway Station. The terminal has left-luggage facilities but will not store anything overnight. Competition between the coach companies is fierce, so shop around to get the best price.

ARRIVING BY CAR

The four major routes into Sydney are the Pacific Highway from the north; the Great Western Highway from the west; the Princes Highway, which follows the coast from Melbourne; and the Hume Highway, which runs inland from Melbourne.

As these routes approach Sydney, they feed into freeways or motorways, which in turn lead to priority routes known as "Metroads" (marked by blue and white hexagonal badges). When you reach the city outskirts, look for the Metroad signs and stay in the lanes marked "city centre".

DIRECTORY

ARRIVING BY AIR

Airport Information
Tel 9667 9111. www.
sydneyairport.com.au

Air Canada
Reservations
Tel 1300 655 767.

Air New Zealand
Reservations
Tel 132 476.

British Airways
Reservations
Tel 1300 767 177.

Emirates
Reservations and flight information
Tel 1300 303 777.

Japan Airlines
Reservations and flight information
Tel 1300 525 287.

Jetstar
Reservations
Tel 131 538.

Qantas Airways
Reservations
Tel 131 313.
Arrivals and departures
Tel 131 223.

REX – Regional Express Airlines
Tel 131 713.

Singapore Airlines
Reservations Tel 131 011.
Arrivals Tel 1300 654 475.

Thai Airways
Reservations
Tel 1300 051 960.

United Airlines
Reservations, arrivals and departures
Tel 131 777.

Virgin Australia
Tel 136 789.

GETTING INTO THE CITY

Airport Connect
Tel 1300 737212.
www.airportconnect.com.au

Airport Link (Train)
Tel 8337 8417.

KST Sydney Airporter
Tel 9666 9988.
www.kst.com.au

ARRIVING BY SEA

Barangaroo Wharf 5
Hickson Rd, Darling Harbour.
Map 4 D1.

Circular Quay
West Circular Quay, Sydney. Map 1 B2.

TRAIN INFORMATION

Central Railway Station
Tel 131 500.

Countrylink
Reservations Tel 132 232.
Arrivals Tel 132 232.

Lost property
Tel 9379 3341.

LONG-DISTANCE COACH STATION

Sydney Coach Terminal
Cnr of Eddy Ave & Pitt St.
Map 4 E5.
Tel 9281 9366.

Getting Around Sydney

Attractions pass

In general, the best way to see Sydney's many sights and attractions is on foot, coupled with use of the public transport system. Buses, trains and the Metro Light Rail system (modern trams) will take visitors to within easy walking distance of anywhere in the inner city. They also serve the suburbs and outlying areas. Passenger ferries provide a fast and scenic means of travel between the city and harbour-side suburbs. The best selection of maps, plus fascinating aerial and satellite views and historical maps, can be found at **Map World**.

Cycling is an eco-friendly way to explore the city

GREEN TRAVEL

The best way to reduce your carbon footprint in Sydney is to travel on foot, by bicycle and on public transport. You can also take the train from Sydney Airport – cutting down on vehicle traffic on this busy corridor. The city is ecologically aware and articulated "bendy" buses, which emit fewer emissions than standard buses, have been introduced on many Sydney routes. To encourage car-pooling, there are several transit lanes (T2 or T3 lanes), which can only be used in peak hours by cars carrying two, three or more passengers.

Many popular walking tracks, such as the Bondi to Bronte Coastal Walk, have filtered water stations along the way so hikers can fill up their bottles rather than discarding them. Emission-free electric bikes are also common. Several operators, including **Sydney Electric Bikes**, sell and rent these bikes, which are powered by a battery and make cycling up hills and long distances easy.

FINDING YOUR WAY AROUND SYDNEY

Sydney is a sprawling metropolis, however, the Central Business District (CBD) is quite small. The city centre lies on the south side of the harbour; the Sydney Harbour Bridge connects it with the north of Sydney. The main shopping area is an easy walk south from the harbour's edge. Darling Harbour is on the city's western edge; the closest beaches, including Bondi are about 9 km (6 miles) to the east of the city and Manly is 11 km (7 miles) northeast (and over the Bridge).

WALKING

Take care when walking around the city. Vehicles are driven on the left and often move quickly. It is wise to use pedestrian crossings; there are two types. Push-button crossings are found at traffic lights. Wait for the green man signal and do not cross at lights if the red warning sign is on or flashing. Zebra crossings are marked by yellow and black signs. Make sure vehicles are stopping before you cross.

GUIDED TOURS

Tours and excursions offer the visitor many different ways of exploring the city and its surroundings – from bus tours for food-lovers to jaunts on the back of a Harley Davidson, guided nature or history walks, cruises on replica tall ships, guided bicycle tours and aerial

adventures by hot-air balloon, seaplane or helicopter. As well as being an easy way to take in the sights, a tour can help you to get a feel for your new surroundings.

Perhaps the most flexible and economical introduction to Sydney's attractions are the unregimented hop-on-hop-off tours in an open-top double decker bus organised by **City Sightseeing**. In addition, visitors can use commuter ferries (*see pp234–5*) as a less costly alternative to commercial harbour cruises, of which there are many.

TICKETS AND TRAVEL PASSES

Sydney's public transport fares and tickets have been streamlined. The previous system has been replaced with MyZone tickets, which include colour-coded MyBus (blue) MyTrain (red), MyFerry (green) and MyMulti tickets (gold). The latter is the best choice for tourists and gives unlimited travel on buses, trains, ferries and Metro Light Rail trams (but not the Monorail, which requires a separate ticket) for either a day, a week, a month or longer, with different tickets covering three different travel zones. The Airport Link train (*see p228*) and sightseeing tours are not included in MyMulti tickets.

The Sydney Attractions Pass, which gains you entry into more than 40 of Sydney's popular sights for a one-off fee, can also be combined with a travel pass (*see p219*).

DRIVING IN SYDNEY

If you are planning to use a car to drive around greater Sydney, you will need a good street directory or an in-car Global Positioning System (GPS), which is usually offered as an option when you hire a car.

It is best to avoid the peak-hour traffic periods (about 7:30–9:30am and 4–7:30pm), if possible. Regular traffic update reports are broadcast on many radio stations.

Petrol is a little more expensive than in North

Traffic crossing Johnstons Bay on Sydney's Anzac Bridge

America, but about half the price of petrol in Europe. Most petrol stations are self-service and will accept major credit cards.

Overseas visitors can use their usual driver's licence to drive in New South Wales, but must have proof that they are only visiting. If your licence is not in English, however, you must carry a translation. Make sure you keep your licence on you at all times when driving

Australians drive on the left-hand side of the road and overtake on the right. Drivers and passengers must wear seatbelts. In the city and suburbs the speed limit is between 40–60 km/h (25–37 mph), and 100–110 km/h (60–65 mph) on motorways, freeways and highways. The maximum speed in a school zone is 40 km/h (25 mph). You must obey the signs relating to these zones as well as bus lanes and T2 and T3 lanes for cars carrying two, three or more passengers.

The 0.05 per cent maximum blood alcohol level for drivers is enforced by random breath tests. A driver found to be over the legal limit will incur

Kerbside Traffic Signs
Always pay strict attention to Sydney's parking and traffic signs as fines for infringements can be very expensive.

a heavy fine, loss of licence and even a prison sentence.

The **NRMA** has a free 24-hour roadside service for members and those who belong to similar organisations overseas such as AAA. Most car hire companies provide free roadside emergency service.

PARKING

Parking in Sydney is strictly regulated with fines for any infringements. In certain areas, particularly along clearways (indicated by signposts), vehicles are towed away if parked illegally. Contact the **Transport Management Centre** to find out where your vehicle has been taken if this happens.

Car parks in the city area charge fees from A$4 to A$25 an hour on weekdays. Look out for the blue and white "P" signs. On-street parking meters vary in price, depending on the time and area.

TAXIS

Taxis are plentiful in Sydney in the city and inner suburbs, although they can be scarce "between shifts" at 2:30–3:15pm. There are taxi ranks at many city locations and taxis are often found outside large hotels. Meters indicate the fare plus any extras, such as booking fees and waiting time. Fares and extra charges are regulated and are more expensive after 10pm.

Taxis designed to accommodate disabled passengers can be booked through any of the major companies.

CYCLING

Visitors should restrict their cycling to designated bicycle tracks, or to areas where motor traffic is likely to be light. They should also remember that wearing a helmet is compulsory. Centennial Park (*see p53*) is a popular biking spot.

Bicycle New South Wales publishes a handbook, *Bike It, Sydney*, which has a map of good cycling routes. The company also provides advice to cyclists. **Bonza Bike Tours** and **Sydney By Bike** offer entertaining guided cycling tours.

Travelling by CityRail, Metro Light Rail and Monorail

MLR logo

Sydney's railway network (operated by CityRail) connects the suburbs with the city and serves a large part of the central business district. A convenient alternative for exploring the museums and shops of Darling Harbour, as well as Chinatown, The Star casino and some inner west suburbs, is the Metro Light Rail (tram). The Monorail is purely a vehicle for tourists. It travels in a loop in one direction above the city, linking the city centre and Darling Harbour attractions.

CityRail train at a platform, Central Railway Station

TRAVELLING BY CITYRAIL

The **CityRail** network covers a vast area and is the quickest way to get into the city from most suburbs, as well as to and from the airport. The City Circle loop runs through the city centre stopping at Central, Town Hall, Wynyard, Circular Quay, St James and Museum stations.

All 16 suburban lines connect with the City Circle at Central Station. The western, northern and southern suburbs are well covered by the network, but it does not extend to the eastern or northern beaches (note: Bondi Junction is covered by the eastern suburb trains but not Bondi Beach).

Fares start at A\$3.20 per ticket. Discounts on return fares apply after 9:30am. Trains run from 4:30am to about midnight. After midnight, NightRide buses travel along rail routes, and all routes pick up from George St and Town Hall. The bus drivers are in contact with taxi firms and can organise a pick up for you.

USING THE METRO LIGHT RAIL TRAMS

The **Metro Light Rail** (MLR) is both a tourist and commuter service. The environmentally friendly trams offer a quicker and quieter way of visiting places of interest between Glebe and Darling Harbour.

The trams travel from Central Station to the western suburb of Lilyfield on a disused goods line, calling at 14 stations, including stops at the The Star casino, the Sydney Fish Markets and Jubilee Park. There are plans to extend the MLR to Dulwich Hill in the west of the city by 2014.

Buy tickets on board from the conductor or use MyMulti tickets (*see p230*), which can be bought from newsagents and convenience stores. The MLR has two zones: Zone 1 from Central to Convention, and Zone 2 from Pyrmont Bay to Lilyfield. A single ticket for Zone 1 or Zone 2 costs A\$3.40, and a single for Zones 1 and 2 costs A\$4.40.

Late night gamblers can take advantage of the Central–The Star–Central trams that run along this limited-stop route 24 hours a day. The all-stops service

---

USING THE CITYRAIL ROUTE MAP

The different CityRail lines are colour-coded and route maps are displayed at all CityRail stations and inside train carriages. Distances shown on the map are not to scale and the routes that lines are seen to take may not be geographically correct.

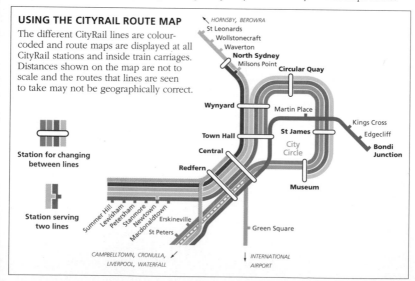

Station for changing between lines

Station serving two lines

HORNSBY, BEROWRA
St Leonards
Wollstonecraft
Waverton
North Sydney
Milsons Point
Circular Quay
Wynyard
Martin Place
Town Hall
St James
Kings Cross
Edgecliff
Central
City Circle
Bondi Junction
Redfern
Museum
Summer Hill
Lewisham
Petersham
Stanmore
Newtown
Macdonaldtown
Erskineville
St Peters
Green Square
CAMPBELLTOWN, CRONULLA, LIVERPOOL, WATERFALL
INTERNATIONAL AIRPORT

Monorail leaving the Central Business District

between Central and Lilyfield operates from 6am–11pm daily (until midnight on Fridays and Saturdays). The daily service runs every 10–15 minutes at peak times, and every 30 minutes between midnight and 6am.

SIGHTSEEING BY MONORAIL

More novel than practical, the **Monorail** runs along a 15-minute scenic loop through central Sydney, Chinatown and Darling Harbour. It offers an easy way to travel and see the sights if you feel like taking a break from walking.

There are seven stops on the Monorail route: City Centre, Darling Park, Harbourside, Convention, Paddy's Markets, World Square and Galeries Victoria. Trains run from 7am–10pm, Monday to Saturday and 8am–10pm Sunday. A Monorail Day Pass allows unlimited rides all day

DIRECTORY

USEFUL INFORMATION

Central Railway Station
Map 4 E5.
Tel 9379 1777.

Circular Quay Railway Station
Map 1 B3.
Tel 9224 3553.

CityRail Information
www.cityrail.info

Metro Light Rail and Monorail
Tel 8584 5288.
www.metrotransport.com.au

Transport Infoline
Tel 131 500
www.131500.com.au

and discounts on certain attractions. There are also multi-day passes and passes for families. Tickets can be bought at any of the monorail information booths. The Monorail is a perfect way to travel on a fun family day out, as well as being convenient for conference delegates staying at central city or Darling Harbour hotels.

MAKING A JOURNEY BY CITYRAIL

1 Study the CityRail route map. Route lines are distinguished by colour, so simply trace the line from where you are to your destination, noting where you need to change and make connections.

2 Buy tickets from ticket dispensing machines or ticket booths at stations (TravelPass tickets can only be bought at stations). To obtain your ticket from a dispensing machine, press the button to indicate destination, then the ticket type (single, return, etc). Insert money into the slot, then collect your ticket and any change.

3 To pass through the ticket barrier, insert your ticket (arrow side up) into the slot at the front of barrier machines (indicated by green arrows). Take your ticket as it comes out of the machine and the barrier gates or turnstile will open.

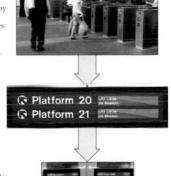

4 To find the right platform, follow the signs with the same colour code as the line you need and the name of the line's final station.

5 On the platform, display signs show all the stations the line travels through. Stations at which the next train will stop are lit up and are announced as the train arrives at the station.

Travelling by Ferry and Water Taxi

Travelling by ferry is a great way to commute between the harbour suburbs. State-run Sydney Ferries provides the majority of services, but it competes with a private operator on the Manly run. The government plans to privatize the entire fleet by the end of 2012, but retain control of fares and routes, as well as ownership of the ferries. Water taxis are a convenient but pricey alternative, and there are numerous sightseeing cruises.

Captain Cook ferry approaching the Sydney Opera House

USING SYDNEY'S FERRIES

There is a constant procession of **Sydney Ferries** traversing the harbour between 6am and midnight daily. The boats cover most of Sydney Harbour and several stops along the Parramatta River. Frequent services run to and from Manly, Darling Harbour, Balmain, Parramatta, Taronga Zoo, Neutral Bay, Pyrmont Bay, Balmain/Woolwich, Mosman, Rose Bay and Watsons Bay, with numerous stops en route. Sydney Buses (see p236) provide convenient connections at most wharves.

Staff at the **Sydney Ferries Information Office** can answer queries and provide ferry timetables. You can also call the **Sydney Ferries Infoline** for advice about connections, destinations and fares.

MAKING A JOURNEY BY FERRY

All ferry journeys start at the Circular Quay Ferry Terminal. Electronic destination boards at the entrance to each wharf indicate the wharf from which your ferry will leave, and also give departure times and all stops made en route.

Tickets can be bought from ticket booths located on the wharves at Circular Quay and from vending machines. MyMulti tickets (for unlimited travel on buses, trains, ferries and MLR trams) can be purchased at several outlets, including newsagents and convenience stores (see p230).

At Circular Quay and Manly Wharf there are automatic ticket barrier machines. To board your ferry, insert the ticket into the slot with the arrow side up and the arrow pointing into the slot. Manly's ferry terminal is serviced by regular ferries and the faster, privately run Manly Fast Ferry. Tickets and information can be obtained from the ticket windows in the centre of the terminal. No food or drink is permitted on the fast ferries. Most, but not all, wharves have wheelchair access.

TYPES OF VESSEL

Sydney Ferries operates six types of vessel: the SuperCats serving Watsons Bay, the RiverCats that travel up river to Parramatta, the HarbourCats, the First Fleet Class for short inner suburb routes, the Lady Class and the large and elegant Freshwaters that pass by the North and South Heads on their way to Manly.

PRIVATE FERRIES

The **Manly Fast Ferry** is owned by a private company; the journey to Manly takes 17 minutes rather than the 30 minutes by Sydney Ferries. The service runs regularly between Circular Quay and Manly in the morning and afternoon peak times, and every hour from 10:50am–3:50pm Monday to Friday. While the peak hour fares are more expensive than Sydney Ferries, fares decrease at non-peak times of the day. The ferry is primarily used by Manly residents who work in

A Sydney Ferries SuperCat

The Freshwater Collaroy en route to Manly

A Sydney Ferries RiverCat

the city, but it does run on the weekend and there's also a service that connects Circular Quay and Darling Harbour with Manly. Timetables change, so check the website. Ferries depart from Wharf 6; tickets can be bought from Wharf 3 at Circular Quay, on board the vessel and at booths at Manly. Passengers can buy individual tickets at around A$8.50 each, or a Smartcard that offers discounted fares.

SIGHTSEEING BY FERRY AND COMMERCIAL OPERATORS

Catching a commuter ferry is a great way to discover the harbour, and no visit to Sydney is complete without seeing the skyline from the water. Close-up views of the Opera House and Fort Denison can be had from any of the North Shore commuter routes, while the Balmain/Woolwich ferry and the RiverCat ferry make a stop at Cockatoo Island (see p106). As well as providing a fascinating glimpse of Sydney's convict history, this island offers perhaps the best vantage point for views of Harbour Bridge and the city skyline.

Other harbour islands can also be visited: the **National Parks and Wildlife Service** runs tours of Fort Denison and Goat Island, while **Captain Cook Cruises** and **Matilda Cruises** operate the hop-on-hop-off Harbour Explorer, which is a 24-hour cruise pass that allows visits

to seven harbour sights including Fort Denison and Shark Island.

Numerous commercial sightseeing cruises cover all budgets, themes and time constraints; most last around 90 minutes. **Australian Travel Specialists** has information on all harbour cruises from Circular Quay and Darling Harbour and they do not charge a booking fee. Many of these leave from Wharf 6 (Circular Quay) so it is worth checking out the day's departures there.

WATER TAXIS

Small, fast taxi boats carry passengers to any number of destinations on the harbour, including harbour islands. You can flag them down like normal cabs if you spot one cruising for a fare. Try Circular Quay near the Overseas Passenger Terminal or King Street Wharf. You can also telephone for a water taxi or book them over the Internet. They will pick up and drop off at any navigable pier. Rates vary, but expect to pay a charge of around A$70 for a journey from Darling Harbour to the Opera House for up to six people.

A water taxi on Sydney Harbour

STATE TRANSIT FERRY ROUTES AROUND SYDNEY HARBOUR

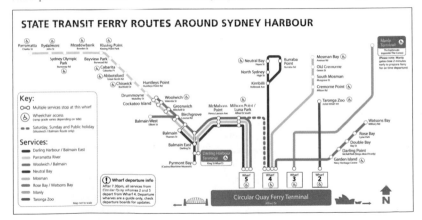

Travelling by Bus

Sydney Buses provides a punctual service that links up conveniently with the city's rail and ferry systems. As well as covering city and suburban areas, there are regular routes that serve the airport *(see p228)* and privately owned hop-on hop-off sightseeing buses. The Transport Infoline *(see p231)* can advise you on routes, fares and journey times for all Sydney buses. Armed with the pull-out map from the inside back cover of this book and a MyMulti ticket; you can avoid the difficulties and expense of city parking.

Automatic stamping machine for validating bus tickets

USING SYDNEY BUSES

The public transport system, including **Sydney Buses**, has been overhauled, and the fleet upgraded. Buses are blue and white, and environmentally friendly "bendy" buses operate on several lines. The route name and number are shown on the front and side of the bus, and the number is also displayed on the rear. An "X" in front of the number means that it is an express bus.

About 25 routes are "pre pay" only, so you must buy a ticket before boarding. All Central Business District (CBD) bus stops are also pre-pay only from 7am–7pm on weekdays to ease congestion. During weekends and out-side these hours, you can pay with cash – try to have the right change for the fare if possible. Among the permanent pre-pay routes is the popular 333 bus to Bondi Beach and on to Watsons Bay. When using a pre-pay MyBus or MyMulti ticket, insert it in the automatic stamping machine as you board. Ensure the arrow is facing you and pointing downwards. Free 555 CBD

Shuttle buses travel in a loop around the CBD from Circular Quay to Central Station along Elizabeth and George streets every 10 minutes.

Front seats on buses must be given up to elderly or disabled people. Eating, drinking, smoking or playing music is prohibited on buses. To signal that you wish to alight, press one of the stop buttons, which are mounted on the vertical handrails, well before the bus reaches your stop.

BUS STOPS

Bus stops are indicated by yellow and black signs dis-playing a profile of a bus and a boarding passenger. Some-times the numbers of the buses travelling along the route are listed below this symbol.

Timetables are usually found on the bus stop sign or are displayed in the nearby shelter. The Sunday timetable also applies to public holidays. While efforts are made to keep bus stop timetables as up-to-date as possible, it is always best to carry a current bus timetable with you. They can be collected from some tourist information facilities and are

also available at Sydney Buses Transit Shop kiosks found at Cicular Quay, Wynward, the Queen Victoria Building and Railways Square in the city, as well as at Bondi Junction and the Manly ferry wharf. Maps and timetables can also be downloaded from the Sydney Buses website.

SIGHTSEEING BY BUS

The brightly coloured City Sightseeing *(see pp230–31)* buses operate a daily hop-on hop-off service that visits 24 Sydney sights in a loop from Circular Quay. The whole journey takes 90 minutes if you don't get off. Stops include Kings Cross, the Botanic Garden, the Australian Museum and Darling Harbour.

The same company runs the Bays & Bondi Explorer that departs from Central Station and calls at 10 stops including Bondi Beach, Double Bay, Rose Bay and Paddington.

The first buses leave at 8:30am and the last finish at 7:30pm, with buses departing every 20 minutes. A combined ticket for both the city and Bondi tours is A$35 for 24 hours, or A$56 for 48 hours.

The great advantage of these services is that you can explore at will, getting on and off the buses as often as you wish. The best way to make the most of your journey is to choose the sights you most want to see and plan a basic itinerary.

Tickets can be bought on the buses at any stop, or from Sydney Visitor Centres *(see p221)*, hotels, travel agencies and ATS at Circular Quay *(see p235)*. They can also be bought online in advance.

A City Sightseeing bus in front of Sydney Harbour Bridge

Travelling beyond Sydney

Sydney is close to several areas of scenic beauty and an excellent wine region. The best way to explore the nearby regions of the Blue Mountains, Hunter Valley and the Southern Highways, or national parks on the edge of Sydney is by car and train. The far north coast New South Wales beach towns and outback and regional centres of western New South Wales are between 1 and 1.5 hours away by plane.

Blue Mountains National Park

DOMESTIC FLIGHTS

Qantas and its subsidiary Qantas Link, Jetstar and Virgin Australia are the main domestic airlines. REX – Regional Express Airlines operates to regional areas in New South Wales from T2 in Sydney Airport *(see pp228–9)*.

Fares can be quite low on competitive routes, and the cheapest rates can often be found online, so shop around before booking. Domestic flights depart from Sydney Airport's terminals 2 and 3; the latter is used exclusively by Qantas.

COUNTRY AND INTER-URBAN TRAINS

The CityRail network *(see p232)* includes InterCity trains that travel to the Blue Mountains, the South Coast (via five stations near the Royal National Park), the Southern Highlands and Newcastle, and the Central Coast. All these services depart from Central Station *(see p229)*.

While the network also includes the Hunter regional line, this does not service the popular wineries near the town of Pokolbin. Passengers wanting to visit the wineries should take the train to Morrisett (on the Newcastle and Central Coast line), then a Rover Coach to Pokolbin.

CountryLink *(see p229)* is a rail and coach network that covers more than 360 destinations in New South Wales, along with Brisbane and Melbourne. On its way out west, the train travels through the Blue Mountains, and trains to Melbourne stop at some Southern Highlands towns.

Tickets can be bought at the Countrylink Travel Centre at Central Railway station, suburban stations in Sydney and at many travel agents, or booked over the phone or online. Trains depart from the main concourse of Central Station, which is upstairs from the suburban train platforms.

LONG-DISTANCE BUS TRAVEL

Long distance bus travel can be cost effective but many journeys are long: for example a coach to Coffs Harbour (considered the midway stop between Sydney and Brisbane) takes over 7 hours. **Greyhound Australia** covers the nation, while other operators, such as **Firefly Express** and **Murrays Coaches**, run services on certain routes.

Competition on the Sydney–Melbourne route are usually quite good and can be as little as A$70 one-way, although it is a long 12- to 14-hour trip. Coaches leave from Central Railway Station.

ROAD TRAVEL

Highways in Sydney and New South Wales are improving all the time. The biggest challenge is knowing which route to take out of the city, so hire a car with a GPS system. Many areas of scenic beauty are within 2 hours' drive of Sydney. Ensure that your hire car comes with roadside breakdown assistance. For more on driving, *see pp230–31*.

CAR HIRE

Rates offered by the major agencies *(see p231)* range from about A$75 a day for a small car to A$100 a day for a larger vehicle. These rates become cheaper over a week's rental and usually include comprehensive insurance. Be sure to read the fine print on hire agreements. **Bayswater Car Rental** has the best rates in Sydney and can be as low as A$28 a day for week's hire.

You must be over 21 years old to hire a car from some companies and if you do not have a credit card, you will need to leave a deposit.

DIRECTORY

USING SYDNEY BUSES

Sydney Buses
Tel 131 500.
www.sydneybuses.info

LONG-DISTANCE BUS TRAVEL

Firefly Express
Tel 1300 950 571.
www.fireflyexpress.com.au

Greyhound Australia
Tel 1300 473 946.
www.greyhound.com.au

Murrays Coaches
Tel 132 251.
www.murrays.com.au

Sydney Coach Terminal
Eddy Avenue and Pitt Street,
Sydney. Map 4 E5.

CAR HIRE

Bayswater Car Rental
Tel 02 9360 3622.
www.bayswatercarrental.com.au

SYDNEY STREET FINDER

The page grid superimposed on the *Area by Area* map below shows which parts of Sydney are covered in this *Street Finder*. Map references given for all sights, hotels, restaurants, shopping and entertainment venues described in this guide refer to the maps in this section. All the major sights are clearly marked so they are easy to locate. A complete index of the street names and places of interest follows on pages 246–9. The key, set out below, indicates the scale of the maps and shows what other features are marked on them, including railway stations, bus terminals, ferry boarding points, emergency services, post offices and tourist information centres.

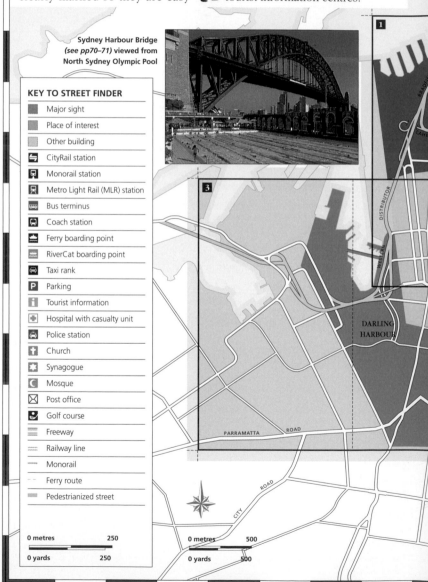

Sydney Harbour Bridge
(see pp70–71) viewed from
North Sydney Olympic Pool

KEY TO STREET FINDER

Major sight
Place of interest
Other building
CityRail station
Monorail station
Metro Light Rail (MLR) station
Bus terminus
Coach station
Ferry boarding point
RiverCat boarding point
Taxi rank
P Parking
Tourist information
Hospital with casualty unit
Police station
Church
Synagogue
Mosque
Post office
Golf course
Freeway
Railway line
Monorail
Ferry route
Pedestrianized street

0 metres 250
0 yards 250

0 metres 500
0 yards 500

DARLING HARBOUR

PARRAMATTA ROAD

Sundial in the Royal Botanic Garden (see pp104–5)

Statues on the Art Deco Anzac Memorial in Hyde Park (see p86)

Enjoying coffee outside Bar Coluzzi in Darlinghurst (see p194)

SYDNEY HARBOUR TUNNEL

THE ROCKS AND CIRCULAR QUAY

BOTANIC GARDEN AND THE DOMAIN

CITY CENTRE

KINGS CROSS AND DARLINGHURST

WILLIAM STREET

NEW SOUTH HEAD ROAD

OXFORD STREET

PADDINGTON

MOORE PARK ROAD

OXFORD STREET

SOUTH DOWLING STREET

ANZAC PARADE

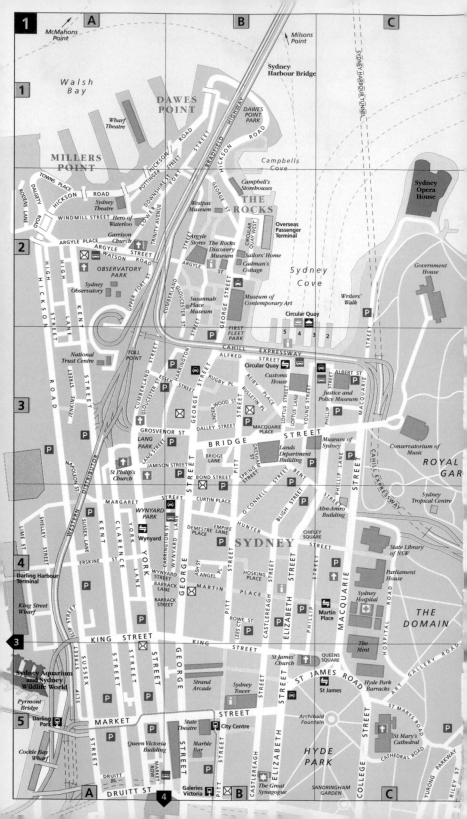

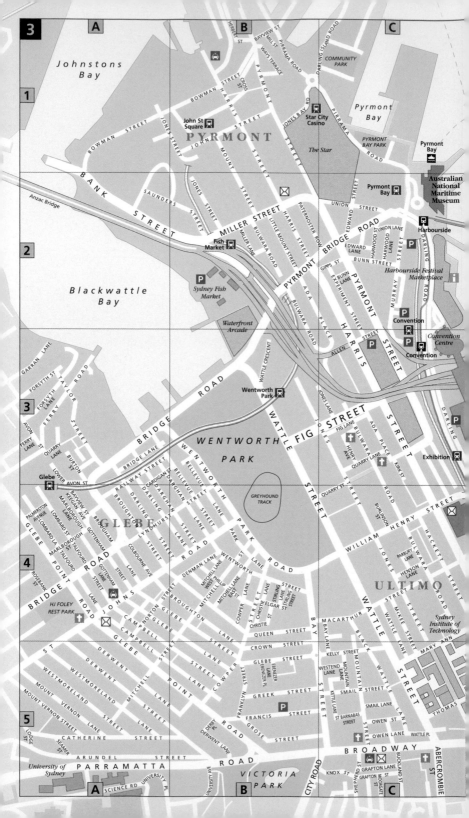

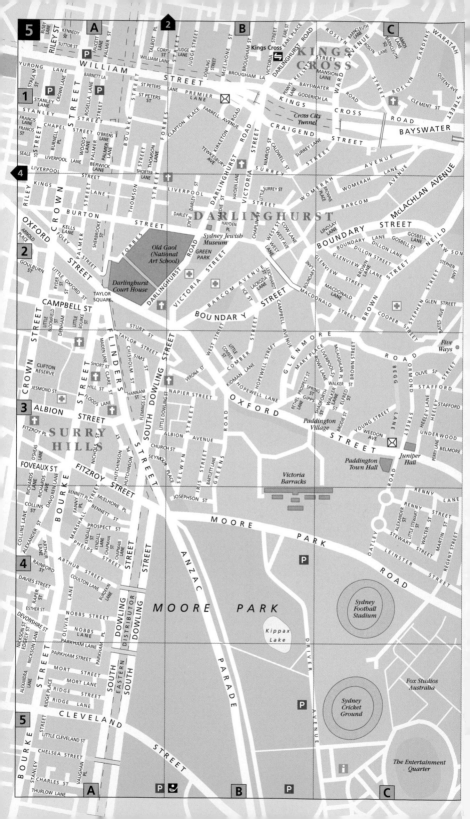

Street Finder Index

General Index

Acknowledgments

Dorling Kindersley would like to thank the following people whose help and assistance contributed to the preparation of this book.

Main Contributors
Ken Brass grew up on Sydney's Bondi Beach. He began his career in journalism with the *Sydney Morning Herald* and later worked as a London correspondent before becoming a staff writer on national daily newspapers in the United Kingdom. Returning home, he worked on the *Australian Women's Weekly, Weekend Australian* newspaper and *Australian Geographic* magazine. His photographs appear regularly in Australian magazines.

Kirsty McKenzie grew up on a sheep station in outback Queensland. She entered journalism after completing an arts degree. After making Sydney her home in 1980, she worked on a number of lifestyle and travel publications. Since becoming a freelance writer in 1987, she has regularly contributed to food, interior design and travel magazines.

Additional Text and Research
Angus Cameron, Leith Hillard, Kim Kitson, Siobhán O'Connor, Rupert Dean.

Additional Photography
Claire Edwards, Leanne Hogbin, Esther Labi, Siobhán O'Connor, Ian O'Leary, Carol Wiley.

Additional Illustrations
Leslye Cole, Stephen Conlin, Jon Gittoes, Steve Graham, Ray Grinaway, Helen Halliday, David Kirshner, Alex Lavroff, Iain McKellar, Chris Orr, Oliver Rennert.

Additional Cartography
Land Information Centre, Sydney.
Dorling Kindersley Cartography, Sydway.

Editorial and Design
DEPUTY EDITORIAL DIRECTOR Douglas Amrine
DEPUTY ART DIRECTORS Gillian Allan, Gaye Allen
MAP CO-ORDINATORS Michael Ellis, David Pugh
PRODUCTION David Proffit
PICTURE RESEARCH Wendy Canning.
DTP DESIGNER Leanne Hogbin
MAPS Gary Bowes, Fiona Casey, Casper Morris, Anna Nilsson, Christine Purcell, Richard Toomey (Era-Maptec Ltd)
EDITORIAL AND DESIGN ASSISTANCE: Emma Anacootee, Charis Atlas, Vandana Bhagra, Jenny Cattell, Louise Cleghorn, Sherry Collins, Stephanie Driver, Mariana Evmolpidou, Joy Fitzsimmons, Clare Forte, Anna Freiberger, Caroline Gladstone, Emily Green, Vinod Harish, Gail Jones, Lisa Kosky, Esther Labi, Jim Marks, Sam Merrell, Rebecca Milner, Sonal Modha, Kylie Mulquin, Rachel Neustein, Louise Parsons, Helen Partington, Alok Pathak, Marianne Petrou, Clare Pierotti, Pure Content, Marisa Renzullo, Ellen Root, Azeem Siddiqui, Susana Smith, Deborah Soden, Rachel Symons, Tracey Timpson, Ros Walford, Dora Whitaker, Carol Wiley.

Index
Jenny Cattell.

Special Assistance
Art Gallery of New South Wales, in particular Sherrie Joseph; Australian Museum, in particular Liz Wilson; Ann-Marie Bulat; the staff of Elizabeth Bay House; Historic Houses Trust; Lara Hookham; Info Direct, in particular Frank Tortora; Professor Max Kelly; Lou MacDonald; Adam Moore; Museum of Sydney, in particular Michelle Andringa; National Maritime Museum, in particular Jeffrey Mellefont and Bill Richards; National Trust of Australia (NSW), in particular Stewart Watters; Bridget O'Regan; Royal Botanic Gardens, in particular Anna Hallett and Ed Wilson; State Transit Authority; Sydney Opera House, in particular David Brown and Valerie Tring; Diane Wallis.

Photography Permissions
Dorling Kindersley would like to thank all those who gave permission to photograph at various cathedrals, churches, museums, restaurants, hotels, shops, galleries and other sights too numerous to thank individually.

Picture Credits
a-above; b-below/bottom; c-centre; f-far; l-left; r-right; t-top.

Works of art have been reproduced with the permission of the following copyright holders:
© MUSEUM OF SYDNEY 1996: *Edge of the Trees* Janet Laurence and Fiona Foley, on the site of FIRST GOVERNMENT HOUSE: 34tr, 85b.

The publisher would like to thank the following individuals, companies and picture libraries for their kind permission to reproduce their photographs:

ACP: 29cb, 30bc; ALAMY IMAGES: John Buxton 222br; Maurice Crooks 235bc; CulturalEyes-AusGS 232cla; frank'n'focus 228cra; Daniel Hewlett 222cr; Network Photographers 180cl; Travel-shots 181t; David Wall 181c; Wildlife Photo Agency/Rob Cleary 219tr; Worldwide Picture Library 10b; ART GALLERY OF NEW SOUTH WALES: *Portrait of Arthur Streeton* (date unknown) Grace Joel oil on canvas on hardboard, 55.6 x 40.7 cm, gift of Miss Joel 1925: 27cb; © Bundanon Trust 1996 *The Expulsion 1947–48* Arthur Boyd (1920-), oil on hardboard 99.5 x 119.6 cm: 33c; © Ms Stephenson-Meere 1996 *Australian Beach Pattern* 1940 Charles Meere (1890–1961) oil on canvas 91.5 x 122 cm: 35tl; © estate of the artist, courtesy Andindilkawa Land Council *Dugong Hunt* (1948) Jabarrgwa (Kneepad) Wurrabadalumba natural pigments on bark 46 x 95cm, gift of the COMMONWEALTH GOVERNMENT 1956: 36b; *Bridge Pattern* Harold Cazneaux (1878–1953), gelatin silver photograph 29.6 x 21.4 cm, gift of the Cazneaux family 1975: 58bc(d); © AGNSW 1996 *Sofala* 1947 Russell Drysdale (1912–81), oil on canvas on hardboard 71.7 x 93.1 cm 108bl; *Sunbaker* (1937) Max Dupain (1911–92), gelatin silver photograph, 37.9 x 42.8 cm: 108cl; *Mars and the Vestal Virgin* 1638 Jacques Blanchard 108cr; © Tiwi Design Executive 1996 *Pukumani Grave Posts, Melville Island* 1958 various artists, natural pigments on wood 165.1 x 29.2 cm, gift of Dr Stuart Scougall 1959: 109tc; A pair of tomb guardian figures (early 7th-century earthenware), each figure 93 x 39 x 23 cm, AGNSW FOUNDATION PURCHASE 1990: 109cra; *The Golden Fleece* (1894) Tom Roberts (1856–1931), oil on canvas, 104 x 158.7 cm: 109crb; *Natives on the Ouse River, Van Diemen's Land* 1838 John Glover, 109bc; © DACS, London 2011 *Study for Self Portrait* 1976 Francis Bacon (1901–92), oil and pastel on canvas 198 x 147.5 cm: 110tr;

© Wendy Whiteley 1996 *The Balcony 2* 1975 Brett Whiteley (1939–92), oil on canvas 203.5 x 364.5 cm: 110bl; *Three Bathers* 1913 Ernst Ludwig Kirchner 110tr; *The Curve of the Bridge* 1928-9 Grace Cossington Smith 110cla, © reproduced by courtesy of Aboriginal Artists Agency *Warlugulong* 1976 Clifford Possum Tjapaltjarri (1932–) and Tim Leura Tjapaltjarri (1939–84), synthetic polymer paint on canvas 168.5 x 170.5 cm: 111tr; *Poster for the Vienna Secession 49th Exhibition* (1918) Egon Schiele (1890–1918), colour lithograph, 67.8 x 53.7 cm: 111bl; AUSTRALIAN INFORMATION SERVICE: 31tl(d); AUSTRALIAN MUSEUM: C. Bento 20tl, 20clb, 20cb, 21tl, 21c, 21crb; 35bl; 89cr, 89cra; AUSTRALIAN PICTURE LIBRARY: John Carnemolla 30clb.

GREG BARRETT: 209bc; BARTEL PHOTO LIBRARY: 160bc; MERVYN G BISHOP: 22crb; Courtesy of BLUETONGUE BREWERY: 183cl; BONZA BIKE TOURS: 230cla; BRUCE COLEMAN: John Cancalosi 45bc; Francisco Futil 44tr; BRIDGECLIMB SYDNEY: 71tl; Bula'bula Arts: Tony Dhanyula *Nyoka* (Mud Crabs), circa 1984, ochres and synthetic polymer on bark, J.W. Power Bequest, purchased 1984 by the MUSEUM OF CONTEMPORARY ART, SYDNEY: 34clb. BRIDGEMAN ART LIBRARY: private collection *Ned Kelly, Outlaw* (1946), oil on panel, Sir Sidney Nolan (1917–92) 31ca; BOTANICAL GARDENS TRUST, SYDNEY: 104cla; CAPTAIN COOK CRUISES: 234cla; CENTREPOINT MANAGEMENT: 83br; courtesy CITY SIGHTSEEING: 236br; COO-EE HISTORICAL PICTURE LIBRARY: 9ca, 61ca, 151ca, 167ca, 217ca; COORBIS: E. O. Hoppé 65cra; Reuters/Mick Tsikas 231tl; Paul Souders 10tc; ANTHONY CRICKMAY: 76cla; David Jones (Australia) P/l: 25crb(D); RUPERT DEAN: 182cl, 182crb; Dixson Galleries, STATE LIBRARY OF NEW SOUTH WALES: 8–9, 20tr, 22blb(D), 26cla, 70tr, 138br; MAX DUPAIN: 77br; DESTINATION NSW-TOURISM: 230tl; Hamilton Lund 221tl; Phase IX 152tr; FAIRFAX PHOTO LIBRARY: 28bl; 52ca; 71bra; 114cl(d); 77tc; ASCUI 51br; Dallen 31cra; Gerrit Fokkema 30br; Ken James 209tr; McNeil 120bl; White 43bl; FIRE AND RESCUE NSW (FRNSW): 222crb; GETTY IMAGES: AFP PHOTO/Greg Wood 226cl; GLOBAL GOSSIP GROUP: 226br; GOVERNMENT PRINTING OFFICE COLLECTION, STATE OF NEW SOUTH WALES: 26clb, 28clb, 76blb; GREAT SOUTHERN RAIL: 228tc; GREAT SYNAGOGUE, SYDNEY: 86tl; HAPPY MEDIUM PHOTOS: 43tc; C MOORE HARDY: 208br; courtesy of HILTON INTERNATIONAL: 168cl; HOOD COLLECTION, STATE LIBRARY OF NEW SOUTH WALES: 71bl, 137br(D); HUGOS GROUP: 178bl; JUSTICE AND POLICE MUSEUM: Ray Joyce 34cla. LAKE'S FOLLY VINEYARDS:159cr; LEONARDO MEDIABANK: 168br; LEURA GARDENS FESTIVAL INC,.: 48cr; LIBERTY WINES: 158cla; LONLEY PLANET IMAGES: Juliet Coombe 11t; Courtesy LUNA PARK TRUST: 129tc; 132cl, 132tc; MAZZ IMAGES: 30–31; MINC COMMUNICATIONS PTY LTD;: Earl Carter Photography 178cr; MEDUSA HOTEL: 171tl; MITCHELL LIBRARY, STATE LIBRARY OF NEW SOUTH WALES: 21br, 21bcb, 22br(d), 22–3, 23tl, 23ca(d), 23cb, 24clb(d), 24cb(d), 24bl, 25tl, 25ca(d), 25bl(d), 26cr, 26bc, 26br, 27tl, 27br, 29ca(d), 29blb, 31cb, 44tl, 71cra, 112tl; DAVID MOORE:

30cla; MOUNT FRANKLIN: 183br; MULTIPLEX PROPERTY SERVICES: 98c; MUSEUM OF CONTEMPORARY ART, SYDNEY: 34cl, 64bl; NATIONAL LIBRARY OF AUSTRALIA, CANBERRA: 24tl, 24cla, 25brb(D), 27bc; NATIONAL MARITIME MUSEUM: 22cl, 36tl, 95 Cra; Nature Focus: Kevin Diletti 47br(D); John Fields 44bl; Pavel German 47tr; NORMAN LINDSAY GALLERY: Photo courtesy National Trust of Australia 161cr; NSW POLICE FORCE: 222cla; OLYMPIC CO-ORDINATOR AUTHORITY: 139t/b.

PARLIAMENT HOUSE: The Hon Max Willis, RFD, ED, LLB, MLC, President, Legislative Council, Parliament of New South Wales. The Hon J Murray, MP, Speaker, Legislative Assembly, Parliament of New South Wales. Artist's original sketch of the historical painting in oils by Algernon Talmage, RA, *The Founding of Australia*. Kindly loaned to the Parliament of New South Wales by Mr Arthur Chard of Adelaide: 73bl; Parramatta City Council: S. Thomas 42tr; PHOTOLIBRARY.COM: David Messent 11b, 229tl; images reproduced courtesy of POWERHOUSE MUSEUM: 22tl, 23br, 24bcb, 26tl, 28tl, 28cla, 28cb, 28bc, 29crb, 29bc, 34t, 34br; 100-1 all, John-Francois Lanzarone 100cla; Penelope Clay 100tl; Sue Stafford 101t; Tyrrell Collection 106tc; Reproduced with permission from RAILCOP NSW AUSTRALIA: 232tl, 233br, 233tl; Phil Carrick 233cra, 233cr; THE ROCKS DISCOVERY MUSEUM: 65tl; ROYAL BOTANIC GARDENS: Jaime Plaza 48bl.

SIMON JOHNSON PURVEYOR OF QUALITY FOODS: 221bl; SOUTHCORP WINES EUROPE: 183tr; STATE LIBRARY OF TASMANIA: 22clb; Stopmotion: 160tr; SUZIE THOMAS PUBLISHING: Thomas O'flynn 74bc, © DACS, London 2011, 76clb; SUPERSTOCK:Digital Vision 10cl; SYDNEY ATTRACTIONS GROUP: 96br, 97cl; SYDNEY FILM FESTIVAL: 51clb; SYDNEY FREELANCE: J Boland 49cl; SYDNEY HARBOUR FORESHORE AUTHORITY: 218br; SYDNEY JEWISH MUSEUM: 35br; SYDNEY OPERA HOUSE TRUST: 74tr, 74cla, 75tc, 75br, 75bl, 76br, 77cla, 77ca, 77cra, 77c; SYDNEY THEATRE: 208cl; SYDNEY WILDERNESS TOURS: 152tr; Willi Ulmer Collection 77bc; TARONGA ZOO: 134tr; TEBUTT'S VII RESTAURANT AND FUNCTION CENTRE:156clb; VINTAGE ESTATES: 159cl; WESTFIELD SYDNEY: 81crb; WESTPAC BANKING CORPORATION: 68br; WILD LIFE SYDNEY: courtesy of Merlin Entertainments Group 97 all, 218tc; YALUMBA WINES: 182cra.

Jacket - Front: ROBERT HARDING PICTURE LIBRARY: Sergio Pitamitz; Back: CORBIS: Lance Nelson tl; DORLING KINDERSLEY: Rob Reichenfield cla, Alan Williams clb; PHOTOLIBRARY: bl; Spine: ROBERT HARDING PICTURE LIBRARY: Sergio Pitamitz t. www.photographersdirect.com

All other images © Dorling Kindersley. For further information see: www.dkimages.com

DORLING KINDERSLEY SPECIAL EDITIONS

DK Travel Guides can be purchased in bulk quantities at discounted prices for use in promotions or as premiums.
We are also able to offer special editions and personalized jackets, corporate imprints, and excerpts from all of our books, tailored specifically to meet your own needs.

To find out more, please contact:
(in the United States) **SpecialSales@dk.com**
(in the UK) **TravelSpecialSales@uk.dk.com**
(in Canada) DK Special Sales at **general@tourmaline.ca**
(in Australia) **business.development@pearson.com.au**